For Dummies
BESTSELLING BOOK SERIES

London For Dummies
1st Edition

London Underground

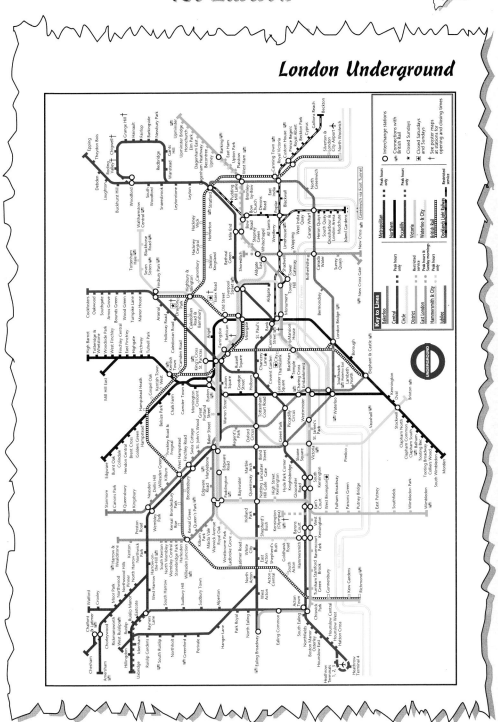

UNDERGROUND

Key to Lines

Bakerloo
Central
Circle
District
East London
Hammersmith & City
Jubilee

Metropolitan
Northern
Piccadilly
Victoria
British Rail
Docklands Light Railway

○ Interchange stations
◉ Connections with British Rail
★ Closed Saturdays and Sundays
See poster maps at stations for opening and closing times

For Dummies™: Bestselling Book Series for Beginners

London For Dummies, 1st Edition

Cheat Sheet

Central London Theaters

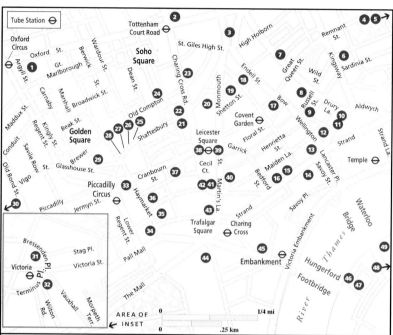

Adelphi **16**	Duchess **12**	National **49**	Royal Opera House **14**
Albery **39**	Duke of York's **43**	New London **7**	St. Martin's **20**
Aldwych **10**	Fortune **8**	Old Vic **47**	Savoy **14**
Almeida **4**	Garrick **42**	Palace **21**	Shaftesbury **3**
Ambassadors **22**	Gielgud **26**	Peacock	Strand **11**
Apollo **27**	Globe **48**	(Sadler's Wells) **6**	Theatre Royal
Apollo Victoria **32**	Her Majesty's **34**	Phoenix **23**	Drury Lane **9**
Barbican **5**	London	Piccadilly **29**	Theatre Royal
Cambridge **19**	Coliseum **40**	The Playhouse **45**	Haymarket **35**
Comedy **36**	London	Prince Edward **24**	Vaudeville **15**
Criterion **33**	Palladium **1**	Prince of Wales **37**	Victoria Palace **31**
Dominion **2**	Lyceum **13**	Queen's **25**	Whitehall **44**
Donmar	Lyric **28**	Royal Court **41**	Wyndhams **38**
Warehouse **18**	Lyric Hammersmith **30**	Royal Festival Hall **46**	

IDG BOOKS WORLDWIDE

For Dummies™: Bestselling Book Series for Beginners

London
FOR
DUMMIES®
1ST EDITION

by Donald Olson

IDG
BOOKS
WORLDWIDE

IDG Books Worldwide, Inc.
An International Data Group Company

Foster City, CA ✦ Chicago, IL ✦ Indianapolis, IN ✦ New York, NY

London For Dummies®, 1st Edition

Published by
IDG Books Worldwide, Inc.
An International Data Group Company
919 E. Hillsdale Blvd.
Suite 400
Foster City, CA 94404
www.idgbooks.com (IDG Books Worldwide Web Site)
www.dummies.com (Dummies Press Web Site)

Library of Congress Control Number: 00-103385

ISBN: 0-7645-6194-4

ISSN: 1531-1457

Printed in the United States of America

10 9 8 7 6 5 4 3 2 1

1B/QV/QZ/QQ/IN

Distributed in the United States by IDG Books Worldwide, Inc.

Distributed by CDG Books Canada Inc. for Canada; by Transworld Publishers Limited in the United Kingdom; by IDG Norge Books for Norway; by IDG Sweden Books for Sweden; by IDG Books Australia Publishing Corporation Pty. Ltd. for Australia and New Zealand; by TransQuest Publishers Pte Ltd. for Singapore, Malaysia, Thailand, Indonesia, and Hong Kong; by Gotop Information Inc. for Taiwan; by ICG Muse, Inc. for Japan; by Intersoft for South Africa; by Eyrolles for France; by International Thomson Publishing for Germany, Austria and Switzerland; by Distribuidora Cuspide for Argentina; by LR International for Brazil; by Galileo Libros for Chile; by Ediciones ZETA S.C.R. Ltda. for Peru; by WS Computer Publishing Corporation, Inc., for the Philippines; by Contemporanea de Ediciones for Venezuela; by Express Computer Distributors for the Caribbean and West Indies; by Micronesia Media Distributor, Inc. for Micronesia; by Chips Computadoras S.A. de C.V. for Mexico; by Editorial Norma de Panama S.A. for Panama; by American Bookshops for Finland.

For general information on IDG Books Worldwide's books in the U.S., please call our Consumer Customer Service department at 800-762-2974. For reseller information, including discounts and premium sales, please call our Reseller Customer Service department at 800-434-3422.

For information on where to purchase IDG Books Worldwide's books outside the U.S., please contact our International Sales department at 317-572-3993 or fax 317-572-4002.

For consumer information on foreign language translations, please contact our Customer Service department at 1-800-434-3422, fax 317-572-4002, or e-mail rights@idgbooks.com.

For information on licensing foreign or domestic rights, please phone +1-650-653-7098.

For sales inquiries and special prices for bulk quantities, please contact our Order Services department at 800-434-4322 or write to the address above.

For information on using IDG Books Worldwide's books in the classroom or for ordering examination copies, please contact our Educational Sales department at 800-434-2086 or fax 317-572-4005.

For press review copies, author interviews, or other publicity information, please contact our Public Relations department at 650-653-7000 or fax 650-653-7500.

For authorization to photocopy items for corporate, personal, or educational use, please contact Copyright Clearance Center, 222 Rosewood Drive, Danvers, MA 01923, or fax 978-750-4470.

About the Author

Donald Olson is a novelist, playwright, and travel writer. His novel *The Confessions of Aubrey Beardsley* was published in the United Kingdom by Bantam Press, and his play, *Beardsley*, was produced in London. His travel stories have appeared in the *New York Times*, *Travel & Leisure*, *Sunset*, and many other national publications. He has also written guidebooks to Italy, Berlin, and Oregon. London is one of his favorite cities.

ABOUT IDG BOOKS WORLDWIDE

Welcome to the world of IDG Books Worldwide.

IDG Books Worldwide, Inc., is a subsidiary of International Data Group, the world's largest publisher of computer-related information and the leading global provider of information services on information technology. IDG was founded more than 30 years ago by Patrick J. McGovern and now employs more than 9,000 people worldwide. IDG publishes more than 290 computer publications in over 75 countries. More than 90 million people read one or more IDG publications each month.

Launched in 1990, IDG Books Worldwide is today the #1 publisher of best-selling computer books in the United States. We are proud to have received eight awards from the Computer Press Association in recognition of editorial excellence and three from Computer Currents' First Annual Readers' Choice Awards. Our best-selling ...For Dummies® series has more than 50 million copies in print with translations in 31 languages. IDG Books Worldwide, through a joint venture with IDG's Hi-Tech Beijing, became the first U.S. publisher to publish a computer book in the People's Republic of China. In record time, IDG Books Worldwide has become the first choice for millions of readers around the world who want to learn how to better manage their businesses.

Our mission is simple: Every one of our books is designed to bring extra value and skill-building instructions to the reader. Our books are written by experts who understand and care about our readers. The knowledge base of our editorial staff comes from years of experience in publishing, education, and journalism — experience we use to produce books to carry us into the new millennium. In short, we care about books, so we attract the best people. We devote special attention to details such as audience, interior design, use of icons, and illustrations. And because we use an efficient process of authoring, editing, and desktop publishing our books electronically, we can spend more time ensuring superior content and less time on the technicalities of making books.

You can count on our commitment to deliver high-quality books at competitive prices on topics you want to read about. At IDG Books Worldwide, we continue in the IDG tradition of delivering quality for more than 30 years. You'll find no better book on a subject than one from IDG Books Worldwide.

John Kilcullen
Chairman and CEO
IDG Books Worldwide, Inc.

Eighth Annual
Computer Press
Awards≥1992

Ninth Annual
Computer Press
Awards≥1993

Tenth Annual
Computer Press
Awards≥1994

Eleventh Annual
Computer Press
Awards≥1995

IDG is the world's leading IT media, research and exposition company. Founded in 1964, IDG had 1997 revenues of $2.05 billion and has more than 9,000 employees worldwide. IDG offers the widest range of media options that reach IT buyers in 75 countries representing 95% of worldwide IT spending. IDG's diverse product and services portfolio spans six key areas including print publishing, online publishing, expositions and conferences, market research, education and training, and global marketing services. More than 90 million people read one or more of IDG's 290 magazines and newspapers, including IDG's leading global brands — Computerworld, PC World, Network World, Macworld and the Channel World family of publications. IDG Books Worldwide is one of the fastest-growing computer book publishers in the world, with more than 700 titles in 36 languages. The "...For Dummies®" series alone has more than 50 million copies in print. IDG offers online users the largest network of technology-specific Web sites around the world through IDG.net (http://www.idg.net), which comprises more than 225 targeted Web sites in 55 countries worldwide. International Data Corporation (IDC) is the world's largest provider of information technology data, analysis and consulting, with research centers in over 41 countries and more than 400 research analysts worldwide. IDG World Expo is a leading producer of more than 168 globally branded conferences and expositions in 35 countries including E3 (Electronic Entertainment Expo), Macworld Expo, ComNet, Windows World Expo, ICE (Internet Commerce Expo), Agenda, DEMO, and Spotlight. IDG's training subsidiary, ExecuTrain, is the world's largest computer training company, with more than 230 locations worldwide and 785 training courses. IDG Marketing Services helps industry-leading IT companies build international brand recognition by developing global integrated marketing programs via IDG's print, online and exposition products worldwide. Further information about the company can be found at www.idg.com.   1/26/00

Dedication

To G and his guiding eyes

And to the memory of Martyn Read, who loved London

Author's Acknowledgments

I'd like to thank **British Airways, Rail Europe,** and **Paul Duboudin** and **Val Austin** of the British Tourist Authority for their generous help while I was researching and writing this guide. Special thanks also go to **Garen Robinson** in London and to **Ron Boudreau,** my editor in New York.

Publisher's Acknowledgments

We're proud of this book; please register your comments through our IDG Books Worldwide Online Registration Form located at http://my2cents.dummies.com.

Some of the people who helped bring this book to market include the following:

Editorial

Editors: Ron Boudreau and Kathleen M. Cox

Copy Editor: Susan Diane Smith

Cartographer: John Decamillis

Editorial Assistant: Jennifer Young

Production

Project Coordinator: Amanda Foxworth

Layout and Graphics: Beth Brooks, Tracy K. Oliver, Kristin Pickett, Jill Piscitelli, Brent Savage, Kathie Schutte, Jeremy Unger

Proofreaders: Laura Albert, Chris Collins

Indexer: Sherry Massey

Special Help
Michelle Conrad, Michelle Hacker, Steve Arany, Robert Annis, Marie Luken

---

General and Administrative

IDG Books Worldwide, Inc.: John Kilcullen, CEO; Bill Barry, President and COO

IDG Books Consumer Reference Group

Business: Kathleen A. Welton, Vice President and Publisher; Kevin Thornton, Acquisitions Manager

Cooking/Gardening: Jennifer Feldman, Associate Vice President and Publisher

Education/Reference: Diane Graves Steele, Vice President and Publisher, Greg Tubach, Publishing Director

Lifestyles: Kathleen Nebenhaus, Vice President and Publisher; Tracy Boggier, Managing Editor

Pets: Dominique Devito, Associate Vice President and Publisher; Tracy Boggier, Managing Editor

Travel: Michael Spring, Vice President and Publisher; Suzanne Jannetta, Editorial Director; Brice Gosnell, Managing Editor

IDG Books Consumer Editorial Services: Kathleen Nebenhaus, Vice President and Publisher; Kristin A. Cocks, Editorial Director; Cindy Kitchel, Editorial Director

IDG Books Consumer Production: Debbie Stailey, Production Director

IDG Books Packaging: Marc J. Mikulich, Vice President, Brand Strategy and Research

♦

The publisher would like to give special thanks to Patrick J. McGovern, without whom this book would not have been possible.

♦

Contents at a Glance

Cartoons at a Glance

By Rich Tennant

page 325

page 43

page 7

page 119

page 199

page 151

page 299

Fax: 978-546-7747
E-mail: richtennant@the5thwave.com
World Wide Web: www.the5thwave.com

Maps at a Glance

Table of Contents

Part VI: Living It Up After Sundown *299*

Chapter 22: Experiencing the
Grand Tradition: London's Theater Scene 301

Chapter 23: The Performing Arts 309

Chapter 24: Enjoying a Pint: Pubs, Clubs, and Bars 315

Introduction

· ·

*F*or all its historic panache, time-honored traditions, quaint corners, and associations with royal pomp and ceremony, London is very much a modern European city (maybe I should say half-European, because the Brits continue to resist full incorporation with the European Union). London is a rich blend of the very old and the very new — from the 900-year-old Tower of London to the just opened Tate Modern gallery and from the Royal Opera House to the British Airways London Eye observation wheel. And it's big, in both size and population; more than 9 million people reside in the 622-square-mile megalopolis known as Greater London.

For first-time visitors, London can be a bit of a challenge. The streets aren't laid out in a grid, and the crowds and traffic in Central London can be intimidating, especially if you're not used to big cities. When you cross the street, you have to look right instead of left; remember that Brits drive on the "wrong" side of the road. And the currency is different. These differences don't present major obstacles, however. If anything, they add to the pleasure of a trip to London because they're reminders that you are, after all, in a different country — albeit one where you (sort of) speak the same language as the natives (see Chapter 1 for a list of British terms that may be unfamiliar).

If you have a bit of advance planning and some useful information under your belt, making the trip will be easier than you thought. London may be far from where you live, but for many people a trip to this city is like going home.

About This Book

London For Dummies is meant to be used as a reference. You can, of course, start at the first page and read all the way through. If you do, you'll end up with an unusually complete knowledge of London essentials. On the other hand, you may not need parts of this guide because you've already been to London and/or know the basics of international travel. You're after quick, easy-to-find specifics. In that case, you can easily flip to the part you need or hone in on a specific chapter — hotels, for example (see Chapter 8). The philosophy behind this book is quite simple. I wanted it to be the kind of guide that I wished I'd had on my first trip to London: informative, practical, down-to-earth, and fun. When you travel, it's the unexpected surprises that create the most memorable moments and provide the stories you take back with you. But the other side of travel is details and planning: What are the most important sights, how can I reach them, what will they cost, and how much time do I need to see them? Where should I eat? Where should I sleep? These aren't small issues when you're away from home. They can make or break a trip — I know that. So what I'm offering here is based on my own experience in traveling, living, and working in London. I don't want you to have a good trip — I want you to have a great one!

You should know, however, that travel information is subject to change at any time — and this is especially true of prices. I, therefore, suggest that you write or call ahead for confirmation when making your travel plans. The authors, editors, and publisher cannot be held responsible for the experiences of readers while traveling. Your safety is important to us, however, so we encourage you to stay alert and be aware of your surroundings. Keep a close eye on cameras, purses, and wallets, all favorite targets of thieves and pickpockets!

Conventions Used in This Book

I recently tried to extract some information from a guidebook and found so many symbols that I needed training in hieroglyphics to inter-pret them all. I'm happy to report that the user-friendly *London For Dummies* travel guide isn't like that. The use of symbols and abbrevia-tions is kept to a minimum, as follows:

- ✔ The credit card abbreviations are AE (American Express), DC (Diners Club), MC (MasterCard), and V (Visa).

- ✔ I list the hotels, restaurants, and top attractions in A-to-Z order, so that moving among the maps, worksheets, and descriptions is easier.

- ✔ I include the London postal area (SW7, for example) in all street addresses in case you want to look up the street in a *London A to Z* or other London street reference map.

- ✔ I give the nearest tube/Underground (subway) stop for all destina-tions (for example, Tube: Piccadilly Circus).

- ✔ I list all prices first in British pounds sterling (£), and then in U.S. dollars ($) rounded to the nearest dollar (when prices are under £3 I don't round them). Though the exchange rate fluctuates daily, in this guide the rate I use is £1 = $1.65.

I've divided the hotels into two categories — my personal favorites and those that don't quite make my preferred list but still get my hearty seal of approval. Don't be shy about considering these "runner-up" hotels if you're unable to get a room at one of my favorites or if your preferences differ from mine — the amenities that the runners-up offer and the services that each provides make all these accommodations good choices to consider as you determine where to rest your head at night.

I also include some general pricing information to help you as you decide where to unpack your bags or dine on the local cuisine. I've used a system of dollar signs to show a range of costs for one night in a hotel or a meal at a restaurant. Check out the following table to decipher the dollar signs:

Cost	Hotel	Restaurant
$	$150 and under	$25 or under
$$	$150 to $225	$25 to $35
$$$	$225 to $300	$35 to $50
$$$$	$300 to $400	$50 and up
$$$$$	$400 and up	

London also has an additional 17.5 percent VAT (value added tax) tax on hotels and restaurant meals. Ask if it's included in the price.

Foolish Assumptions

While writing this book, I made some assumptions about you, dear reader. I'm assuming that either you've never been to London and want to learn about it from scratch, or you've been there already and want a convenient and up-to-date reference.

Maybe you just don't have much time to spend on trip planning and don't want to wade through a ton of boring, brain-numbing information. You want an easy-to-use reference where you can quickly find the answers you need and where you aren't faced with hundreds of choices that all sound similar. You want expert advice on how to maximize your time and enjoy a hassle-free trip. If you've been frustrated using conventional travel guides, *London For Dummies* is the book you've been looking for. And I'm assuming that you won't object to *readable text*, with a bit of humor and London gossip, and some real opinions thrown in.

How This Book Is Organized

London For Dummies is divided into seven parts plus an appendix. If you read the parts in sequential order, they can guide you through all the advance-planning aspects of your trip and then get you off and running after you're in the City by the Thames.

  ✔ **Part I: Getting Started** introduces London and gives you some excellent reasons for going there. I help you decide on the best time of year for your visit, give you sound advice on planning a realistic budget, and provide special tips for families, travelers with disabilities, seniors, and gays and lesbians.

✔ **Part II: Ironing Out the Details** helps take some of the wrinkles out of trip planning. You can find all the options for airlines and tips on how to get the best fare, plus the lowdown on package tours and whether they can save you money. (They certainly can!) The thumbnail sketches of London neighborhoods help you decide where you want to stay. I explain what kind of accommodation you can expect for your money, provide details on booking a room, and describe London's best hotels. This part helps you tie up any pretrip loose ends (passports and so on) *before* you enter the aircraft and fasten your seatbelts for the flight to London.

✔ **Part III: Settling into London** tells you what you need to know after you arrive. A bit of airport orientation is in order, followed by detailed information on the ways, means, and costs of getting from the airport into the city. To help you get your bearings, I provide another quick rundown of London's diverse neighborhoods. I tell you everything you need to know about getting around town — whether you travel on foot, on the Underground or bus, or in a taxi. And because you must use pounds and pence, I talk money, such as where to find a currency exchange or an ATM.

✔ **Part IV: Dining in London** begins with an appetizing survey of London's dining scene before moving on to the delectable main course: London's best restaurants, complete with easy-to-use indexes for price, location, and type of cuisine. This part ends with some suggestions for meals on the run and special places to go for tea, fish-and-chips, or a picnic.

✔ **Part V: Exploring London** is dedicated to seeing the sights — from the absolute must-sees (Buckingham Palace, Westminster Abbey, and the British Museum) to lesser-known haunts and fascinating places nearby (Hampton Court and Windsor Castle). I suggest all kinds of guided tours and provide shopping coverage that steers you to a whole range of big stores (yes, Harrods) and small specialty shops I think that you'd like to know about. I also provide sample daily itineraries that won't leave you gasping for breath. And if you want to explore beyond London, check out my five great day or overnight trips from the city (Bath, Stonehenge, and more).

✔ **Part VI: Living It Up After Sundown** is dedicated to the theater scene, the performing arts, and all manner of after-dark entertainment possibilities. I clue you in to the best sources for finding out what's going on around town and tell you how to get tickets. Then I fill you in on some of the city's best pubs, clubs, bars, and discos.

✔ **Part VII: The Part of Tens** allows me to squeeze in some extra places and sights I think are special but don't really fit in elsewhere in the book. My tens lists include ten-plus reasons to visit the South Bank, ten famous London statues, ten special London churches, and ten historic pubs.

✔ The appendix, **Quick Concierge,** is an A-to-Z directory of fast facts you need to know, such as how the telephone system works, what numbers to call in an emergency, and what taxes you must pay. I include a list of toll-free telephone numbers and Web sites for airlines and hotel chains serving London. I also tell you where to go for more information on London. I provide names, addresses, and phone numbers and/or Web sites of relevant agencies and sources.

I've also included a bunch of *worksheets* to make your travel planning easier — among other things, you can determine your travel budget, create specific itineraries, and keep a log of your favorite restaurants so you can hit them again next time you're in town. You can find these worksheets easily because they're printed on yellow paper.

Icons Used in This Book

These five icons appear in the margins throughout this book:

 Bargain Alert is my favorite icon — and I suspect it may be yours, too. I'm not cheap, but I love to save money. I love to know about special deals. Every time I tell you about something that can save you money, I include the Bargain Alert icon.

 The Tip icon highlights useful bits of information that can save you time or enhance your London experience. A Tip alerts you to something (like a special guided tour or a way to avoid standing in long lines) you may not otherwise consider or even know about.

 I'm not an alarmist, so you won't find too many Heads Up icons. If you see one, it means that I want you to be aware of something, such as the ticket agencies claiming to sell "reduced-price tickets" or the double-tipping scam you may encounter in a restaurant. London, you'll be pleased to know, isn't the kind of city that requires too many warning labels.

 Traveling with children? Keep your eyes peeled for the Kid Friendly icon. If the icon is in front of a hotel name, the hotel welcomes families with children and may even provide extras for kids. If it's in front of a restaurant name, the kids will enjoy the food or the atmosphere and the staff will be welcoming to youngsters. And if the icon is in front an attraction name, kids will (probably) enjoy something about the place.

 When was the last time you read a travel book that filled you in on local gossip as well as all the mundane facts? For the London Tattler icon (named after the famous London newspaper *The Tatler,* published from 1709 to 1711), I include only the most newsworthy scandals — I mean stories — to report on. I throw in these tidbits about well-known Londoners and curious bits of London lore just for the fun of it.

Where to Go from Here

To London, of course! This book is a very good place to start your journey, giving you the tools you need to make the most of your trip. You can also take it with you if you visit a travel agent or reference it as you look into various tours or package deals. Because it covers all the basics, it's an excellent guide to help you plan, anticipate, and understand exactly what you want to see and do in London. Whatever you do, and wherever you go in London, I hope that you'll think of me as your guide or companion on the journey. I love London. My goal is to help you have a great time while you're there — however you read the book and plan out your trip.

Part I
Getting Started

The 5th Wave
By Rich Tennant

"And how shall I book your flight to London — First Class, Coach, or Medieval?"

In this part . . .

Are you a stranger to London? Well, it's time you were introduced, and this part helps you put a face to the place. In Chapter 1, I give a general overview of this great city, sketching in some details so you'll know what you'll find there — including the newest attractions. If you haven't decided when to go, Chapter 2 fills you in on what London offers during each season and why some times may be better than others for a visit. Chapter 3 is about planning your budget — a workable budget based on real London prices — and includes cost-cutting tips. And Chapter 4 is full of special advice for London-bound families, seniors, travelers with disabilities, and gays and lesbians.

Chapter 1

Discovering the Best of London

* *

* *

So, you're going to London. Gives you a thrill just thinking about it, right? The capital of the United Kingdom is one of the world's top destinations, visited year-round by millions from all corners of the globe. Once you arrive, you'll be making your way through one of the most historic, cultured, and exciting cities on earth. There's every reason to feel a tingle of anticipation.

But maybe you're not absolutely certain London will be your cup of Earl Grey. "What's it *really* like?" you want to know. So I start by talking a bit about London's flavor — or flavour, as the Brits spell it. What will you find in the City by the Thames?

From Londinium to London: Landmarks of History

Did you know you can see **Roman ruins** in London? Two millennia ago, London was Londinium, a colony of the Roman Empire. On one London street you can actually see the excavated remains of a temple where Roman soldiers worshiped a Persian god named Mithras. Though it's one of London's oldest archaeological sites, the **Temple of Mithras** is relatively unknown to visitors.

On the other hand, some of London's sights have percolated through most people's consciousness because they've seen them in countless movies or photos, heard about them from friends, or read about them somewhere. Places like the **Tower of London** and **Westminster Abbey** have a legendary quality, but they're quite real — and they're open to visitors throughout the year. The Tower and the Abbey represent almost *1,000 years* of history. And that's why the great landmarks in London stir the imagination: They've been witness to so much — from glorious triumphs to bloody tragedies.

When visiting the Tower, you're walking on a piece of ground where the great dramas and terrors of a turbulent kingdom were played out, where Elizabeth I was held captive while still a princess and where Sir Thomas More and Ann Boleyn (second wife of Henry VIII and mother of the future Elizabeth I) were beheaded. When stepping into Westminster Abbey, you're entering the place where England's kings and queens have been crowned since William the Conquerer claimed the throne in 1066. In this guide, all of London's great historic landmarks are described in Chapters 16 and 17.

The Royals: Pomp, Ceremony, and Scandal

I never really gave much thought to royalty, except as a footnote to history, until one day several years ago. I was passing St. James's Palace just as Princess Diana and Princess Anne were being hustled into a waiting limousine. There they were, two famous princesses, going about the mysterious routines of royalty. I glimpsed them for maybe 3 seconds and stood there like a slack-jawed yokel as the limo pulled away.

In London, the royals are spied on the way movie stars are in America. The paparazzi furor lessened a bit after Princess Diana's death but seems to be revving up again now that Prince William has turned 18 and is fair game. From the Queen on down, the monarchy is a huge business, and you can't avoid it. Buy a London paper any day you're there and you'll find some juicy tidbit about the Queen Mother, Prince Edward, Princess Margaret, Prince William, or some other member of what Brits call The Firm. (I provide a few gossipy items of my own in this guide with my "London Tattler" asides.)

Okay, so you're probably not going to get invited to the Queen's Garden Party or be asked to go on a hunt with Prince Charles and Camilla Parker-Bowles. But it's still fun to see **Buckingham Palace,** the royal seat of power and intrigue (see Chapter 16), and to traipse through **Windsor Castle** (see Chapter 17), an hour away. Although you can't see the rooms where Diana actually lived, you can get into **Kensington Palace** and see the **Princess Diana Memorial Playground** in Kensington Gardens (see Chapter 16).

I was in London during the Queen's Silver Jubilee celebrations and still remember the parties and festive brouhaha throughout the city. Another big royal event is coming up in 2002, the year the Queen celebrates her 50th anniversary on the throne. I'm interested in seeing how London celebrates that one. The only other monarch to hold the throne for that long was Queen Victoria.

Cool Britannia: 21st-Century London

Trend-setting London is to the United Kingdom what New York City is to the United States: the place where it happens first (or ultimately ends up). London is where you can put the eyeball on what's hot, British style. You see the latest hardcore street fashions side by side with the quintessentially traditional. And this ancient city is now as high-tech as a hyperlink, with mobile phones, cybercafes, and e-communications part of everyday life.

With Greenwich, the center of time, just minutes away, London decided to celebrate the arrival of 2000 in a big way. The **Millennium Dome** (see "Greenwich" in Chapter 17) and the **British Airways London Eye** observation wheel (see Chapter 16) are just two of the new large-scale attractions. Even more exciting is the **Tate Modern** art gallery (see Chapter 16). A new **Millennium Bridge** now spans the Thames between Tate Modern and St. Paul's Cathedral. Sleek new Underground (subway) stations have opened on the **Jubilee Line.** The courtyard of the hallowed British Museum has been transformed into a stunning glass-roofed **Great Court,** adding much needed space. And **Hertford House,** home of the Wallace Collection (see Chapter 17), has opened its new interior atrium.

Food, Glorious Food

Once upon a time, you could always count on getting lousy meals in London, not to mention the entire United Kingdom. The cooking — all too often dull, insular, and uninspired — was the joke of Europe. That began to change in the 1980s, with the influx of new cooking trends that favored foods from France and Italy. Since then, London has become a food capital (allegedly with more Michelin-starred restaurants than Paris). It's certainly the best place to find restaurants serving inventive Modern British cuisine. But don't despair: All those wonderful "Old English" faves are still around — eggs, kippers, beans, and fried tomatoes for breakfast; bubble and squeak; roast beef and Yorkshire pudding; meat pies; fish-and-chips; toad in the hole; cottage pie; sticky toffee pudding; and trifle.

And don't forget that London boasts more ethnic restaurants than anywhere else in the United Kingdom, so almost any kind of cuisine can be literally on the tip of your tongue. For more about English food, see Chapter 13. My recommended restaurants are in Chapter 14, with tips for teas and cakes and more informal meals in Chapter 15.

Mind your teas and queues

When you're in London, you speak English. American English is perfectly fine, of course. Like a major credit card, it's accepted everywhere. But British English (or English English if you prefer) does differ a bit from the English spoken in the New World. You also see some minor spelling variants: cheque, colour, theatre, and so on. Here are a few general terms you'll probably encounter (see Chapter 13 for food terms):

English English	American English
Bonnet	Hood of a car
Boot	Trunk of a car
Brilliant	All-purpose enthusiastic superlative
Brolly	Umbrella
Cheers	Goodbye (or when raising a glass in a toast)
Cinema	Movie ("Theatre" is only live theater.)
Coach	A long-distance bus
Concessions	Special discounts for students, seniors, and the disabled
Cooker	Stove (Sometimes called an Aga, a brand name.)
First floor	Second floor (and so on)
Flat	Apartment
Fortnight	Two weeks
Ground floor	First floor
Jumper	Sweater
'Kew	Thank you
Knackered	Tired
Knickers	Underwear ("Don't get your knickers in a twist.")
Lift	Elevator
Loo	Toilet/restroom ("I need to use the loo.")
Lorry	Truck
Mate	Male friend
Nappy	Diaper
Peckish	Hungry
Petrol	Gasoline
Queue	To line up (The Brits are excellent queuers.)

English English	American English
Quid	One pound sterling
Mac (short for macintosh)	Raincoat
Return ticket	Round-trip ticket
Ring	Call on the phone ("Ring me in the morning.")
Rubber	Eraser
Serviette	Napkin
Single ticket	One-way ticket
Subway	Underpass
Ta	Thank you
Tea time	Between 3:30 and 6 p.m.
Tights	Pantyhose
Torch	Flashlight
Underground/the Tube	Subway

From Harrods to the Portobello Market: The Shopping Scene

It's not just my credit cards speaking. I'm here to tell you that London is one of the world's great shopping cities. Possibly the greatest. Why? The sheer variety of what's available. From mighty Harrods and Fortnum & Mason to the super-chic boutiques of Bond Street, from the 200-year-old shops on Jermyn Street to the wonderland of bookstores on Charing Cross Road, London offers a seemingly endless array of goods and goodies.

Custom-made shirts and suits, hand-tooled leather shoes, high-quality woolens from all over the United Kingdom — in London, you can still find such things. You can hunt for an old engraving, paw through bric-a-brac at an outdoor market stall, or wander through the London silver vaults in your quest for a soup ladle. In Chapter 19, I put you onto some of the best shopping in London.

Parks for Perambulating

I love big cities. I love being right in the thick of it. But at times, the urban rumble and roar get to be a bit much, and then I instinctively seek out a place where there's peace and quiet and lots of green. Fortunately, London is blessed with marvelous parks.

You may have heard of them: **Hyde Park, Kensington Gardens, St. James's Park, Green Park,** and **Regent's Park** (see Chapter 16). These carefully groomed havens, where you can stroll beneath stately trees, lounge on the grass, watch ducks in a pond, or admire the color of the spring-time daffodils, were former royals-only hunting grounds. Now they're part of every Londoner's life and life's blood, the green lungs of an otherwise congested city.

Charming Streets and Squares for Exploring

What could be more fun than just wandering around London's streets? Try it. Pick a neighborhood. The City? Soho? Chelsea? Then just stroll at will, taking note of the wealth of architectural styles, the curious reminders of days gone by, the blue "famous-person-lived-here" plaques on housefronts. On some streets, you can almost hear the horses' hooves clopping on the cobblestones as they did up until about 1915.

Since the Great Fire of 1666 burned down most of medieval London, the building and house styles you see tend to range from the sober neo-classical of the early 18th century to the more elegantly light-hearted Regency style of the early 19th century to the heavier and less graceful Victorian period of the mid- to the late 19th century. The human scale of London streets, with their long terraces of attached brick, stone, and stucco homes built around leafy squares, gives the city a charm and character that intrigues and delights the eye. London grew from a series of villages, and that village-like character is still found in many London neighborhoods (for a list of them, see Chapters 6 and 10).

So Many Magnificent Museums, So Little Time

What can I say about London's magnificent museums? If you're a dedicated museum maven, London's selection will keep you going for days, weeks, months, even years. This city is loaded with every conceivable kind of treasure from all over the world.

If you tire of the great Western European masterworks hanging in the **National Gallery,** you can walk next door to see images of pop icons like Elton John and Princess Di in the **National Portrait Gallery** (see Chapter 16 for both). London's South Bank (see Chapter 25) is really buzzing now that the stunning **Tate Modern** (see Chapter 16) has opened; it shows an international roster of contemporary greats. You can also enjoy masterpieces in museums that were built as private palaces, such as **Spencer House,** former home of Princess Diana's family; **Apsley House,** home of the first duke of Wellington; and **Hertford House,** home of the Wallace Collection (all described in Chapter 17).

Among the "museum museums," the venerable **British Museum** (see Chapter 16), with its unparalleled collection of antiquities, comes out on top — the magnificent Parthenon sculptures (formerly called the Elgin Marbles) understandably hold pride of place there. If you're keen on decorative and applied arts, you can head over to the **Victoria & Albert Museum** (see Chapter 16), a linchpin in the cluster of great South Kensington museums. And you can also tour the **Museum of London,** probably the world's most comprehensive city museum, and **Tate Britain,** formerly the Tate Gallery, holding the world's greatest collection of British art.

Many London museums are favorites with kids as well as adults. The dinosaurs (and the gemstones) at the **Natural History Museum** are dazzling. One of the exhibits in the **Science Museum** is the scorched and battered Apollo 10 Command Module. You can find a whole slew of intriguing museum possibilities in Chapters 16 and 17.

All the City's on Stage: Theater, Performing Arts, and the Club Scene

It's one of my deepest, darkest secrets. *I grew up longing to speak with a cultured English accent.* I don't know where this weird desire came from, unless it was from watching too many old British movies on TV. I've since discovered thousands (if not millions) of Americans, who, like me, who never tire of listening to those magnificently distinctive voices, whether it be East End cockney or upper-crust Queen's English. (If you're puzzled about East End, West End, and other parts of town, see Chapter 6.)

That's why, when I'm in London, I go to the theater every chance I have. On my last trip, in less than a week, I saw productions with Vanessa Redgrave, John Hurt, Zoe Wanamaker, Alan Bates, and Dame Maggie Smith. When actors of this caliber are on the boards — as they always are in London — you don't need to think twice about going to the theater. You just go.

The London theater scene is phenomenal, and seeing a West End play adds to any trip's enjoyment. Take your pick (you have to because so much is available): long-running international-hit musicals, Gilbert & Sullivan operettas, light comedies, hard-hitting dramas, everything from Shakespeare to Wilde to Mamet and beyond. Theater is so much a part of London that I devote all of Chapter 22 to it. Culture vultures can also flip to Chapter 23 for a run-down on the other performing-arts possibilities — grand opera, symphony concerts, chamber music, and dance. And don't forget, ticket prices are lower in London than they are in New York.

But that's only part of the story. Are you a club person? Do you want to slip into your slinkiest gown and go dance to a band or listen to a DJ spinning the latest sounds? Or maybe having a pint or two in a neighborhood pub is more to your taste? Or would you like to dress up in your swellest clothes and glide into one of London's legendary hotel bars for a cocktail? For your after-dark entertainment, you'll also find jazz joints, blues bars, cabarets, gaming clubs, and more. Have a look at what's on offer in Chapter 24.

Chapter 2

Deciding When to Go

*L*ondon is one of those cities that's popular year-round. So popular, in fact, that according to the British Tourist Authority, nearly 12.3 *million* tourists from around the globe visited London in 1998 (the last year for which figures are available), with more than 2.3 million of them from the States.

Arriving in London at any time of year without advance hotel reservations is not a wise idea. If you're planning your trip between April and mid-October, planning ahead is *essential*. Although you can find agencies in London that can help you find a hotel or a B&B in peak season (see Chapter 7), the lines are usually long, and you never know quite what you'll be getting or where it'll be. In Chapter 8 you find descriptions of my recommended London hotels.

The Secrets of the Seasons: What to Expect

London weather is what you might call "changeable." It's hard to predict just what the weather will be like in any given season: Remember that England is an island, and the seas surrounding it, as well as its northerly location, determine its weather patterns. In general, however, the climate is fairly mild year-round, rarely dipping below freezing or rising above 80°F/27°C (at least for extended periods). Table 2-1 gives you an idea of the London's temperature and rainfall variations.

London can be drizzly, it can be muggy, it can be dry and hot, it can be clammy, and it can be glorious. Some days you get a combination. Whatever the weather, whatever the season, London is well worth seeing. The following sections let you know what's happening in London season by season so you can pick the best time for you.

Table 2-1 London's Average Temperatures and Rainfall											
	Jan	*Feb*	*Mar*	*Apr*	*May*	*Jun*	*Jul*	*Aug*	*Sept*	*Oct*	*Nov* *Dec*
Temp (°F/°C)	40/4	40/4	44/7	49/9	55/13	61/16	64/18	64/18	59/15	52/11	46/8 42/6
Rainfall (in.)	2.1	1.6	1.5	1.5	1.8	1.8	2.2	2.3	1.9	2.2	2.5 1.9

A-bloom in the spring

London is at its green, blooming best in April and May. Springtime is when you find the great London parks and gardens and the surrounding countryside at their peak of lushness, which is why the Chelsea Flower Show is the quintessential London spring event.

During the half-term school holidays in late February and for 3 weeks around Easter, visitors pour into London. During those periods, the major attractions have longer lines (*queues* in Britspeak) and hotel rooms may be harder to find. Public transportation is reduced and many museums, stores, and restaurants are closed on Good Friday, Easter, and Easter Monday.

Summer fun in the sun

The heat's on, and it's always nice to be warm in notoriously chilly London. When the summer weather is fine, it's very fine indeed, and the city moves outdoors to take advantage of it with alfresco theaters, concerts, and festivals you can enjoy (see Chapters 22 and 23). Summer evenings in London are deliciously long and often cool, even if the day has been hot. It stays light until 9 p.m.

July and August are the months of highest rainfall in London, so skies then can stay gray and cloudy. On the other hand, occasional summer heat waves can drive the mercury into the 80s and even 90s, making July and August hot and muggy. To make matters worse, many businesses and budget-class hotels don't have air-conditioning. Exacerbated by London's soot and gas and diesel fumes, a hot spell can lead to excessive air pollution.

Most overseas visitors (30 percent of travelers) converge on the city from July to September. Lines for major attractions can be interminably long, and you may bump into your next-door neighbor from Poughkeepsie. Centrally located hotels are more difficult to come by, and their high-season rates apply. If you're traveling in summer, booking your hotel in advance is essential (see Chapter 8).

Chock full of culture in the fall

The golden glow of autumn casts a lovely spell over London. Falling leaves skitter down the streets and through the squares, there's a crispness in the air, and the setting sun gives the old stone buildings and church spires a mellow patina. And London's cultural calendar springs to life.

Yes, autumn can bring rain (every season may do that in London), but you're just as likely to encounter what Americans call "Indian Summer." After mid-September, fewer tourists are around, so the city feels less crowded and you may encounter more Londoners than visitors. Airfares and hotel rates are usually lower.

Wonderful winter

Londoners love to be cozy, and there's no better time for coziness than winter. Interestingly, though most overseas visitors to London arrive in July and August, the number of visitors from *within* the United Kingdom is highest between January and March. What do they know that you should know?

London in winter is a bargain. London's off-season is November 1 to December 12 and December 25 to March 14. Winter off-season rates for airfares and hotels can sometimes be astonishingly low — airline package deals don't get any cheaper (see Chapter 5). At these times, hotel prices can drop by as much as 20 percent. If you arrive after the Christmas holidays, you can also take advantage of London's famous post-Christmas sales (more on this in Chapter 19).

And, although the winter winds may blow, nothing in London stops — in fact, everything gets busier. Why? Because 'tis "the season." Everyone's social calendar is packed, and the arts (theater, opera, concerts, gallery shows) are in full swing. London boasts a lovely buzz during the Christmas season: The stores decorate, lights are lit, carols are sung, special holiday pantomimes are performed, and the giant Norwegian spruce goes up in Trafalgar Square.

Naturally, winter has its downsides. Although the Yuletide holidays are always jolly, they also add up to another peak London tourist season from mid-December to Christmas. You know what that means: bigger crowds and higher prices. The city is virtually shut down on December 25 and 26 and January 1. Stores, museums, and other attractions are closed; on December 26 (Boxing Day), it's difficult to find any kind of restaurant open.

Wintertime London may be gray and wet for weeks on end; by midwinter, the skies get dark by about 3:30 p.m. The British usually keep their thermostats set about 10° lower than do Americans. Rather than turn up the heat, they don their woollies. You should do the same — or be prepared for a chronic case of goose pimples.

London Calendar of Events

London hums with festivals and special events of all kinds, some harking back to centuries past. Before you leave for London, write or call the **British Tourist Authority** (see the Appendix at the back of this book for addresses and phone numbers) and request a copy of its monthly *London Planner*, which lists major events, including theater and the performing arts.

For recorded information on weekly London events while in London, call the London Tourist Board's 24-hour **London Line** at ☎ **09068-663-344;** calls cost 60 pence (about $1) per minute. You can't call the London Line from outside the United Kingdom.

January

In January, the **London Parade** features marching bands, floats, and the Lord Mayor of Westminster traipsing in a procession from Parliament Square to Berkeley Square. Call ☎ **020-8566-8586** for more details. January 1 (noon–3pm).

February

February brings in the **Chinese New Year,** marked by colorful street celebrations on and around Gerrard Street in Soho's Chinatown. Date varies.

March

St. Patrick's Day is a big to-do in London, which has the third-largest Irish population after New York and Dublin. There are no parades, but you'll see lots of general merriment. March 17.

The **Chelsea Antiques Fair** draws antiques lovers to Chelsea Old Town Hall (King's Road) for 10 days. For more information, call ☎ **01444-482-514.** Mid-March (also held in mid-September).

April

At the **Oxford and Cambridge Boat Race** between Putney Bridge and Mortlake Bridge, rowing eights from the two famous universities compete for the Beefeater Cup. A good viewing spot is the Hammersmith Mall. First Saturday in April (check local press for exact date).

The **London Marathon** was first held in 1981 and has become one of the most popular sporting events in the city. In 2000, an estimated 32,000 runners took part, men and women, champion athletes and first-timers. The 26.2-mile race begins in Greenwich, winds its way past the Tower of London and along the Thames, and finishes in The Mall in front of Buckingham Palace, one of the best viewing spots. For more information, call ☎ **020-7620-4117.** Mid-April.

May

The **Football Association FA Cup Final** is held at Wembley Stadium. Remember that *football* in the United Kingdom is soccer, and tickets are difficult to obtain given the sport's popularity. Contact the Box Office, Wembley Stadium Ltd., Wembley HA9 0DW, ☎ **020-8902-0902.** Mid-May.

One of London's most famous spring events, the **Chelsea Flower Show,** held on the grounds of the Chelsea Royal Hospital, draws tens of thousands of visitors from around the world. It's a good idea to order tickets in advance; in the States you can order them from Keith Prowse at ☎ **800-669-7469** or 914-328-2357. For more information, call the Royal Horticultural Society at ☎ **020-7834-4333.** Late May.

June

The juried **Royal Academy Summer Exhibition** presents more than 1,000 works of art by living artists from all over the United Kingdom. For more information, call the Royal Academy at ☎ **020-7439-7438.** Early June to mid-August.

June 4 is the **Queen's birthday,** but her birthday parade, Trooping the Colour, takes place about a week later. The Horse Guards celebrate "Ma'am's" birthday in Whitehall with an equestrian display full of pomp and ceremony. For free tickets, send a self-addressed stamped envelope from January 1 to February 28 to Ticket Office, Headquarters, Household Division, Chelsea Barracks, London SW1H 8RF, ☎ **020-7414-2279.** Mid-June.

Kenwood, a lovely estate at the top of Hampstead Heath, is the bucolic setting for the **Kenwood Lakeside Concerts,** a summer season of Saturday-night open-air concerts. For more information, call ☎ **020-8233-7435.** Mid-June to early September.

The world's top tennis players whack their rackets at the **Wimbledon Lawn Tennis Championships,** held at Wimbledon Stadium. Getting a ticket to this prestigious event is complicated. August 1 to December 31, you can apply to enter the public lottery for next year's tickets by sending a self-addressed stamped envelope to All England Lawn Tennis Club, P.O. Box 98, Church Rd., Wimbledon, London SW19 5AE. For more information, call ☎ **020-8944-1066** or 020-8946-2244 (recorded information) or visit www.Wimbledon.com on the Web. Late June to early July.

The **City of London Festival** presents a series of classical concerts, poetry readings, and theater in historic churches and buildings, including St. Paul's Cathedral and the Tower of London. For more information, call ☎ **020-7377-0540** or 020-7638-8891 (box office). Late June to mid-July.

July

In July, you can see the much-loved **BBC Henry Wood Promenade Concerts.** Known as The Proms, this series of classical and popular concerts is held at the Royal Albert Hall. To book by credit card, call the box office at ☎ **020-7589-8212.** Mid-July to mid-September.

August

Buckingham Palace opens to the public August through September.

During the **Notting Hill Carnival,** steel bands, dancing, and Caribbean fun take over in the streets of Notting Hill (Portobello Road, Ladbroke Grove, All Saints Road). This enormous street fair is one of Europe's largest. For more information, call ☎ **020-8964-0544.** Bank Holiday weekend in August (last Monday in August).

September

The **Thames Festival** celebrates the mighty river, with giant illuminated floats. For more information, call ☎ **020-7401-2255.** Mid-September

The **Chelsea Antiques Fair** draws antiques lovers to Chelsea Old Town Hall (King's Road) for 10 days. For more information, call ☎ **01444-482-514.** Mid-September (also held in mid-March).

November

Although based at the National Film Theatre on the South Bank, the London Film Festival presents screenings all over town. Call ☎ **020-7928-3232** in November for recorded daily updates on what's showing where. Throughout November.

On **Guy Fawkes Night,** bonfires and fireworks commemorate Guy Fawkes's failure to blow up King James I and Parliament in 1605. Check *Time Out* for locations. November 5.

For the **State Opening of Parliament,** the Queen in all her finery sets out from Buckingham Palace in her royal coach and heads to Westminster, where she reads out the government's program for the coming year. (This event is televised.) For more information, call ☎ **020-7971-0026.** First week in November.

The new Lord Mayor of London goes on the grand **Lord Mayor's Procession** through the City from Guildhall to the Royal Courts of Justice in his gilded coach; festivities include a carnival in Paternoster Square and fireworks on the Thames. For more information, call ☎ **020-7971-0026.** Early November.

December

Christmas lights go on in Oxford Street, Regent Street, Covent Garden, and Bond Street. Early December.

The **lighting ceremony** of the huge Norwegian spruce Christmas tree in Trafalgar Square officially announces the holiday season. Early December.

Trafalgar Square is the focus of **New Year's Eve** celebrations. December 31.

Chapter 3

Planning Your Budget

. . . .

In This Chapter

▶ Planning a realistic budget for your trip

▶ Pricing things in London

▶ Uncovering hidden expenses

▶ Using credit cards, traveler's checks, and ATMs

▶ Considering money-saving tips

. . . .

*O*kay, you want to go, you're all excited about it, but can you really afford it? You need a financial reality check to be sure you bring along enough for the ride. If you've never been to London, you need to know without a doubt that it's an expensive city. But even though you may think the trip would be prohibitively expensive because of the transatlantic flight, you can often find bargain airfares to this popular spot that, in some cases, may be cheaper than what you'd pay when flying within the States. Adding everything up, your trip to London can actually be comparable in cost to a trip to New York, San Francisco, or Los Angeles (also expensive cities to visit). And you get an experience that's rich in history and priceless in ambiance.

Adding Up the Elements

You can easily budget for your London trip, but holding down costs while you're in London may be another matter. Everything is so enticing (and did I say expensive?). Use the worksheets at the back of this book to get an approximate idea of what you'll spend throughout your trip. A good way to get a handle on all costs is to keep a tally from the moment you leave home. Walk yourself mentally through the trip:

✔ Begin with transportation to your nearest airport.

✔ Add flight costs, the price of getting from the London airport to your hotel, the hotel rate per day, and an allotment for meals and snacks (exclude breakfast if it's included in the hotel rate).

✔ Figure in costs for public transportation (you really don't want to drive in London) and admission prices to museums, the theater, and other entertainment expenses (don't forget the cost of film and processing).

✔ Determine what you'd like to spend on souvenirs.

After you've done all that, tack on another 15 percent to 20 percent for good measure.

When you arrive at the airport in London, you may be asked by the Immigration authorities how much money you have with you. In order to enter the United Kingdom, you must have sufficient means (cash, traveler's checks, credit cards) to maintain and accommodate yourself and any dependents without recourse to public funds (of course, you may not be asked this either; see Chapter 5) .

Lodging: Your biggest expense

The biggest bite from your budget comes from the cost of your hotel or other accommodation. Fortunately, you'll know what you need to spend because you'll want to book your rooms well in advance of your trip, as London hotels fill up fast. Many mid-range London hotels and all B&Bs (bed-and-breakfast inns) include at least a continental breakfast as part of the room rate, so you can save a few pounds there.

Read Chapter 6 to get an idea of London neighborhoods and their suitability as your home base. Chapter 7 discusses what you can expect for your money and how to get the best rate. Once you get a firm handle on the benefits of price and location, peruse Chapter 8 for my recommendations of top-notch B&Bs and hotels in all price ranges and locations. Plus, if you make the mistake of not booking your rooms in advance, you find which places can help.

Rates vary considerably from B&B to B&B, so giving a reliable average can't really be done. For the recommendations in this guide, however, the rate at a B&B will *generally* be $125 to $150, a moderate hotel $150 to $225, and an expensive hotel $225 to $300. After that, you hit the stratosphere of $300-plus luxury, and in that price range, saving money may not be your optimum goal.

Transportation: Save with Travelcards

Here's some good news: You won't need to rent a car in London, and that'll save you a bundle (however, if you want to rent a car to explore London's environs, see Chapter 9). The London Underground (called *the tube*) is fast, convenient, and easy to use. Special reduced-price transportation passes, called *Visitor Travelcards* (see Chapter 11 for cards you can buy in London), make getting around the city relatively inexpensive.

You can buy your Visitor Travelcards in the United States and Canada before you leave home. Two are available: the *All Zone* and the *Central Zone*. Both allow unlimited travel on the tube and bus and are available in 3-, 4-, or 7-day increments. Prices for the Central Zone card are $21 for adults and $9 for children for 3 days; $26 for adults and $11 for children for 4 days; and $32 for adults and $13 for children for 7 days. You can buy Visitor Travelcards by contacting a travel agent, by calling **Rail Europe** at ☎ **888-382-7245,** or by going online at www.raileurope.com.

If you plan to travel around England by train, consider getting a BritRail pass. You must buy these passes before you arrive, but they offer considerable savings over individual fares. There's a slew of options: a choice of either first or second class, senior passes for those over 60, travel-time periods from 8 consecutive days to 1 month, and Flexipasses allowing you to travel a certain number of days within a set time period. The cost for first-class travel for any 3 days in an 8-day period is $94 adults and $27 children (5 to 15 years); second-class is $69 adults and $18 children. You can order BritRail passes from BritRail Travel International, 500 Broadway, New York, NY 10036 (☎ **888-BRITRAIL** in the U.S. or **800-555-BRIT** in Canada). You can also call Rail Europe at ☎ **888-382-7245** or order through the Rail Europe Web site at www.raileurope.com.

Dining: Experience London's new cuisine

The food in England used to be the butt (or shank) of many a joke, but in recent years London has emerged as one of the great food capitals of the world. Of course, that means eating at the top restaurants is going to cost you. However, you can find countless pubs and restaurants where you can dine cheaply and well — and where you can enjoy your meal along with the locals. In addition, many of the best London restaurants offer special fixed-price meals that can be real bargains.

If you eat lunch and dinner at the moderately priced restaurants recommended in Chapter 14, you can expect to pay $30 to $70 per person per day for meals, not including wine (assuming that breakfast is included in your hotel rate). If you eat breakfast at a café instead and are content with coffee and a roll, expect to pay about $4 to $5. Depending on the restaurant, an old-fashioned English breakfast with eggs, bacon or sausage, toast, and tea or coffee can run anywhere from $8 to $15. Likewise, a simple afternoon tea at a cafe (see Chapter 15 for these lighter meals) will set you back about $7 or $8, but a lavish high tea at one of the great London hotels may total $30 or more.

Sightseeing: Pay as you go

Your budget for admission fees depends on what you want to see, of course. But you may not want to cut costs when it comes to sightseeing. After all, the sights are what you came all this way to see. Sure, it costs $18 to get into the **Tower of London,** but would you really want to miss out on seeing this historic landmark and the extraordinary Crown Jewels housed there? Keep in mind that if you're a senior or a student, you can often get a reduced-price admission.

Check out the sights in Chapters 16 and 17 and determine which are on your list of "must sees." Then add them to the worksheet at the back of this book. Some of the top sights — the **British Museum, National Gallery, National Portrait Gallery, Tate Britain,** and **Tate Modern** — are free. And it costs nothing to stroll through London's great parks or to view **Buckingham Palace** (okay, from the outside) and see the **Changing of the Guard.** Some museums, particularly those in South Kensington, offer free admission after 4:30 p.m. (but this means you have only an hour for your visit).

Shopping and nightlife: Control costs here

Shopping and entertainment are the most flexible parts of your budget. You don't have to buy anything at all, and you can hit the sack right after dinner instead of seeing a play or dancing at a club. You know what you want. Flip through the shopping options in Chapter 19 and the entertainment and nightlife venues in Chapters 22, 23, and 24. If anything strikes you as something you can't do without, budget accordingly. (Keep in mind that a pint in a pub will set you back about $3.50, while a theater ticket can go for anywhere between $25 and $95.)

Table 3-1 gives you an idea of what things typically cost so you can avoid some culture shock.

Table 3-1	What Things Cost in London
Item	*Cost in U.S. $*
Transportation from airport to Central London	
From Heathrow by Underground	$5.75
From Gatwick by train	$17.00
One-way Underground fare within Central London	$2.50
Double room at the Savoy (very expensive)	$553.00–$586.00
Double room at Hazlitt's (expensive)	$280.00
Double room with breakfast at Hotel La Place (moderate)	$173.00–$272.00
Double room at Hotel 167 B&B (inexpensive)	$149.00–$163.00
Double room at Aston's Apartments (self-catering)	$140.00–$198.00
Pub meal for one at Museum Tavern (inexpensive)	$12.00
Meal for one at Oxo Tower, excluding wine (expensive)	$60.00
Set-price dinner for one at Rules, excluding wine (moderate)	$26.00
Dinner for one at The Oratory, excluding wine (inexpensive)	$22.00
Pizza at Gourmet Pizza Company (inexpensive)	$11.00
Afternoon tea for one at the Lanesborough (expensive)	$34.00
Coffee and cake at Pâtisserie Valerie (inexpensive)	$8.00
Pint of beer at a pub	$3.50
Admission to the Tower of London (adult/child)	$18.00/$12.00
Admission to Madame Tussaud's (adult/child)	$17.00/$11.00
Theater ticket	$25.00–$95.00

This statistic may be of some use when planning your budget. In 1998 (the latest year for which figures are available), U.S. visitors to London spent an average of £98 ($162) per day. The figure for all overseas visitors averages out to £74 ($122) per day. The figures include expenditures only while in London. So, for example, if visitors paid in advance for their accommodations as part of a package tour, that payment wasn't included in the figure, but if they paid for the room in London, the payment was included.

Keeping the VAT and Hidden Costs in Check

Let me introduce you to Britain's version of a sales tax, called the *value-added tax (VAT)*. Brace yourself: It amounts to 17.5 percent. The VAT is part of the reason why London prices are so high. The tax is added to the total price of consumer goods (the price on the tag already includes it) and to hotel and restaurant bills. It's not a hidden expense, but not all quoted room rates, especially in the luxury tier, include it. Make sure to ask if your quoted room rate is inclusive or exclusive of VAT. (I give this information for every recommended hotel in Chapter 8.)

 If you're not a resident of the European Union, you can get a VAT refund on purchases made in the United Kingdom (this doesn't include hotels and restaurants). See Chapter 19 for details.

 On top of the VAT, a few restaurants add a service charge of 12.5 to 15 percent to your bill. If they do this, the menu must state this policy. This charge amounts to mandatory tipping, so if your receipt comes back with a space for you to add a tip, put a line through it. This is one of those little things that's important for you to be aware of, so I mention it again in Chapter 13.

As a general rule, except for tips in restaurants (12.5 to 15 percent) and to cab drivers (15 percent), London isn't a city where you'll be tipping excessively. Unless, of course, you're staying in an expensive hotel with porters who carry your bags (£1 per bag carried) and doormen who'll hail you a cab (£1).

Choosing Traveler's Checks, Credit Cards, ATMs, or Cash

Money makes the world go round, but dealing with an unfamiliar currency can make your head spin. In London, you'll be paying for things in pounds and pence, meaning you'll have to convert your own currency into British pounds sterling (see Chapter 12 for detailed information about pounds, pence, and your pennies). When it comes to getting cash in London, should you bring traveler's checks or use ATMs? What about paying with credit cards? In this section, I talk about the special things you may need to know.

Toting traveler's checks: Safer than cash

Today, *traveler's checks* (*cheques* in the U.K.) are something of an anachronism from the days when people used to write personal checks all the time instead of using credit cards or going to the not-yet-invented ATMs. These days, you don't really need traveler's checks because London, like most European cities, have 24-hour ATMs linked to a national network that most likely includes your bank at home (see the next section "Using ATMs: They're everywhere"). Still, if you want the security of traveler's checks and don't mind the hassle of showing your passport every time you want to cash one, you can get them at almost any bank before you leave home.

Your traveler's checks will be denominated in dollars or whatever your local currency is. After you arrive, you need to convert them to pounds and pence. I explain the transaction process in Chapter 12.

Never pay for hotels, meals, or purchases with traveler's checks denominated in any currency other than British pounds. You get a bad exchange rate if you try to use them as cash.

Using ATMs: They're everywhere

Ten years ago, a bank card in Europe was a piece of useless plastic. Now ATMs have revolutionized the money side of travel. You can travel to London with as little as $20 in your pocket, using your bank card to withdraw the cash you need, in pounds, on arrival. ATMs offer a cheap, fast, and easy way to exchange money at the bank's bulk exchange rate, which is better than any rate you'd get on the street. If you withdraw only as much cash as you need every couple of days, you won't feel insecure carrying around a huge wad of bills.

If you're planning to use ATMs, make certain you have a PIN before you arrive. You'll need a four-digit PIN to use ATMs in London — if you have a six- or an eight-digit PIN, you need to have a new one assigned. (You can also use ATMs to get credit-card cash advances, but you'll need a PIN suitable for overseas use. Check with your bank or credit-card company for details.)

You find 24-hour ATMs all over London: outside banks, in large supermarkets, and in some Underground (tube) stations. *Cirrus* (☎ 800-424-7787; www.mastercard.com/atm) and *Plus* (☎ 800-843-7587; www.visa.com/atms) are the most popular networks; check the back of your ATM card to see which network your bank belongs to. The toll-free numbers and Web sites give you locations of ATMs where you can withdraw money while on vacation.

Many U.K. banks impose a fee of 50¢ to $3 every time you use an ATM. Your own bank may also charge you a fee for using ATMs from other banks. Obviously, you need to think twice about the amount you're withdrawing to keep bank fees low by limiting your need to use an ATM.

If you try to withdraw cash from an ATM and get a weird message saying your card isn't valid for international transactions, most likely the bank just can't make the telephone connection to check it (occasionally this epidemic can be citywide). Don't panic. Try another ATM or wait until the next day.

Paying with plastic: Classy and convenient

Credit cards are invaluable when traveling — they're a safe way to carry money and provide a convenient record of all your travel expenses. American Express, Diners Club, MasterCard, and Visa are widely accepted in London. A Eurocard or Access sign displayed at an establishment means it accepts MasterCard.

When traveling, I've come to rely more and more on credit cards to pay for hotel rooms, meals, theater and concert tickets, and many other purchases. I do this not because I'm a chargeaholic; I just find it much easier than carrying around a wad of pound notes, stopping to cash traveler's checks, or using ATMs all the time.

Credit-card purchases are usually translated from pounds to dollars at a favorable rate and show up on your monthly statement, so it's easier to keep track of expenditures.

You can also use credit cards to get cash advances at any bank or from ATMs (see the preceding section, "Using ATMs: They're everywhere"), though you start paying interest on the advance the moment you receive the cash. (You won't receive frequent-flyer miles on an airline credit card, either.)

British retailers now have the option to charge more for goods and services paid for by credit card, though they're obliged to display a clear indication that differentiated pricing applies.

Bringing cash: Always appropriate

Britain has no exchange controls, so you can bring as much cash and as many traveler's checks into the country as you wish. Some folks like to change a small amount (say $100) of currency into pounds before leaving. It's like a small emergency fund, and it's always enough to cover transportation from the airport to the hotel. You can do this at currency exchanges in airports offering international flights to the United Kingdom.

Nowadays, though, it may be simpler to wait until you arrive in London before changing money. The currency-exchange windows at Heathrow and Gatwick (see Chapter 10) will almost certainly be open when your flight arrives, or you can use one of the ATMs. Getting and changing money in London has never been so convenient.

Cutting Costs

Throughout this book, Bargain Alert icons highlight money-saving tips and/or great deals. Here are some additional cost-cutting strategies:

- ✔ **Go in the off-season.** If you can travel at non-peak times (October to mid-December or January to March), you'll find hotel prices can be as much as 20 percent less than during peak months.

- ✔ **Travel on off days of the week.** Airfares vary depending on the day of the week. If you can travel on a Tuesday, Wednesday, or Thursday, you may find cheaper flights to London. When you inquire about airfares, ask if you can obtain a cheaper rate by flying on a specific day.

- ✔ **Try a package tour.** For popular destinations like London, you can book airfare, hotel, ground transportation, and even some sight-seeing by making just one call to a travel agent or packager — and you'll pay a lot less than if you tried to put the trip together yourself (see Chapter 5).

- ✔ **Reserve a hotel room with a kitchen (in London these are called "self-catering units") and do at least some of your own cooking.** You may not feel as if you're on vacation if you do your own cooking and wash your own dishes, but you'll save money by not eating in restaurants two or three times a day.

- ✔ **Always ask for discount rates.** Membership in AAA, frequent-flyer plans, trade unions, AARP, or other groups may qualify you for discounts on plane tickets, hotel rooms, or even meals.

- ✔ **Ask if your kids can stay in your room with you.** A room with two double beds usually doesn't cost any more than one with a queen-size bed. And many hotels won't charge you the additional person rate if that person is pint-sized and related to you. Even if you have to pay a few pounds extra for a rollaway bed, you save hundreds by not taking two rooms.

- ✔ **Try expensive restaurants at lunch instead of dinner.** At most top restaurants, prices at lunch are considerably lower than those at dinner, and the menu often includes many of the dinnertime specialties. Also, look for the fixed-price menus.

- ✔ **Walk a lot.** London is large but eminently walkable. A good pair of walking shoes can save you money in taxis and other local transportation. As a bonus, you get to know the city and its inhabitants more intimately, and you can explore at a slower pace.

- ✔ **Skip the souvenirs.** Your photographs and your memories should be the best mementos of your trip. If you're worried about your budget, do without the T-shirts, key chains, tea mugs, and other "royal" trinkets.

Chapter 4

Planning Ahead for Special Travel Needs

*M*any of today's travelers have special interests or needs. Parents may want to take their children along on trips. Seniors may like to take advantage of discounts or tours designed especially for them. People with disabilities may need to ensure that sites on their itineraries offer wheelchair access. And gays, lesbians, and bisexuals may want to know about welcoming places and events. In response to these needs, this chapter offers advice and resources.

Taking Your Children Along

Traveling with children, from toddlers to teens, is a challenge — no doubt about it. It can put a strain on the budget and the kinds of activities you choose to fill up your day. But in the end, isn't it great to share your experiences as a family?

Look for the Kid Friendly icon as you flip through this book. I use it to highlight hotels, restaurants, and attractions that are particularly family friendly. Zeroing in on these places can help you plan your trip more quickly and easily.

In addition, the following resources can help you plan your trip:

✔ **About Family Travel** (424 Bridge St., Ashland, OR 97520; ☎ **800-826-7165** or 541-488-3074. Fax: 541-488-3067. e-mail: aft@ about-family-travel.com. Internet: www.about-family-travel. com) can tailor a tour specifically for families traveling to London. Its service includes arranging airfares, hotel rooms, transportation, and theater tickets, as well as providing tips on sights and destinations.

> ✔ **Family Travel Forum** (☎ **212-665-6124.** Fax: 212-661-6136.
> Internet: `www.familytravelforum.com`) offers a call-in service for
> subscribers. You can order a subscription ($48 per year) by writing
> FTF, 891 Amsterdam Ave., New York, NY 10025, or call to request its
> information packet, including a sample newsletter, for $2.95.

Locating family-friendly accommodations

Most hotels will happily accommodate your family if you reserve your
rooms in advance and make the staff aware that you're traveling with
kids. The establishment may bring in an extra cot or let you share a
larger room; these types of arrangements are common. Smaller B&Bs
may present problems such as cramped rooms and shared toilet facilities — and some places don't accept children. Ask questions before
you reserve. Be sure to check out Chapter 8 to find hotels that are particularly family friendly.

London has plenty of American-style fast-food places, including **Burger
King, McDonald's, Pizza Hut,** and **KFC.** Younger teens will probably
want to check out the **Hard Rock Café** in Mayfair or the scene at the
Pepsi Trocadero in **Piccadilly Circus,** which offers theme restaurants
such as **Planet Hollywood** and the **Rainforest Café** (see Chapter 17).

Expensive restaurants are less welcoming toward young children. The
menus aren't geared to the tastes of U.S. youngsters, the prices can be
high, and the staff can be less than accommodating. Keep costs down
by eating at a restaurant with a pre-theater fixed-price menu (usually
served 5:30 to 7 p.m.). Your time in London may also be the time and
place to introduce your kids to some delicious and exotic cuisines they
haven't tried — for example, Chinese or Indian. You can find family-
friendly restaurants in Chapters 14 and 15.

If the weather is fine, a picnic in **Kensington Gardens** or **Hyde Park**
may be just the ticket for an enjoyable afternoon (see Chapter 15 for
more suggestions). Renting a self-catering flat with a kitchen is also an
option (as long as you don't mind cooking while on holiday).

Planning your trip together

Your children may be more excited about their London trip if they
know some of the special sights and events in store for them. Before
you leave, sit down with your kids and make a plan. Go over the sights
and activities in Chapters 16 and 17, and let your children list a few of
the things they'd like to see and do, in order of preference. Make a
similar list of your own. Older children may want to do some London
research on the Internet. Together, plot out a day-by-day schedule that
meets everyone's needs.

You can generate excitement about the trip by letting your younger
children read *Peter Pan* or *Peter Pan in Kensington Gardens,* telling them
about his statue there. If they've already read the *Harry Potter* series,

they'll know that Harry lives in London — in fact, he leaves from Paddington Station to go off to sorcerer's school. Older children may enjoy thinking about traveling around London in the Underground (the tube, or subway) or taking a boat trip down the **Thames.** Incite your kids' curiosity about historic sites such as the **Tower of London** and **H.M.S.** *Cutty Sark.* And most young people would enjoy the prospect of a meal at the **Hard Rock Café** and a trip to **Madame Tussaud's** wax museum.

Some kids and adult activities can easily overlap. You may want to spend one afternoon in **Kensington Gardens.** After you all visit **Kensington Palace,** the kids can blow off steam in the new **Princess Diana Memorial Playground.** Many kid-oriented activities in London are just as interesting for parents. From the dinosaur exhibit in the **Natural History Museum** to the animatronic robots re-creating historic scenes in **Madame Tussaud's,** you and your kids will have plenty to look forward to.

Don't overschedule your days with your children. You can't enjoy your trip if both you and your children are worn out.

Preparing for a long trip

The shortest international trip to London (from New York) is about 6 hours (unless you're traveling on the Concorde); air time from Australia may be 25 hours. This is a lot of time for kids to sit still and be quiet. Although they can spend some of the journey time watching a movie (or two) offered by the airlines, come prepared with extra diversions: games, puzzles, books — whatever you know will keep your kids entertained. Request a special kids' menu at least a day in advance. If your child needs baby food, bring your own and ask a flight attendant to warm it. Dealing with jet lag can be hard on adults but even harder on small children. Don't schedule too much for your first day in London. Get everyone comfortably settled and take it from there.

Hiring a baby-sitter while on your trip

What you really need is a relaxing evening at the opera and a romantic late dinner. But you can't take Junior along on this special evening. What are your options? Ask your hotel staff if they can recommend a local baby-sitting service. Most of the hotels marked with a Kid Friendly icon in Chapter 8 will arrange for baby-sitting. London also has several respected and trustworthy baby-sitting agencies that provide registered nurses and carefully screened mothers, as well as trained nannies, to be sitters. Check the London Yellow Pages.

A fully licensed children's care facility, **Pippa Pop-ins** (430 Fulham Rd., SW6 1DU; ☎ **020-7385-2458.** Fax: 020-7385-5706) provides a lovely toy-filled nursery (staffed by experienced caregivers) where you can safely park the little ones. Baby-sitting is available at £8.50 ($14) per hour before 11:30 p.m.; they'll care for your child for the day for a fee of £50 ($82).

Admission prices for most London attractions are generally reduced for children 5 to 16 years old. Under-5s almost always get in for free. If you're traveling with one or two children 5 to 15, always check to see whether the attraction offers a money-saving family ticket, which considerably reduces the admission price for a group of two adults and two children.

Taking Advantage of Bargains and Tips for Seniors

London won't present any problems for you if you're a senior who gets around easily. If not, when you plan your trip, be aware that not all hotels — particularly less expensive B&Bs — have elevators. The steep staircases in some places are a test for *anyone* with luggage. When you reserve a hotel, ask whether or not you'll have access to an elevator or "lift," as they're called in England.

Although London is often crowded, people are generally polite and courteous. The British are orderly when standing in lines (*queueing up*), and they usually respect personal space. And you don't need to be overly concerned about crime. Yes, it does occur, but with far less frequency than in many other major cities.

In most cities, including London, being a senior often entitles you to some terrific travel bargains, such as reduced admission at theaters, museums, and other attractions. Carrying ID with proof of age can pay off in all these situations. *Note:* In London and the United Kingdom, you may find that some discounts are available only to members of a British association; public transportation reductions, for example, are available only to U.K. residents with British Pension books. But always ask, even if the reduction isn't posted.

The following sources can provide information on discounts and other benefits for seniors:

- ✔ **AARP (American Association of Retired Persons**, 601 E St. NW, Washington, DC 20049; ☎ **800-424-3410;** Internet: www.aarp.org), offers member discounts on car rentals and hotels. It offers $8 yearly ($20 for 3 years) memberships that include discounts of 12 percent to 25 percent on Virgin Atlantic flights to London from eight U.S. cities.

- ✔ **National Council of Senior Citizens** (8403 Colesville Rd., Suite 1200, Silver Spring, MD 20910; ☎ **301-578-8800**), a nonprofit group, offers memberships ($12 per couple) that include a bimonthly magazine and discounts on hotels, car rentals, and pharmacy purchases.

✔ **Elderhostel** (75 Federal St., Boston, MA 02110-1941; ☎ 877-426-8056; Internet: www.elderhostel.org) offers people 55 and older a variety of university-based educational programs in London and throughout England. These courses are value-packed, hassle-free ways to learn while traveling. The price includes airfare, accommodations, meals, tuition, tips, and insurance. And you'll be glad to know that there are no grades. Popular London offerings have included "Inside the Parliament," "Legal London," "Classical Music and Opera in London," and "Treasures of London Galleries."

✔ **SAGA International Holidays** (222 Berkeley St., Boston, MA 02116; ☎ 877-265-6862) offers inclusive tours for those 50 and older. Though its tours cover places outside London (such as Cornwall), you can get a pre- or post-tour London extension.

✔ **Grand Circle Travel** (347 Congress St., Boston, MA 02210; ☎ 800-597-3644) is another agency that escorts tours for mature travelers. Write for its publication *101 Tips for the Mature Traveler* or order online at www.gct.com.

Most of the major domestic airlines, including American, United, Continental, US Airways, and TWA, offer discount programs for senior travelers — be sure to ask whenever you book a flight.

Accessing London: Information for People with Disabilities

A disability needn't stop anybody from traveling because more options and resources are available than ever before. London is much more accessible to travelers in wheelchairs than it used to be. Many hotels and restaurants are happy to accommodate people with disabilities. All the top sights in Chapter 16 and many of the attractions in Chapter 17 are wheelchair accessible (call first to make arrangements and get directions to special entrances and/or elevators). Theaters and performing-arts venues are often wheelchair accessible as well (again, call first).

However, the United Kingdom doesn't yet have a program like the Americans with Disabilities Act — though by 2002, some form of legislation may be in place. So if you have any kind of disability, a trip to this huge metropolis is going to require intensive planning.

Contact the British Tourist Authority (see the Appendix for addresses and phone numbers) to be mailed a copy of its *Disabled Traveler Fact Sheet*. RailEurope's British Travel Shop (551 Fifth Ave., 7th floor, New York, NY 10176; ☎ 212-490-6688) sells *Access in London* ($19.95), the best and most comprehensive London guide for the disabled and anyone with a mobility problem. It provides full access information for all the major sites, hotels, and modes of transportation. The book costs £7.95 ($13) in the United Kingdom and is available at many London bookstores.

A World of Options, a 658-page book of resources for disabled travelers, covers everything from biking trips to scuba outfitters. It costs $35 and is available from Mobility International USA (P.O. Box 10767, Eugene, OR, 97440; ☎ 541-343-1284, voice and TDD. E-mail: miusa@igc.apc.org. Internet: www.miusa.org). For more personal assistance, call the Travel Information Service at ☎ 215-456-9603 or 215-456-9602 (for TTY).

Access to Travel (P.O. Box 43, 29 Bartlett Lane, Delmar, NY 12054-1105; ☎ 518-439-4146. Fax: 518-439-9004) is a magazine providing practical information for travelers with disabilities.

Here are some other helpful resources in the United States:

- ✔ **Travel Information Service** at ☎ 215-456-9603 or 215-456-9602 (TTY) or on the Web at www.mossresourcenet.org provides general information and resources for the disabled traveler.

- ✔ The **Society for the Advancement of Travel for the Handicapped** (347 Fifth Ave., Suite 610, New York, NY 10016; ☎ 212-447-7284. Fax: 212-725-8253. E-mail: sathtravel@aol.com. Internet: www.sath.com) is a membership organization with names and addresses of tour operators specializing in travel for the disabled. You can call to subscribe to its magazine, *Open World.*

- ✔ **American Foundation for the Blind** (11 Penn Plaza, Suite 300, New York, NY 10001; ☎ 800-232-5463; Internet: www.afb.org) offers information on traveling with seeing-eye dogs; it also issues ID cards to the legally blind.

For United Kingdom information and advice on suitable accommodations, transportation, and other facilities, contact the Holiday Care Service (2nd Floor, Imperial Buildings, Victoria Road, Horley RH6 7PZ; ☎ 01293-774-535 or 01293-776-943 for hearing impaired; Fax: 01293-784-647).

Here are some other resources in the United Kingdom:

- ✔ **Tripscope, The Courtyard** (Evelyn Road, London W4 5JI; ☎ 020-8994-9294) provides travel and transport information and advice, including airport facilities.

- ✔ **RADAR (Royal Association for Disability and Rehabilitation,** 12 City Forum, 250 City Rd., London EC14 8AF; ☎ 020-7250-3222. Fax: 020-7250-0212) publishes information for disabled travelers in Britain.

> ✔ **Artsline** at ☎ **020-7388-2227** provides advice on the accessibility of London arts and entertainment events. The Society of Lond on Theatres (32 Rose St., London WC2E 9ET; Internet: www. officiallondontheatre.co.uk) offers a free guide called *The Disabled Guide to London's Theatres.*

Be sure to discuss with your travel agent the means of travel that will accommodate your physical needs (train, plane, tour groups, and so on); special accommodations or services you may require (transportation within the airport, help with a wheelchair, and special seating or meals); and the type of special assistance you can expect from your transportation company, hotel, tour group, and so on.

Considering the benefits of escorted tours

You can find tours designed to meet the needs of travelers with disabilities. One of the best operators is **Flying Wheels Travel** (143 West Bridge, P.O. Box 382, Owatonna, MN 55060; ☎ **800-525-6790;** Internet: www.flyingwheels.com), which offers various escorted tours and cruises, as well as private tours in minivans with lifts.

Here are some other tour operators for London-bound travelers with disabilities:

> ✔ **Accessible Journeys** (☎ **800-846-4537.** Fax: 610-521-6959. E-mail: sales@disabilitytravel.com. Internet: www.disabilitytravel. com) offers tours of Britain and London in minibuses or motorcoaches.
>
> ✔ **Accessible Tours** (☎ **800-533-5343** or 914-241-1700. Fax: 914-241-0243. Internet: www.travel-cruises.com), a division of Directions Unlimited Travel, offers individual customized travel and tours.
>
> ✔ **The Guided Tour** (☎ **800-783-5841.** Fax: 215-635-2637. E-mail: gtour400@aol.com) has 1- and 2-week guided tours for individuals, with one staff member for every three travelers.
>
> ✔ **Undiscovered Britain** (☎ **215-969-0542.** Fax: 215-969-9251. E-mail: ann@undiscoveredbritain.com. Internet: www. undiscoveredbritain.com) provides specialty travel and tours for individuals, small groups, or families traveling with a wheelchair user.

Dealing with access issues

Although London's streets and sidewalks are generally kept in good repair, it's an old city so you won't find many modern curb cuts. Public transportation is going to be a concern for people with disabilities: Some stations of the Underground (subway) have elevators and ramps, but public buses aren't wheelchair accessible. However, the black London cabs are roomy enough for wheelchairs.

London Transport's Unit for Disabled Passengers (172 Buckingham Palace Rd., SW1 9TN; ☎ **020-7918-3299.** Fax: 020-7918-3876) publishes a free brochure called *Access to the Underground*. It also provides information on the wheelchair-accessible midibus service (called Stationlink) between all the major BritRail stations, and Victoria Coach Station in Central London has Braille maps.

Trains throughout the United Kingdom now have wide doors, grab rails, and provisions for wheelchairs. To get more information or to obtain a copy of the leaflet *Rail Travel for Disabled Passengers*, contact The Project Manager (Disability), British Rail, Euston House, Eversholt St., London NW1 1DZ; ☎ **020-7922-6984**.

Wheelchair Travel (1 Johnston Green, Guildford, Surrey GU2 6XS; ☎ **1483-233-640.** Fax: 1483-237-772. E-mail: info@wheelchairtravel. co.uk. Internet: www.wheelchair-travel.co.uk) is an independent transport service for the disabled traveler arriving in London. It has self-drive cars and minibuses (although I'd strongly discourage anyone, disabled or not, from driving in London) and can provide wheelchairs. Driver guides are also available on request. Bring your own disabled stickers and permits from home if you're going to rent a self-drive vehicle.

Not all hotels and restaurants provide wheelchair ramps. Most of the less expensive B&Bs and older hotels don't have elevators, or the elevators are too small for a wheelchair. Ask about this issue when you reserve, or use a travel agency specializing in travel for people with disabilities.

All of London's better-known museums and attractions (see Chapter 16) are accessible, and a number of the sites described in Chapter 17 are fully or partially wheelchair accessible, but in some cases you must use a different entrance. Call the attraction to find out about special entrances, ramps, elevator locations, and general directions.

Persons with disabilities are often entitled to special discounts at sightseeing and entertainment venues. These discounts are called concessions (often shortened to "concs") in Britain.

Taking health precautions

Before you leave on your trip, talk to your physician about your general physical condition and your prescriptions for the time you're traveling, medical equipment you should take, and how to get medical assistance when you're away. Carry all prescription medicines in their original bottles with the contents clearly marked, along with a letter from your doctor.

Make a list of the generic names of your prescription drugs in case you need to replace or refill them during your visit. Pack medications in your hand luggage. If you're in a wheelchair, have a maintenance check before your trip and take some basic tools and extra parts if necessary. If you don't use a wheelchair but have trouble walking or become easily tired, consider renting a wheelchair to take with you as checked baggage.

Finding Sites and Events Friendly to Gays, Lesbians, and Bisexuals

London has always been a popular destination for gays, lesbians, and bisexuals, even in the days (up to 1967) when homosexuality was a criminal offense in Britain. Today, with a more tolerant government at the helm, gay pride is prominent. The city government has actually *spent money* to promote gay tourism. You can find gay theaters, gay shops, more than 100 gay pubs, famous gay discos, and gay community groups of all sorts.

Old Compton Street in Soho is the heart of London's Gay Village, filled with dozens of gay pubs, restaurants, and upscale bars/cafes. The Earl's Court area, long a gay bastion, has several gay/lesbian/bi hotels and restaurants, including the **Philbeach Hotel** and the **New York Hotel** (see Chapter 8).

Lesbigay events in London include the **London Lesbian and Gay Film Festival** in March, the **Pride parade** and celebrations in June, and the big outdoor bash known as **Summer Rites** in August. You can obtain information and exact dates by phone or online from the London Lesbian and Gay Switchboard (later in this section).

Brighton, (which I describe in Chapter 21) is one of the gayest seaside resort towns in Europe. From London, you can get there on the train in under an hour.

You may want to check out the following Web sites as you plan your trip. All are specifically geared to gay and lesbian travelers to London and the United Kingdom:

- ✔ www.pinkpassport.com
- ✔ www.demon.co.uk/world/ukgay
- ✔ www.gaytravel.co.uk
- ✔ www.gayguide.co.uk
- ✔ www.gaybritain.co.uk
- ✔ www.timeout.com, the online edition of *Time Out* magazine, with a gay and lesbian section

London's Lesbian and Gay Switchboard at ☎ **020-7837-7324** also has a Web site (accessed on Yahoo!) at www.llgs.org.uk.

The newest and most useful travel guide — covering London, Brighton, and lots of other hot European destinations — is *Frommer's Gay & Lesbian Europe* (published by IDG Books Worldwide, Inc.), available at most bookstores.

In addition, several gay magazines, useful for their listings and news coverage, are available in gay pubs, clubs, bars, and cafes. The most popular are *Boyz, Pink Paper*, and *QX* (*Queer Xtra*; www.qxmag.co.uk). *Gay Times* (www.gaytimes.co.uk) is a high-quality monthly news-oriented mag available at most newsagents. *Gay to Z*, the United Kingdom's "pink telephone directory," can be accessed on the Web at www.freedom.co.uk/gaytoz. Indispensable for its city-wide listings (including gay listings), *Time Out* appears at newsagents on Wednesdays.

Gay's the Word (66 Marchmont St., WC1; ☎ **020-7278-7654;** Tube: Russell Sq.) is the city's only all-round gay and lesbian bookstore; it stocks a fine selection of new and used books and current periodicals.

Part II
Ironing Out the Details

THE FARGO FAMILY DESTROYS ANOTHER CULTURAL LANDMARK

Okay—everyone say Abbey Road...

In this part . . .

This part is all about the nitty-gritty of trip planning. How will you get to London and where will you stay once you've arrived? Chapter 5 covers the pros and cons of using a travel agent and gives you some tips on package tours and airlines. Chapter 6 describes the kinds of accommodations you'll find and discusses London neighborhoods where you might want to stay. Finding a good hotel for the best rate possible is the focus of Chapter 7. You might want to skip all those and turn directly to Chapter 8, my list of London's best hotels, all described and cross-indexed by price and location. And Chapter 9 goes through some last-minute details and ties up a bunch of loose ends: getting a passport, making advance reservations, packing, and more.

Chapter 5

To London, To London: Getting There

*Y*ou just wanted to take a nice little trip to London. But now you are overwhelmed trying to make all the necessary decisions. Do you need a travel agent? Do you want to travel with a tour group and have all the decisions made for you, or do you want to strike out on your own? How do you find the best airfares to London? This chapter can help you iron out the details, so you can go back to happily dreaming about your trip to London.

Travel Agents: The Good News and the Bad News

A travel agent can help you find a bargain airfare, hotel room, or rental car. The best travel agents can tell you how much time to budget for a destination, find you a cheap flight that doesn't require you to change planes a few times in strange airports, get you a better hotel room for about the same price, and even give recommendations on restaurants.

The best way to find a good travel agent is by word of mouth. Check with family members, neighbors, or friends who've had experiences with travel agents. Make sure that you pick an agent who knows London.

Travel agents work on commission. The good news is that *you* don't pay the commission; the airlines, accommodations, and tour companies do.

The bad news is that you may run into some unscrupulous travel agents who will try to persuade you to book the vacations that bring them the highest commissions.

To make sure that your travel agent meets your needs, find out all you can about London (you've already made a sound decision by buying this book) and pick out some hotels and attractions you think you'll like. If necessary, get a more comprehensive guide such as *Frommer's London* or *Frommer's London from $75 a Day* (both published by IDG Books Worldwide, Inc.). If you have access to the Internet, check prices on the Web in advance so you can look out for your own interests. Then take your guidebook and Web information to a travel agent and ask him or her to make the arrangements for you.

Because an agent has access to more resources than even the most complete Web travel site, he or she should be able to get you a better price than you could get by yourself. And an agent can issue your tickets and vouchers on the spot. If the agent can't get you into the hotel of your choice, ask for an alternative recommendation; then look for an objective review in your guidebook while you are still at the travel agency.

 Some airlines and resorts have begun limiting or eliminating travel agent commissions altogether. The immediate result has been that agents don't bother booking these services unless the customer specifically requests them. If more airlines and companies throughout the industry lower commissions, travel agents may have to start charging customers for their services.

Escort Service: Should You Join a Tour Group?

When you travel, do you like to let a bus driver worry about maneuvering through the traffic and locating the destination — while you sit in comfort and listen to a tour guide describe the sights? Or do you prefer heading out on foot and following your intuition, even if you don't catch all the highlights? Do you plan each day's events, or would you rather improvise? The answers to these questions determine whether you should choose the guided tour or travel on your own.

Some people love escorted tours, which are formally defined as groups brought together by an agency for purposes of travel and supplied with transportation, guides, admission fares, and commentaries. The tours free tourists from spending lots of time getting from one place to the next. Tour guides take care of all the details and describe each attraction. Escorted tours disclose the costs up front so travelers don't get many surprises. Escorted tours can take you to the maximum number of sights in the minimum amount of time with the least amount of hassle, and most of the guides are wonderfully knowledgeable about the city and its sights so you probably get more information in less time than you could gather on your own.

Other people need total freedom and spontaneity. They prefer to explore a destination on their own time and at their own pace. They don't mind losing their way to a museum, or getting caught in a thunderstorm without an umbrella (*brolly* in Britspeak), or finding that a recommended restaurant has disappeared. To them, these mishaps make up the adventure of travel.

Dozens of companies offer escorted tours to London. Many of them cater to special interests, such as theater or history buffs, and others are more general. Your best bet is to check with a travel agent or to scan the travel section in your local paper. American Express and many of the airlines offer escorted tours.

If you plan to join an escorted tour, ask a few important questions before you sign up:

- ✔ **What is the cancellation policy?** Do you need to place a deposit? When do you pay in full? Can they cancel the trip if not enough people sign up? If they do cancel, will you get a refund? What if you can't go? How late can you cancel and still get some kind of a refund?

- ✔ **How jam-packed is the schedule?** Are 25 hours of activities stuffed into a 24-hour day (forget the sleep), or will you have time for relaxing or shopping? If you don't enjoy getting up at 7 a.m. every day and not returning to your hotel until 6 or 7 p.m., certain escorted tours may not be for you.

- ✔ **How big is the group?** The smaller the group, the more flexible the schedule will be and the less time you'll spend waiting for people to get on and off the bus. Tour operators may be evasive about this information, because they may not know the exact size of the group until all the reservations are in, but you should be able to get a rough estimate. Some tours have a minimum group size and the tour company may cancel the tour if they don't book enough people. Again, be sure you know their refund policy on cancellations.

- ✔ **What's included?** Don't assume that anything not specifically spelled out is included in your fee. And you may need to ask; they don't always volunteer the information. For example, you may have to pay to get yourself to or from the airport. You may get a box lunch on a day trip, but drinks may cost extra. Beer may be free but wine may not. Admission to attractions may or may not be included, as well as side trips or social events.

- ✔ **How much choice do you have?** Can you opt out of certain activities or does the bus leave once a day, no exceptions? Are all your meals planned in advance? Can you choose your entree at dinner or does everybody get the same meal? Are vegetarian options available?

If you're taking an escorted tour, I recommend that you purchase travel insurance, especially if the tour operator asks you to pay up front. But don't buy insurance from the tour company! If they don't fulfill their obligation to provide you with the vacation you've paid for, they probably won't fulfill their insurance obligations either. Get travel insurance through an independent agency (see Chapter 9).

Forget the Escort: Weighing the Benefits of Package Tours

Package tours are different from escorted tours. *Package tours* are only a way of buying your airfare and accommodations at the same time. And for popular destinations such as London, they're really the smart way to go, because you can save a *ton* of money.

A London package tour that includes airfare, hotel, and transportation to and from the airport may cost less than the hotel alone if you book the room yourself. That's because packages are sold in bulk to tour operators, who resell them to the public.

Packages vary considerably. Some offer a better class of hotel than others. Some offer the same hotels for lower prices. Some offer flights on scheduled airlines; others book charters. Your choices of accommodations and travel days may be limited. Some packages let you choose between escorted vacations and independent vacations; others allow you to add on just a few excursions or escorted day trips (also at prices lower than if you book them yourself) without booking an entirely escorted tour.

Each destination usually has one or two packagers that offer better deals than the rest because they buy in even greater volume. The time you spend shopping around will be well rewarded.

Picking the proper package

The best place to start looking for a good travel package is the travel section of your local Sunday newspaper. Also check the ads in the back of national travel magazines such as *Travel & Leisure, National Geographic Traveler,* and *Condé Nast Traveler.* One of the biggest tour packagers in the Northeast is **Liberty Travel** (☎ **888-271-1584** to find the store nearest you; www.libertytravel.com) and it usually boasts a full-page ad in Sunday papers. You won't get much in the way of service, but you will get a good deal. Another option is **American Express Vacations** (☎ **800-241-1700;** travel.americanexpress.com/travel/personal).

If you're planning a package tour (always a bargain, no matter what time of year you travel), make certain that you check the rates carefully. Some package rates are good all year, but others charge more or less depending on the season. Package rates also vary according to the type of hotel you stay in.

Checking out airlines and hotels

The airlines are good source of London package tours, because they package their flights together with accommodations. When you pick the airline, you can choose the one that has frequent service to your hometown and the one (or its partner) on which you accumulate frequent-flyer miles.

Although disreputable packagers are uncommon, they do exist; by buying your package from an airline, you can be fairly sure that the company will still be in business when your departure date arrives. Among the London airline packages, options include the following:

- **American Airlines Vacations** (☎ **800-321-2121**; www. aavacations.com)

- **British Airways Holidays** (☎ **800-AIRWAYS**; www.britishairways. com/holiday)

- **Continental Airlines Vacations** (☎ **800-634-5555**; www. flycontinental.com)

- **Delta Vacations** (☎ **800-872-7786**; www.deltavacations.com)

- **Northwest Airlines World Vacations** (☎ **800-800-1504**; www. nwaworldvacations.com)

- **Trans World Airlines Getaway Vacations** (☎ **800-438-2929**; www.twa.com)

- **United Airlines Vacations** (☎ **800-328-6877**; www. unitedvacations.com)

To give you an idea of what you're facing, here's a quick look at some sample airline package prices — based on per person, double occupancy. Single supplements are available for solo travelers, but they increase the price considerably (aggravating, isn't it?).

The following packages were available at press time; they may or may not be available when you travel, but they can give you an idea of typical offerings:

- **British Airways:** "A Taste of London" packages are $499 to $1,199 for 4 days/3 nights and $619 to $1,689 for 7 days/6 nights. Prices include airfare, transportation to your hotel from Heathrow or Gatwick, accommodations, and an open-top bus tour.

    "Treasures of London," a 7-day/6-night package for $729 to $1,809, adds a 7-day Travelcard for the bus and Underground (subway) and a more comprehensive sightseeing tour.

    Starting at $699 per adult and $389 per child for 4 days/3 nights, "London Family Vacations" offer a meal at Planet Hollywood and a choice of a GoSee museum pass, a theater ticket, or a sightseeing tour.

✔ **TWA:** The "Majestic London" package — at $1,829 to $2,249 depending on the season and point of departure — includes airfare, chauffeur-driven airport-to-hotel transfers, a chauffeured sightseeing tour of the West End (or private car and driver at your disposal for 6 hours), 3 nights in a deluxe hotel, and two dinners.

✔ **Delta:** "City Stay" London theater packages range from $789 to $1,159, including airfare, hotel accommodations for three nights, and a top-price ticket to a West End show.

✔ **Continental Airlines:** Its "London City Stay" package includes round-trip airfare and 3 nights in a hotel for $449 to $1,079, depending on the city of departure and class of hotel. Many add-ons are available, including tours and theater tickets.

✔ **Virgin Atlantic:** For $909 to $1,789, the 7-day/6-night London packages include airfare, airport transfers, accommodations, two London tours, a theater pass, and an afternoon tea.

These packages don't include airport taxes and surcharges, which typically amount to about $80. All hotels have private bathrooms (with tubs or shower stalls) and include breakfast.

The biggest hotel chains also offer packages. The following are among large hotel groups with properties in London:

✔ **Forte & Meridien Hotels & Resorts** (☎ 800-225-5843)

✔ **Hilton International** (☎ 800-HILTONS)

✔ **Hyatt** (☎ 800-228-3336)

✔ **Inter-Continental Hotels & Resorts** (☎ 800-327-0200)

✔ **Sheraton** (☎ 800-325-3535)

✔ **Thistle Hotels Worldwide** (☎ 800-847-4358)

If you already know where you want to stay, call the hotel and ask whether it can offer land/air packages.

Rates Aloft: Getting the Best Airfare

Airfares are capitalism at its purest. All the passengers in the same cabin on an airplane rarely pay the same fare; they pay what the market will bear.

Business travelers pay the premium rate — known as the *full fare* — if they want the flexibility to buy their tickets at the last minute, to change their itineraries at a moment's notice, or to get home before the weekend. Passengers pay the least — usually a fraction of the full fare — if they can book their tickets long in advance, don't mind staying over Saturday night, or are willing to travel on a Tuesday, Wednesday, or Thursday.

Airlines often lower the prices on their most popular routes (such as London). These fares have advance-purchase requirements and date-of-travel restrictions, but you can't beat the price — usually no more than $400 for a transatlantic flight to London from the East Coast. Watch for these sales as you're planning your vacation, and if you find them, grab them. The sales tend to take place in seasons of low travel volume. Sales are almost never available around the peak months of July and August.

Airfares during London's peak season (late April to mid-October) are higher than those during the off-season (November 1 to December 12 and December 25 to March 14). See the next section for information on how the airlines' Web sites can save you even more!

Flying high with the Net

Another way to find the cheapest fare is to search the Internet. That's what computers do best: search through millions of pieces of data and return information in ranked order. The number of virtual travel agents on the Internet has increased exponentially in recent years. Agencies now compete the way locksmiths do in the yellow pages for the first alphabetical listing. At this writing, 007Travel, 1st Choice Travel, and 1Travel.com all preceded A Plus Travel in an alphabetical listing of online travel agents.

There are too many companies to mention them all, but the following are a few of the respected ones:

- ✔ **Travelocity** (incorporates Preview Travel; `www.travelocity.com`; `www.previewtravel.com`; `www.frommers.travelocity.com`): Travelocity is Frommer's online travel planning/booking partner. It uses the SABRE system to offer reservations and tickets for more than 400 airlines, plus reservations and purchase capabilities for more than 45,000 hotels and 50 car-rental companies. An exclusive feature is its Low Fare Search Engine, which automatically searches for the three lowest-priced itineraries based on your criteria. Travelocity's Destination Guide includes updated information on some 260 destinations worldwide — supplied by Frommer's.

- ✔ **Microsoft Expedia Travel** (`www.expedia.msn.com`): Expedia's site will e-mail you the best airfare deal once a week if you want.

- ✔ **Yahoo! Travel** (`travel.yahoo.com/destinations`): The Yahoo! site has a feature called "Fare Beater," which checks flights on other airlines or at different times or dates in hopes of finding an even cheaper fare.

Because Web information is subject to change without notice, and each site has different benefits and requirements, check out the site for more specific information when you're ready to travel.

Great last-minute deals are available directly from the airlines through a free e-mail service called E-savers. Each week, the airline sends members a list of discounted flights, usually leaving the upcoming Friday or Saturday and returning the following Monday or Tuesday. You can sign up for all the major airlines at once by logging on to **Smarter Living** (www.smarterliving.com), or you can go to each individual airline's Web site (see the Appendix). These sites offer schedules, flight booking, and info on late-breaking bargains. Another site that can help you reel in big savings is **Priceline** (www.priceline.com). At this site, you bid for your tickets; if your bid is accepted, the service immediately purchases the tickets with the credit-card number you've provided; tickets can't be exchanged, transferred, or cancelled.

Considering consolidators: How low can they go?

Consolidators, also known as *bucket shops,* act as wholesalers, buying up blocks of unused seats directly from the airlines and reselling them to the public at cut rates. Their prices are much better than the fares you could get yourself — usually 10 percent to 30 percent lower than the published rates — and are often even lower than the rates your travel agent can get. Consolidators' ads appear in the small boxes at the bottom of the page in the Sunday travel section. Reliable consolidators include ☎ **1-800-FLY-4-LESS** and **1-800-FLY-CHEAP.** Another good choice, **Council Travel** (☎ **800-226-8624;** www.counciltravel.com) caters to young travelers, but its bargain-basement prices are available to people of all ages.

Happy Landing: Getting Comfy with Your Airport

Your London adventure really begins when you land, and where you land can make a difference in how easy it is to get about. Four airports serve regularly scheduled flights to the London metropolitan area, with a fifth airport that's less frequently used. Public transportation service is available into Central London from all five airports (see Chapter 10).

Where you arrive depends on the city you're flying from and your airline. If you're on a regularly scheduled international flight from the States, you'll arrive at Heathrow or Gatwick. If you're on a flight from the Continent, you may land at Heathrow, Gatwick, Stansted, or London City. Luton is much smaller than the others and is used mostly for charter flights from the Continent. Here's a brief description of each of the five airports:

✓ **Heathrow,** the main international airport, is about 15 miles west of Central London. It's served by Air New Zealand, American, British Airways, Continental, Delta, Icelandair, United, and Virgin Atlantic. You can get into London on the Underground (the tube) in about 40 minutes for £3.50 ($6). The Heathrow Express Train

> travels between Heathrow and Paddington rail station (in 15 minutes) for £12 ($20) and the Airbus to Victoria and Euston rail stations (in about 75 minutes) for £7 ($12).
>
> ✔ **Gatwick** is a smaller airport about 25 miles south of London. It's served by American, British Airways, Delta, Continental, Northwest, Icelandair, TWA, and Virgin Atlantic. Gatwick Express trains travel from the airport to Victoria Station in Central London in about half an hour for £10.20 ($17).
>
> ✔ **Stansted,** about 50 miles northeast of London, is used for national and European flights. The Stansted Sky Train to Liverpool Street Station takes 45 minutes and costs £10 ($17).
>
> ✔ **London City,** only 6 miles east of Central London, services European destinations. A bus charges £5 ($8) to take passengers on the 25-minute trip from the airport to Liverpool Street Station.
>
> ✔ **Luton,** 28 miles northwest of London, services mostly charter flights. Travel by train from the airport to King's Cross Station for £10 ($17); the trip takes about an hour.

Channel or Chunnel?

If you're traveling to London from another destination in Europe, flying isn't the only way to get there. Train and car ferries and high-speed Hovercrafts cross the English Channel throughout the year from ports in France, Holland, and Belgium. And the Eurostar, a high-speed train, zips beneath the Channel through the Chunnel, a tunnel beneath the English Channel.

Taking the train

London has several train stations, and the one you arrive at depends on your point of departure from the Continent. The fabulous 3-hour Eurostar service connecting Paris and Brussels to London via the Chunnel arrives at **Waterloo International Station** (some Eurostar trains even offer a drive-on/drive-off service for people heading to London in a car). Trains from Amsterdam arrive at **Liverpool Street Station.** People traveling to London from elsewhere in the United Kingdom may arrive at **Victoria, Paddington, King's Cross,** or **Euston Station.** Every London train station has an Underground link.

The trains in the United Kingdom are separate from those in the rest of Europe, so a Eurail pass isn't valid there. If you're going to travel within the United Kingdom, check out the various BritRail passes available by calling ☎ **888-BRITRAIL** (in the United States) or ☎ **800-555-BRIT** (in Canada) or by checking out www.raileurope.com.

Travel with a queen

You can sail from New York to Southampton, 77 miles from London, on board the Cunard Line's *Queen Elizabeth II*. There is one departure a month in May, two crossings in June, and one crossing per month from July to November. The trip takes 6 days. For more information, contact Cunard Line ☎ **800-5CUNARD**.

Several types of Eurostar fares are available. Senior fares for those over 60 and Youth fares for those under 26 can cut the price of a first-class fare ($239 at press time) by 20 percent or more. The same reductions apply for passengers traveling with validated Eurail and BritRail passes. Check out current and special promotional fares for Eurostar by visiting Rail Europe's Web site at www.raileurope.com.

Taking the ferry or hovercraft

Crossing time for the car, train, and passenger ferries that regularly criss-cross the English Channel can be anywhere from 90 minutes to 5 hours, depending on the point of departure. Various hovercrafts skim over the water in as little as half an hour. The price of these Channel crossings is figured into any train ticket that has London as its final destination.

- ✔ **P&O European Ferries** (☎ **561-563-2856** in the United States or 1705-301-200 in the United Kingdom; Internet: www.poportsmith.com) offers daily ferry/car crossings between Cherbourg and Portsmouth (crossing time 5 hours) and Le Havre and Portsmouth (crossing time 5½ hours).

- ✔ **P&O Stena Line** (☎ **561-563-2856** in the United States or 1304-864-003 in the United Kingdom; Internet: www.posl/com) operates ferries between Calais and Dover (crossing time 75 minutes).

- ✔ **Sea France Limited** (☎ **01304-212-696** in the United Kingdom) runs ferries between Dover and Calais (crossing time 90 minutes).

- ✔ **Hoverspeed UK Limited** (☎ **01304-865-000** in the United Kingdom; Internet: www.hoversped.co.uk) operates hovercrafts that zip across the Channel between Calais and Dover in 35 minutes; the SuperseaCats (jet-propelled catamarans) run between Newhaven and Dieppe in 55 minutes. Frequent train service to London is available from all the Channel ports.

Chapter 6

Choosing Your Neighborhood Base

- -

In This Chapter

▶ Finding out what kinds of accommodations London offers

▶ Choosing a neighborhood to stay in

▶ Knowing what to expect in a hotel in your price range

- -

*L*ondon hotel rooms run the gamut from a basic tiny bedroom with a shared bathroom down the hall to elegant, sumptuous splendor that you need a bucket full of bucks to pay for.

Are you the kind of person who would be depressed by a small, dreary hotel room on an air shaft? Do you require some creature comforts to make your vacation enjoyable? Or is your room nothing more than a place to sleep and change clothes, and you're utterly unaffected by your surroundings?

For purposes of helping you choose the accommodations that are right for you in the neighborhood of your choice, I'm assuming that dumps are out — both in hotel rooms and in neighborhoods. In Chapter 8, I give you details about specific hotels and B&Bs that I can heartily recommend. In this chapter, I provide details about London's downtown neighborhoods that will help you select a location as quiet or noisy, as off or on the beaten track as you prefer.

Determining Your Kind of Place

Accommodations in London are available in varying price ranges and degrees of luxury. Places to stay generally fit into one of two categories: hotels and bed-and-breakfast inns (B&Bs). Nothing is going to be as inexpensive as that low-rate motel on the freeway back home, but London offers good budget hotels and plenty of B&Bs that won't render you unconscious when you see the bill. If you have a few more dollars (whoops, that is, *pounds*) to throw around, you can choose among unique boutique hotels, large chain hotels, and several ultra-luxurious places known the world over. The following sections provide a rundown on the quirks and perks of each type of accommodation.

Understanding the pros and cons of B&Bs

Bed-and-breakfast inns (B&Bs) in Europe are different from what you may have come to expect in the United States. Most are former homes (some are current homes; you stay with the family) — usually old homes — and the comfort and service varies widely. The plumbing can be unpredictable, as can the water temperature. Space is often scarce. But they do offer a slice of domestic London life that you can't get anywhere else.

Because B&Bs are often private homes and not hotels, typical amenities can also vary widely, especially in the bathroom facilities. Nearly all B&B rooms contain wash basins, but you may have to share a bathroom down the hall. The facilities are usually kept scrupulously clean, but many U.S. travelers prefer private bathrooms for their private business. Keep in mind, however, that "en-suite" baths (in the room) are generally so small you'll feel as if you haven't left the airplane, and the super-small showers may make you claustrophobic.

The decor in many of the lowest-priced B&Bs is fairly unimpressive. Coming back to a small room with thrown-together furniture, avocado walls, and a tiny bathroom down the hall with no hot water may be a price you're willing to pay for saving money, but I don't recommend any such places in Chapter 8. The more popular and well-appointed B&Bs are, of course, more expensive. But I believe they're worth the price in comfort and convenience.

What about the breakfast part of the B&B? Well, gone are the days when the staff of every B&B cooked you up a "full English breakfast" (also known as a *fry-up*) of eggs, sausages, bacon, fried tomatoes, and beans. Some still do, but others put out a *continental buffet,* which is a breakfast of cereals, fruits, and breads. That's why some B&B descriptions in Chapter 8 say "English breakfast included" and others say "Continental breakfast included."

Licensed B&Bs, like hotels, are inspected regularly, and the quality of B&Bs has improved considerably over the years. I recommend them for people who don't require a lot of extras, though the most successful B&Bs continually upgrade their services or offer some enticing extras. For example, many B&Bs now provide cable TVs and direct-dial phones in the rooms.

If you want to do some additional B&B research, the following two agencies have useful Web sites:

- ✔ **Worldwide Bed & Breakfast Association:** www.londonbandb.com (☎ **800-852-2632** in the United States).

- ✔ **London Bed and Breakfast Agency Ltd.:** www.londonbb.com (☎ **020-7586-2768** in London).

If you're physically disabled or in any way infirm, B&Bs may not be the choice for you. B&Bs usually don't have elevators, so you may have to carry your luggage up steep narrow stairs. Be sure to check how accessible the B&B is before you make your reservations.

Exploring hotel choices

London boasts a wide choice of hotels. Some inexpensive ones provide breakfast with a room rental; others charge an additional fee for this most important meal of the day. At a four- or five-star hotel, you'll pay a hefty price to eat breakfast on the premises. At a self-catering hotel, you make your own breakfast in your room.

London offers a few *boutique hotels*. These hotels are mid-range in size but not price; sumptuously furnished, they offer state-of-the-art amenities and full service. The **Covent Garden Hotel** and the **Dorset Square Hotel** in Marylebone are two of the best.

A more traditional choice is one of London's older deluxe hotels. The **Cadogan** in Knightsbridge, the **Gore** in South Kensington, and **Hazlitt's 1718** in Soho have all been around for a century or more. These hotels offer a distinctly English kind of style, full of charm and character.

The older deluxe hotels are offset by the hippest-of-the-hip: the **St. Martin's Hotel,** an Ian Schrager concoction in a converted office block.

But maybe you *always* stay at one of the chain hotels — a **Hyatt,** a **Sheraton,** or a **Marriott,** places that are basically the same no matter where they are: They rely on their brand-name, no-surprise approach to win customers. Well, London is chock full of chain hotels, if that's what you fancy. Most of them cater to large groups, and you may feel rather anonymous in them. On the other hand, these hotels are usually well equipped for people with disabilities and families with children.

At the top of the hotel spectrum, in both price and prestige, are the landmark hotels: the **Dorchester, Claridge's,** the **Park Lane,** and the **Savoy.** These famous hotels are among the best in the world. In each of these, you can expect glamorous public salons (and glamorous fellow guests), a generously proportioned and well-decorated room with a large private bath, an on-site health club or access to one nearby, and top-of-the-line service.

You can also consider staying at a *self-catering hotel*, where *you* do the cooking in your own hotel room. For short stays and for one or two people, self-catering hotels don't always beat the competition's price. But for families and those who can't afford or don't want to eat every meal out, self-catering hotels can be a budget-saver. I note the best in Chapter 8.

London Accommodations Overview

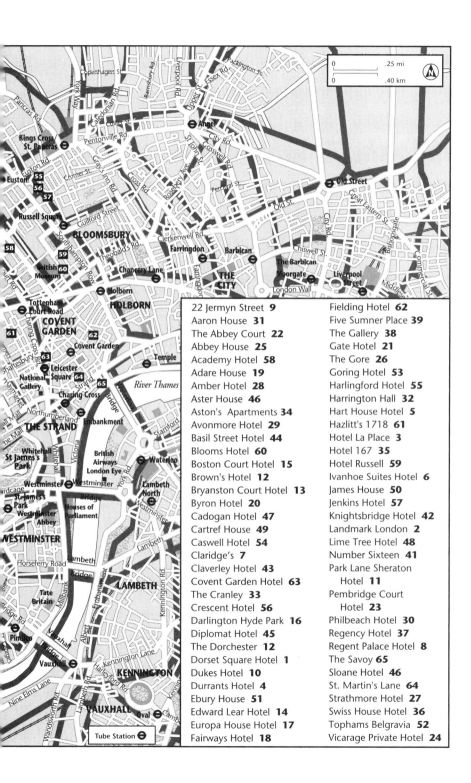

22 Jermyn Street **9**
Aaron House **31**
The Abbey Court **22**
Abbey House **25**
Academy Hotel **58**
Adare House **19**
Amber Hotel **28**
Aster House **46**
Aston's Apartments **34**
Avonmore Hotel **29**
Basil Street Hotel **44**
Blooms Hotel **60**
Boston Court Hotel **15**
Brown's Hotel **12**
Bryanston Court Hotel **13**
Byron Hotel **20**
Cadogan Hotel **47**
Cartref House **49**
Caswell Hotel **54**
Claridge's **7**
Claverley Hotel **43**
Covent Garden Hotel **63**
The Cranley **33**
Crescent Hotel **56**
Darlington Hyde Park **16**
Diplomat Hotel **45**
The Dorchester **12**
Dorset Square Hotel **1**
Dukes Hotel **10**
Durrants Hotel **4**
Ebury House **51**
Edward Lear Hotel **14**
Europa House Hotel **17**
Fairways Hotel **18**

Fielding Hotel **62**
Five Sumner Place **39**
The Gallery **38**
Gate Hotel **21**
The Gore **26**
Goring Hotel **53**
Harlingford Hotel **55**
Harrington Hall **32**
Hart House Hotel **5**
Hazlitt's 1718 **61**
Hotel La Place **3**
Hotel 167 **35**
Hotel Russell **59**
Ivanhoe Suites Hotel **6**
James House **50**
Jenkins Hotel **57**
Knightsbridge Hotel **42**
Landmark London **2**
Lime Tree Hotel **48**
Number Sixteen **41**
Park Lane Sheraton
  Hotel **11**
Pembridge Court
  Hotel **23**
Philbeach Hotel **30**
Regency Hotel **37**
Regent Palace Hotel **8**
The Savoy **65**
Sloane Hotel **46**
St. Martin's Lane **64**
Strathmore Hotel **27**
Swiss House Hotel **36**
Tophams Belgravia **52**
Vicarage Private Hotel **24**

Brits, and Europeans in general, are not as committed to smokefree environments as Americans are, though this cultural trait is beginning to change. For now, however, many London hotels and B&Bs don't have no-smoking rooms (although some do, and some reserve a floor for nonsmokers). To find out if your hotel is nonsmoker-friendly, simply ask whether no-smoking rooms are available. In the hotel descriptions in Chapter 8, I always note any hotels that are completely smoke-free.

Choosing the Neighborhood You Need

You can make your trip to London work more smoothly if you pay some attention to the neighborhood you wish to stay in. Can you get a good night's sleep there? Is it close to attractions or public transportation? Can you take a brisk walk at night without fear? This section gives you the pluses and minuses of London's chief hotel neighborhoods, so you can match the amenities and drawbacks against your own needs.

Central London, considered the city center, is divided into three areas: *The City,* the *West End,* and *West London* (or Central London beyond the West End). The following sections provide brief descriptions of the Central London neighborhoods containing the hotels I recommend in Chapter 8. I don't cover all of Central London because it's unlikely that you'll stay in The City (which is the home of many tourist sites but few hotels) or Holborn (London's legal heart). Crime is less prevalent in London than in many other major cities, and all the neighborhoods in the following list are safe areas. For a more complete description of Central London's neighborhoods, see Chapter 10.

The West End

The West End (that is, west of The City) is what you might loosely call "downtown" London. Most people think of the West End as synonymous with the theater, entertainment, and shopping areas around Piccadilly Circus and Leicester Square. The following sections describe West End areas and attractions.

Covent Garden and The Strand

Covent Garden is the home of the **Royal Opera House** and **Covent Garden Market,** one of the city's most popular gathering spots. The entire area is chock-a-block with shops, restaurants, and pubs, but not many hotels. However, the **Fielding,** one of London's most centrally located budget hotels, and the **Covent Garden Hotel,** a luxurious boutique hotel created from an old hospital, are both here. The Covent Garden and Leicester Square tube (subway) stops provide the closest access, but you can easily walk to anywhere in the West End or neighboring Soho. South of Covent Garden is *The Strand,* a major street flanked with theaters, shops, and restaurants. Architecturally, however, it's far less distinctive than the Covent Garden area. The **Savoy** is the most famous hotel on The Strand. If you stay in this area, you should know:

> ✔ It's in the heart of the West End, close to theaters, shopping, and entertainment.
>
> ✔ It's busy all day long and far into the night, so noise could be a problem.

Bloomsbury

North of Covent Garden is the *Bloomsbury* district, location of the **British Museum,** the **University of London,** and many other colleges and bookstores. The formidably Victorian **Hotel Russell** peers down on **Russell Square,** the largest park in Bloomsbury. The streets around the square, especially Cartwright Gardens, are lined with hotels and B&Bs long-favored by budget travelers. Tottenham Court Road and Goodge Street are Bloomsbury's major shopping streets and, with Russell Square, the main Underground (subway) stops. This centrally located area tends to be quiet and rather staid, but offers many restaurants and pubs. If you stay in this area, you should know:

> ✔ It's close to the British Museum and within walking distance of the West End.
>
> ✔ You'll need to go elsewhere for your nightlife.'

Piccadilly Circus, Leicester Square, and Charing Cross

Central London's major theater, entertainment, and shopping streets are to the west of Covent Garden. *Piccadilly Circus* is one of the world's best-known tourist meccas, full of megastores, glitzy arcades, and restaurants catering to the hordes. Commercial West End theaters and first-run movie palaces lie on or adjacent to *Leicester Square* and Shaftesbury Avenue. *Charing Cross Road* is famed for its bookstores and booksellers. The **Regent Palace Hotel** is one of the older tourist hotels in this area, where the streets tend to be crowded, noisy, and rather anonymous. The state-of-the-art **St. Martin's Lane,** designed by Philippe Starck, is the area's newest and coolest hot spot. Transportation is easy, with tube (subway) stations at Piccadilly Circus, Leicester Square, and Charing Cross Road. If you stay in this area, you should know:

> ✔ It's in the commercial heart of London, close to major shopping streets and entertainment.
>
> ✔ Be prepared for lots of street action, day and night. On weekends, this area can become boisterous and rowdy.

Soho

The warren of densely packed streets east of Leicester Square is *Soho.* It's always been known for its restaurants and clubs but had a seedy air until about a decade ago, when gentrification took over big-time. Soho remains a major tourist hub for shopping, eating, and nightclubbing. It has also become London's Gay Village, with dozens of gay pubs, restaurants, and upscale cafe/bars around Old Compton Street. London's Chinatown is centered around Gerrard Street. Soho isn't particularly known for its hotels, but there are a few, including **Hazlitt's 1718,** one of London's oldest and most charming. The closest tube (subway) stops are Leicester Square, Covent Garden, and Tottenham Court Road. If you stay in this area, you should know:

- ✔ The West End theaters and museums are minutes away.

- ✔ It's a nightclub, restaurant, and café mecca, with a few porn shops and strip clubs thrown into the mix.

- ✔ The narrow streets can be confusing, and they're often packed and noisy far into the night.

Westminster and Victoria

Westminster has been the seat of British government since 1050, when Edward the Confessor moved his court there. **Trafalgar Square,** a famous gathering point for tourists (and pigeons) across from the **National Gallery,** marks its northern periphery. From there, the Westminister area extends south, running beside the Thames and east of St. James's Park to **Westminster Abbey** and the **Houses of Parliament.**

The *Victoria* area around massive **Victoria Station** is a good spot to track down convenient and moderately priced B&Bs and hotels, especially on Ebury Street, the site of old favorites such as the **Lime Tree Hotel.** Victoria Station is one of London's major transportation hubs, a nucleus for the Underground (subway), BritRail, and Victoria Coach Station. If you stay in this area, you should know:

- ✔ Inexpensive to moderately priced hotels and B&Bs are plentiful along Ebury Street.

- ✔ You may feel slightly out of the loop in this area, especially at night, even though the public transportation options are great. For some, that's a real plus.

St. James's

St. James's is the site of many tony hotels, including **22 Jermyn Street,** an elegant boutique hotel. Named after the Court of St. James's, this posh neighborhood, which begins at Piccadilly Circus and moves southwest to include **Pall Mall, the Mall, St. James's Park,** and **Green Park,** is often called Royal London. The Queen herself lives here, at **Buckingham Palace.** It might be the most convenient area in the West End, because it includes the American Express office on the Haymarket and upscale shopping emporiums such as **Fortnum & Mason** (one of the Queen's grocers) on Regent Street. If you stay in this area, you should know:

- ✔ It's near the seats of royal power and privilege and some great shopping, as well as two lovely parks.

- ✔ You'll pay top dollar (or pound, I should say) for the choice location.

Mayfair

Luxury hotels cluster along the quiet streets of *Mayfair,* an area filled with elegant Georgian townhouses and exclusive shops. The **Park Lane,** one of London's most famous (and expensive) hotels, overlooks Green Park. Marvelous little finds such as the inexpensive **Ivanhoe Suites** allow the rest of us to stay in this posh neighborhood. Mayfair is the most fashionable section of London, but offers no major tourist attractions. The **American Embassy** is at **Grosvenor** (pronounced *Grove*-nur) **Square** and, according to song legend, a nightingale once sang in **Berkeley** (pronounced *Bark*-lee) **Square.** You can access Mayfair to the north by the Bond Street or Marble Arch Underground (subway) station and to the south by Hyde Park Corner or Green Park station. If you stay in this area, you should know:

✔ You'll be in a lovely place — if you can afford it. Most of the hotels are luxury establishments and extremely expensive.

✔ You'll have to go elsewhere for your fun.

Marylebone

Marylebone (pronounced *Mar*-lee-bone), which includes **Regent's Park** (home of the **London Zoo**), is north of Bloomsbury and Mayfair. Here you can find that perennial tourist favorite, **Madame Tussaud's** wax museum. **Baker Street** continues to draw sleuthing Sherlock Holmes aficionados. Dating from Mr. Holmes's era is the gigantic **Landmark London,** a luxuriously restored railway hotel; **Durrants,** a traditional English small hotel, is even older. Marylebone has some lovely squares, such as **Portman Place,** laid out in the late 18th century, but later development robbed the area of much of its village character. If you stay here, you should know:

✔ Marylebone offers plenty of shopping and restaurants, as well as a huge park that's great for kids.

✔ You'll find this neighborhood less convenient if you're going to spend every night seeing a West End show. The area is business oriented, so the side streets are generally deserted after 8 p.m.

Central London beyond the West End

The following are considered West London (as opposed to the West End) neighborhoods. All in Central London, they contain some prime shopping, beautiful parks and gardens, and popular museums.

Knightsbridge

A fashionable and fashion-conscious area south of Hyde Park and west of Green Park, *Knightsbridge* is famed for its shopping. **Harrods,** one of the world's great department stores, is located there. Expensive chic boutiques and upscale restaurants are found along Beauchamp (pronounced *Beech*-um) Place, dating from the Regency era. The area has some superexpensive high-rise and boutique hotels and a few midrange hotels, such as the **Claverley Hotel** and **Knightsbridge Hotel.** If you stay in this area, you should know:

  ✔ It's close to Hyde Park.

  ✔ Hotels are generally in the expensive-plus category.

  ✔ Surprisingly little nightlife is available for ordinary folks, although
    the area is an upscale-shopper's and gourmand's dream.

Belgravia

Extending south of Knightsbridge to the river, *Belgravia* has been a residential quarter for London aristocrats since Queen Victoria's time. It
rivals Mayfair for poshness and wealth and, like Mayfair, doesn't have any
major museums or tourist attractions. **Belgrave Square,** its centerpiece,
was completed in 1835. The hotels here tend to be on the upper-end of
the price scale, with just a few moderately priced possibilities such as the
Diplomat Hotel, sprinkled into the mix. If you stay in this area, these tips
will be helpful:

  ✔ Be prepared for steep prices and empty streets at night (but
    plenty of quiet, and you can pretend you're a *toff* (Britspeak for
    the upper class).

  ✔ This area is London's version of Embassy Row.

Chelsea

Full of expensively charming town houses and quiet mews (former
stables converted into residences), *Chelsea* flanks the river to the southwest of Belgravia. Upper crusts (including the late Princess Diana before
her marriage) who lived and/or shopped around **Sloane Square,**
Chelsea's northern boundary, were called the "Sloane Rangers" in the
1980s. In the 19th century, Chelsea was the preferred place of residence
for artistic and literary luminaries and "bohemians." Flamboyant person-
alities such as Oscar Wilde and actress Lillie Langtry held court in the
Cadogan Hotel, today one of London's most delightfully old-fashioned
establishments. The lovely 17th-century **Chelsea Physic Garden** is
found on the grounds of the Chelsea Royal Hospital, which also plays
host to the annual Chelsea Flower Show. Trendy **King's Road,** Chelsea's
major shopping (and traffic) artery, has been in the forefront of contemporary London street fashion since the 1960s. Here are some tips when
considering a stay in this area:

  ✔ Although the area is charming, getting to and from the West End
    can be time consuming.

  ✔ King's Road is a hip shopping street, but it closes down after 6 p.m.

Kensington and Holland Park

The Royal Borough of *Kensington* lies west of **Kensington Gardens,** one
of London's most beautiful parks. In the park itself is **Kensington
Palace,** former home of the late Princess Diana and current home of
Princess Margaret and other lesser royals. The Kensington area is tra-
versed by two major shopping streets, Kensington High Street to the
south and Kensington Church Street to the east. Nearby **Holland Park,**
another tony neighborhood, boasts an open-air theater and is a lovely

place for a quiet stroll. The **Vicarage Private Hotel, Abbey House,** and the **Avonmore Hotel** are all fine inexpensive places in converted Victorian townhouses. If you stay in this area, you should know:

✔ Its nearness to Kensington Gardens and Holland Park, along with the abundance of shopping, make this a great area during the daytime.

✔ You may feel a bit lonely at night when the shops close and the neighborhood's residential nature takes over. In addition, you need to allot extra time for getting to and from the West End.

South Kensington

A busy residential neighborhood south of Kensington Gardens, *South Kensington* is prime hotel and restaurant territory. Popular with European and American travelers, its streets and squares are lined with frequently identical Victorian terrace houses, many of them converted into B&Bs and small hotels. Four Victorian houses form **Aston's Apartments,** a good choice for those interested in self-catering rooms; the **Strathmore** is the former residence of 14th earl of Strathmore, the Queen Mother's late dad. The Gloucester Road tube station provides easy access into the rest of London and is a stop on the Piccadilly Line from Heathrow airport. South Kensington is the other major tube station in the area. South Ken is frequently referred to as *Museumland* because the **Natural History Museum,** the **Victoria & Albert Museum,** and the **Science Museum** are all there. So is **Royal Albert Hall,** a landmark concert hall. **Kensington Gardens** is never more than a few minutes' walk from anywhere in South Ken. All in all, this is one of the best areas to stay in London. Here are some tips to help you decide whether to stay in this area:

✔ South Ken offers an abundance of reasonably priced hotels and B&Bs.

✔ The major museums are a short walk away, as are a number of restaurants.

✔ Kensington Gardens and Kensington shopping are nearby.

Earl's Court

South of Kensington (and west of South Kensington) is *Earl's Court,* sometimes called Kangaroo Court for the preponderance of Australians who favor its budget hotels and nonswanky pubs and restaurants. Visitors pour in to the concerts and major exhibitions held at the **Earl's Court Exhibition Centre.** For decades the neighborhood has been home to a sizeable gay community, and though much of the action has moved to Soho, Earl's Court still has several gay pubs, restaurants, and hotels, such as the **Philbeach** and the **New York.** Earl's Court, a bit tattered in places, is undergoing gentrification, but it's still your best bet for truly inexpensive places to stay and eat. Earl's Court is the area's primary Underground (tube) station. If you stay in this area, you should know:

✔ Earl's Court is noted for its inexpensive lodgings and long-settled gay/lesbian ambience.

✔ Overall, it's not the prettiest part of town, but it has some nice areas.

Paddington and Bayswater

The *Paddington* area, north of Kensington Gardens and Hyde Park, has **Paddington Station** as its focal point, where children's book favorite *Paddington Bear* made his debut. (Sorry, you won't see him there.) Norfolk Square and Sussex Gardens are crammed with inexpensive B&Bs, such as **Adare House.** Quaint Paddington ain't; it's busy rather than lively, and no major tourist sites are located here.

Bayswater, south of Paddington Station, is another area to look for B&Bs. Most are found in Victorian terrace houses around large squares. You'll find moderately priced establishments, such as the **Byron Hotel.** Like Paddington, Bayswater has no major tourist sites but is close to **Hyde Park.** The tube stations are Paddington, Bayswater, Queensway, Lancaster Gate, and Marble Arch. If you stay in this area, you should know:

- ✔ Budget hotels are plentiful, but Paddington and Bayswater aren't very distinguished.

- ✔ You won't end up spending a great deal of your precious time in either area, except to sleep.

Notting Hill

Notting Hill, with busy Bayswater Road to the north and Kensington to the west, has become a hot spot in recent years, particularly the neighborhood of Notting Hill Gate. Once a place to be avoided, now it's a place to be seen, drawing visitors to restaurants and clubs. Portobello Road (the Hugh Grant/Julia Roberts film *Notting Hill* was shot here) is the site of one of London's most famous Saturday street markets and also the tiny **Gate Hotel** and its talkative parrot Bilko. The nicer parts of Notting Hill are filled with small late-Victorian houses and mansions sitting on quiet, leafy streets. The tube station is Notting Hill Gate.

Here are some things to know about staying in this area:

- ✔ The main streets have a youthful edge and energy.

- ✔ It isn't really known for its hotel scene, but there are some B&Bs and the quaint 6-room Gate Hotel.

- ✔ It's close to Portobello Market, but you won't spend more than a few hours there on Saturday.

- ✔ Getting to/from the West End at night requires extra time.

Index of recommended hotels by location

Here's a listing of the hotels I recommend by neighborhood and price ($ = least expensive; $$$$$ = most expensive). For a complete description of these hotels, see Chapter 8.

Bayswater

Byron Hotel, $$

Belgravia

Diplomat Hotel, $$

Bloomsbury

Academy Hotel, $$
Blooms Hotel, $$$$
Crescent Hotel, $
Harlingford Hotel, $
Hotel Russell, $$$
Jenkins Hotel, $

Chelsea

Cadogan Hotel, $$$$
Sloane Hotel, $$$

Covent Garden

Covent Garden Hotel, $$$$$
Fielding Hotel, $

Earl's Court

Aaron House, $
Amber Hotel, $$
Philbeach Hotel, $

Kensington

Abbey House, $
Avonmore Hotel, $
Vicarage Private Hotel, $

Knightsbridge

Basil Street Hotel, $$$$
Claverley Hotel, $$
Knightsbridge Hotel, $$$

Marylebone

Boston Court Hotel, $
Bryanston Court Hotel, $$
Dorset Square Hotel, $$$
Durrants Hotel, $$
Edward Lear Hotel, $
Hart House Hotel, $
Hotel La Place, $$
Landmark London, $$$$$

Mayfair

Ivanhoe Suites Hotel, $
Park Lane Hotel, $$$$$

Notting Hill

The Abbey Court, $$$
Gate Hotel, $
Pembridge Court Hotel, $$$

Paddington

Adare House, $
Darlington Hyde Park, $$
Europa House Hotel, $
Fairways Hotel, $

Piccadilly Circus

Regent Palace Hotel, $$
St. Martin's Lane, $$$$$

Soho

Hazlitt's 1718, $$$

South Kensington

Aster House, $$
Aston's Apartments, $$
The Cranley, $$$
Five Sumner Place, $$$
The Gallery, $$
The Gore, $$$$
Harrington Hall, $$$
Hotel 167, $
Number Sixteen, $$$
Regency Hotel, $$$
Strathmore Hotel, $$$
Swiss House Hotel, $

St. James's

Dukes Hotel, $$$$
22 Jermyn Street, $$$$

The Strand

The Savoy, $$$$$

Westminster & Victoria

Caswell Hotel, $
Ebury House, $
Goring Hotel, $$$$
James House & Cartrel House, $
Lime Tree Hotel, $$
Tophams Belgravia, $$

Chapter 7

Off the Rack: Booking Your Room

Chant this as a general mantra: "I will not arrive in London without a hotel reservation." This is especially important if you're planning your trip from mid-April to early October (high season). Hotels in the inexpensive-to-moderate range are always the first ones to be snapped up, but space can be tight everywhere, at any time of year, if a major trade show or convention is coming to the city.

The maximum rate that a hotel charges for a type of room is the *rack rate*. If you walk in off the street and ask for a room for the night, the hotel may charge you this top rate. Sometimes the rate is posted on the fire/emergency exit diagrams on the back of your door.

Be aware that you don't have to pay the rack rate! Hardly anybody does. Just ask for a cheaper or discounted rate. The result is often favorable when savvy travelers make this request at larger hotels. However, prices aren't generally negotiable at smaller hotels and B&Bs. Some of them do offer special rates for longer stays, however.

Getting the Best Room at the Best Rate

The rate you pay for a room depends on many factors and the way you make your reservation is the most important. A travel agent may be able to negotiate a better room rate than you could get by yourself. (The hotel gives the agent a discount in exchange for steering his or her business toward that hotel.)

Before you make your hotel reservation, I recommend that you call both the U.S. toll-free number and the local London number for the prospective hotel. I know that calling both sources takes time and money, but the quoted rates can vary so widely you could save a bundle. (Smaller and less expensive B&Bs and hotels generally don't have toll-free numbers in the States, so you'll have to call, fax, or e-mail the establishment directly.)

Room rates change with the season and as occupancy rates rise and fall. You're less likely to receive discount rates if a hotel is close to full, but if it's close to empty, you may be able to negotiate a significant discount. Expensive hotels catering to business travelers are most crowded on weekdays and usually offer discounts for weekend stays. If you make your reservation with a large chain hotel, be sure to mention membership in AARP, frequent-flyer programs, and any other corporate rewards program. Budget hotels and small B&Bs rarely offer these organization discounts, but you never know when the mention may be worth a few pounds off your room rate in larger hotels.

You may be able to save 20 percent or more by traveling *off-season,* which is mid-October to mid-December and January to March (see Chapter 2). Always ask if any special discounts are in effect. For example, you may be able to stay for 7 nights for the price of 6, or if you're with your kids, a child under 12 may be able to stay free in your room. If you're willing to share a bathroom, you can save money that way, too. The best rates of all will probably be with an air/hotel package (see Chapter 5). With these packages, which are sometimes astonishingly cheap, you'll have to choose a hotel that's part of the package. Airline package hotels tend to be larger chains. So what? The money you save may amount to hundreds of dollars.

Hotels almost never consider a room reservation confirmed until they receive partial or full payment (this policy varies from hotel to hotel). You can almost always confirm your reservations immediately with a credit card; otherwise, you must mail in your payment (generally using an International Money Order available at most banks). Before booking, always ask about the cancellation policy. If your plans change, you don't want pay for a room you've never slept in. At some hotels you can get your money back if you cancel a room with 24 hours notice; in others, you must notify the hotel 5 or more days in advance. After you've booked the room, request a written confirmation by fax, e-mail, or post and be sure to take it along on your trip.

Sorry, you can't escape that annoying 17.5 percent *value-added tax (VAT).* In general, the quoted room rate includes the VAT (except for rooms at the upper end of the price scale). Be sure to ask, though, so you won't get an unpleasant surprise when you're checking out. Unless otherwise noted (the listing will say "Rates don't include 17.5 percent VAT"), the VAT is included in the rates for my recommended hotels.

The telephone in your hotel is convenient, but I recommend that you avoid using it if you're on a budget. A local call that costs 20 pence at a phone booth may cost you £1 ($1.65) or more from your hotel phone. If you plan to make a number of calls, get a phone card (see the details under "Telephone" in the Appendix) and use a phone outside the hotel.

Surfing the Web for Hotel Deals

Although the major travel-booking Web sites (Travelocity, Expedia, Yahoo!, and Priceline; see Chapter 5 for details) offer hotel booking, you may be better off using a site devoted to lodging because more general sites don't list all types of properties. Some lodging sites specialize in a particular type of accommodation, such as bed-and-breakfast inns, which aren't on the more mainstream booking services. Other services, such as TravelWeb, offer weekend deals on major chain properties that cater to business travelers and have more empty rooms on weekends. Here are some good all-purpose Web sites you can use to track down London hotels and make online reservations:

✔ **Hotel Reservations Network** (www.180096hotel.com) lists bargain rates at hotels in U.S. and international cities, including London. Because it prebooks blocks of rooms, HRN sometimes has rooms at hotels that are "sold out." If you click "London" and input your travel dates, the site provides a list of the best prices for a selection of hotels in various neighborhoods. Descriptions include an image of the property and a locator map. To book online, click "Book Now." The toll-free number is printed all over this site, so call if you want more options than the Web site lists online.

✔ **TravelWeb** (www.travelweb.com) lists more than 16,000 hotels worldwide, focusing on chains such as Hyatt and Hilton, and you can book almost 90 percent of these online. Its Click-It Weekends, updated each Monday, offers weekend deals at many leading chains. TravelWeb is the online home for Pegasus Systems, which provides transaction processing systems for the hotel industry.

✔ **Hotel-U.K. Reservations Service** (www.demon.co.uk/hotel-uk) features Best Value hotels of the month and other moneysaving promotions.

✔ **British Hotel Reservation Centre** (www.bhrc.co.uk) lists seasonal specials at selected London hotels.

✔ **All Hotels on the Web** (www.all-hotels.com) doesn't actually include *all* the hotels on the Web, but it does have tens of thousands of listings throughout the world, including London. Bear in mind that each hotel in the list has paid a small fee ($25 and up) for placement, so the list is not objective, but more like online brochures.

✔ **London Tourist Board hotel** (www.londontown.com) Web site has a long list of properties to choose from, but it doesn't tell you if any are offering special rates.

✔ **SeniorSearch U.K.** (www.ageofreason.com) is a site for seniors looking for special hotels and other forms of accommodation, including home and apartment exchanges.

✔ **InnSite** (www.innsite.com) provides B&B listings for inns in the States and dozens of countries around the globe, including the United Kingdom. You can find a B&B in London, look at images of the rooms, check prices and availability, and then e-mail the innkeeper if you have questions. This extensive directory includes listings only if written by the innkeeper (getting on the list is free), who usually includes a link to the inn's own Web site.

No Room at the Inn? Arriving without a Reservation

Whatever your hotel choice in London, I want to remind you again: *Booking ahead is important!* However, if you do arrive without a reservation, your first option is to start calling the hotels directly — try to get into town in the morning, so you can begin your room search early.

You can also book rooms through the following trustworthy agencies, but the first two don't have phone service so you must show up in person (in high season, expect long lines at both):

✔ The **Britain Visitor Centre** is at 1 Regent St. (Tube: Piccadilly Circus); it's open Monday to Friday 9 a.m. to 6:30 p.m. and Saturday and Sunday 10 a.m. to 4 p.m.

✔ The **Tourist Information Centre** is in the forecourt of Victoria Station (Tube: Victoria); Easter to October, it's open daily 8 a.m. to 7 p.m. November to the day before Easter, it's open Monday to Saturday 8 a.m. to 6 p.m. and Sunday 9 a.m. to 4 p.m.

✔ The London Tourist Board's **Accommodation Bookings Hotline** at ☎ **020-7932-2020** or 020-7604-2890 is open Monday through Friday 9:30 a.m. to 5:30 p.m.; with this service you must book with a credit card.

The following private agencies can also help you find a room:

✔ **British Hotel Reservation Centre** (☎ **020-7828-0601.** E-mail: sales@bhrc.co.uk) offers a 24-hour phone line. It provides free reservations and discounted rates at all the leading hotel groups and the major independents. It operates a reservations desk (open daily 6 a.m. to midnight) at the Underground station of Heathrow Airport.

✔ **First Option Hotel Reservations** (☎ **0345-110-011.** Fax: 020-7945-6016) is another hotel booking service. It operates kiosks at the following Central London rail stations: Victoria, by Platform 9 (☎ **020-7828-4646**); Kings Cross, by Platform 8 (☎ **020-7837-5681**); Euston (☎ **020-7388-7435**); Paddington (☎ **020-7723-0184**); and Charing Cross (☎ **020-7976-1171**).

✔ **Worldwide Bed & Breakfast Association** (☎ 020-8742-9123) — the London office — can arrange a London B&B room for you.

✔ **London Bed & Breakfast** (☎ **800-852-2632** in the United States or 020-8742-9123. Fax: 020-8749-7084 in the United Kingdom) can provide inexpensive accommodations in select private homes.

✔ **The London Bed and Breakfast Agency Limited** (☎ **020-7586-2768**) also offers inexpensive accommodations in select private homes.

Of course, even if you find a room (which you probably will, somewhere), you can't be choosy about price or location when you literally arrive on the fly without a reservation. Keep all your options open, and book ahead.

Chapter 8

London's Best Hotels and B&Bs

*W*hen you choose a London hotel or B&B, price and location are the key considerations. After you look over the neighborhood descriptions in Chapter 6 and decide on a location and a price range, you can begin your search for the perfect accommodations for you.

In this chapter, I give you my hotel recommendations that cover all kinds of accommodations in all price ranges, from the simple to the opulent. I've tried to put in as many distinctive small hotels as possible. And I've weighted my list with mid-range choices.

All the hotels in this chapter provide private bathrooms, unless I note otherwise in the description. Private bathrooms don't necessarily include both a shower and a tub, though; you may get one or the other (more often a shower). If having a tub is important to you, request one when you make your reservation. Don't expect American-sized bathrooms, especially in B&Bs; some of the baths are so compact you can almost fit them into your luggage.

The Kid Friendly icon in front of a hotel name indicates that the hotel is suitable for families with children. These hotels have rooms with three or four beds (called *triples* or *quads*) or adjoining rooms and/or include baby-sitting among their services.

I don't have room in this guide to describe more than a sampling of London hotels. If my top recommendations are full, you can check out "Runner-Up Choices" at the end of this chapter, which lists additional trustworthy and recommendable hotels arranged from most to least expensive. Or you can contact one of the hotel or B&B reservation services I list at the end of Chapter 7.

Criteria for Recommendations

In Chapter 7, I explain the kinds of hotels you can find; in Chapter 6, I describe the neighborhoods most convenient for visitors. In this chapter,

I provide an index of hotels by price. Then I list and describe the recommended hotels alphabetically, noting both price and location. You can record your choices in the hotel worksheet at the back of this book.

You may be wondering what critical yardsticks I use for recommending the hotels in this chapter. Here they are:

- First, I've stayed in my share of dumps over the years, and I sure didn't enjoy the experience. I don't think you would either. So I dumped the dumps. You won't find any on this list.

- Next criterion? Cleanliness. These hotels are well maintained; you won't find old cigarette butts on the floor or rings around the bathtubs.

- Next criterion? That old friend, location. All the hotels are in Central London and accessible to Underground station (tube) stops.

- Finally, they all have a little something extra, so they stand out from the crowd of London hotels.

Every recommended hotel has a $ symbol to help you hone in on your price limit. These symbols are based on the rack rate (no discounts), and prices are based on an average conversion rate of £1 = $1.65; exchange rates vary from day to day, so these prices are only a guide. (*Note:* Dollar sign icons reflect the *average* of a hotel's high- and low-end rack rates.) Room rates are subject to change without notice, so even the rates quoted in this book may be different from the actual rate you receive when you make your reservation. Don't be surprised if the rate you're offered is lower than the rack rates listed here; likewise, don't be too alarmed if the price has crept up slightly.

$ ($150 and under) — This category covers many B&Bs and some small hotels. You get breakfast, served in a dining room, but no room service. Your room has a wash basin and perhaps a built-in shower, but you may have to share a bathroom down the hall. (More and more B&Bs are installing private baths, however miniscule, in their rooms.) Expect tight spaces and a basic no-frills approach to decorating. You may have to carry your own bags, and there'll probably be no elevator or air-conditioning. You may or may not have a TV and a direct-dial phone in your room.

$$ ($150–$225) — The B&Bs and hotels in this price range generally show a bit more flair than the ones in the $ category, but the rooms may still be small and there may not be an elevator. Most places include breakfast, usually served in a dining room; room service is unlikely. There probably is no air-conditioning, but most likely a telephone and a TV is in every room. And chances are you can have a private bathroom — though it may be small and have only a shower. There may be some amenities like hair dryers, trouser presses, and tea/coffeemakers.

Chapter 8

London's Best Hotels and B&Bs

*W*hen you choose a London hotel or B&B, price and location are the key considerations. After you look over the neighborhood descriptions in Chapter 6 and decide on a location and a price range, you can begin your search for the perfect accommodations for you.

In this chapter, I give you my hotel recommendations that cover all kinds of accommodations in all price ranges, from the simple to the opulent. I've tried to put in as many distinctive small hotels as possible. And I've weighted my list with mid-range choices.

All the hotels in this chapter provide private bathrooms, unless I note otherwise in the description. Private bathrooms don't necessarily include both a shower and a tub, though; you may get one or the other (more often a shower). If having a tub is important to you, request one when you make your reservation. Don't expect American-sized bathrooms, especially in B&Bs; some of the baths are so compact you can almost fit them into your luggage.

The Kid Friendly icon in front of a hotel name indicates that the hotel is suitable for families with children. These hotels have rooms with three or four beds (called *triples* or *quads*) or adjoining rooms and/or include baby-sitting among their services.

I don't have room in this guide to describe more than a sampling of London hotels. If my top recommendations are full, you can check out "Runner-Up Choices" at the end of this chapter, which lists additional trustworthy and recommendable hotels arranged from most to least expensive. Or you can contact one of the hotel or B&B reservation services I list at the end of Chapter 7.

Criteria for Recommendations

In Chapter 7, I explain the kinds of hotels you can find; in Chapter 6, I describe the neighborhoods most convenient for visitors. In this chapter,

I provide an index of hotels by price. Then I list and describe the recommended hotels alphabetically, noting both price and location. You can record your choices in the hotel worksheet at the back of this book.

You may be wondering what critical yardsticks I use for recommending the hotels in this chapter. Here they are:

 ✔ First, I've stayed in my share of dumps over the years, and I sure didn't enjoy the experience. I don't think you would either. So I dumped the dumps. You won't find any on this list.

 ✔ Next criterion? Cleanliness. These hotels are well maintained; you won't find old cigarette butts on the floor or rings around the bathtubs.

 ✔ Next criterion? That old friend, location. All the hotels are in Central London and accessible to Underground station (tube) stops.

 ✔ Finally, they all have a little something extra, so they stand out from the crowd of London hotels.

Every recommended hotel has a $ symbol to help you hone in on your price limit. These symbols are based on the rack rate (no discounts), and prices are based on an average conversion rate of £1 = $1.65; exchange rates vary from day to day, so these prices are only a guide. (*Note:* Dollar sign icons reflect the *average* of a hotel's high- and low-end rack rates.) Room rates are subject to change without notice, so even the rates quoted in this book may be different from the actual rate you receive when you make your reservation. Don't be surprised if the rate you're offered is lower than the rack rates listed here; likewise, don't be too alarmed if the price has crept up slightly.

$ (**$150 and under**) — This category covers many B&Bs and some small hotels. You get breakfast, served in a dining room, but no room service. Your room has a wash basin and perhaps a built-in shower, but you may have to share a bathroom down the hall. (More and more B&Bs are installing private baths, however miniscule, in their rooms.) Expect tight spaces and a basic no-frills approach to decorating. You may have to carry your own bags, and there'll probably be no elevator or air-conditioning. You may or may not have a TV and a direct-dial phone in your room.

$$ (**$150–$225**) — The B&Bs and hotels in this price range generally show a bit more flair than the ones in the $ category, but the rooms may still be small and there may not be an elevator. Most places include breakfast, usually served in a dining room; room service is unlikely. There probably is no air-conditioning, but most likely a telephone and a TV is in every room. And chances are you can have a private bathroom — though it may be small and have only a shower. There may be some amenities like hair dryers, trouser presses, and tea/coffeemakers.

$$$ ($225–$300) — The hotels in this category offer pretty lobbies, with elevators, and staff to carry your bags. Breakfast or afternoon tea may be included but generally isn't; there probably is an on-site restaurant with room service. The rooms are larger, with better furnishings, telephones, air-conditioning (usually), and double-glazed windows to cut down on noise (unless the hotel is on the Historic Register). The TVs are likely hooked up to a satellite dish or cable network. The private bathrooms are generally roomy and comfortable, depending on the age of the hotel and how recently it's been refurbished. Amenities like hair dryers, trouser presses, tea/coffeemakers, and special soaps and shampoos are standard.

$$$$ ($300–$400) — In this range, expect even fancier lobbies and elevators and more staff. Breakfast won't be included, but you can order whatever you want from a high-priced room service menu or eat in a good on-site restaurant. The rooms are large and well decorated, with minibars, satellite/cable TVs, telephones (perhaps two or more), air-conditioning, double-glazed windows if possible, and even modem jacks for personal computers. A full range of amenities and entertainment options is in every room. The bathrooms are spacious and generally equipped with tubs *and* showers and deluxe toiletries. Security is monitored.

$$$$$ ($400 and up)— In this range, you're paying for the name, the location, and the prestige. At these Rolls-Royce hotels, you find sumptuous lobbies and salons, an extensive staff at your beck and call, one or more bars, gourmet restaurants, 24-hour room service, and probably access to a spa or health club (if not on the premises, then nearby). You also encounter the rich and perhaps even the famous. The opulent rooms have everything you can imagine, from plush furniture to multiple phones (perhaps one in the bath) to modem jacks to full entertainment centers to heated towel racks and ultradeluxe toiletries in the oversized bathrooms. Security is tight.

Unless otherwise noted, the prices include value-added tax (VAT). For those listings that don't include VAT, you need to add another 17.5 percent to the quoted rate (generally, this addition is necessary only for luxury hotels).

Index by Price

$
Aaron House (Earl's Court)
Abbey House (Kensington)
Adare House (Paddington)
Avalon Hotel (Bloomsbury)
Avonmore Hotel (Kensington)
Boston Court (Marylebone)
Caswell Hotel (Westminster & Victoria)
Crescent Hotel (Bloomsbury)

Ebury House (Westminster & Victoria)
Edward Lear Hotel (Marylebone)
Europa House Hotel (Paddington)
Fairways Hotel (Paddington)
The Gate (Notting Hill)
Harlingford Hotel (Bloomsbury)
Hart House Hotel (Marylebone)
Hotel 167 (South Kensington)
Ivanhoe Suites Hotel (Mayfair)

James House & Cartrel House
(Westminster & Victoria)
Jenkins Hotel (Bloomsbury)
Philbeach Hotel (Earl's Court)
Swiss House (South Kensington)
Vicarage Private Hotel (Kensington)

$$

Academy Hotel (Bloomsbury)
Amber Hotel (Earl's Court)
Aster House (South Kensington)
Aston's Apartments (South Kensington)
Bryanston Court Hotel (Marylebone)
The Byron (Paddington & Bayswater)
Claverley Hotel (Knightsbridge)
Darlington Hyde Park (Paddington)
Diplomat Hotel (Belgravia)
Durrants Hotel (Marylebone)
Fielding Hotel (Covent Garden)
The Gallery (South Kensington)
Hotel La Place (Marylebone)
Lime Tree Hotel (Westminster &
Victoria)
Regent Palace Hotel (Piccadilly Circus)
Tophams Belgravia (Westminster &
Victoria)

$$$

The Abbey Court (Notting Hill)
The Cranley (South Kensington)
Dorset Square Hotel (Marylebone)

Five Sumner Place (South
Kensington)
Harrington Hall (South Kensington)
Hazlitt's 1718 (Soho)
Hotel Russell (Bloomsbury)
Knightsbridge Hotel (Knightsbridge)
Number Sixteen (South Kensington)
Pembridge Court (Notting Hill)
Regency Hotel (South Kensington)
Sloane Hotel (Chelsea)
Strathmore Hotel (South Kensington)

$$$$

22 Jermyn Street (St. James's)
Basil Street Hotel (Knightsbridge)
Blooms Hotel (Bloomsbury)
Cadogan Hotel (Chelsea)
Dukes Hotel (St. James)
The Gore (South Kensington)
Goring Hotel (Westminster &
Victoria)

$$$$$

Covent Garden Hotel (Covent
Garden)
Landmark London (Marylebone)
Park Lane Hotel (Mayfair)
The Savoy (The Strand)
St. Martin's Lane (Piccadilly Circus)

Recommended London Hotels

22 Jermyn Street

$$$$ St. James's

This chic 18-room boutique hotel is a Victorian townhouse near
Piccadilly Square — on an exclusive street where almost every shop has
a Royal Warrant. The guest rooms are richly appointed in traditional
English style, replete with fresh flowers and chintz. The bathrooms are
equally tasteful. Many amenities and 24-hour room service are available.

22 Jermyn St. (just south of Piccadilly Circus), London SW1Y 6HL; ☎ ***800-682-7808***
in the United States or 020-7734-2353. Fax: 020-7734-0750. E-mail: office@
22jermyn.com. *Internet:* www.22jermyn.com. *Tube: Piccadilly Circus (take
Lower Regent St. exit; Jermyn St. is the 1st right outside the station). Rack rates:
£241 ($398) double. AE, DC, MC, V.*

A Night at the Palace?

Looking for a place to stay that's truly unique? Consider **Hampton Court Palace,** described in Chapter 17 and located in East Moseley, Surrey, 13 miles west of London on the north side of the Thames. Believe it or not, two self-contained, self-catering locations in the palace are available for 4- and 7-day rentals.

Fish Court is an apartment in the Tudor wing, which was once home to the Officers of the Pastry. It's cozy, with two single rooms, a twin, and a double, as well as a kitchen and a living room. It might be expensive for two (£108/$178 per person per night for a week), but if you're traveling in a group of six in peak season, that comes to only £36 ($59) per person per night for a week.

On a grander scale is the imposing **Georgian House,** built on the palace grounds in 1719 for George, Prince of Wales. There you have your own walled garden and magnificent views over the palace roofs from the attic windows. The rooms (two singles, two twins, and one double, plus a kitchen, a sitting room, and a dining room) are airy and spacious, with antique and classic furnishings. If you're traveling with a group of eight, that comes to around £33 ($54) per person per night.

Reserve both through **Landmark Trust,** Shottesbrooke, Maidenhead, Berks, SL6 3SW (☎ **01628-825-925**; Internet: www.landmarktrust.co.uk).

Aaron House

$ **Earl's Court**

This former family home on a Victorian square is a standout among the many Earl's Court B&Bs. Although modernized and upgraded, friendly and convenient, Aaron House still retains its original tile entry and ornately carved interior staircase leading to the 23 comfortable and well-kept guest rooms. The largest rooms overlook the garden square and street, which can be noisy.

17 Courtfield Gardens London SW5 OPD; ☎ *020-7373-3834. Fax: 020-7373-2303. E-mail:* reservations@aaronhousehotel.co.uk. *Internet:* www.aaronhousehotel.co.uk. *Tube: Earl's Court (then a 5-minute walk east on Earl's Court Gardens Rd. to Courtfield Gardens). Rack rates: £50 ($83) double without bathroom, £61 ($101) double with bathroom. Continental breakfast included. MC, V.*

The Abbey Court

$$ **Notting Hill**

This graceful hotel is located in a renovated mid-Victorian townhouse near Kensington Gardens. With a flower-filled front patio and a rear conservatory where breakfast is served, this hotel has 22 charming guest rooms that feature 18th- and 19th-century country antiques and marble bathrooms equipped with Jacuzzi tubs, showers, and heated towel racks. You can take advantage of the services of the concierge, and babysitting can be arranged.

West End Hotels

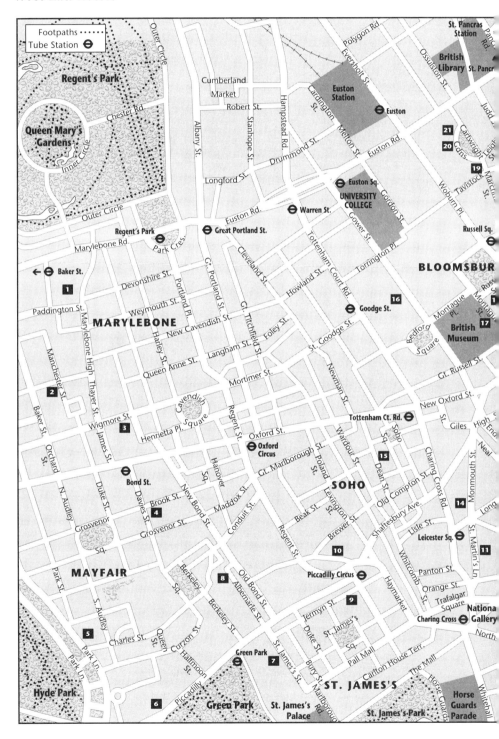

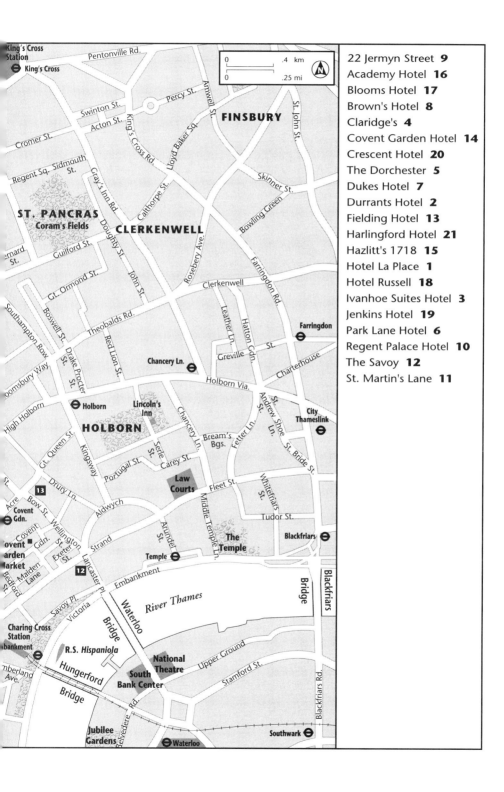

22 Jermyn Street **9**
Academy Hotel **16**
Blooms Hotel **17**
Brown's Hotel **8**
Claridge's **4**
Covent Garden Hotel **14**
Crescent Hotel **20**
The Dorchester **5**
Dukes Hotel **7**
Durrants Hotel **2**
Fielding Hotel **13**
Harlingford Hotel **21**
Hazlitt's 1718 **15**
Hotel La Place **1**
Hotel Russell **18**
Ivanhoe Suites Hotel **3**
Jenkins Hotel **19**
Park Lane Hotel **6**
Regent Palace Hotel **10**
The Savoy **12**
St. Martin's Lane **11**

20 Pembridge Gardens, London W2 4DU; ☎ **020-7221-7518.** *Fax: 020-7792-0858. E-mail:* info@abbeycourthotel.co.uk. *Internet:* www.abbeycourthotel. co.uk. *Tube: Notting Hill Gate (then a 5-min. walk north on Pembridge Gardens Rd.) Rack rates: £145–£165 ($239–$272) double. AE, MC, V.*

Abbey House

$ Kensington

For tranquillity and affordability in a great location (next to Kensington Gardens and Palace), this small family-run B&B can't be beat. Although modernized, the 1860s-era building retains many original features. The 16 spacious guest rooms (some triples and quads) have central heating and washbasins; every two units share a bathroom. The decor is cheerful and charming, although a bit frilly.

11 Vicarage Gate (off Kensington Church St.), London W8 4AG; ☎ **020-7727-2594.** *Tube: High Street Kensington (then a 5-minute walk east on Kensington High St. and north on Kensington Church St.). Rack rates: £68–£74 ($112–$122) double without bathroom. English breakfast included. No credit cards accepted.*

Academy Hotel

$$ Bloomsbury

You can easily walk to the British Museum, the theater district, and Covent Garden from this freshly refurbished 55-unit hotel that takes up three Georgian row houses. The abundance of nice features include original glass panels, colonnades, intricate exterior plasterwork, an elegant bar, a library room, a secluded patio garden, and a restaurant serving modern European food. The bathrooms tend to be small.

17–25 Gower St.(near the British Museum), London WC1E 6HG; ☎ **800-678-3096** *in the United States or 020-7631-4115. Fax: 020-7636-3442. Tube: Goodge St. (then a 10-minute walk east on Chenies St. and south on Gower St.). Rack rates: £145 ($239) double. English breakfast included. AE, DC, MC, V.*

Adare House

$ Paddington

This well-maintained refurbished property retains a modest homey ambience. Most of the 20 guest rooms are small, but immaculately clean and comfortably furnished; the bathrooms come with showers. Hyde Park is within easy walking distance.

153 Sussex Gardens (near Paddington Station), London W2 2RY; ☎ **020-7262-0633.** *Fax: 020-7706-1859. E-mail:* adare.hotel@virgin.net. *Tube: Paddington Station (then a 5-min. walk south on London St. and west on Sussex Gardens Rd.). Rack rates: £69–£76 ($96–$125) double. English breakfast included. MC, V.*

Westminster and Victoria Hotels

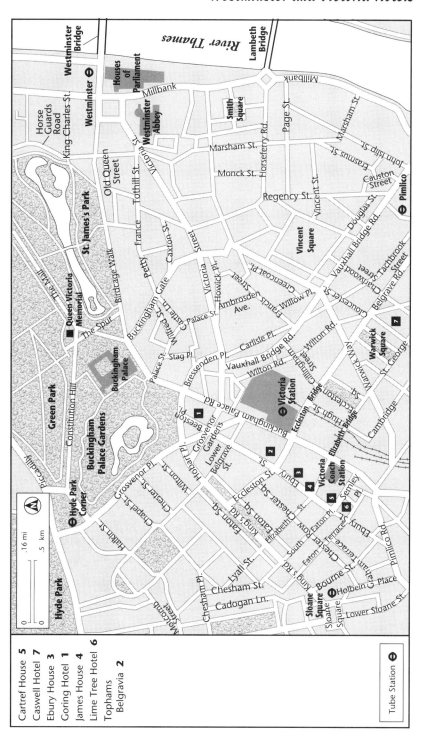

Cartref House **5**
Caswell Hotel **7**
Ebury House **3**
Goring Hotel **1**
James House **4**
Lime Tree Hotel **6**
Tophams
Belgravia **2**

Tube Station ⊖

Hotels from Knightsbridge to Earl's Court

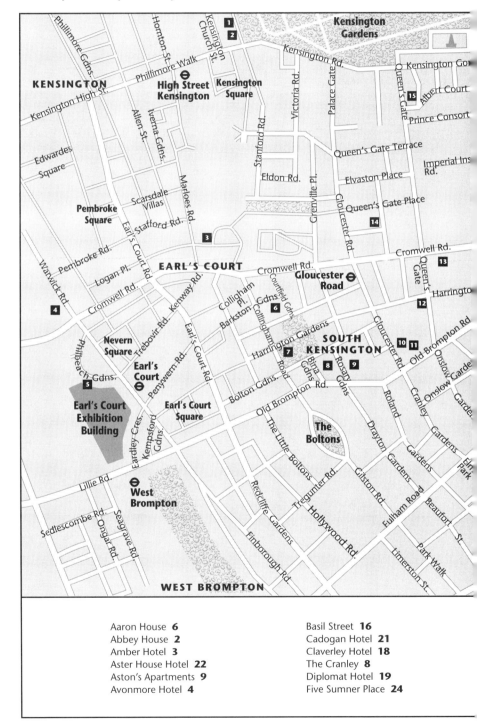

Aaron House **6**
Abbey House **2**
Amber Hotel **3**
Aster House Hotel **22**
Aston's Apartments **9**
Avonmore Hotel **4**

Basil Street **16**
Cadogan Hotel **21**
Claverley Hotel **18**
The Cranley **8**
Diplomat Hotel **19**
Five Sumner Place **24**

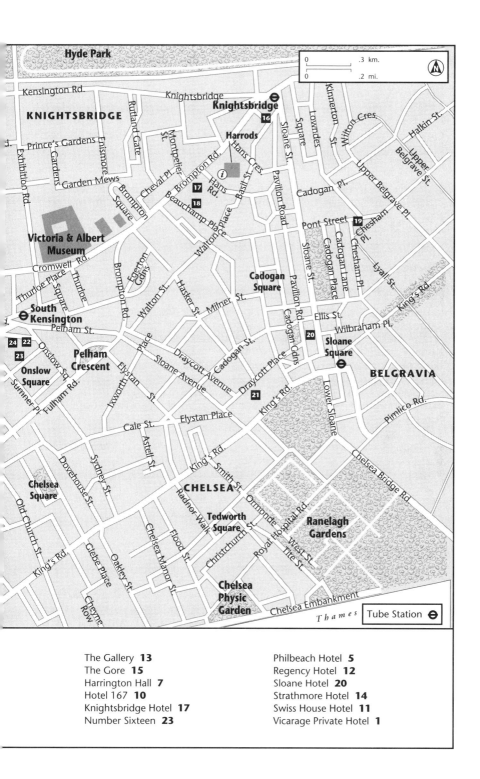

The Gallery **13**

The Gore **15**

Harrington Hall **7**

Hotel 167 **10**

Knightsbridge Hotel **17**

Number Sixteen **23**

Philbeach Hotel **5**

Regency Hotel **12**

Sloane Hotel **20**

Strathmore Hotel **14**

Swiss House Hotel **11**

Vicarage Private Hotel **1**

Aster House

$$ South Kensington

Found at the end of an early Victorian terrace, this 12-unit no-smoking-allowed B&B is a charmer, especially for the price. It's so discreet that the location isn't even marked by a sign. Aster House reopened in April 2000 after a complete renovation. Each guest room is individually decorated in English country-house style, many with four-poster, half-canopied beds and silk wallpaper. The new bathrooms come with power showers. The breakfasts, served in the glassed-in garden conservatory, are more health-conscious than is traditional from an English B&B.

3 Sumner Place (near Onslow Sq.), London SW7 3EE; ☎ *020-7581-5888. Fax: 020-7584-4925. E-mail:* asterhouse@btinternet.com. *Tube: South Kensington (then a 5-minute walk west on Old Brompton Rd. and south on Sumner Place). Rack rates: £135–£165 ($223–$272) double. Buffet continental breakfast included. MC, V.*

Aston's Apartments

$$ South Kensington

In three carefully restored Victorian redbrick townhouses, Aston's offers value-packed self-catering accommodations, some ideal for families. Each studio has a compact kitchenette, a small bathroom, and bright functional furnishings. The more expensive designer studios feature larger bathrooms, more living space, and extra pizzazz in the decor. If you like the idea of having your own cozy London apartment (with daily maid service), you can't do better. The owners have just added another property on nearby Queen's Gate; you can book a self-catering room there through the main Aston's number.

31 Rosary Gardens (off Hereford Sq.), London SW7 4NQ; ☎ *800-525-2810 in the United States or 020-7590-6000. Fax: 020-7590-6060. E-mail:* sales@ astons-apartments.com. *Internet:* www.astons-apartments.com. *Tube: Gloucester Rd. (then a 5-min. walk south on Gloucester Rd. and west on Hereford Sq.; Rosary Gardens is 1 block further west). Rack rates: £85–£120 ($140–$198) double. Rates don't include 17.5 percent VAT. AE, MC, V.*

Avonmore Hotel

$ Kensington

This small hotel is in a quiet neighborhood easily accessible to West End theaters and shops. You'd be hard-pressed to find more for your money: Each of the nine guest rooms offers a tasteful decor and an array of amenities not usually found in this price range. This establishment was once voted London's best private hotel by the Automobile Association (AA). An English breakfast is served in a cheerful breakfast room; a bar and limited room service are also available.

66 Avonmore Rd. (northwest of Earl's Court), London W14 8RS; ☎ *020-7603-4296. Fax: 020-7603-4035. E-mail:* avonmore.hotel@dial.pipex.com. *Internet:* www.avonmore.hotel.dial.pipex.com. *Tube: West Kensington (then a*

5-minute walk north on North End Rd. and Mattheson Rd. to Avonmore Rd.). Rack rates: £80 ($132) double without bathroom, £90 ($148) double with bathroom. English breakfast included. AE, MC, V.

Blooms Hotel

$$$$ Bloomsbury

With its cozy fireplace and period art, this 27-room hotel evokes a luxurious country-home atmosphere. Guests in this beautifully restored and tastefully furnished townhouse can take morning coffee or light summer meals in a walled garden overlooking the British Museum. The guest rooms are individually designed, with traditional elegance and muted colors. Ground-floor rooms are available for the disabled. The specially priced weekend package rate is a real bargain.

7 Montague St. (next to the British Museum), London WC1B 5BP; ☎ ***020-7323-1717.** Fax: 020-7636-6498. E-mail:* blooms@mermaid.co.uk. *Tube: Russell Sq. (then a 5-minute walk west on Bernard St. and around Russell Sq. to Montague Place, at the northwest corner of the square). Rack rates: £195–£205 ($322–$338) double. English breakfast included. AE, DC, MC, V.*

Boston Court Hotel

$ Marylebone

Within walking distance of Oxford Street shopping and Hyde Park, this 13-unit hotel on a street brimming with B&Bs offers affordable accommodations in a centrally located Victorian-era building. The guest rooms are small and utilitarian, showing a no-nonsense bright approach to decorating, but all have private showers and small refrigerators.

26 Upper Berkeley St. (near Marble Arch), London W1H 7PF; ☎ ***020-7723-1445.** Fax: 020-7262-8823. E-mail:* info@boston-court-hotel.com. *Internet:* www. boston-court-hotel.com. *Tube: Marble Arch (then a 10-minute walk west on Bayswater Rd., north on Edgware Rd., and east on Upper Berkeley St.). Rack rates: £55 ($91) double with shower only, £75 ($124) double with bathroom. Continental breakfast included. MC, V.*

Bryanston Court Hotel

$$ Marylebone

Located in a neighborhood with many attractive squares, this 200-year-old hotel is one of Central London's finest in the moderate price range. The refurbished hotel has 54 small guest rooms (and equally small bathrooms) that are comfortably furnished and well maintained. You can find a welcoming bar with a fireplace in the back of the lounge.

56–60 Great Cumberland Place (near Marble Arch), London W1H 7FD; ☎ ***020-7262-3141.** Fax: 020-7262-7248. E-mail:* hotel@bryanstonhotel.com. *Internet:* www.bryanston.com. *Tube: Marble Arch (then a 5-min. walk north on Great Cumberland Place to Bryanston Place). Rack rates: £110 ($182) double. Continental breakfast included. AE, DC, MC, V.*

Marylebone, Paddington, Bayswater, and Notting Hill Hotels

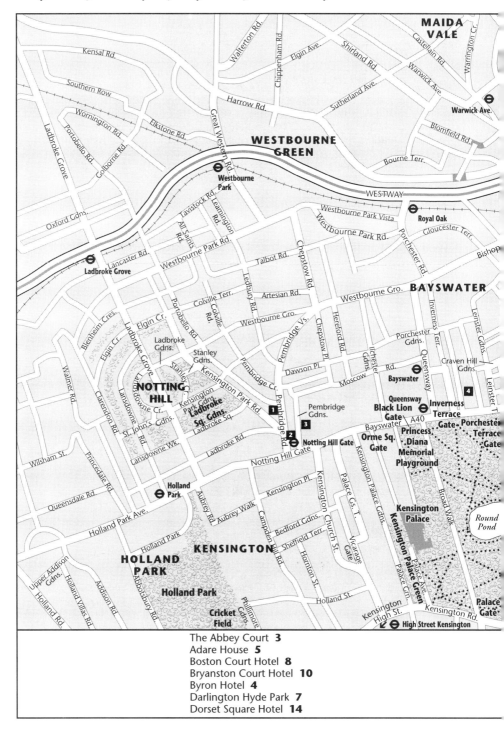

The Abbey Court **3**
Adare House **5**
Boston Court Hotel **8**
Bryanston Court Hotel **10**
Byron Hotel **4**
Darlington Hyde Park **7**
Dorset Square Hotel **14**

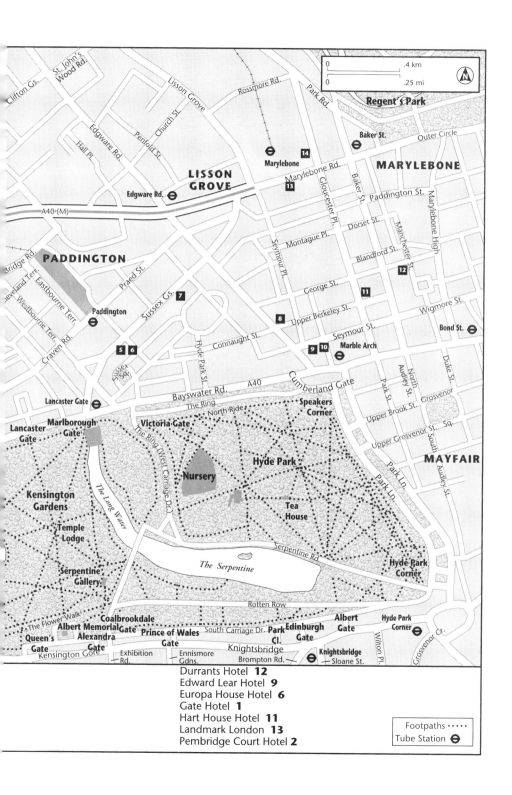

Durrants Hotel **12**
Edward Lear Hotel **9**
Europa House Hotel **6**
Gate Hotel **1**
Hart House Hotel **11**
Landmark London **13**
Pembridge Court Hotel **2**

Byron Hotel

$ Bayswater

The family-run 45-room Byron occupies a Victorian house that's been thoroughly modernized but hasn't lost its traditional atmosphere. The guest rooms have ample closets, tile baths, and good lighting. Breakfast is served in a cheery dining room. The staff members are pleasant and helpful. Considering the amenities offered, this establishment offers an especially good value.

36–38 Queensborough Terrace (off Bayswater Rd.), London W2 3SH; ☎ 020-7243-0987. Fax: 020-7792-1957. E-mail: byronhotel@capricorn.com. *Tube: Queensway (then a 5-min. walk east on Bayswater Rd. and north on Queensborough Terrace). Rack rates: £105 ($173) double. English or continental breakfast included. AE, DC, MC, V.*

Cadogan Hotel

$$$$ Chelsea

You'll feel transported back to the Victorian era with guests such as the legendary actress Lillie Langtry if you stay at this beautiful 69-room hotel, with a wood-paneled small lobby and sumptuous drawing room (good for afternoon tea), close to all the exclusive Knightsbridge shops. The Cadogan (pronounced Ca-*dug*-en) is the hotel where poet, playwright, and novelist Oscar Wilde was staying when he was arrested (room 118 is the Oscar Wilde Suite). The large guest rooms, many overlooking the Cadogan Place gardens, are quietly tasteful and splendidly comfortable, with large bathrooms. The sedate Edwardian restaurant is known for its excellent cuisine.

75 Sloane St. (near Sloane Sq.), London SW1X 9SG; ☎ 800-260-8338 in the United States or 020-7235-7141. Fax: 020-7245-0994. E-mail: info@cadogan.com. *Internet:* www.cadogan.com. *Tube: Sloane Sq. (then a 5-min. walk north on Sloane St.). Rack rates: £190–£225 ($313–$377) double. Rates don't include 17.5 percent VAT. AE, MC, V.*

Caswell Hotel

$ Westminster & Victoria

This 18-room hotel lies on a quiet cul-de-sac in an otherwise bustling area. The decor is understated, except for the abundance of chintz in the lobby. Four floors of nicely furnished guest rooms offer amenities usually found in higher-priced hotels, however many are without bathrooms. The extremely thoughtful and considerate staff accounts for a great deal of repeat business.

25 Gloucester St. (near Warwick Sq.), London SW1V 2DB; ☎ 020-7834-6345. Tube: Victoria Station (then a 10-minute walk southeast on Belgrave Rd. and southwest on Gloucester St.). Rack rates: £54 ($89) double without bathroom, £75 ($124) double with bathroom. English breakfast included. MC, V.

Claverley Hotel

$$ Knightsbridge

On a quiet Knightsbridge cul-de-sac a few blocks from Harrods, this cozy place is considered one of London's best B&Bs. The public rooms feature Georgian-era accessories, 19th-century oil portraits, elegant antiques, and leather-covered sofas. Most of the 29 guest rooms have wall-to-wall carpeting, upholstered armchairs, and marble bathrooms with power showers. You'll enjoy the excellent English breakfast.

13–14 Beaufort Gardens (off Brompton Rd.), London SW3 1PS; ☎ *800-747-0398 in the United States or 020-7589-8541. Fax: 020-7584-3410. E-mail:* claverleyhotel@ netscapeonline.co.uk. *Tube: Knightsbridge (then a 2-min. walk south past Harrods on Brompton Rd. to Beaufort Gardens). Rack rates: £130–£195 ($214–$321) double. English breakfast included. AE, DC, MC, V.*

Covent Garden Hotel

$$$$$ Covent Garden

Created from an 1850s French hospital and dispensary, this boutique hotel surrounds guests in luxury. No two of the 50 guest rooms are alike. Many rooms have large windows with rooftop views. The decor is a lush mix of antiques and fine contemporary furniture, and the granite-tiled bathrooms with glass-walled showers and heated towel racks are among the best in London. The wood-paneled public rooms are just as impressive. Brasserie Max serves up eclectic bistro food and is a chic place to lunch. If you don't get enough exercise touring London, you can keep in shape at the small gym on the premises.

10 Monmouth St. (near Covent Garden Market), London WC2H 9HB; ☎ *800-553-6674 in the United States or 020-7806-1000. E-mail:* covent@firmdale.com. *Internet:* www.firmdale.com. *Tube: Leicester Sq. (then a 5-minute walk north on St. Martin's Lane, which becomes Monmouth St.). Rack rates: £220–£280 ($363–$462) double. Rates don't include 17.5 percent VAT. AE, DC, MC, V.*

The Cranley

$$$ South Kensington

On a quiet street near South Kensington's museums, the Cranley is housed in a trio of restored 1875 townhouses. Luxuriously appointed public rooms and 37 high-ceilinged guest rooms with original plasterwork and concealed kitchens make this a standout. The white-tiled bathrooms are large and nicely finished, with tubs and showers. Suites on the ground (first) floor open onto a charming private garden and have Jacuzzis. Breakfast, available for £9.95 ($16), is served in a pleasantly tony dining room.

10–12 Bina Gardens (off Brompton Rd.), London SW5 0LA; ☎ *800-448-8355 in the United States or 020-7373-0123. Fax: 020-7373-9497. E-mail:* thecranley@ writeme.com. *Internet:* www.thecranley.co.uk. *Tube: Gloucester Rd. (then a 5-min. walk south on Gloucester Rd., west on Brompton Rd., and north on Bina Gardens). Rack rates: £160–£180 ($264–$297) double. AE, DC, MC, V.*

Crescent Hotel

$ Bloomsbury

North of Russell Square in the heart of academic London, this comfortably elegant hotel has seen four decades of travelers returning to this 200-year-old building. The 27 guest rooms include small singles with shared bathrooms in addition to more spacious twin, double, and family rooms that have private bathrooms (which tend toward the minuscule). The furnishings are simple but include many thoughtful extras. Guests have access to the adjacent gardens with private tennis courts.

49–50 Cartwright Gardens (near Tavistock Sq.), London WC1H 9EL; ☎ *020-7387-1515. Fax: 020-7383-2054. Tube: Russell Sq. (then a 10-minute walk north on Marchmont St, which becomes Cartwright Gardens). Rack rates: £82 ($135) double with bathroom. English breakfast included. MC, V.*

Diplomat Hotel

$$ Belgravia

Belgravia is a very expensive area, so guests of the Diplomat consider themselves lucky to find such a reasonably priced small hotel in this section of London. The lobby area features a partially gilded circular staircase and a cherub-studded Regency-era chandelier. The 27 high-ceilinged guest rooms are tastefully done in a Victorian style. The hotel isn't state-of-the-art but is very well maintained and a cut above the average for this price range.

2 Chesham St. (just south of Belgrave Sq.), London SW1X 8DT; ☎ *020-7235-1544. Fax: 020-7259-6153. E-mail:* Diplomat.Hotel@btinternet.com; *Internet:* www.btinternet.com/~diplomat.hotel. *Tube: Sloane Sq. (then a 5-min. walk northeast on Cliveden and north on Eaton Place, which becomes Chesham St.). Rack rates: £125–£140 ($192–$231) double. English buffet breakfast included. AE, DC, MC, V.*

Dorset Square Hotel

$$$ Marylebone

This sophisticated 38-room luxury boutique hotel occupies a beautifully restored Regency townhouse overlooking Dorset Square, a private garden surrounded by graceful buildings. Inside and out, this hotel is the epitome of traditional English style. Each guest room is unique, filled with a superlative mix of antiques, original oils, fine furniture, fresh flowers, and richly textured fabrics. The bathrooms are marble and mahogany (just remember that some of those enticing little "extras" aren't free).

39–40 Dorset Sq. (just west of Regent's Park), London NW1 6QN; ☎ *800-553-6674 in the United States or 020-7723-7874. Fax: 020-7724-3328. E-mail:* Dorset@firmdale.com. *Internet:* www.firmdale.com. *Tube: Marylebone (then a 2-min. walk east on Melcombe to Dorset Sq.). Rack rates: £140–£240 ($231–$396) double. Rates don't include 17.5 percent VAT. AE, MC, V.*

Durrants Hotel

$$ Marylebone

Opened in 1789 off Manchester Square, this 92-room hotel provides an atmospheric London retreat. The 18th-century letter-writing room shows that it's quintessentially English, as do the pine- and mahogany-paneled public areas and a wonderful Georgian room that serves as a restaurant. The wood-paneled guest rooms are generously proportioned (for the most part) and nicely furnished, with decent-sized bathrooms.

George St. (across from the Wallace Collection), London W1H 6BJ; ☎ *020-7935-8131. Fax: 020-7487-3510. E-mail:* reservations@durrantshotel. com. *Tube: Bond St. (then a 5-min. walk west on Oxford St. and north on Duke St. and Manchester St.). Rack rates: £130–£135 ($215–$223) double. AE, MC, V.*

Edward Lear Hotel

$ Marylebone

One of the two 1780 brick townhouses that make up this popular budget hotel was the home of the 19th-century artist/nonsense poet Edward Lear (famed for "The Owl and the Pussycat," among other delightful rhymes). His illustrated limericks decorate the walls of the sitting room. Steep stairs lead to the 31 guest rooms, which are small but comfortable. Fewer than half the rooms have private bathrooms, and the area — close to Marble Arch — has a lot of traffic noise. The rear rooms are quieter.

28–30 Seymour St. (near Marble Arch), London W1H 5WD; ☎ *020-7402-5401. Fax: 020-7706-3766. E-mail:* edwardlear@aol.com. *Internet:* www.edlear. com. *Tube: Marble Arch (then 1 block north to Seymour St.). Rack rates: £64.50 ($106) double without bathroom, £89.50 ($148) double with bathroom. English breakfast included. MC, V.*

Europa House Hotel

$ Paddington

If you want a private shower in your room but don't want to pay too much for the luxury, this family-run budget hotel may be your best choice. As in most B&Bs along Sussex Gardens, the guest rooms are small, but they're well kept and were refurbished in 1999. Some of the 18 rooms are custom-built for groups, with three, four, or five beds. A hearty English breakfast is served in the bright dining room.

151 Sussex Gardens (near Paddington Station), London W2 2RY; ☎ *020-7402-1923 or 020-7723-7343. Fax: 020-7224-9331. E-mail:* europahouse@enterprise.net. *Tube: Paddington Station (then a 5-min. walk south on London St. to Sussex Gardens). Rack rates: £55–£68 ($91–$112) double. English breakfast included. AE, MC, V.*

Fielding Hotel

$$ Covent Garden

The Fielding, named for author Hemry Fielding (famous for *The History of Tom Jones*), is on a beautiful old street (now pedestrian only) lit by 19th-century gaslights and across from the Royal Opera House. The stairways are steep and narrow (the hotel has no elevator), and the 24 rather cramped guest rooms are undistinguished in decor, but they do have showers and toilets. Those quibbles aside, this quirky hotel is an excellent value. A small bar is on the premises, and the area is loaded with cafes, restaurants, and fabulous shopping.

4 Broad Court, Bow St., London WC2B 5QZ; ☎ *020-7836-8305. Fax: 020-7497-0064. E-mail:* reservations@the-fielding-hotel.co.uk. *Internet:* www.the-fielding-hotel.co.uk. *Tube: Covent Garden (then a 5-min. walk north on Long Acre and south on Bow St.). Rack rates: £100–£130 ($165–$214) double. AE, DC, MC, V.*

Five Sumner Place

$$$ South Kensington

This 14-room charmer — one of the best B&Bs in Kensington — occupies a landmark Victorian terrace house that has been completely restored in an elegant English style. The guest rooms are comfortably and traditionally furnished; all have bathrooms (a few have refrigerators as well). You can enjoy a full range of services, including breakfast in a Victorian-style conservatory.

5 Sumner Place (just east of Onslow Sq.), London SW7 3EE; ☎ *020-7584-7586. Fax: 020-7823-9962. E-mail:* reservations@sumnerplace.com. *Internet:* www.sumnerplace.com. *Tube: South Kensington (then a 3-minute walk west on Brompton Rd. and south on Sumner Place). Rack rates: £141–£151 ($233–$249) double. English breakfast included. AE, MC, V.*

The Gallery

$$ South Kensington

This relatively unknown 36-room hotel is near the cultural and retail attractions in South Kensington and Knightsbridge. The splendid hotel occupies two completely restored and converted Georgian residences. The elegant guest rooms are individually designed and include half-canopied beds and marble-tiled bathrooms. A team of butlers cares for your every need. The lounge, with its rich mahogany paneling and moldings and deep colors, has the ambience of a private club.

8–10 Queensberry Place (opposite the Museum of Natural History), London SW7 2EA; ☎ *0171-915-0000. Fax: 0171-915-4400. E-mail:* gallery@eeh.co.uk. *Internet:* www.eeh.co.uk. *Tube: South Kensington (then a 5-min. walk west on Thurloe St. and Harrington Rd. and north on Queensberry Place). Rack rates: £120–£145 ($198–$239) double. Rates don't include 17.5 percent VAT. Continental breakfast included. AE, DC, MC, V.*

Gate Hotel

$ Notting Hill

This tiny three-story building dates from the 1820s (when people were much smaller), so the six color-coordinated guest rooms are cramped but atmospheric, and the stairs are steep. The Gate is the only hotel along the length of Portobello Road, with its antiques shops and Saturday bric-a-brac stalls. Kensington Gardens is a 5-minute walk away.

6 Portobello Rd., London W11 3DG; ☎ *020-7221-0707. Fax: 020-7221-9128. E-mail:* reservations@gatehotel.co.uk. *Internet:* www.gatehotel.com. *Tube: Notting Hill Gate (then a 5-min. walk north on Pembridge Rd. and northwest on Portobello Rd.). Rack rates: £80–£90 ($132–$148) double. Continental breakfast included. MC, V.*

The Gore

$$$$ South Kensington

If you dream of the days of Queen Victoria, you'll definitely appreciate the old-world charm of the Gore, which has been in more or less continuous operation since 1892. On a busy road near Kensington Gardens and the Royal Albert Hall, the Gore is loaded with historic charm: walnut and mahogany paneling, oriental rugs, and 19th-century prints. Each of the 54 guest rooms is unique, filled with high-quality antiques and elegant furnishings. Even the toilets, concealed in old commodes, are remarkable. Bistro 190 is hip and popular (see Chapter 10).

189 Queen's Gate (south of Kensington Gardens), London SW7 5EX; ☎ *800-637-7200 in the United States or 020-7584-6601. Fax: 020-7589-8127. E-mail:* reservations@ gorehotel.co.uk. *Internet:* www.gorehotel.com. *Tube: Gloucester Rd. (then a 10-min. walk east on Cromwell Rd. and north on Queen's Gate). Rack rates: £170–£255 ($280–$421) double. Rates don't include 17.5 percent VAT. AE, DC, MC, V.*

Harlingford Hotel

$ Bloomsbury

You can get lost in the array of staircases (no elevators) and halls in the three 1820s town houses that join to make up this amenable hotel. The 44 guest rooms (all unique) are pleasantly comfy, some graced with floral prints and double-glazed windows to cut down on noise; the best rooms are on the second and third levels. The bathrooms are very small, however. Guests have use of the tennis courts in Cartwright Gardens.

61–63 Cartwright Gardens (north of Russell Sq.), London WC1H 9EL; ☎ *020-7387-1551. Fax: 020-7387-4616. Tube: Russell Sq. (then a 10-minute walk northwest on Woburn Place, east on Tavistock Sq. and north on Marchmont St.). Rack rates: £85 ($140) double. English breakfast included. AE, DC. MC, V.*

Harrington Hall

$$$ South Kensington

Welcome to one of the most inviting addresses in the South Kensington area. This six-story terrace house is well represented by the beautifully designed classical lobby that sets the tone for the 200 stylish guest rooms (some much larger than others). Flowery fabrics and patterned carpets create a High English ambience. Other amenities include a fitness center with a gym, a sauna, and showers.

5–25 Harrington Gardens (south of Kensington Gardens), London SW7 4JW; ☎ *800-44-UTELL in the United States or 020-7396-9696. Fax: 020-7396-9090. E-mail:* harringtonsales@compuserve.com. *Internet:* www.harringtonhall. co.uk. *Tube: Gloucester Rd. (then a 2-min. walk south on Gloucester Rd. and west on Harrington Gardens). Rack rates: £180–£220 ($297–$363) double. AE, DC, MC, V.*

Hart House Hotel

$ Marylebone

Cozy and well preserved, this Georgian-mansion-turned-hotel is within easy walking distance of West End theaters, shopping areas, and parks. The immaculately clean 16 guest rooms are done in a combination of styles and furnishings ranging from Portobello antique to modern. Room 7 is a triple with a big bathtub and shower; number 11, on the top floor, is light and bright.

51 Gloucester Place, Portman Sq. (just north of Marble Arch), London W1H 3PE; ☎ *020-7935-2288. Fax: 020-7935-8516. E-mail:* reservations@harthouse.co.uk. *Internet:* www.harthouse.co.uk. *Tube: Marble Arch (then a 5-min. walk north on Gloucester Place). Rack rates: £98 ($161) double. English breakfast included. AE, MC, V.*

Hazlitt's 1718

$$$ Soho

Built in 1718 (you may have guessed it from the name), this intimate 23-room gem offers old-fashioned atmosphere and a hip Soho location. Recent restoration that exposed original wooden paneling and other features hidden for years didn't add an elevator, but the Georgian-era guest rooms are charming. They feature mahogany and pine furnishings and antiques as well as lovely bathrooms, many with clawfoot tubs. The back rooms are quieter; the front rooms are lighter, but without the quieting effect of double-glazed windows, you do hear the street noise. Continental breakfast is £7.25 ($12).

6 Frith St., Soho Sq. (just west of Charing Cross Rd.), London W1V 5TZ; ☎ *020-7434-1771. Fax: 020-7439-1524. E-mail:* reservations@hazlitts.co.uk. *Internet:* www.hazlitts.co.uk. *Tube: Tottenham Court Rd. (then a 10-min. walk west on Oxford St. and south on Soho St. to Frith St. at the south end of Soho Sq.). Rack rates: £170 ($280) double. Rates don't include 17.5 percent VAT. AE, DC, MC, V.*

Hotel 167

$ South Kensington

Hotel 167 (no, it wasn't built in 167; it just occupies that spot on the street) attracts hip young visitors drawn by the price and business people who like its central location. This fashionable hotel is bright and attractive, offering 16 guest rooms, each with a decent-sized bathroom (some with showers, others with tubs). The rooms are furnished with a mix of fabrics and styles, mostly beiges and browns. Nearby tube stations make it convenient to the rest of London, and the busy neighborhood itself is fun to explore.

167 Old Brompton Rd., London SW5 0AN; ☎ *020-7373-0672. Fax: 020-7373-3360. E-mail:* enquiries@hotel167.com. *Internet:* www.hotel167.com. *Tube: South Kensington (then a 10-min. walk west on Old Brompton Rd.). Rack rates: £90–£99 ($149–$163) double. Continental breakfast included. AE, DC, MC, V.*

Hotel La Place

$$ Marylebone

This desirable hotel, north of Oxford Street, caters to women traveling alone. The interior has been upgraded to boutique-hotel standards (although the exterior isn't especially impressive); the 21 moderately sized guest rooms are done in classic English style, with mahogany furnishings, brocades, and opulent curtains. The bathrooms are as nice as the rooms. The hotel's Jardin is a chic, intimate wine bar/restaurant. Madame Tussaud's is nearby.

17 Nottingham Place (near the southwest corner of Regent's Park), London W1M 3FF; ☎ *020-7486-2323. Fax: 020-7486-4335. E-mail:* reservations@hotellaplace. com. *Internet:* www.hotellaplace.com. *Tube: Baker St. (then a 5-min. walk east on Marylebone Rd. and south on Nottingham Place). Rack rates: £105–£165 ($173–$272) double. English breakfast included. AE, DC, MC, V.*

Hotel Russell

$$$ Bloomsbury

This huge red brick hotel has been looking down on Russell Square in the heart of Bloomsbury for about a century. Built in the grand Victorian style, with a marble staircase, wood paneling, and crystal chandeliers, the hotel's multimillion-pound refurbishment, completed in 2000, restored a rich elegance to the 330 guest rooms. Virginia Woolf would turn over in her grave if she knew the hotel had a restaurant named after her serving burgers and grills. In addition, **Fitzroy Doll's** is a fine-dining restaurant.

Russell Sq., London WC1B 5BE; ☎ *020-7837-6470. Fax: 020-7837-2857. Internet:* www.principalhotels.co.uk. *Tube: Russell Sq. (the hotel is right on the square). Rack rates: £182 ($300) double. AE, MC, V.*

Ivanhoe Suites Hotel

$ Mayfair

Located above a restaurant on a pedestrian street of boutiques and restaurants, and close to even more shopping on New and Old Bond streets, this townhouse hotel has eight stylishly furnished guest rooms with sitting areas and refrigerator/bars. You can enjoy an unusual number of services for a hotel this small and inexpensive, including breakfast served in your room. Hyde Park is 5 minutes away.

*1 St. Christopher's Place, Barrett St. Piazza (just north of Oxford St.), London W1M 5HB; ☎ **020-7935-1047.** Fax: 020-7224-0563. Tube: Bond St. (then a 5-min. walk north on Gees Court to St. Christopher's Place). Rack rates: £79 ($130) double. Continental breakfast included. AE, DC, MC, V.*

James House & Cartref House

$ Westminster & Victoria

James House and Cartref House (across the street from each other, with a total of 11 rooms) deserve their reputation among the top ten B&Bs in London. Both are completely smoke-free. Each guest room is individually designed; some of the large ones contain bunk beds that make them suitable for families. Fewer than half have private bathrooms. The English breakfast is hearty, and the place is remarkably well kept. There's no elevator, but guests don't seem to mind. It doesn't matter to which house you're assigned; both are winners.

*108 and 129 Ebury St. (near Victoria Station), London SW1W 9QD; James House ☎ **020-7730-7338;** Cartref House ☎ **020-7730-6176.** Fax: 020-7730-7338. E-mail: jandchouse@cs.com. Tube: Victoria Station (then a 10-min. walk north on Grosvenor Gardens and south on Ebury St.). Rack rates: £65 ($107) double without bathroom, £78 ($129) double with bathroom. English breakfast included. AE, MC, V.*

Jenkins Hotel

$ Bloomsbury

The good news is that this no-smoking hotel offers a bit of Georgian charm, a great location near the British Museum and West End theaters, a nice comfortable atmosphere, a full breakfast, and a wonderfully low price. The bad news is that the 15 guest rooms are small, the hotel provides no elevator, fewer than half the units have private bathrooms, and there's no reception or sitting room. But it *is* a place where you can settle in and feel at home.

*45 Cartwright Gardens (just south of Euston Station), London WC1H 9EH; ☎ **020-7387-2067.** Fax: 020-7383-3139. E-mail: reservations@jenkinshotel. demon.co.uk. Internet: www.jenkinshotel.demon.co.uk. Tube: Euston Station (then a 5-minute walk east on Euston Rd. and south on Mabledon Place to the south end of Cartwright Gardens). Rack rates: £68 ($112) double without bathroom, £78 ($129) double with bathroom. English breakfast included. MC, V.*

Knightsbridge Hotel

$$$ Knightsbridge

If you want a place convenient to many of the city's top theaters and museums, consider the recently renovated Knightsbridge. This family-run hotel sits on a tree-lined, traffic-free square between fashionable Beauchamp Place and Harrods. Small and unpretentious, with a subdued Victorian ambience, the hotel's 40 well-furnished guest rooms offer many amenities and a good value.

12 Beaufort Gardens (just south of Harrods), London SW3 1PT; ☎ **020-7589-9271.** *Fax: 020-7823-9692. E-mail:* reception@knightsbridgehotel.co.uk. *Internet:* www.knightsbridgehotel.co. *Tube: Knightsbridge (then a 5-min. walk west on Brompton Rd. and south on Beaufort Gardens). Rack rates: £150 ($248) double. English breakfast included. AE, MC, V.*

Landmark London

$$$$$ Marylebone

In 1899, when the Landmark opened, it was the finest Victorian railway hotel in England. An enormous investment of millions of pounds have restored it beyond its former glory. When you book a room, ask what's on offer; almost nobody pays the rack rates, and you may get a bargain. Built around a Winter Garden atrium, the hotel is in a great location, particularly if children are traveling with you; the Landmark is less than a 5-minute walk from Madame Tussaud's and Regent's Park. Its 299 guest rooms are among London's largest, graced with marble bathrooms, blond wood furnishings, and modern paintings; special rooms are available for the disabled. You can find just about every amenity, including a large health club, baby-sitting, and an indoor pool.

222 Marylebone Rd. (half a block from Madame Tussaud's), London NW1 6JQ; ☎ **800-323-7500** *in the United States or 020-7631-8000. Fax: 020-7631-8080. E-mail:* reservations@thelandmark.co.uk. *Internet:* www.landmarklondon. co.uk. *Tube: Marylebone (the hotel is just a few steps away). Rack rates: £305–£335 ($503–$553) double. Rates don't include 17.5 percent VAT. AE, DC, MC, V.*

Lime Tree Hotel

$$ Westminster & Victoria

This cozy brick-fronted town house is near Buckingham Palace, Westminster Abbey, and the Houses of Parliament. The 26 guest rooms are simply furnished but generally larger and with more amenities than are usually available in this price range, making this hotel a wise choice for travelers on a budget. The bathrooms are small. The front rooms have small balconies overlooking Ebury Street; the rear rooms are quieter and look out over a small garden.

135–137 Ebury St. (near Victoria Station), London SW1W 9RA; ☎ **020-7730-8191.** *Fax: 020-7730-7865. Tube: Victoria Station (then a 5-minute walk north on Grosvenor Gardens and south on Ebury St.). Rack rates: £100–£110 ($165–$181) double. Generous English breakfast included. AE, DC, MC, V.*

Number Sixteen

$$$ South Kensington

Flower fans will drool over the award-winning gardens at this luxurious B&B in four early-Victorian town houses. The 36 guest rooms are decorated with an eclectic mix of English antiques and modern paintings, and the bathrooms are large by London standards. On chilly days, you'll find a fire crackling in the drawing-room fireplace. Breakfast is served in the rooms, but if the weather's fine you can have it in the garden and enjoy the fish pond and the bubbling fountain.

16 Sumner Place (north of Onslow Sq.), London SW7 3EG; ☎ ***800-592-5387** in the United States or 020-7589-5232. Fax: 020-7584-8615. E-mail:* reservations@ numbersixteenhotel.co.uk. *Internet:* www.numbersixteenhotel.co.uk. *Tube: South Kensington (then a 5-min. walk west on Brompton Rd. and south on Sumner Place). Rack rates: £135 ($223) double without bathroom, £170–£195 ($280–$322) double with bathroom. Continental breakfast included. AE, DC, MC, V.*

Park Lane Sheraton Hotel

$$$$$ Mayfair

Sometimes called the "Iron Lady of Piccadilly" because it's so well built, this landmark hotel was opened in 1927. The cheapest of the 305 guest rooms (not yet remodeled) are fairly spacious but old-fashioned and lack air-conditioning. Americans may prefer the renovated executive rooms and suites, all of which are decorated with a warm mix of classic English furnishings and have beautiful marble bathrooms. The price goes up according to location (particularly if it's a suite overlooking Green Park), size, and decor. Every conceivable amenity is available. The **Palm Court Lounge** is a swank place for afternoon tea (see Chapter 15), and two restaurants are on the premises.

Piccadilly (across from Green Park), London W1Y 8BX; ☎ ***800-325-3535** in the United States or 020-7499-6321. Fax: 020-7499-1965. Internet:* www.sheraton.com/ parklane. *Tube: Green Park (then a 3-min. walk southwest along Piccadilly). Rack rates: £275–£325 ($454–$536) double. AE, DC, MC, V.*

Philbeach Hotel

$ Earl's Court

The Philbeach is the largest and most established of the Earl's Court gay-friendly hotels. It's a large Victorian house on a Victorian crescent, and the atmosphere is more relaxed than at the gay-friendly **New York Hotel** (☎ **020-7244-6884**) next door. The decor is slightly baroque, bringing together an eclectic mix of paintings and furniture. About half the 40 rooms have bathrooms that include tiny showers. Guests can enjoy a TV lounge, an intimate basement bar, and a glass-walled dining room off the garden for breakfast; in the evening, the last becomes a good French restaurant called Wilde About Oscar. Men will probably be more comfortable here than women. A two-night minimum is required on weekends.

30–31 Philbeach Gardens (near the Earl's Court Exhibition Centre), London SW5 9EB; ☎ *020-7373-1244. Fax: 020-7244-0149. Internet:* www.philbeachhotel. freeserve.co.uk. *Tube: Earl's Court (take the Warwick Rd. exit; the hotel is a 5-min. walk north on Warwick St. and west on Philbeach Gardens). Rack rates: £65 ($107) double without bathroom, £85 ($140) double with bathroom. Continental breakfast included. AE, DC, MC, V.*

Regency Hotel

$$$ South Kensington

This refitted hotel occupies six Victorian terrace houses. The establishment exemplifies English elegance, demonstrated by a Chippendale fireplace and five Empire chandeliers suspended vertically, one on top of the other, in one of the stairwells. The 209 modern guest rooms are subdued and attractive, with good-sized bathrooms. Visit the health club with steam rooms, saunas, or the sensory-deprivation tank (if that kind of experience is your cup of tea).

100 Queen's Gate (near the Museum of Natural History), London SW7 5AG. ☎ *800-328-9898 in the United States or 020-7370-4595. Fax: 020-7370-5555. E-mail:* info@regency-london.co.uk. *Internet:* www.regency-london.co.uk. *Tube: South Kensington (then a 5-min. walk west on Pelham St. and Harrington Rd. to Queen's Gate). Rack rates: £152 ($251) double. Rates don't include 17.5 percent VAT. AE, DC, MC, V.*

Regent Palace Hotel

$$ Piccadilly Circus

One of Europe's largest hotels, the 920-room Regent Palace sits at the edge of Piccadilly Circus. After having staunchly adhered to its utilitarian 1915 design, it's now being upgraded — about a quarter of the guest rooms contain bathrooms; the others have sinks in the rooms and shared facilities in the halls. With a lobby that looks like an airport ticket counter (expect lines) and an endless flow of tourists, it's easy to feel anonymous here. But step out the door and you're in the exciting heart of the West End. Rates are lower midweek.

12 Sherwood St. (just north of Piccadilly Circus), London W1A 4BZ; ☎ *020-7734-7000. Fax: 020-7734-6435. E-mail:* rml003@forte-hotels.com. *Internet:* www.forte-hotels.com. *Tube: Piccadilly Circus (then a 2-min. walk north on Sherwood St.). Rack rates: £59–£84 ($97–$139) double without bathroom; £99–£109 ($163–$180) double with bathroom. AE, DC, MC, V.*

The Savoy

$$$$$ The Strand

An opulent eight-story landmark from 1889, the Savoy boasts 15 types of guest rooms, including some famous art deco ones with their original features. They're all spacious and splendidly decorated. The bathrooms, as large as some hotel rooms, are clad in red-and-white marble and have enormous glass-walled showers and heated towel racks. The most expensive rooms offer river views; others look out over the hotel courtyard. The **Savoy Grill** is one of London's most famous restaurants (see Chapter 14), and in the Thames Foyer you can get a superlative English tea (see Chapter 15); the Savoy Theatre, where Gilbert and Sullivan operettas are performed, is connected to the hotel.

The Strand (just north of Waterloo Bridge), London WC2R 0EU. ☎ *800-63-SAVOY in the U.S. or 020-7836-4343. Fax: 0171-240-6040. E-mail:* info@the-savoy.co.uk. *Internet:* www.savoy-group.co.uk. *Tube: Charing Cross (then a 5-minute walk east along The Strand). Rack rates: £335–£355 ($553–$586) double. Rates don't include 17.5 percent VAT. AE, DC, MC, V.*

Sloane Hotel

$$$ Chelsea

This captivating full-service hotel makes an ideal spot for a luxurious, romantic hideaway. The 12 individually decorated guest rooms feature antique treasures and rich fabrics; the larger rooms have sitting areas, and the bathrooms are marble. On the rooftop terrace you can have breakfast (£9 to £12/$15 to $20), afternoon tea, or evening cocktails.

29 Draycott Place (west of Sloane Sq.), London SW3 2SH; ☎ *800-324-9960 in the United States or 020-7581-5757. Fax: 020-7584-1348. E-mail:* sloanehotel@ btinternet.com. *Internet:* www.premierhotels.com. *Tube: Sloane Sq. (then a 5-min. walk west on Symons St., at the northwest corner of the square, to Draycott Place). Rack rate: £149–£185 ($231–$305) double. Rates don't include 17.5 percent VAT. AE, DC, MC, V.*

St. Martin's Lane

$$$$$ Piccadilly Circus

An Ian Schrager–developed hotel, St. Martin's Lane opened in 1999 and is *the* new in place to stay if you have the bucks and are into trendy high design. This once-nondescript office block has become a haven for the hip, now boasting an ultracool, almost surreal lobby; 3 restaurants; and 204 beautifully minimalist all-white guest rooms designed by trendy Philippe Starck. The bathrooms are roomy and luxurious and the windows floor-to-ceiling; every room has its own color-lighting panel, so you can control the mood. Weekend rates are available.

45 St. Martin's Lane (next to the English National Opera), London WC2N 4HX; ☎ *020-7300-5500. Fax: 020-7300-5501. Tube: Leicester Sq. (then a 2-min. walk east on Court to St. Martin's Lane). Rack rates: £235–£255 ($388–$421) double. Rates don't include 17.5 percent VAT. AE, DC, MC, V.*

Strathmore Hotel

$$$ South Kensington

This hotel overlooks a private garden square just minutes from the South Ken museums and was formerly the residence of the 14th earl of Strathmore, the Queen Mum's father. The high-ceilinged spaciousness of its 80 guest rooms is particularly appealing. The fabrics and furnishings (lots of handcarved rosewood furniture) were chosen with care, and the bathrooms have tubs and showers. The special summer rate of £89 ($146) per night, including breakfast, gives the Strathmore a distinct high-season edge over other area hotels.

41 Queen's Gate Gardens (at the southeast corner of the gardens), London SW7 5NB; ☎ ***020-7584-0512.*** *Fax: 020-7584-0246. E-mail:* strathmore@grangehotels. co.uk. *Internet:* www.grangehotels.co.uk. *Tube: Gloucester Rd. (then a 2-min. walk north on Gloucester Rd. and east on Queen's Gate Gardens). Rack rates: £155–£169 ($256–$279) double. AE, MC, V.*

Swiss House Hotel

$ South Kensington

Swiss House is a comfortable bargain B&B. It lacks an elevator and isn't stylish, but the 16 guest rooms are clean and nice, with pale walls, floral-print bedspreads, and small but serviceable bathrooms. The rear rooms are quieter and have views out into a garden. Located in the heart of South Ken (next door to Hotel 167), this hotel is well known to budget travelers, so book your reservations early. The hotel staff can arrange for baby-sitting.

171 Old Brompton Rd. (south of the Gloucester Rd. tube station), London SW5 0AN; ☎ ***020-7373-2769.*** *Fax: 020-7373-4983. E-mail:* recep@swiss-hh.domon.co.uk; *Internet:* www.webscape.co.uk/swiss-house/index.html. *Tube: Gloucester Rd. (then a 5-min. walk south on Gloucester Rd. and west on Old Brompton Rd.). Rack rates: £80–£90 ($132–$149) double. Continental breakfast included. AE, DC, MC, V.*

Tophams Belgravia

$$ Westminster & Victoria

Completely renovated in 1997, Tophams comprises five interconnected small row houses. The flower-filled windowboxes in the front add a bit of charm. The best of the 40 guest rooms are comfortably appointed, with private bathrooms and four-poster beds. The restaurant offers both traditional and modern English cooking for lunch and dinner. The location is convenient for travelers planning to explore London by tube or train.

28 Ebury St. (around the corner from Victoria Station), London SW1W 0LU; ☎ ***020-7730-8147.*** *Fax: 020-7823-5966. E-mail:* tophams_belgravia@ compuserve.com. *Internet:* www.tophams.co.uk. *Tube: Victoria Station (then a 5-min. walk north on Grosvenor Gardens and south on Ebury St.). Rack rates: £110 ($182) double without bathroom, £130–£170 ($214–$281) double with bathroom. English breakfast included. AE, DC, MC, V.*

Vicarage Private Hotel

$ Kensington

The family-run Vicarage offers old-world English charm, hospitality, and a good value. The hotel is on a residential garden square close to High Street Kensington and Kensington Palace. The 18 guest rooms, individually furnished in Victorian style, can accommodate up to four; room 19 on the top floor is particularly charming. Some of the double and twin rooms now have bathrooms. Many guests return here year after year.

10 Vicarage Gate (west of Kensington Gardens), London W8 4AG; ☎ **020-7229-4030.** *Fax: 020-7792-5989. E-mail:* reservations@londonvicaragehotel.com. *Internet:* www.londonvicaragehotel.com. *Tube: Kensington High St. (then a 10-min. walk east on Kensington High St. and north on Kensington Church St.). Rack rate: £74 ($122) double without bathroom, £98 ($162) double with bathroom. English breakfast included. No credit cards.*

Runner-Up Choices

Basil Street Hotel

$$$$ Knightsbridge

8 Basil St., London SW3 1AH; ☎ **020-7581-3311.** *Fax: 020-7581-3693. E-mail:* thebasil@aol.com. *An Edwardian hotel that's practically on Harrods doorstep and offers baby-sitting service.*

The big splurge

In this chapter I supply entries for several deluxe **$$$$$** hotels, among them the **Park Lane, The Savoy,** and the **St. Martin's.** If you're looking for the plushest of the plush, here are a few more suggestions:

✔ **Brown's Hotel** (29 @nd 34 Albemarle St., near Berkeley Square; ☎ **020-7493-6020.** Fax: 020-7493-9381. E-mail: brownshotel@ukbusiness.com. Internet: www.brownshotel.com).

✔ **Claridge's** (Brook Street, near Grosvenor Square; ☎ **800-223-6800** in the U.S. or 020-7629-8860. Fax: 020-7499-2210. E-mail: info@claridges.co.uk. Internet: www.savoy-group,co.uk).

✔ **The Dorchester** (53 Park Lane, at the east side of Hyde Park; ☎ **800-727-9820** in the U.S. or 020-7629-8888. Fax: 020-7409-0114. E-mail: info@dorchesterhotel.com.

Dukes Hotel

$$$$ St. James's

35 St. James's Place, London SW1A 1NY; ☎ **800-381-4702** *in the United States or 020-7491-4840. Fax: 020-7493-1264. E-mail:* dukeshotel@compuserve.com. *Internet:* www.dukeshotel.co.uk. *Charm, style, and tradition in a 1908 townhouse; babysitting is just one of many amenities offered.*

Goring Hotel

$$$$ Westminster & Victoria

15 Beeston Place, Grosvenor Gardens, London SW1W 0JW; ☎ **020-7396-9000**. *Fax: 020-7834-4393. E-mail:* reception@goringhotel.co.uk. *Internet:* www.goringhotel.co.uk. *Great location just behind Buckingham Palace, with top-notch service.*

Pembridge Court Hotel

$$$ Notting Hill

34 Pembridge Gardens, London W2 4DX; ☎ **020-7229-9977**. *Fax: 020-7727-4982. E-mail:* reservations@pemct.co.uk. *Lovely hotel furnished with antiques, located in Notting Hill Gate.*

Amber Hotel

$$ Earl's Court

101 Lexham Gardens, London W8 6JN; ☎ **020-7373-8666**. *Fax: 020-7835-1194. A Victorian charmer in Earl's Court with a private garden in back.*

Darlington Hyde Park

$$ Paddington

111–117 Sussex Gardens, London W2 2RU; ☎ **020-7460-8800**. *Fax: 020-7460-8828. E-mail:* darlinghp@aol.com. *Internet:* www.members.aol.com/darlinghp. *A Paddington area hotel that's a bit short on style but a good value.*

Ebury House

$ Westminster & Victoria

102 Ebury St., London SW1W 9QD; ☎ **020-7730-1350**. *Fax: 020-7259-0400. A B&B near Victoria Station known for the warmth of its hospitality.*

Fairways Hotel

$ Paddington

186 Sussex Gardens, London W2 1TU; ☎ **020-7723-4871**. *Fax: 020-7723-4871. E-mail:* fairwayshotel@compuserve.com. *Internet:* www.scoot.co.uk/fairways_ hotel. *A B&B boasting a homelike atmosphere and bargain rates.*

Chapter 9

Tying Up Loose Ends: Passports and More

● ●

In This Chapter

▶ Reading the fine print: Passports, customs, and insurance

▶ Taking care of your health: Medications and emergencies

▶ Making reservations for the things you just can't miss

▶ Packing light: what to take and what to leave

● ●

*B*efore you depart for London to take that boat ride on the river Thames or visit the Old Royal Observatory ("the center of time and space"), you have some loose ends to tie up. Do you have an up-to-date passport? Have you taken steps to meet your health needs while you're on your trip? Have you made reservations for the restaurant you have to try, and do you have your tickets for the play you just can't miss? Do you know what to pack for a trip to London? This chapter answers all your nagging questions and helps you take care of the last-minute details.

Dealing with Passports, Visas, and Health Certificates

A valid passport is the only legal form of identification accepted around the world. You can't cross an international border without it. Getting a passport is easy, but the process takes some time.

The *U.S. State Department's Bureau of Consular Affairs* maintains www.travel.state.gov, a Web site that provides everything you ever wanted to know about passports (including a downloadable application), customs, and other government-regulated aspects of travel.

Applying for a passport

Apply for your passport at least a month, preferably two, before you plan to leave on your trip. The processing takes an average of 3 weeks, but it can run longer during busy periods (especially in spring). For people over age 15, a passport is valid for 10 years; for those 15 and under, it's valid for 5 years.

If you're a U.S. citizen applying for a first-time passport and are 13 years of age or older, you need to apply in person at one of the following locations (see "Applying for Canadian, Australian, and New Zealand passports" later in this chapter for info on how to apply in other countries):

- ✔ One of the 13 passport offices throughout the United States — in Boston, Chicago, Honolulu, Houston, Los Angeles, Miami, New Orleans, New York City, Philadelphia, San Francisco, Seattle, Stamford (Connecticut), and Washington, D.C. Check the telephone directory or call the National Passport Information Center at ☎ **900-225-5674** (35 cents per minute) or 888-362-8668 ($4.95 per call) for the addresses of these offices.

- ✔ A federal, state, or probate court.

- ✔ A major post office. (Not all accept applications; call the phone number in the following paragraph to find the ones that do.)

To apply for your first passport, fill out *form DSP-11*. To renew your passport, you need *form DSP-82.* You can obtain these applications at the locations in the preceding list or by mail from *Passport Services,* Office of Correspondence, Department of State, 1111 19th St. NW, Washington, DC 20522-1705. You can also download the application off the Internet at www.travel.state.gov. For more information and to find your regional passport office, call the *National Passport Information Center* at ☎ **900-225-5674** (35 cents per minute) or 888-362-8668 ($4.95 per call) or log on to the Web site.

For first-time passports, children 14 to 18 years of age must apply in person (just like you) and need the same application and documents in the preceding list. Parents or guardians of children under 13 can obtain passports for them by presenting two photos of each child. Children's passports are valid for 5 years.

Bring the following when you apply for your first passport or to renew an old one:

- ✔ **Completed passport application**. You can fill out this form in advance to save time. However, **do not sign** the application until you present it in person at the passport agency, court, or post office.

- ✔ **Application fee**. For people over age 15, a passport costs $60 ($45 plus a $15 handling fee); for those 15 and under, it costs $40 total.

✔ **Proof of U.S. citizenship.** Bring your old passport if you're renewing; otherwise, bring a certified copy of your birth certificate with registrar's seal, a report of your birth abroad, or your naturalized citizenship documents.

✔ **Proof of identity.** Among the accepted documents are a valid driver's license, a state or military ID, a student ID (if you're currently enrolled), an old passport, or a naturalization certificate.

✔ **Two identical 2-inch by 2-inch photographs with a white or off-white background.** You can get these taken in just about any corner photo shop; these places have a special camera to make the photos identical. Expect to pay up to $12.50 for them. You can't use the strip photos from one of those photo vending machines.

When you have your passport photos taken, get an additional set (of you and your children) to take along with you. You need a photo to buy a 7-day or longer London Travelcard. And your child needs one to apply for a Child Photocard, which qualifies children to pay reduced prices on buses (see Chapter 11 for more details). Having extra photos on hand saves you the time, bother, and expense of having them taken in London.

If you're 18 or older and renewing a passport issued no more than 12 years go, you don't have to apply in person; you can do it all by mail. Include your expired passport, pink renewal form DSP-82, two identical photos (see the preceding bulleted list), and a check or money order for $45 (no extra handling fee). Send it (registered, just to be safe) to one of the agencies listed on the back of the application form. Allow at least 4 to 6 weeks for your application to be processed and your new passport to be sent.

Need your passport in a hurry, perhaps to take advantage of that incredibly low airline fare to London? To expedite your passport (to receive it in 5 business days), visit an agency directly or go through the court or post office and have them send the application via overnight mail. This process costs an extra $35. For more information, call the *National Passport Information Center* at ☎ **900-225-5674** (35 cents per minute) or 888-362-8668 ($4.95 per call).

Applying for Canadian, Australian, and New Zealand passports

The following list offer more information for citizens of Canada, Australia, and New Zealand:

✔ **Canadians** can pick up passport applications at the central Passport Office (Department of Foreign Affairs and International Trade, Ottawa, ON K1A 0G3; ☎ **800-567-6868**), one of the 28 regional passport offices, most travel agencies, or from www.dfait-maeci.gc.ca/passport (downloadable forms). A child under 16 may be included on a parent's passport, but needs his or her own passport to travel unaccompanied. Applications must be accompanied by two identical 2-inch-by-2-inch photos and a birth certificate or Certificate of Canadian Citizenship. Passports are valid for 5 years and cost $60, and processing takes 5 to 10 days if you apply in person or 10 days to 3 weeks by mail.

✔ **Australians** can visit a local post office or passport office, call toll free ☎ **131-232**, or log on to www.dfat.gov.au/passports for details on how and where to apply. Adult passports cost AUS$128 and passports for travelers under 18 are AUS$64.

✔ **New Zealanders** can pick up passport applications at any travel agency, online at www.passports.govt.nz, or at the Passport Office, P.O. Box 10-526, Wellington (☎ **0800-225-050**). Adult passports cost NZ$80 and passports for travelers under 16 are NZ$40. Mail the completed form, along with the pair of identical 50-mm by 40-mm photos and proof of citizenship, to the Wellington office.

Understanding passport rules

If you're a citizen of the United States, Canada, Australia, or New Zealand, you must have a passport with at least 2 months remaining validity to enter the United Kingdom. Citizens of European Union (EU) countries supposedly do not need a passport to visit other EU countries, but in reality they do need one if their country doesn't issue identity cards. You'll need to show your passport at the Customs and Immigration area when you arrive at a London airport. After your passport is stamped, you can remain in the United Kingdom as a tourist for up to 3 months.

Keep your passport with you at all times. The only times to give it up are at the bank or currency exchange when you're converting traveler's checks or foreign currency. Present your passport to the hotel clerk when you check in; after examining it, the clerk will return it to you. If you're not going to need your passport for currency exchange, ask whether the hotel has a safe where you can keep it locked up.

Dealing with a (gulp) lost passport

Don't worry; if you lose your passport in London, you won't be sent to the Tower, but you need to take steps to replace it *immediately*. Go directly to the nearest consulate or high commission office. Bring all available forms of personal ID, and the staff will get started on generating you a new passport. For the addresses of consulates and high commissions, see the appendix.

Getting visas and health certificates

No visa is required if you're going to stay in the United Kingdom for less than 3 months. The U.S. Department of State's Bureau of Consular Affairs operates a phone line for current visa information: ☎ 202-663-1225 (Monday through Friday 8:30 a.m. to 4 p.m.). Or you can check its Web site at www.travel.state.gov.

Likewise, you don't need an International Certificate of Vaccination to enter the United Kingdom, as you would if traveling to Southeast Asia or parts of Africa. The country is notoriously concerned about rabies, but that doesn't apply to you (I hope), only to the pet you will *not* be bringing along (under any circumstances) because it would be quarantined if you did.

Deciding Insurance Needs

Three kinds of travel insurance are available: trip-cancellation insurance, medical insurance, and lost luggage insurance. Here is my advice on all three:

✔ **Trip-cancellation insurance** is a good idea if you've signed up for an escorted tour and paid a large portion of your vacation expenses up front (for information on escorted tours, see Chapter 5).

✔ Buying **medical insurance** for your trip doesn't make sense for most travelers. Your existing health insurance should cover you if you get sick while on vacation (though if you belong to an HMO, check to see whether you're fully covered while in the United Kingdom).

✔ **Lost luggage insurance** is not necessary for most travelers. Your homeowner's or renter's insurance should cover stolen luggage if you have off-premises theft coverage. Check your existing policies before you buy any additional coverage. If an airline loses your luggage, it is responsible for paying $1,250 per bag on domestic flights and $635 per bag (maximum of two bags) on international flights. If you plan to carry anything more valuable than that, keep it in your carry-on bag.

Some credit cards (American Express and some gold and platinum Visa and MasterCards, for example) offer automatic flight insurance against death or dismemberment in case of an airplane crash. If you still feel you need more insurance, try one of the following companies:

✔ **Access America,** 6600 W. Broad St., Richmond, VA 23230 (☎ 800-284-8300).

✔ **Mutual of Omaha,** Mutual of Omaha Plaza, Omaha, NE 68175 (☎ 800-228-9792).

> ✔ **Travel Guard International,** 1145 Clark St., Stevens Point, WI
> 54481 (☎ **800-826-1300;** www.travel-guard.com).
>
> ✔ **Travel Insured International, Inc.,** P.O. Box 280568, East Hartford,
> CT 06128 (☎ **800-243-3174;** www.travelinsured.com).

Don't pay for more insurance than you need. For example, if you need only trip-cancellation insurance, don't buy coverage for lost or stolen property. Trip-cancellation insurance costs about 6 to 8 percent of the total value of your vacation.

Taking Care of Your Health

Getting sick will ruin your vacation, so I strongly advise against it (of course, last time I checked, the bugs weren't listening to me any better than they probably listen to you).

Talk to your doctor before leaving on a trip if you have a serious and/or chronic illness. If you have a serious condition, such as heart disease, epilepsy, or diabetes, wear a Medic Alert identification tag, which will immediately alert any doctor to your condition and give him or her access to your medical records through Medic Alert's 24-hour hot line (a worldwide toll-free emergency response number is on the tag). Membership is $35, plus a $15 annual fee. Contact the *Medic Alert Foundation,* P.O. Box 1009, Turlock, CA 95381-1009 (☎ **800-825-3785;** www.medicalert.org).

Bring all your medications with you, as well as prescriptions for more (in generic, not brand name, form) if you worry that you'll run out. If you have health insurance, be sure to carry your insurance card in your wallet. If you worry about getting sick away from home, buy medical insurance (see the preceding section on insurance). It'll cover you more completely than your existing health insurance.

If you fall ill while traveling, ask the concierge at your hotel to recommend a local doctor (if the concierge seems stymied, you can even ask for the name of his or her own physician). If you can't locate a doctor, contact your country's embassy or consulate (see the Appendix for addresses and phone numbers). If the situation is serious and as a last resort, dial ☎ **999** (no coins required), the number for police and medical emergencies. If the situation is life-threatening, go to the emergency or accident department at the local hospital.

Under the United Kingdom's nationalized health care system, you're eligible only for free *emergency* care. If you're admitted to a hospital as an in-patient, even from an accident and an emergency department, you must pay unless you're a U.K. resident or resident of the European Economic Area. This financial obligation is true for follow-up care as well. See the Appendix for the names, addresses, and phone numbers of hospitals offering 24-hour emergency care.

Most U.S. health insurance plans and HMOs cover at least part of the out-of-country hospital visits and procedures if insurees become ill or are injured while out of the country. Most require that you pay the bills up front at the time of care, issuing a refund after you return and file all the paperwork.

Before leaving home, obtain a directory of U.K. doctors from the *International Association of Medical Assistance to Travelers (IAMAT)*. Its address in the United States is 417 Center St., Lewiston, NY 14092 (☎ **716-754-4883**) and in Canada is 40 Regal Rd., Guelph, Ontario N1K 1B5 (☎ **519-836-0102**). It's on the Web at `www.sentex.net/~iamat`.

Not Renting a Car in London

Having a car in London is far more of a hassle than a help for the following reasons:

- Maneuvering through London's congested and complicated maze of streets can be an endurance test even for Londoners.

- Finding your way through the city in heavy traffic while driving on the *left-hand side* of the road can turn even the best American driver into a gibbering nut case.

- Parking is difficult to find and expensive (street meters cost £1/$1.65 for 20 minutes).

- Gas (*petrol* in Britspeak) costs about $4 a gallon.

- Public transportation — especially the Underground (subway) — will get you everywhere you want to go at a fraction of the cost.

Do yourself a favor: Forget about renting a car. If you want to be with Londoners on their own turf (or in their own tunnels), the tube (Underground) is a great way to do it. Even if you're planning excursions outside London, the trains are a better option. (However, see Chapter 21 for details on renting a car for day-tripping.)

Getting Reservations and Tickets Before You Leave Home

If your time in London is limited and you don't want to miss specific plays, concerts, or top restaurants, make your reservations or buy your tickets in advance.

For advance reservations, call the restaurant directly from home (the restaurant listings in Chapters 14 and 15 include phone numbers), but keep in mind the time change (London is 5 hours later than Eastern Standard, so when it's noon in New York, it's 5 p.m. in London). You can also ask your hotel concierge to make the reservation for you after you arrive, but be sure to do so far enough ahead (you may have to reserve a couple of days or even a week or two in advance for some trendy places).

If you're planning on a high tea at the Ritz or one of the other elegant London hotels that serve legendary afternoon teas (I list them in Chapter 15), you may have to book that reservation in advance as well. For a list of hot restaurants in London that require advance booking, see Chapter 13.

Two on the aisle: Prebooking tickets

Every London theater has a row (or more) of house seats that are kept until the last possible moment. Those seats as well as any returns generally go on sale on the day of the performance — in the morning or an hour before curtain time. Your chances of getting a seat to a sold-out show are good if you go directly to the box office.

You may be looking forward to a specific event, and missing it would ruin your trip. On my last trip, my must-see was Dame Maggie Smith in Alan Bennett's new play, *The Lady in the Van.* Every day in front of the box office, a long queue of theater lovers desperately hoped to snag a return ticket. Dame Maggie, as they say, was the hottest show in town. So I was glad I'd booked a seat in advance.

You can book in advance (and pay an additional commission) before you leave home by contacting one of the following:

✔ **Keith Prowse.** The New York office of this London-based ticket agency (☎ **800-669-7469** or 914-328-2357; e-mail: tickets@ keithprowse.com; Internet: www.keithprowse.com) handles West End shows, the English National and Royal Opera, pop concerts, and events such as the Chelsea Flower Show and the British Open. After payment is received, the agency sends you a voucher to be exchanged for tickets at the box office.

✔ **Albemarle**. This respected booking agency (at 74 Mortimer St., London, W1N 8HL; ☎ **020-7637-9041;** fax: 020-7631-0375; e-mail: sales@albemarle-london.com; Internet: www.albemarle-london.com) maintains a definitive London Theatre Web site with listings of all current West End shows, opera, ballet, and rock and pop concerts. If you see a performance you like, you can book it via e-mail. The prices include a booking fee of 23 percent plus tax. Albemarle sells the best seats to most shows for £44.10 ($73); the face value of the ticket is £35 ($58). If there's time, the company will mail tickets worldwide; otherwise, you can pick them up at the theater or have them delivered to your hotel.

If you want to attend an opera or a ballet at the **Royal Opera House**, prebook months, not days, in advance. Check out the major performing-arts venues in Chapter 23; if the group has a Web site, I list it. Usually you can book directly online.

What's playing and where

The ticket-booking agencies in the preceding section will tell you what's currently on. The following Web sites are also useful for finding out what's playing in London:

- ✔ **The Society of London Theatre** (www.officiallondontheatre.co.uk) offers a comprehensive listing of plays, opera, and dance in the West End.

- ✔ *Time Out* (www.timeout.com) provides online theater, music, dance, and other events listings. You can browse through and find everything that's currently playing, including smaller venues.

- ✔ **Electronic Telegraph** (www.telegraph.co.uk), the online version of the *Daily Telegraph*, reviews theater and other performance events in its "Arts & Books" section.

- ✔ **The Net edition of the *London Times* and the Sunday Times** (www.sunday-times.co.uk) offers reviews and listings of West End shows and other events. Look under "Arts" and "Culture."

- ✔ **The online version of the *Evening Standard* newspaper** (www.thisislondon.co.uk) has listings of current theater and music events.

Packing It Up and Taking It on the Road

Before you start packing, think realistically about what you'll need for the length of time you'll be gone. And think practically. A sauce stain on a white silk dress or dress shirt will render it unwearable (I hope). In general, plan to dress in *layers*. Pack *nonwhite* clothing. And unless you're going to London in the height of summer (perhaps even then), consider that the temperature will probably be between *45 degrees Fahrenheit and 60 degrees Fahrenheit, and the climate is often damp.*

The English favor woolens because they're warm, they're practical, and they hold their shape even after a drenching downpour. Many hotel rooms are equipped with trouser presses, which will get out the wrinkles and save you the hassle of toting along a travel iron. Remember that London is one of the great shopping cities of the world. If you forget a critical item, you can buy it in London.

According to 18th-century writer (and Londoner) Dr. Johnson, "When two Englishmen meet, their first talk is of the weather." Things haven't changed much since then. The unpredictability of the English climate has led to another sound British maxim: "There is no such thing as bad weather, there is only inappropriate clothing."

Deciding what to bring

Start packing by compiling everything that you think you'll need on your trip. Then get rid of half of it. You don't want to injure yourself by lugging half your house around with you. Getting from the airport and your hotel can be difficult; but if you're staying in a B&B without an elevator, lugging a heavy load of suitcases up and down narrow London stairways can be a royal pain in the gluteus max.

If you ask me, packing is a spiritual exercise. It teaches you a great deal about yourself and your basic needs. It's about lightening your load.

Some essentials for your trip include

- ✔ Comfortable walking shoes

- ✔ A versatile sweater (gray or dark colored)

- ✔ A waterproof jacket or coat (preferably one with a hood)

- ✔ Something to sleep in (London thermostats are often set about 10 degrees lower than those in the States.)

You need a formal suit or fancy dress only if you plan to attend a board meeting, a funeral, a wedding, or some similar occasion, or you want to dine in one of the city's finest restaurants. For daily wear around the city, a pair of jeans or khakis will do. You may want to consider a couple of cotton pullovers you can wear under a sweater or sweatshirt.

London can be blusteringly cold in winter and drizzly at any time of the year, so packing a collapsible umbrella (or *brolly* as the Brits call them) is always a wise idea. If you're traveling to London in late fall or winter, a lined raincoat and a heavy sweater will be put to good use, as will a pair of gloves and a scarf.

Dressing like a Londoner

London — like Paris, Milan, and New York — is a fashion-conscious city. This doesn't mean that you *must* be fashionable, only that you *can* be, and that if you are, other fashionable people may notice you. If you plan to eat in any upscale restaurants, you'll encounter a "smart but casual" dress code. You won't be let in if you try to enter the dining room wearing jogging shoes, sweatpants, or blue jeans.

Smart but casual men need to bring along a pair of dressy but comfortable trousers and a sports jacket (or a suit if you like), a shirt and tie (or dressy sweater), and leather shoes (preferably with a nice patina). Smart but casual women can wear a dress, a skirt and blouse, a suit with skirt and jacket, or a pants-suit. One thing you might want to know: As in New York, the big color in London is black. So if you're wondering what color is in this and every season, it's noir, noir, Nanette.

Packing smart

Before you choose a suitcase for your trip, decide what kind of traveling you intend to do. A bag with wheels makes sense for walking with luggage on hard floors. Wheels won't help you carry baggage on uneven roads or up and down stairs. A foldover garment bag is a nuisance if you pack and unpack often, but it can help keep dressy clothing wrinkle-free. Hard-sided luggage protects breakable items better but weighs more than soft-sided bags.

Airlines allow you two pieces of carry-on luggage, both of which must fit in the overhead compartment or beneath the seat in front of you. Each airline defines its own dimension limits for carry-ons, but the limits usually average around 60 inches total (10 by 14 by 36 inches). Your carry-on should contain a book (this one, of course), any medications you use, any breakable items you don't want to put in your suitcase, a snack in case you don't like the airline food (the flight will be at least 6 hours), and your vital documents (such as return tickets and passport).

Select a backpack or shoulder bag as one of your carry-ons. It can double as an all-purpose carry-along bag — for your guidebooks, maps, and camera — while you're in London.

Leaving electronics at home

When I'm on an exciting trip, the last thing I want is to tune myself *out* of what is going on around me. I want to enjoy the sights and atmosphere. People today think that they need to haul along every new electronic toy or gadget wherever they go. Trust me, doing so won't add anything to your trip — in fact, it'll detract from it. Even the mobile phone that's glued to your ear at home can be turned off and left behind. (You'll notice, though, that every other Londoner now seems to be talking while walking.)

Some electronic items may be necessary — a laptop, for example, if you have to work while in London. Except for the absolute necessities, leave all the other electronic devices at home.

If you think that you won't enjoy your trip without a few electrical gadgets, here's what you need to know: You can't plug an American appliance into a British outlet without frying your appliance and/or blowing a fuse. American current runs 110V, 60 cycles; the standard voltage throughout Britain is 240V AC, 50 cycles. You need a current converter or transformer to bring the voltage down and the cycles up. Two-pronged American plugs won't fit into the three-pronged square British wall sockets, so you also need a three-pronged square adapter and/or converter if you use U.S. appliances in Britain. Plug adapters and converters are available at most travel, luggage, electronics, and hardware stores. Some plug adapters are also current converters. Most contemporary laptop computers automatically sense the current and adapt accordingly (check the manual, bottom of the machine, or manufacturer first to make sure that you don't destroy your data and/or equipment).

Count down: Ten things to do before you leave

For peace of mind on your trip, make sure that you take care of some housekeeping details before you leave. Though most are fairly obvious, they are easy to overlook in the excitement of getting ready for a trip:

✔ Get someone to look after your pets (or kennel them) and water the plants.

✔ Put a hold on your mail and newspaper deliveries.

✔ Empty/defrost your refrigerator.

✔ Put several lights in the house on timers (dining room at dinner time, TV room during prime time, and so on).

✔ Lock all windows and doors (don't forget the basement and garage).

✔ Arrange for a friend or taxi to take you to the airport (this method is cheaper and better than leaving your car in the airport garage).

✔ Reconfirm your plane's seat reservation and your hotel bookings.

✔ Call the airline to double-check that your flight is on time.

✔ Get to the airport at least 2 hours before your flight.

✔ Sit back on the plane, take a deep breath, and tell yourself: "I'm on my way to London!" Cheerio! Have a great time.

Travel-sized versions of hair dryers, irons, shavers, and so on are dual voltage, which means that they have built-in converters (usually you have to turn a switch to go back and forth). If you insist on lugging your own hair dryer or electric shaver to London, make sure that it's dual voltage or that you carry along a converter. Hotels black out on a regular basis when someone from the United States plugs in a 110V hair dryer, and the appliance explodes in an impressive shower of sparks or melts in his or her hands. To avoid voltage issues, use a straight-edge razor for shaving, unless you have a battery-operated electric shaver. However, most hotels have a special plug for low-wattage shavers *and shavers only.*

Part III
Settling into London

"Morris, please stop screaming 'Give me liberty or give me death!' That's not going to get the door unstuck, and people are beginning to stare."

In this part . . .

Daydreaming about going to a place is cheap, convenient, and lots of fun: You don't have to concern yourself with how to get from point A to point B without wasting time and money. But when you actually reach London, reality will set in. You won't be familiar with how the Underground runs, how the bus system works, when the trains run, or how to get a taxi. In this part, I guide you from the airport into the city and then introduce you to London's neighborhoods (see Chapter 10). In Chapter 11, I tell you everything you need to know about public transportation, including ways to save a bundle on bus and tube tickets. A quick and easy primer on U.K. currency follows in Chapter 12.

Chapter 10

Finding Your Way Around London

. . . .

In This Chapter

▶ Traveling from the airport (or train station) to your hotel

▶ Getting yourself oriented to the London neighborhoods

▶ Finding help and information after you've arrived

. . . .

*A*lthough London is among the world's largest cities, in both size and population, many of its neighborhoods were once small villages. With its roots deep within Roman times, London's not the easiest city to find your way around in; the streets aren't arranged in an organized design and, though most have been paved and modernized, some remain cobblestoned. This quaint, village-like quality is one reason for London's enduring charm, but charm is little comfort when you're lost in a strange place, so let me help you get your bearings. Neighborhood boundaries come later in this chapter. First, you need to get from the airport (or train station) into Central London.

From the Plane into London

Heathrow and Gatwick airports handle the bulk of London's international flights. The airports are accustomed to handling thousands of customers every day, so you needn't fear any unpleasant surprises.

Proceeding through Passport Control and Customs

Have your passport ready because your first stop after deplaning will be Passport Control (for details on getting a passport, see Chapter 9). It's a fairly routine procedure. On the plane you'll fill out a *landing card* that asks for your name, home address, passport number, and the address you'll be staying at in London. Present this completed form with your passport to the official at Passport Control. The official may ask for the following information:

- ✔ How long you'll be staying (under 3 months if you don't have a visa)

- ✔ Where you plan to stay

- ✔ Whether the trip is for business or pleasure (don't be afraid to say pleasure)

- ✔ What your next destination will be

- ✔ How much money you have with you

Although you may think that the question about your finances is snoopy impertinence, there's a good reason for it. Officials want to verify that people entering the country won't apply for some kind of welfare or National Health insurance benefits and become a burden on the country.

Generally, however, they stamp your passport without asking a thing. After your passport is stamped, proceed to pick up your luggage. From there, you'll wind your way out through the Customs Hall.

At the Customs area, you get two choices: "Nothing to Declare" and "Goods to Declare." Chances are you won't be declaring anything, in which case you walk right through. Limits on imports for visitors 17 and older entering England include

- ✔ 200 cigarettes, 50 cigars, or 250 grams (8.8 oz.) of loose tobacco

- ✔ 2 liters (2.1 qt.) of still table wine

- ✔ 1 liter of liquor over 22 percent alcohol content or 2 liters of liquor under 22 percent

- ✔ 2 fluid ounces of perfume

If you fall within these limits, go through the "Nothing to Declare" area at Customs. You may, however, be stopped for a random luggage search. Don't take it personally if this happens. Unless you're smuggling in contraband, you have nothing to worry about. For information on duty-free shopping and limits on what you can bring back home, see Chapter 19.

Arriving at busy Heathrow

About 15 miles west of Central London, Heathrow (☎ **020-8759-4321**) is the largest of London's airports as well as the world's busiest, with four passenger terminals serving flights from around the globe. Moving walkways and signposts that mark just about everything make the trek through the long corridors easier and less confusing. You probably will arrive at Terminal 3 or 4:

- ✔ Terminal 3 is for non-British long-haul flights.

- ✔ Terminal 4 is for British Airways intercontinental flights and the superfast Concorde.

After clearing Customs (see the preceding section), you enter the main concourse of your terminal. You can pick up a free map and general info from the *Tourist Information Centre* in the Terminal 3 Arrivals Concourse (open daily 6 a.m. to 11 p.m.) or in the Underground concourse of Terminals 1, 2, and 3 (open daily 8 a.m. to 6 p.m.). Other available services include ATMs, hotel booking agencies (see Chapter 7), theater booking services, and several banks and bureaux de change (where you can swap your dollars or traveler's checks for pounds and pence).

You have several options for getting into the city. The London Underground (☎ 020-7222-1234), called the *Underground* or the *tube*, is the London subway system and the cheapest mode of public transportation for most Central London destinations (see the Cheat Sheet at the front of this book for a map of the Underground system). All terminals at Heathrow link up with the tube system. Follow the Underground signs to the ticket booth. The Piccadilly Line gets you into Central London in about 45 minutes for a fare of £3.50 ($6). Underground trains run from all four Heathrow terminals every 5 to 9 minutes Monday through Saturday 5:30 a.m. to 11:30 p.m. and Sunday 6 a.m. to 11 p.m.

The one potential hassle with the Underground is that the tube trains don't have luggage racks. Stash your bags as best you can — behind your legs, on your lap, or near the center doors where there's more space. If it's rush hour, the trains become increasingly packed as you get closer to London. To reach your hotel on the Underground, you may have to change trains or take a cab from the Underground station closest to your destination.

For more information on the Underground, including discount passes (called *Travelcards*), check out Chapter 11.

If the Underground is closed, you can ride the N97 night bus from Heathrow to Central London. Buses (located in front of the terminals) run every 30 minutes Monday through Saturday midnight to 5 a.m. and Sunday 11 p.m. to 5:30 a.m. The trip takes about an hour; a one-way fare is £1.50 ($2.50) before 4:30 a.m. or £1 ($1.65) after 4:30 a.m.

The Airbus Heathrow Shuttle (☎ 020-8400-6655) may be a better alternative to the Underground if you have lots of heavy luggage. Two routes are available: The A1 goes from Heathrow to Victoria Station via Cromwell Road, Knightsbridge, and Hyde Park Corner; the A2 goes to Kings Cross Station via Bayswater, Marble Arch, Euston, and Russell Square. Travel time for both is about 75 minutes, and the fare is £7 ($12), payable on the bus. Up to three buses an hour depart daily 4 a.m. to 11:23 p.m. from the front of Heathrow's terminals.

The Heathrow Express (☎ 0845-600-1515) is a dedicated train line running from all four Heathrow terminals to Paddington Station in only 15 minutes. The trains have air-conditioning, ergonomically designed seating, and lots of luggage space. Using this service requires a simple bus-to-train transfer. You can catch a Heathrow Express bus outside your arrival terminal. The bus will take you directly to the train. The fare is £12 ($20) Express class or £20 ($33) first class, and you can buy tickets at the airport or on board the train. Service runs Monday through Saturday 5:07 a.m. to 11:47 p.m. and Sunday 5:03 a.m. to 11:48 p.m.

If you're travel-weary, you may want the luxury of taking a taxi (☎ **020-8745-7487**) directly to your hotel. Taxis are especially cost effective if four or five people are traveling together. You can order one at the Taxi Information booths in all four terminals. Expect to pay about £35 ($58) plus tip for a trip of about 45 minutes. Cabs are available 24 hours a day. Wheelchair facilities are available at all times for the disabled.

Getting in at calmer Gatwick

Gatwick (☎ **01293-535-353**) is considerably smaller than Heathrow but provides the same services, except that the British Tourist Authority doesn't have an office there. Gatwick is about 28 miles south of Central London. Once used only for charters, Gatwick now handles international flights from some U.S. airlines; international flights come in at the South Terminal. Gatwick also has a North Terminal.

If you land at Gatwick instead of Heathrow, you have fewer means of transportation into Central London. The highway system from Gatwick into London is far less efficient than from Heathrow, so buses, mini-vans, or cabs can end up taking 2 to 3 hours in heavy traffic.

Your quickest way of getting into Central London is the convenient Gatwick Express train (☎ **0990-301-530**) You can board the train right in the South Terminal, and in about 30 minutes, you'll be at Victoria Station. Cost is £10.20 ($17). Trains run daily every 15 minutes from 5 a.m. to midnight; they run hourly throughout the night.

Slightly less expensive is the local Connex South-Central train (☎ **01332-387-601**), which also runs to Victoria Station and usually takes about 5 minutes longer; its fare is £8.20 ($14). Four trains run each hour during the day; from midnight to 5 a.m., they run every half-hour.

Another train service is the Thameslink (☎ **0845-748-4950**), running between Gatwick and King's Cross Station for £9.50 ($16). Service is every 15 minutes daily 3:45 a.m. to 12:15 a.m.; trip time is about 45 minutes.

For 24-hour taxi service between Gatwick and Central London, call

- ✔ Gatwick Airport Cars (☎ **01293-562-291**)
- ✔ Gatwick Goldlines Cars (☎ **01293-568-368**)

You can order a taxi at the Taxi Information booth when you arrive at Gatwick Airport. Fares for both companies are the same: £60 ($99) plus tip for the journey that takes about 90 minutes.

Landing at another airport

You can arrive at airports other than Heathrow and Gatwick. The following sections help you navigate from these less-used facilities.

Stansted: For national and European flights

Stansted (☎ **01279-680-500**) is a single-terminal airport used for national and European flights. It's about 33 miles northeast of Central London. The Stansted Skytrain (☎ **01332-387-601**) to Liverpool Street Station takes 45 minutes and costs £10.70 ($18). Trains run every half-hour daily 6 a.m. to 11:59 p.m. Taxi fare into the city averages about £60 ($99) plus tip.

London City Airport: European destinations only

London City Airport (☎ **020-7646-000**) is a mere 6 miles east of the city center, but it services only European destinations. A Red Route shuttle bus (☎ **020-7646-0000**) takes passengers from the airport to Liverpool Street Station in 25 minutes for £5 ($8). The buses run every 10 minutes daily 6 a.m. to 9:30 p.m. A taxi to the vicinity of Marble Arch will cost about £25 ($41) plus tip.

Luton: Serving European charters

Luton (☎ **01582-405-100**) services European charter flights. It's a small, independent airport about 33 miles northwest of the city. The Greenline 757 Bus (☎ **0990-808-080**) runs from the airport to the Victoria Coach Station on Buckingham Palace Road every hour daily 5:30 a.m. to midnight; the trip takes about 75 minutes and costs £7 ($12).

You can also take the 24-hour Railair Coach Link to Luton Station (3 miles away), which connects with the Luton Flyer train to King's Cross Station in Central London. The fare is £10 ($17); trip time is 1 hour.

Taxis into the city cost about £50 ($83) plus tip.

Arriving at the Channel Ports

If coming from the Continent by train and ferry or hovercraft, you cross the English Channel and disembark at one of the United Kingdom's Channel ports. The ports closest to London are *Dover, Ramsgate,* and *Folkestone* to the east and *Southampton, Portsmouth,* and *Newhaven* to the south. The *QEII* cruise ship also docks at Southampton.

From whichever port you're at, you take another train into London. Trains connecting with ferries on the U.K. side of the Channel generally go to Liverpool Street Station, Victoria Station, or Waterloo International. Waterloo is also where the Eurostar Chunnel trains arrive from Paris and Brussels. On the Eurostar, you don't have to make any train-to-boat-to-train transfers along the way. For more on the Eurostar, see Chapter 5.

All London stations link to the Underground system. Just look for the Underground symbol (a circle with a line through it). Here's how they connect:

- ✔ **Waterloo** is linked to the Northern and Bakerloo lines.

- ✔ **Victoria** is on the District, Circle, and Victoria lines.

- ✔ **Liverpool Street** is on the Circle, East London, Metropolitan, and Central Lines.

Taxi ranks stand outside all train stations. See Chapter 11 for more information on the London Underground and taxis.

London's train stations are swarming with activity. You find bookstores, bureaux de change (currency exchange facilities), restaurants, newsagents, and many of the services airports traditionally offer. See the section "Getting Guidance in London" later in this chapter for information about the tourist information centers that you find in several London train stations. You can stock up on maps and brochures and, if you arrived in London without a hotel reservation, you can book a room from Victoria and several other train stations (see Chapter 7 for details).

Keep in mind that the United Kingdom, like the rest of Europe, uses the 24-hour clock for rail and other timetables. That means 0530 is 5:30 a.m., 1200 is noon, and 1830 is 6:30 p.m. Don't be confused: just continue counting up from noon: 1300 = 1 p.m., 1400 = 2 p.m., 1500 = 3 p.m., and so on up to 2400 (midnight). In this guide, I stick to the American a.m. and p.m. system. Like most of the rest of the world, London goes on Daylight Saving Time from April through October.

Resetting your internal clock

Passengers flying to London generally experience *jet lag,* so you need to try and reset your internal clock. On a 6-hour flight from the East Coast, for example, you move through 5 hours of time change. When you arrive at 7 a.m. *your* time, it'll be noon *London* time. My best advice is to try and get acclimated to London time immediately. Reset your watch before you get off the plane. Don't keep looking for a clock and trying to figure out what time it is back home.

Stay up as long as you can your first day in London, and then wake up at a normal time (well, try to, anyway) the second day. Drink plenty of water both days, as well as on the plane, to avoid dehydration and to help keep you regular. Try to eat at usual London meal times. I've always found that walking a lot on my first day in London helps me to beat jet lag and get me in synch with the city.

Figuring Out the Neighborhoods

Orienting yourself to London's prime neighborhoods will help you plan your days (and nights) so that you can make the most of your time in this fascinating jigsaw of a city.

Londoners orient themselves by neighborhood (see the map "London Neighborhoods"). Sounds simple enough, but with London's confusing and sometimes oddly named streets and its seemingly endless plethora of neighborhoods, you may have a hard time telling where one neighborhood begins and another leaves off. For orientation purposes, I give you major streets as boundary markers. But be aware that the neighborhoods frequently bleed beyond these principal arteries.

To help you find your way around, I strongly suggest that you buy a copy of *London A to Z* (ask for *London A to Zed*, because *z* is pronounced "zed"). You can pick up this indexed London street map at just about any bookstore or newsagent (you may want to get it while you're at the airport).

Although Greater London encompasses a whopping 622 square miles, the main tourist portion is only a fraction (25 square miles at the most) of that distance. Most sites within this 25-mile range are convenient to the Underground system (the tube). You may have a short (10 minute or less) walk from the tube stop to your destination) but London is flat, and for walkers it's a dream.

London is divided into postal districts, like ZIP codes in the United States. All London street addresses include a designation such as SW1 or EC3. (In London, the postal districts are related to where they lie geographically from the original post office, which was at St. Martin-le-Grand in The City.) Addresses in the City of London, the easternmost portion of Central London, have designations such as EC2, EC3, or EC4. As you move west, the codes change to W, WC, SW, NW, and so on.

You don't need to bother yourself with postal districts except when you're looking up streets in *London A to Z* (many streets in different parts of London have the same name) or sending something by mail. When you actually hit the streets, the postal district designations aren't as important as the nearest tube stop.

London is a huge city. Getting your bearings is easier if you visualize the city in sections.

Remember that London grew up along the north and south banks of the river Thames, which snakes through the city in a long, loose S curve. This great river played a fundamental role in London's development and continues to be critical to the city's growth and prosperity. London's major tourist sights, hotels, and restaurants are on the river's north bank, and many of the city's famous performing-arts venues are on the South Bank.

London Neighborhoods

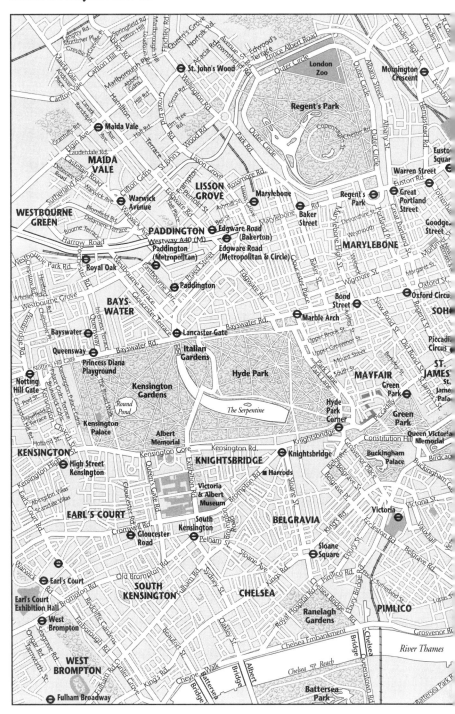

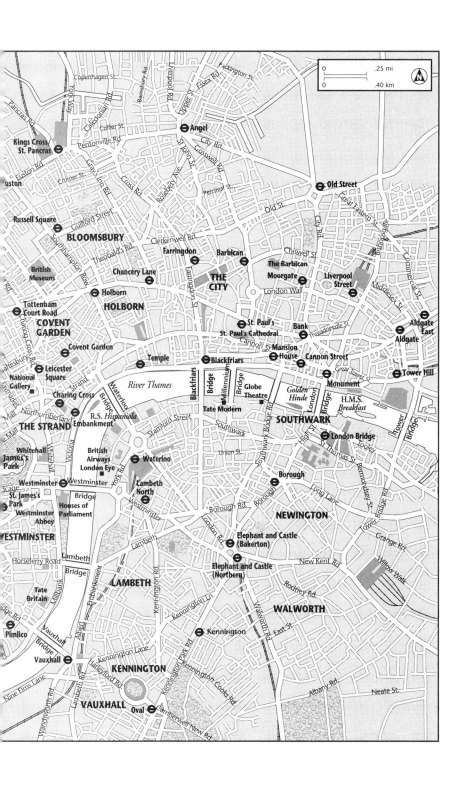

Central London, on the north bank of the Thames, is considered to be the *city center,* the area covered by the Circle Line Underground route. Paddington Station anchors the northwestern corner, Earl's Court marks the southwestern corner, Tower Hill sits at the southeastern corner, and Liverpool Street Station anchors the northeastern corner. Central London is divided into three areas: The City, the West End, and West London. I start at The City and move west from there. Check out Chapter 6 if you think that you'd like to stay in one of these neighborhoods and you need more information.

The City of London: The heart of it all

A self-governing entity that extends south from Chiswell Street to the river Thames, the City of London is bounded on the west by Chancery Lane and to the east by the **Tower of London,** the city's most important historic monument.

Fleet Street, associated with printing and publishing since the 1500s but now a little forlorn since the departure of most of its newspaper tenants, cuts through the center of the district to Ludgate Circus, where it becomes Ludgate. Follow that road and you get to **St. Paul's Cathedral,** its massive dome beautifully illuminated at night. St. Paul's is just one of the buildings perched on the ancient area known as *The City.*

Covering the original 1 square mile that the Romans called Londinium, The City encompasses the territory between Moorfields to the north and the Thames to the south and from Aldgate to the east and Temple Bar to the west. Today this area is the Wall Street of England, home to the **Bank of England,** the **Royal Exchange,** and the **Stock Exchange,** as well as the new **Lloyds of London** building and the **NatWest Tower,** London's second tallest building. It's also where you can find the **Museum of London,** the remains of the **Roman Temple of Mithras,** the church of **St. Stephen Walbrook** (designed by Christopher Wren), the Wren-designed **Monument** that commemorates the Great Fire of London in 1666, and the **Barbican Centre,** a mega-arts complex of theaters and concert halls.

Liverpool Street Station is the main rail terminus in this area. The major tube stops are Blackfriars, Tower Hill, St. Paul's, Liverpool Street Station, Bank, Barbican, and Moorgate.

The West End: Downtown London

The West End (that is, west of The City) is "downtown" London. The West End is known for the theater, entertainment, and shopping areas around Piccadilly Circus and Leicester Square. But a host of neighborhoods make up the West End. I describe them briefly in sections that follow.

Holborn

Abutting the City of London to the west is the old borough of Holborn, the legal heart of London and home to the **Inns of Court, Lincoln's Inn Fields,** and **Royal Courts of Justice** and **Old Bailey.**

This "in-between" district is bounded roughly by Theobald's Road to the north, Farringdon Road to the east, the Thames to the south, and Kingsway, Aldwych, and Lancaster Place to the west. The major tube stops are Holborn, Temple, Blackfriars, and Aldwych.

The Strand and Covent Garden

The northern section of The Strand, the area west of Holborn, is Covent Garden, with Shaftesbury Avenue as its northern boundary. Covent Garden has many theaters, eateries, and shops and is home to the **Royal Opera House** and **Covent Garden Market,** one of the busiest shopping areas in London. Covent Garden is really an area for strolling, shopping, and stopping for tea or a meal.

Formerly one of the premier streets in England, The Strand runs from Trafalgar Square to Fleet Street; it's the principal thoroughfare along the southern edge, with Charing Cross Road to the west and Kingsway, Aldwych, and Lancaster Place to the east. **Cleopatra's Needle,** dating from about 1475 B.C. and moved to England in 1878, is located in the Victoria Embankment on the north side of the Hungerford Bridge. The major tube stops are Covent Garden, Leicester Square, and Charing Cross.

Bloomsbury

Just north of Covent Garden, New Oxford Street and Bloomsbury Way mark the beginnings of the Bloomsbury district, home of the **British Museum** and several colleges and universities, as well as the only surviving London home of novelist Charles Dickens.

This intellectual pocket of Central London was home to the famed Bloomsbury Group, whose members included novelist Virginia Woolf and historian Lytton Strachey. Bloomsbury is bounded to the east by Woburn Place and Southampton Row, to the north by Euston Road, and to the west by Tottenham Court Road. The major tube stops are Euston Square, Russell Square, Goodge Street, and Tottenham Court Road.

Soho

This lively area is full of restaurants, cafes, bars, pubs, and nightclubs and is popular with the gay community. London's **Gay Village** is centered around Old Compton Street. Gerrard Street is one of the main streets of Chinatown. Much of Soho used to be a down-to-earth Italian neighborhood, then it became known for its strip joints and porn palaces. You'll still see remnants of the sex 'n' sleaze era, but most of it is now gone and things are going upscale.

The Soho neighborhood occupies the warren of densely packed streets north of Shaftesbury Avenue, west of Charing Cross Road, east of Regent Street, and south of Oxford Street. The major tube stops are Leicester Square, Covent Garden, and Tottenham Court Road.

Piccadilly Circus, Leicester Square, and Charing Cross

This area, just west of The Strand, is "downtown" London or Theatreland. Piccadilly Circus, with its landmark figure of Eros, is the area's major traffic hub and best-known tourist destination, feeding into Regent Street and Piccadilly. The **Royal Academy of Arts** is just west of Piccadilly Circus. A few minutes' walk to the east puts you at Leicester Square and Shaftesbury Avenue, where you find most of the West End theaters. From Leicester Square, Charing Cross Road runs south to **Trafalgar Square** with its delightful fountains and four immense bronze lions guarding its corners. Around the square, you see the **National Gallery.** Charing Cross Road is well known for its bookshops. The tube stops are Piccadilly Circus, Leicester Square, and Charing Cross.

Mayfair

Elegant and exclusive, Mayfair is luxury-hotel and luxury-shopping land. It's nestled in between Regent Street on the west, Oxford Street on the north, Piccadilly on the south, and Hyde Park on the west. The major tube stops are Piccadilly Circus, Bond Street, Marble Arch, and Hyde Park Corner.

Marylebone

In a sense, Marylebone (pronounced *Mar*-lee-bone) is "Medical London," because it has several hospitals and the famous **Harley Street Clinic.** But perhaps the most famous street is Baker Street, home of the fictional Sherlock Holmes. **Madame Tussaud's** wax museum is on Marylebone Road.

Marylebone is the neighborhood north of Mayfair and Bloomsbury and is capped to the north by giant **Regent's Park** (Marylebone, Road runs south of the park). Great Portland Street is the eastern boundary and Edgware Road the western.The major tube stops are Baker Street, Marylebone, and Regent's Park.

St. James's

St. James's is "Royal London," a posh green haven beginning at Piccadilly and moving southwest to include **Green Park** and **St. James's Park,** with **Buckingham Palace** between them and **St. James's Palace** across from St. James's Park.

Pall Mall (pronounced *Pel Mell*), lined with exclusive "gentlemen's clubs," runs roughly east-west into the area and meets the north-south St. James's Street. Regent Street is the eastern boundary. The tube stops are St. James's Park and Green Park.

Westminster

East and south of St. James's, Westminster draws visitors to **Westminster Abbey** and the **Houses of Parliament,** the seat of British government.

Westminster extends from Northumberland Avenue just south of Charing Cross to Vauxhall Bridge Road, with the Thames to the east and **St. James's Park** to the west. Victoria Station, on the northwestern perimeter, is a kind of axis for Westminster, Belgravia, and Pimlico. The tube stops are Westminster, St. James's Park, and Victoria.

Pimlico

The pie-shaped wedge of London extending west from Vauxhall Bridge Road to Buckingham Palace Road is Pimlico. Crowning it to the north is Victoria Station, and here you can also find the **Tate Britain** gallery. The tube stops are Pimlico and Victoria.

Belgravia

A posh quarter long favored by aristocrats, Belgravia is where many foreign embassies are located. Beginning west of Victoria Station and Green Park, Belgravia extends south to the river and west to Sloane Street; it's bounded to the north by **Hyde Park.**The tube stops are Victoria, Hyde Park Corner, and Sloane Square.

Central London: Harrods and more

Naturally, after leaving the West End, you go beyond the West End, to Central London's residential, cultural, and shopping attractions, including beautiful gardens, and popular museums.

Knightsbridge

West of Belgravia is the fashionable residential and shopping district of Knightsbridge, bounded to the north by **Hyde Park** and to the west by Brompton Road. Here you can find **Harrods,** the famed department store that has been a London shopping staple for a century and a half. Running through the neighborhood is Beauchamp Place (pronounced *Beech*-um). The tube stops are Knightsbridge and Sloane Square.

Chelsea

South of Knightsbridge and west of Belgravia, artsy, trendy Chelsea begins at Sloane Square and runs south to Cheyne Walk and Chelsea Embankment that run along the Thames. The famous King's Road acts as its northern boundary and Chelsea Bridge Road its eastern border. To the west it extends as far as Earl's Court Road, Redcliffe Gardens, and Edith Grove. In Chelsea you'll find **Carlyle's House** and the lovely and historic **Chelsea Physic Garden.** The annual Chelsea Flower Show is held on the grounds of Chelsea Royal Hospital. The tube stop is Sloane Square.

South Kensington

Forming the green northern boundary of South Kensington are **Kensington Gardens** and **Hyde Park.** South Ken is London's museum capital. along with a bevy of hotels and restaurants.Tourists in droves enjoy the attractions of the **Natural History Museum, Science Museum,** and **Victoria & Albert Museum.**

South Kensington is bounded to the south by Brompton Road, to the west by Gloucester (pronounced *Glos*-ter) Road and to the east by Fulham Road. The tube stops are Gloucester Road and South Kensington.

Kensington

The residential neighborhood of Kensington fills in the gap between **Kensington Gardens** and **Holland Park,** with Notting Hill Gate and Bayswater Road marking it off to the north. Kensington Church Street runs north-south between Notting Hill Gate and Kensington High Street. The tube stop is High Street Kensington.

Earl's Court

This neighborhood has long been a haven for budget travelers (particularly Australians, hence its nickname Kangaroo Court) and for gays and lesbians. It's gradually being renovated, but many streets are in disrepair. This area offers no major tourist attractions.

This down-to-earth neighborhood begins south of West Cromwell Road and extends down to Lillie Road and Brompton Road is the down-to-earth Earl's Court neighborhood. Its western boundary is North End Road and its eastern boundary Earl's Court Road. The tube stop is Earl's Court.

Notting Hill

Beginning north of Holland Park, Kensington Gardens, and Hyde Park (Holland Park Avenue and Bayswater Road run along the northern perimeter of the parks) are the antiques shops of Notting Hill and the rising subneighborhood of Notting Hill Gate.

The area is bounded by Clarendon Road to the west, Queensway to the east, and Wesbourne Grove to the north. The most famous street, Portobello Road, runs north-south through the center. The tube stops are Notting Hill Gate, Bayswater, and Queensway.

Bayswater and Paddington

Picking up where Notting Hill ends, Bayswater runs east to meet Marylebone at Edgware Road. The roaring A40 (Westway) highway acts as its northern boundary. Paddington Station is in the northwestern corner of Bayswater.

This is a commercial area and is not much to look at. The neighborhood offers no major tourist attractions but many budget B&Bs. The tube stops are Paddington, Lancaster Gate, Marble Arch, and Edgware Road.

The South Bank

You most likely won't be staying on the South Bank, but you may go there for a play, an exhibition, or a concert at one its internationally known arts and performance venues or museums. The tube stops are Waterloo, London Bridge, and Southwark.

The **Royal National Theatre,** the **South Bank Centre** (which contains the **Royal Festival Hall** and two smaller concert halls), the **Hayward Gallery,** and the **National Film Theatre** are all clustered beside the river within easy walking distance of Waterloo Station. Closer to

Westminster Bridge is the city's newest high-rise attraction: the **British Airways London Eye observation wheel.**

For a scenic route to the South Bank, take the tube to Embankment, on the north bank, and walk across the Thames on the Hungerford pedestrian bridge. The **Jubilee Walkway,** a breezy riverside path, extends south from the arts complexes to the **London Aquarium** and north to the new **Tate Modern** and the **Globe Theatre** (a re-creation of the Elizabethan outdoor theater used by William Shakespeare), **Southwark Cathedral,** and **Tower Bridge.** The new pedestrian-only **Millennium Bridge** spanning the Thames from **Tate Modern** to **St. Paul's** should be completed by the time you arrive.

Getting Guidance in London

You can find hotel- and theater-booking agencies, a currency exchange, and lots of free brochures on river trips, walking tours, and day trips from London at the *Britain Visitor Centre,* 1 Regent St., Piccadilly Circus, SW1 (Tube: Piccadilly Circus), which provides tourist information to walk-in visitors (no phone assistance is available). The office is open Monday through Friday 9 a.m. to 6:30 p.m. and Saturday and Sunday 10 a.m. to 4 p.m.

An excellent bookshop is among the features of the main *Tourist Information Centre,* run by the London Tourist Board and located in the forecourt of Victoria Station (Tube: Victoria). Open daily 8 a.m. to 7 p.m., it also offers booking services and free literature on London attractions and entertainment. Other Tourist Information Centres are in the Liverpool Street Underground Station (open daily 8 a.m. to 6 p.m.); the Arrivals Hall of the Waterloo International Terminal (open daily 8:30 a.m. to 10:30 p.m.); the Terminal 1, 2, and 3 Underground station (open daily 8 a.m. to 6 p.m.), and the Terminal 3 Arrivals concourse (open daily 6 a.m. to 11 p.m.) at Heathrow Airport.

The *London Line* at ☎ **09068-663-344** provides 24-hour information, updated daily, on scheduled events. At 60p (90¢) per minute, this service isn't cheap, but it's reliable.

A London Underground map is as indispensable as the *London A to Z* (which includes an Underground map). You can pick up a free tube and bus map up at any Underground ticket office — and you can use the Underground map on Cheat Sheet at the front of this guide. For current listings and reviews of plays and other events, consider buying a copy of *Time Out.* It hits the newsstands each Wednesday and costs £1.95 ($3).

If you're traveling with kids, you may find *Kidsline* helpful; call ☎ **020-7222-8070** (Monday through Friday 4 to 6 p.m. and summer holidays 9 a.m. to 4 p.m.) for tips on kid-friendly places to go and things to see. The London Tourist Board's children's information line at ☎ **0839-123-404** is a recorded service that provides details about events and exhibitions that children will enjoy; it costs 39p to 49p (65¢ to 80¢) per minute.

Chapter 11

Getting Around London

In This Chapter

▶ Going with the flow: Using London's mass transit

▶ Getting around by taxi

▶ Getting around on foot

*L*ondon is a mess to drive in, so don't even think about renting a car when you're in the city (see Chapter 21 for information about renting a car for day trips outside the city). Even more difficult than driving in London is finding a place to park; if you park illegally, you'll be fined and you may even have your car immobilized by a wheel clamp or towed away and impounded. Play it safe; public transportation is fine, so take the bus, tube, or taxi. Or take a leisurely stroll and enjoy the views. This chapter provides the information you need to get around London by public transportation or on foot, so you can leave the driving to the Brits.

For general London travel information, call ☎ 020-7222-1234. You can get free bus and Underground maps and buy Travelcards and bus passes (see the next section) at any major Underground (subway) station or at the London Travel Information Centres in the stations at King's Cross, Liverpool Street, Oxford Circus, Piccadilly Circus, St. James's Park, Victoria, and Heathrow Terminals 1, 2, and 3.

Tube Travel: Going Underground

The London subway system — commonly referred to as the *tube* or the *Underground* — is fast and convenient, and nearly everyone but the royals uses it. Millions of residents and visitors ride it daily. Thirteen tube lines criss-cross the city and intersect at various stations where passengers can change from one train to the next. On Underground maps, every line is color-coded (Bakerloo is brown, Piccadilly dark blue, and so on). Each tube stop is marked by a red circle with a horizontal line through it. Nearly every place in London is near a tube stop. The system is simple and comprehensive, so planning your route is easy.

All you need to know is the name of your stop and the direction you're heading. After you figure out which line you need to take, look on the map for the name of the last stop in the direction you need to go. The name of the last stop on the line is marked on the front of the train (it's easy to read) and sometimes on electronic signboards that display which train is arriving. Inside all but the oldest trains are electronic signs and/or recorded voices that announce the name of each approaching stop. London's Underground stations often have newspaper kiosks and small shops in them or directly outside. You'll rarely encounter a panhandler in a tube station.

Check out the Cheat Sheet at the beginning of this guide for a handy color map of the Underground on one side. The tube stations vary considerably. Some, such as Covent Garden and Gloucester Road, have elevators to the trains (and optional stairways). Others, such as Leicester Square and Piccadilly Circus, provide very long escalators. Some offer stairways only. In major stations handling more than one line, long (but clearly marked) tunnels extend from one line to another. Most of the trains are new or have been updated. The older trains have upholstered seats.

The trains aren't air-conditioned, however, so during packed weekday rush hours (8 to 9:30 a.m. and 5 to 7 p.m.), they can be stuffy. Smoking isn't permitted. As with any transit system this enormous, occasional glitches and delays occur. The only time to think twice about taking the tube is Friday and Saturday after 10:30 p.m., when drinkers are leaving pubs. Inebriated louts can be obnoxious. The Underground service ends at around midnight (a little earlier on less used lines). Keep this in mind when you're out painting the town red. You'll have to take a taxi or one of the night buses.

Most of the Underground system operates with automated entry and exit gates. A passenger feeds a ticket into the slot, it disappears and then pops up again like a piece of toast, the gate bangs open, and the traveler removes the ticket and passes through. Passengers go through the same process to get out, but the machine keeps the ticket (unless it's a Travelcard, which is returned). Some stations outside of Central London employ ticket collectors.

Opened in 1999, the *Jubilee Line* is the newest tube line. Architecture buffs may want to check out some of the new stations (such as London Bridge and Southwark) built for it. And London's oldest Underground line? The system's first tube train began operating almost 150 years ago. You can see one of the first (dark, primitive) Underground cars and a fantastic collection of original horse-drawn omnibuses at the **London Transport Museum** (see Chapter 17 for details).

You've got a ticket to ride

You can get tickets for the Underground at the ticket window or from one of the automated machines found in most stations (machines can change £5, £10, and £20 notes). Fares to every station are posted.

The city is divided into zones for purposes of setting fares. Zone 1 covers all of Central London. Zone 6 extends as far as Heathrow to the west and Upminster to the east. Make sure that your ticket covers all the zones you'll be traveling through (no problem if you're staying in Central London). If it doesn't, you may have to pay a £10 ($17) penalty fare.

A single-fare one-way ticket within one zone costs £1.50 ($2.50) for an adult and 60p ($1) for a child 5 to 15. This amount is the maximum that passengers must pay to reach any sight in Central London (provided that they're staying in Central London). Tickets are valid on the day of issue only.

If you plan to travel by Underground, you can save time and money by buying a book of 10 tickets, called a *carnet.* Carnet tickets are valid in one zone only. The price is £11 ($18) for an adult and £5 ($8) for a child. With a carnet, you can save £4 ($7) over single fares and won't have to wait in line to buy tickets. With a Travelcard, you can save even more.

Travelcards: The best fare going and coming

For the best rate — if you plan on using London's public transportation system extensively — consider buying the 1-day, weekend, 7-day, or 1-month *Travelcard,* allowing unlimited travel by Underground *and* bus.

- ✔ A **1-day Travelcard for Zones 1 and 2** (everything in Central London) costs £3.90 ($7) for an adult and £2 ($3.30) for a child; it's valid after 9:30 a.m. weekdays and all day Saturday and Sunday.

- ✔ The **weekend Travelcard for Zones 1 and 2** costs £5.80 ($10) for an adult and £3 ($5) for a child.

- ✔ A **7-day Travelcard for Zone 1** is useful if you're going to be in London for week and aren't planning any trips outside Central London; it costs £15.30 ($25) for an adult and £6.50 ($11) for a child.

- ✔ A **1-month Travelcard for Zone 1** is £58.80 ($97) for an adult and £25 ($41) for a child.

The *Family Travelcard* is good for families or groups of one or two adults traveling with one to four children; it's valid after 9:30 a.m. Monday through Friday and all day Saturday and Sunday. Rates for 1 day of travel in Zones 1 and 2 are £2.60 ($4.30) for an adult and 80p ($1.30) for a child.

You and your children will need passport-sized photos to buy 7-day or longer Travelcards in London. The photo is affixed to a separate ID card. No photos are required for *Visitor Travelcards* purchased in the States, however (see Chapter 3).

Traveling by Bus: London's Famed Double-Deckers

Taking a bus in London is a good-news, bad-news proposition. The bad news is that, unless you have plenty of time or have a claustrophobic aversion to the Underground, you'll arrive at your destination faster by taking the tube or walking (during rush hour, buses creep along at about the same pace as a pedestrian). Also, you need to know the streets of London so you can exit the bus at the correct stop. Get a free bus map at one of the Travel Information Centres (see the introduction to this chapter) or you could become quite lost.

The good news is that riding the bus is cheaper than taking the tube; you don't need to use escalators, elevators, or tunnels; and you get to see the sights as you travel. London is known for its big red double-decker buses, and most tourists want to ride on top of one at least once; it's just plain fun.

Each bus stop is clearly marked by a concrete post with a red or white sign on top reading "London Transport Bus Service." Another sign shows the routes of the buses that stop there. Here's what the colors mean: If the sign on top is

- **Red:** It's a *request stop,* and you must hail the approaching bus as you would a taxi (don't whistle, just put up your hand).
- **White:** The bus will stop automatically. Be sure to check the destination sign in front of the bus to make certain that it's going the entire route.

Playing the fare game

The bus network was recently divided into two fare zones to simplify cash transactions:

- **Zone 1** covers all of Central London, including all the main tourist sites.
- **Zone 2** is everything beyond Zone 1.

If you're traveling by bus into, from, within, and across Central London (Zone 1), the bus fare for adults is £1 ($1.65). For any bus journey you take in outer London (Zone 2), the fare is 70p ($1.15). Children pay a 40p (65¢) flat rate good for both zones. *Note:* No child fares are in effect between 10 p.m. and 4:30 a.m. Children 14 and 15 years old must have a Child Photocard to obtain the child rate; that means they'll need a passport-sized photo and will have to obtain this free ID card at a tube station or one of the Travel Information Centres (see the introduction to this chapter).

In the past, a conductor on board went around and collected fares with a polite "'kew" (thank you). Today, the driver often doubles as the conductor. Have some coins with you because the driver isn't allowed to change banknotes.

If you plan to travel extensively by bus, purchase a 1-day bus pass. You can use it all day (before 9:30 a.m., even on weekdays, unlike the Travelcard), but it isn't valid on *N-prefixed night buses,* discussed in the next section. You can purchase 1-day and longer bus passes at most Underground stations, selected newsagents, and the Travel Information Centres. A 1-day bus pass for all of Central London costs £3 ($5) for an adult and £1 ($1.65) for a child 5 to 15. A 7-day bus pass for Central London costs £11.50 ($18) for an adult and £4 ($7) for a child 5 to 15. A monthly bus pass is £44.20 ($73) for an adult and £15.40 ($25) for a child. *Note:* Children must have a Child Photocard ID in order to buy and use any of these tickets; the card is free at major tube stations and Travel Information Centres but requires a passport-size photograph.

Painting the town red: Night buses

If you live in large, urban areas of the United States, you are accustomed to the bars staying open until near dawn. However, in London, the pubs close at 11 p.m., the tube stops running about 11:30 p.m., and at midnight the buses become *night* (*N*) *buses,* changing their routes and increasing their Central London fares to £1.50 ($2.50). You can't use a 1-day bus pass and family or weekend Travelcard on a night bus; you can, however, use a Visitor Travelcard (see Chapter 3) or a 7-day or longer Travelcard. Nearly all night buses pass through Trafalgar Square, Central London's late-night mecca for insomniacs.

Paying the Cab Tab

You can still find the old-fashioned, roomy black London taxis, but smaller and newer cabs also roam London's busy streets. London cabs aren't cheap, whatever their size or color. The fare starts at £1.40 ($2.30) for one person, with 40p (70¢) for each additional passenger. The meter leaps 20p (35¢) every 111 yards or 90 seconds. You may also need to pay surcharges: 10p (17¢) per item of luggage, 60p ($1) weeknights 8 p.m. to midnight and 90p ($1.50) throughout the night, and 60p ($1) Saturdays and Sundays until 8 p.m. and 90p ($1.50) after that. Tipping the cabbie 15 percent of the total fare is customary.

You can hail a cab on the street. If a cab is available, its yellow or white "For Hire" sign on the roof will be lit. You can order a cab in advance, called a *radio cab,* by calling ☎ **020-7272-0272** or 020-7253-5000. Just remember that if you do order a radio cab, the meter starts ticking when the taxi receives notification from the dispatcher.

London is one city where you don't have to worry about whether or not the cabdriver knows how to reach your destination. Extensive training, which includes an exhaustive street test called "The Knowledge," makes London cabbies among the most adept in the world at finding a street address.

Pounding the Pavement: Walkies

You're cheating yourself out of experiencing the true essence of London if you don't take some time on foot to explore the city's side streets, country lanes, little mews dwellings (former stables converted into homes), and garden squares.

London architecture spans some 2,000 years of history, and as you walk though its streets, you see building styles that incorporate everything from remnants of the original brick-and-mortar walls and a fort erected by the Romans to the late-postmodern **Canary Wharf Tower,** at 800 feet the city's tallest building. Wedged into this dense urban landscape you can find ancient bastions of power such as the **Tower of London,** Gothic glories such as 900-year-old **Westminster Abbey,** tidily elegant Regency terraces in Mayfair, private palaces in St. James's, and Victorian townhouses in Kensington.

If you want to take a detailed stroll or two around the city, focusing on your private interests, such as Dickens's London or Westminster and Whitehall, check out the 11 tours in *Frommer's Memorable Walks in London,* published by IDG Books Worldwide, Inc.

What walkers need to know

When you're walking in London (or anywhere in the United Kingdom) remember that:

- ✔ **Traffic moves on the opposite side of the street**. When you cross any street, look in the direction opposite from the one you're accustomed to. That is, look right as you cross most streets, instead of left (as you would automatically do in the States or elsewhere in the world). This advice sounds simple enough on paper, but in practice you need to keep reminding yourself.

- ✔ **Pedestrian crossings are marked by striped lines (called zebra crossings) on the road.** Flashing lights near the curb indicate that drivers must stop and yield the right of way if a pedestrian has stepped out into the zebra crossing to cross the street.

Although London is a walker's paradise, Central London is much too large to cover on foot. But parts of it are wonderfully compact and intimate, so be sure to give yourself some time to wander about.

Walkers' sites in Central London

One place you can best explore on foot is *Chelsea:* Start at Sloane Square or busy King's Road and meander southwest toward Cheyne Walk along the river.

You can also meander through cafe-laden *Soho,* just north of Shaftesbury Avenue, and the pedestrian-only precincts of the *Covent*

Garden area just south of it. And *South Kensington,* with its great museums, is full of charming side streets and squares.

Even more atmospheric is the area in and around **Lincoln's Inn Fields** in Holborn, where the traditions of old London pervade the beautiful 17th-century courts of law. At night, the **Houses of Parliament,** the clock tower containing the bell known as **Big Ben,** and **Westminster Abbey** are all floodlit and form an impressive sight. To get there, walk down Whitehall from Charing Cross.

Parks and other scenic walks

London is home to some of the world's most beautiful parks, and you really must experience them on foot. That's what they're there for.

The Green Park tube stop provides convenient access to **Green Park** from the north; from the tube stop you can walk down to Constitution Hill, a major thoroughfare closed to traffic on Sundays, and on to **Buckingham Palace.** Continue east into **St. James's Park** via Pall Mall (also traffic free on Sundays), passing **Clarence House** (home of the Queen Mum) and **St. James's Palace** (London home of Prince Charles and the boys, Prince William and Prince Harry), or stroll along the shores of **St. James's Park Lake.**

You can enter **Hyde Park** from the Hyde Park Corner tube stop; head west into this massive green lung via the paths paralleling the north and south banks of the Serpentine, Hyde Park's lake. After you cross the Serpentine Bridge, you're in **Kensington Gardens;** the famous statue of Peter Pan is to the north. **Kensington Palace** (home to Princess Margaret and several other royals) is on the western perimeter, beyond the Round Pond. Marylebone, to the north, is where you can find **Regent's Park,** with the **London Zoo** in the northern section and **Queen Mary's Gardens** roughly in the center.

In July 2000, a 7-mile walk commemorating the life of Princess Diana opened. The walk passes through four of London's royal parks: **St. James's Park, Green Park, Hyde Park,** and **Kensington Gardens.** Along the way are 70 plaques pointing out sites associated with Diana, including **Kensington Palace** (her home for 15 years), **Buckingham Palace, St. James's Palace** (where she once shared an office with Prince Charles), and **Spencer House** (once her family's mansion and now a museum — see Chapter 17).

One of the best scenic walks in London is the **Jubilee Walkway,** marked on the London map distributed free by the British Tourist Authority. It runs along the South Bank from Lambeth Bridge to Tower Bridge, offering great Thameside views of the north bank along the way, and continues on the north bank from the **Tower of London** all the way down to the **Houses of Parliament.** The walk will take you a good half day, but provides an opportunity to see a large and important area of London.

Chapter 12

Pounds and Pence: Talking Money

. . . .

. . . .

*T*ravelers to foreign destinations, especially first-time travelers, have big money worries — they don't worry so much about having enough money as they do about the difference between money in their home countries and money abroad. What are the conversion rates? Where can they change one currency into another for the best rate? Are traveler's checks better than credit cards or ATM cards? Will their home PIN work in a foreign country? Travelers have a seemingly endless list of money matters to consider.

You can't avoid these questions because you'll spend money every day of your trip, often in ways that you don't spend it at home. British currency is different, I'll grant you that, but you can certainly get the hang of it. In this chapter, I explain the basic money matters you'll run into. Refer also to Chapter 3 for information on purchasing traveler's checks before you go and using credit cards and ATMs in London.

Making Sense of Pounds and Pence — and the New Euro

Britain's unit of currency is the *pound sterling (£)*. Every pound is divided into *100 pence (p)*. Coins come in denominations of 1p, 2p, 5p, 10p, 20p, 50p, £1, and £2. Notes are available in £5, £10, £20, and £50 denominations. As with any unfamiliar currency, British pounds and pence take a bit of getting used to. The coins have different sizes, shapes, and weights according to value. Each banknote denomination has its own color and bears a likeness of the Queen. All currency is drawn on the Bank of England.

The fate of British currency in its pounds-and-pence form is one of the most hotly debated topics in the United Kingdom today. You may have heard about the single European currency, called the *euro,* that was adopted by 11 European countries on January 1, 1999. Cautious, contentious Britain has opted out from switching over to the euro just yet. During 2000 and 2001, even if you're traveling from London to other countries in the European Union, you won't have to worry about the euro. The changeover has so far been basically between financial institutions and businesses (however, if you travel to EU countries, you may notice that prices are given in both the national currency and euros). The various national currencies won't be homogenized into euros (or *ecus,* European Currency Units) until mid-2002. Even then, it's anyone's guess whether or not Britain will adopt the plan.

Managing the Exchange

The *exchange rate,* which fluctuates every day, is the rate you get when you use your own currency to buy pounds sterling (see Table 12-1). In general, **$1 = 67p (or £1 = $1.65).** These are *approximate* figures, but they're what I use for all prices in this guide (rounded off to the nearest dollar). When you are about to leave on your trip, check with your bank or look in the newspaper to find out the current rate.

Table 12-1	Simple Currency Conversions		
U.S.	*U.K.*	*U.K.*	*U.S.*
$1	67p	£1	$1.65
$5	£3.35	£2	$3.30
$10	£6.70	£5	$8.25
$20	£13.40	£10	$16.50
$50	£33.50	£20	$33
$100	£67	£50	$82.50

Changing money (either cash or traveler's checks) into a foreign currency makes many people nervous, especially if they're changing money for the first time. You needn't fear. Changing money is really a fairly simple operation. Just remember that every time you exchange money you'll need to show your passport.

Bureaux de change and the banks of England

If you want some pounds in hand when you arrive at the airport (to pay for a taxi perhaps), you can exchange currency before you leave home at many banks and at foreign exchange services at international airports (see Chapter 3). Otherwise, you can easily change cash or traveler's checks in London by using a currency-exchange service called a *bureau de change*. These services are available at major London airports, at any branch of a major bank, at all major rail and Underground stations in Central London, at post offices, and at American Express or Thomas Cook offices. Unless located in a bank or travel agency, most bureaux de change are open daily 8 a.m. to 9 p.m.

Every major bank in Central London has a foreign currency window where you can exchange traveler's checks or cash. Weekday hours for banks are generally 9:30 a.m. to 4:30 p.m., but a few open earlier. Some banks (usually based in busy shopping areas) are open all day Saturday. All banks are closed on public holidays, but many branches have 24-hour banking lobbies with ATMs and/or ATMs on the street outside. Banking is a volatile business, with mergers, acquisitions, and name changes occurring all the time. The big names in London include *Barclays Bank* (☎ **020-7441-3200**), *Midland Bank* (☎ **020-7599-3232**), and *NatWest* (☎ **020-7395-5500**). These banking companies all have branches throughout the city.

Reputable London banks and bureaux de change exchange money at a competitive rate but charge a commission (typically 1 percent to 3 percent of the total transaction) and a small additional fee (usually £3/$5). Some currency-exchange services now guarantee you the same exchange rate when you return pounds for dollars (keep your receipt if this service is offered and you want to make use of it).

 All U.K. bureaux de change and other money-changing establishments are required to clearly display exchange rates and full details of any fees and rates of commission with equal prominence. Rates must be displayed at or near the entrance to the premises. Rates fluctuate from place to place and so do fees, so it sometimes pays to shop around.

 Steer clear of bureaux de change that offer good exchange rates but charge a heavy commission (up to 8 percent). You find them in major tourist sections of London (some are open 24 hours). Some hotels also cash traveler's checks, but their commission is often considerably higher than at a bank or bureaux de change. Before exchanging your money, always check to see the exchange rate, how much commission will be charged, and whether additional fees apply.

 You can avoid paying a second commission fee by using American Express traveler's checks and cashing them at American Express, 6 Haymarket, SW1 (☎ **020-7930-4411**; Tube: Piccadilly). Its foreign exchange bureau is open Monday through Friday 9 a.m. to 5:30 p.m., Saturday 9 a.m. to 6 p.m., and Sunday 10 a.m. to 5 p.m. American Express has other foreign exchange offices in heavily touristed areas throughout Central London, including

✔ 78 Brompton Rd., Knightsbridge SW3; ☎ **020-7584-3431**; Tube: Knightsbridge

✔ 84 Kensington High St., Kensington W8; ☎ **020-7795-8703**; Tube: Kensington High St.

✔ 51 Great Russell St., Bloomsbury WC1; ☎ **020-7404-8700**; Tube: Russell Sq.

✔ 1 Savoy Court, The Strand WC2; ☎ **020-7240-1521**; Tube: Charing Cross

ATMs

You can find ATMs all over London, strategically located at every commercial juncture and byway: inside and/or outside banks, in large supermarkets and department stores, and even in some Underground stations. For convenience, they can't be beat. Using your bank or credit card and a PIN (check with the company to determine whether your PIN will work in Europe; you may need to get a new one), you can immediately access British pounds and avoid the hassle of a bureau de change entirely. U.S. banks in London tend to be for corporate business accounts rather than personal banking, so be prepared to use another banks ATM and pay a fee. See Chapter 3 for more detailed information on using your bank or credit card in London's ATMs.

Citibank customers using ATMs at *Citibank International* (☎ **020-7234-5678**) — with branches at 332 Oxford St., W1 (Tube: Marble Arch), and 336 Strand, WC2 (Tube: Charing Cross) — pay no transaction fee.

Some big British banks came under fire in 2000 when they announced new and outrageously high user fees of £2.50 ($4) per transaction for "disloyal" customers using the ATMs at other banks. The outcry from the public, press, and politicians was so strong that the banks began backpedaling. The issue hadn't been settled by press time.

Traveling Smart: Handling Loss or Theft

Horrors! You reach for your money and find that it's missing. Or you've fallen afoul of a thief. London is a fairly safe city, but crime happens. You can minimize the risk that crime will happen to you by following three basic rules:

✔ Keep your wallet or purse out of sight, but not in your back pocket or in your backpack.

✔ Don't leave your purse, briefcase, backpack, or coat unattended in any public place.

✔ Don't flash your money or credit cards around.

In the unlikely event that your wallet or purse is stolen, you need to cancel all your credit cards. It's probably wise to do this even before you call the police (call directory assistance ☎ **192** free from public payphones or look under "Police" in the London phone directory for the police station nearest you). The same advice applies if you lose a credit card. If you can think back to where you had it last, call that place. Some good soul may have found it and turned it in. If it's a lost cause, however, cancel your card so no one else can use it.

Almost every credit card company has an emergency toll-free number you can call if your card is lost or stolen. The company will cancel the card number immediately, and may also be able to wire you a cash advance; in many places, you can get an emergency replacement card in a day or two. See the Appendix for the U.K. numbers to call if your credit card gets lost or stolen while you're in London.

If you carry traveler's checks (see Chapter 3), be sure to keep a record of their serial numbers (keep the record separate from the checks, of course). Write down the numbers of the checks as you cash them. If the checks are stolen, you need to be able to report exactly which checks are gone in order to get them replaced. The check issuer will tell you where to pick up the new checks.

If your purse or wallet is gone, the police aren't likely to recover it for you. However, after you cancel your credit cards, call to inform the police. You may need the police report number for credit card or insurance purposes later.

Taxing matters: So just where is this added value?

No discussion of money matters in London would be complete without a reference to the odious and ubiquitous *value-added tax (VAT)*, Britain's version of a sales tax. It amounts to 17.5 percent and is added to the total price of all consumer goods (the price tag already includes it) as well as hotel and restaurant bills. If you're not a resident of the European Union, you can get your VAT refunded on purchases made in the United Kingdom (but not the VAT paid at hotels and restaurants). See Chapter 19 for details.

Part IV
Dining in London

The 5th Wave By Rich Tennant

"I don't know why you're so surprised.
The waiter <u>told</u> you the fish and chips
were 7 pounds."

In this part . . .

Sometimes I wonder if I love to travel so much because I like to eat but hate to cook. Traveling, after all, is the perfect excuse to *eat out all the time*. But even though dining out is one of the great pleasures of any trip, it can also be a big hassle in a strange city if you don't know where to go or what to order. (Kippers may sound cute and delicious, but do you really like smoked fish?) In this part, it's time to sit down and raise our forks for some delicious victuals.

In Chapter 13, I give an appetizing introduction to London's dining scene — the kinds of restaurants you'll find (from pubs and fish-and-chips joints to the hottest haute havens) and the variety of cuisine you'll encounter. I give some tips on how to eat well for less (we're all trying to lose a few pounds, after all) and other tasty morsels of useful information. If you don't know the difference between a crisp and a chip or think a sultana is the wife of a sultan, you'll find my brief food glossary very helpful. My A-to-Z list of recommended London restaurants is in Chapter 14. I've tried to include as many low- to moderate-priced places as possible, but if you're a real "foodie" you'll find some fabulous places where you can sink your choppers and curl your tongue around a truly great gourmet meal. In Chapter 15, I provide still more options: places for a spot of tea, for quick(er) bites, and for something to satisfy your sweet tooth.

Chapter 13

Dining in London: Oh, the Possibilities

*Y*ou can still find traditional English dishes in London: Yorkshire pudding, fish-and-chips, or bangers and mash. So if you want to sample the old cuisine, you won't be disappointed. But London now offers a vast array of culinary choices; over 5,700 restaurants prepare the cuisines of more than 60 countries. This chapter explains what you need to know about new trends, ethnic cuisines, and dining bargains. The information was accurate as this book went to press, but keep in mind that the restaurant scene changes all the time.

As a general rule, breakfast is served 7:30 to 9:30 a.m., lunch (often called dinner) is 12:30 to 2:30 p.m., and dinner (often called supper) is served 7 to 9:30 p.m. Afternoon tea is served 3:30 to 5:30 or 6 p.m. Brunch is generally served 11 a.m. to 4 p.m. on weekends.

Some Like It Haute: Eating Trendy

To be trendy and talked about, a London restaurant must have a celebrity owner, a celebrity chef, a solid reputation, a great view, a chic location, and/or unmistakable ambience — and, of course, memorable food helps, too.

Sir Terence Conran is a proven leader at creating hot London restaurants. His **Oxo Tower Restaurant** and the adjacent **Oxo Tower Brasserie** perch above the Thames on the South Bank. Sir Terence is also the name behind **Le Pont de la Tour** overlooking Tower Bridge; the bright **Bluebird** in Chelsea; and the showy below-ground **Quaglino's** in St. James's (when I last ate there, the five diners at the table across from me were all on their cell phones at the same time).

Other hot haute spots include the super-trendy **Asia de Cuba** in Ian Schrager's new St. Martin's Lane hotel; Chelsea's **Aubergine,** where the classic French cooking has earned two Michelin stars; the **Savoy Grill,** a downplayed power-player hangout in the Savoy hotel; **Zafferano,** a superlative Italian restaurant in tony Knightsbridge; **Vong,** a French-Thai fave, also in Knightsbridge; the stylish **L'Odeon,** where window tables provide a bird's-eye view of Piccadilly Circus; and **The Ivy,** a long-time Soho favorite for chic-seekers.

The preceding restaurants require booking more than a week in advance, and you can find their telephone numbers and full descriptions in Chapter 14. At all but the "smartest" London restaurants, it's usually possible to get a table on fairly short notice during the week, especially if you're willing to dine before 7 p.m. or after 9 p.m. Some of the mega-eateries hold up to several hundred diners at one time.

Looking at Food: Modern British to the Best Ethnic Eats

London is the hallmark of culinary evolution. The local food horizon expanded as the postwar generation began to travel outside of England, experiencing new cuisines, and as "exotic" foods became more readily available in the markets.

The traditional hearty, but sometimes thought of as dull, "plain English cooking" is certainly still prevalent in London, and it's even enjoying renewed interest and respect. Londoners still enjoy their fish-and-chips, steak-and-kidney pies, and bangers and mash. And the best dishes — game, lamb, meat and fish pies, and roast beef with Yorkshire pudding — are readily available. But Modern British cuisine takes old standards and deliciously reinvents them with foreign influences and ingredients, mostly from France (sauces), the Mediterranean (olive oil, oregano, and garlic), and northern Italy (pasta, polenta, and risotto). Besides Modern British, London foodies continue to favor classic French and Italian cuisines in their own right.

Other new influences making their way into Modern British cooking come from Thailand and Morocco (couscous). Indian cooking, one of the more pleasant reminders of the Empire, has been a favorite ethnic food for some time. London is filled with Indian restaurants (about 1,500 of them) serving curries and dishes cooked in clay tandoori pots. *Balti*, a thick curry from Pakistan, is the one of the more recent ethnic must-try dishes in London.

Index by Cuisine

British/Continental
The Stockpot — Piccadilly Circus & Leicester Square, $

British/French
The Ivy — Soho, $$
Langan's Bistro — Marylebone, $$
Shepherd's — Westminster & Victoria, $$$
R.S. Hispaniola — The Strand, $$$

British (Modern)
Founders Arms — South Bank, $
The Oratory — Knightsbridge, $$

British (Traditional)
Clarke's — Notting Hill, $$$
Devonshire Arms — Kensington, $
Dickens Inn by the Tower — The City, $
Fortnum & Mason — St. James's, $$
Fox & Anchor — The City, $
The George — The Strand, $
The George & Vulture — The City, $$
The Granary — Piccadilly Circus & Leicester Square, $
Maggie Jones — Kensington, $$
The Museum Tavern — Bloomsbury, $
Porter's English Restaurant — Covent Garden, $$
Rules — Covent Garden, $$$
Savoy Grill — The Strand, $$$$
Simpson's-in-the-Strand — The Strand, $$$
Veronica's — Bayswater, $$
Ye Olde Cheshire Cheese — The City, $$

Chinese
Ken Lo's Memories of China — Wesminster & Victoria, $$$$
Poons in the City — The City, $$$

Cuban/Asian
Asia de Cuba — Piccadilly Circus & Leicester Square, $$$

French
Aubergine — Chelsea, $$$$
Brasserie St. Quentin. — South Kensington, $$
L'Odeon — Piccadilly Circus & Leicester Square, $$$$
Oxo Tower Brasserie — South Bank, $$$

French/Thai
Vong — Knightsbridge, $$$

Hungarian
The Gay Hussar — Soho, $$$$

Indian
Café Spice Namaste — The City, $$
Noor Jahan — South Kensington, $$

International
Chelsea Kitchen — Chelsea, $
Ebury Wine Bar — Westminster & Victoria, $$
Le Pont de la Tour — South Bank, $$$$

Italian
San Lorenzo — Knightsbridge, $$$
Zafferano — Knightsbridge, $$$

Japanese
Wagamama Noodle Bar — Soho, $

Modern European
Bluebird — Chelsea, $$$$
Quaglino's — St. James's, $$$$

North American
Ed's Easy Diner — Soho, $
Hard Rock Café — Mayfair, $$
Joe Allen — Covent Garden, $$

Pacific Rim/International
Café Suze — Marylebone, $$

Pizza/Pasta

Gourmet Pizza Company —
St. James's, $
Pizzeria Condotti — Mayfair, $

Seafood

North Sea Fish Restaurant —
Bloomsbury, $$

Thai

Chiang Mai — Soho, $$

Vegetarian

Crank's In London — Mayfair, $
Food for Thought — Covent Garden, $

Locating the Best Restaurants

London offers a nice mix of restaurants; you can enjoy a wide variety of foods throughout the city. Soho and neighboring Covent Garden offer the most choices in the West End, with British, African, Caribbean, Mongolian, American (North and South), French, Italian, Spanish, Thai, Korean, Japanese, Middle Eastern, Eastern European, Modern European, Turkish, and vegetarian all represented. South Kensington is another eclectic grab bag of culinary choices.

Unlike in some other large cities, ethnic restaurants aren't grouped together within specific areas of London. However, several Chinese restaurants are clustered along Lisle, Wardour, and Gerrard streets in Soho's Chinatown. And Notting Hill has long been a standby for low-price Indian and Caribbean restaurants.

Index by Location

Bayswater

Veronica's — Traditional British, $$

Bloomsbury

The Museum Tavern — Traditional
British, $
North Sea Fish Restaurant — Seafood, $$

Chelsea

Aubergine — French, $$$$
Bluebird — Modern European, $$$$
Chelsea Kitchen — International, $

The City

Café Spice Namaste — Indian, $$
Dickens Inn by the Tower — Traditional
British, $
Fox & Anchor — Traditional British, $
The George & Vulture — Traditional
British, $$

Poons in the City — Chinese, $$$
Ye Olde Cheshire Cheese — Traditional
British, $$

Covent Garden

Food for Thought — Vegetarian, $
Joe Allen — $$
North American Porter's English
Restaurant — Traditional British, $$
Rules — Traditional British, $$$

Holborn

The George — Traditional British, $$

Kensington

Clarke's — Modern European, $$$
Devonshire Arms — Traditional
British, $
Maggie Jones — Traditional British, $$

Knightsbridge

The Oratory — Modern British, $$
San Lorenzo — Italian, $$$
Vong — French/Thai, $$$
Zafferano — Italian, $$$

Marylebone

Café Suze — Pacific Rim/
    International, $$
Langan's Bistro — British/
    French, $$

Mayfair

Hard Rock Café — North
    American, $$

Piccadilly Circus & Leicester Square

Asia de Cuba — Cuban/Asian, $$$
The Granary — Traditional British, $
L'Odeon — French, $$$$
The Stockpot — British/
    Continental, $

Soho

Chiang Mai — Thai, $$
Crank's In London — Vegetarian, $
Ed's Easy Diner — North American, $
The Gay Hussar — Hungarian, $$$$
The Ivy — British/French, $$
Wagamama Noodle Bar — Japanese, $

South Bank

Founders Arms — Modern Br
Le Pont de la Tour —
    International, $$$$
Oxo Tower Brasserie — French, $.

South Kensington

Brasserie St. Quentin — French, $$
Noor Jahan — Indian, $$

St. James's

Fortnum & Mason — Traditional
    British, $$
Gourmet Pizza Company —
    Pizza/Pasta, $
Quaglino's — Modern European, $$$$

The Strand

The George — Traditional British, $
R.S. Hispaniola — British/French, $$$
Savoy Grill — Traditional British, $$$$
Simpson's-in-the-Strand — Traditional
    British, $$$

Westminster & Victoria

Ebury Wine Bar — British/
    International, $$
Ken Lo's Memories of China —
    Chinese, $$$$
Shepherd's — Traditional British or
    British/French, $$$

Pricing Your Favorites

In the Index that follows, you see a list of my favorite restaurants arranged by price. Turn to Chapter 14 for a full description of each restaurant. The listings in Chapter 14 give two price elements for each restaurant: the price range of the menu's main courses and a dollar symbol that gives you an idea of the average cost of dinner for one person, including an appetizer (a *starter*), a main course (a *main*), dessert (*afters* or *pudding*), a drink (not wine or beer), tax, and tip. At places marked with $, the average dinner price is $25 or less. Plan to shell out between $25 and $35 at places marked with $$. Restaurants with $$$ will set you back $35 to $50. Is price no object? Expect to pay $50 and more at $$$$ restaurants.

Please bear in mind that the $ symbols denote the average price for a meal; if you order the most expensive entree and a bottle of wine, a $$ restaurant can easily become a $$$$ restaurant. On the other hand, if you order from a set-price menu, a $$$$ restaurant tab might dip down to $$.

 Sirloin, so the story goes, got its name from James I when he was a guest at Houghton Tower in Lancashire. When a succulent leg of beef was placed before him, he knighted it with his dagger, crying, "Arise, Sir Loin."

Index by Price

$$$$

Aubergine — Chelsea
The Gay Hussar — Soho
Ken Lo's Memories of China — Wesminster & Victoria
Le Pont de la Tour — South Bank
L'Odeon — Piccadilly Circus & Leicester Square
Quaglino's — St. James's
Savoy Grill — The Strand

$$$

Asia de Cuba — Piccadilly Circus & Leicester Square
Clarke's — Kensington
Oxo Tower Brasserie — South Bank
Poons in the City — The City
R.S. Hispaniola — The Strand
Rules — Covent Garden
San Lorenzo — Knightsbridge
Shepherd's — Westminster & Victoria
Simpson's-in-the-Strand — The Strand
Vong — Knightsbridge
Zafferano — Knightsbridge

$$

Brasserie St. Quentin — South Kensington
Café Spice Namaste — The City
Café Suze — Marylebone
Chiang Mai — Soho
Ebury Wine Bar — Westminster & Victoria
Fortnum & Mason — St. James's

The George & Vulture — The City
Hard Rock Café — Mayfair
The Ivy — Soho
Joe Allen — Coven Garden
Langan's Bistro — Marylebone
Maggie Jones — Kensington
Noor Jahan — South Kensington
North Sca Fish Restaurant — Bloomsbury
The Oratory — Knightsbridge
Porter's English Restaurant — Covent Garden
Veronica's — Bayswater
Ye Olde Cheshire Cheese — The City

$

Chelsea Kitchen — Chelsea
Crank's In London — Soho
Devonshire Arms — Kensington
Dickens Inn by the Tower — The City
Ed's Easy Diner — Soho
Food for Thought — Covent Garden
Founders Arms — South Bank
Fox & Anchor — The City
The George — The Strand
Gourmet Pizza Company — St. James's
The Granary — Piccadilly Circus & Leicester Square
The Museum Tavern — Bloomsbury
Pizzeria Condotti — Mayfair
The Stockpot — Piccadilly Circus & Leicester Square
Wagamama Noodle Bar — Soho

Budget-Friendly Dining

If the thought of paying $50 dinner tabs gives you heartburn, you can visit pubs, cafes, sandwich bars, pizza places, and fast-food restaurants to get edible, economical food. Another alternative: Many of London's top restaurants offer two- and three-course fixed-priced meals that won't make you wince when you get the bill. Sometimes these bargains are called pre- or post-theater menus, which means that they're served only from about 5:30 to 7 p.m. and after 9:30 p.m. Wine is generally fairly expensive, so forgo that if price is an issue. And try your splurge dining at lunch, when prices are often one-third less than those at dinner and the food is the same.

Americans ask for the check, but Brits ask for the bill. That annoying 17.5 percent VAT (value-added tax) will automatically be added. A moderate cover charge for bread (even if you don't eat it) may be tacked on as well.

Look at the menu to see whether a service charge has been added to your tab. Plenty of unwary tourists double tip without realizing it. Be aware that the words "service charge" on a bill mean a gratuity has already been added. If it has, you're not expected to leave any further tip. Some restaurants add a service charge to your bill and also have a tip area on the credit-card receipt you sign. If you've already paid a service charge, don't leave a tip as well. If the menu says "service not included," then leave a tip of at least 15 percent.

Pub grub

Pubs are your best bet for getting a good meal for a low price. The food will generally be traditional and down-to-earth: meat pies and mash (mashed potatoes), fish-and-chips, mixed grills (sausages and a chop or cutlet), salads, sandwiches, and the famous *ploughman's lunch* (bread and cheese or pâté). Pub food may be prepackaged and frozen, then microwaved. However, more and more pubs resemble casual restaurants — except that more people are drinking. The food may be fresh, more adventurous, and better prepared at the better pubs.

Pubs are drop-in places, and finding a table at lunchtime isn't always easy. Pubs don't accept reservations. Order your food from the serving counter and your drinks from the bar, and then seat yourself. Pub grub is generally washed down by beer, the British national drink. Draft beer in Britain is served at room temperature, as are most soft drinks. Bottled imported beer, served cold, is generally available but more expensive.

Unless a pub has a special *children's certificate,* kids under 14 are allowed only into the gardens and separate family rooms. The legal drinking age in the United Kingdom is 18, although restaurants can serve beer or cider to kids over 16 who order a meal. Pubs tend to be smoky.

What in the world is an aubergine?

Food is one area where the mother tongue often differs from American English. You may encounter a few unfamiliar words in food-related conversations, in the supermarket, or on restaurant menus. Here are a few of them:

English English	American English
Afters	Dessert
Aubergine	Eggplant
Bangers	Sausages
Bap	Soft sandwich bun
Bill	Restaurant check
Biscuit	Cracker or cookie
Black or white	Refers to how you want your coffee (white is coffee with cream)
Broad bean	Lima bean
Bubble and squeak	Mashed potatoes mixed with cabbage or meat and then fried
Chicory	Endive
Chips	French fries
Cornish pasties	Pastry filled with meat, onions, and vegetables
Cottage pie	Ground meat and mashed potatoes baked in a pie
Courgette	Zucchini
Crisps	Potato chips
Crumpet	Holier version of an "English muffin"
French beans	Green beans
Fry-up	Big English breakfast of eggs, sausage/bacon, baked beans, tomatoes, and so on
Gateau	Cake
Jacket potato	Baked potato with various toppings
Jelly	Gelatin dessert
Joint	Meat roasted on the bone
Kipper	Smoked fish
Haricots vert	Green beans
Liquor	A salty, parsley-based green gravy
Mains	Main courses

English English	American English
Mange tout	Snow peas
Marrow	Squash
Mash	Mashed potatoes
Mince	Ground meat, usually beef
Ploughman's lunch	Pub grub consisting of crusty bread, cheese, or pâté
Pudding	Dessert
Rasher	Slice of bacon
Rocket	Arugula
Salt beef	Corned beef
Scotch egg	Hard-boiled egg fried in jacket of ground sausage and bread crumbs
Shepherd's pie	Baked pie of meat and vegetables covered with gravy and mashed potatoes
Spirits	Hard alcohol
Sponge	Sponge cake
Spotted dick	Sponge cake with fruit and raisins steamed and served with custard sauce
Starter	Appetizer
Steak-and-kidney pie	Pastry-topped pie of steak, kidneys, and mushrooms in gravy
Sticky toffee pudding	Spotted dick (see previous entry) without the fruit and served with warm butterscotch sauce
Sultana	Raisin
Sweet	Dessert
Toad-in-the-hole	Sausage or beef baked in popover batter
Top-up	Refill
Treacle	Molasses
Trifle	Sponge cake soaked in sherry, layered with raspberry preserves, covered with custard sauce, and capped with whipped cream.
Welsh rarebit	Melted cheddar cheese and mustard or Worcestershire sauce served on toast
Whitebait	Small whole deep-fried fish

Dressing to dine

Fashion-conscious Londoners are quick to spot the gauche and the gaudy. They tend to play down garish Hollywood-style glamour in favor of sedate stylishness. But London is becoming a bit more casual. You can wear what's comfortable for you at most restaurants. However, at a hot spot or any $$$ and $$$$ restaurant, I suggest that you dress up rather than down. Assume that a "smart but casual" dress code is in effect in these places and leave the running shoes and blue jeans back at the hotel. Here are my recommendations:

✓ **Men:** Wear a sports jacket and dress trousers (or a suit) with a shirt and tie.

✓ **Women:** A basic black dress or tailored suit is appropriate if you're going to "swan about" in tony eateries.

Gays and lesbians on the lookout for low-priced meals in groovy gay-friendly environments flock to Soho's newest phenomenon: the gay cafe/bar. These trendy hangouts serve good, low-priced meals and pay serious attention to decor.

Wine bars and cafes

Wine bars are more upscale than pubs and usually less smoky. As in pubs, children under 14 aren't permitted in wine bars except in gardens or family rooms. Be aware that a meal in a wine bar will cost more than a similar meal in a pub. Of course, you can order wine instead of beer.

London's cafes generally serve light, inexpensive food and offer limited menus. Most people enjoy a cup of coffee or pot of tea and a sandwich. You may be tempted by the cakes and other sweets.

Chapter 14

London's Best Restaurants

· ·

In This Chapter

▶ Getting full reviews of my favorite restaurants in London

▶ Finding out how to dress, what to order, and how much money to bring with you

· ·

*L*ondon is the home of more than 5,700 restaurants. As you can imagine, choosing which establishments to include in this chapter of my favorites is a monumental task. I try to cover as much of Central London as possible (see the map, "Restaurants in and around The City"). All the establishments are easy to get to, and you can reach all of them by taking the Underground (tube) system and perhaps walking a bit.

If you can't get a dinner reservation, try for lunch instead (lunch will probably be less expensive anyway). If smoking bothers you, always ask when you're booking a table whether a no-smoking section is available. If not, you may be enveloped in a gray haze.

What the $ Symbols Mean

The dollar signs I list with the restaurant description denote the *average* cost of dinner for one person, including an appetizer (a *starter*), a main course (a *main*), a dessert (an *after* or a *pudding*), a drink (not wine or beer), tax, and a tip. Estimating what an average meal will cost is difficult, because everyone eats differently. In addition, many places have set-price meals that are less expensive than average. But I indicate general price ranges with these symbols:

▸ $ $25 or under

▸ $$ $25 to $35

▸ $$$ $35 to $50

▸ $$$$ $50 and up

The following section includes my restaurant recommendations designed to satisfy all tastes and budgets. For those of you who want to get the flavor of merry old England, I include some of the oldest and most respected London restaurants serving traditional English food. For the more chic and trendy among you, I include restaurants that serve the best of Modern British cuisine as well as hybrids of British/ French and British/Continental. For people on a budget — or who just want to eat in a down-to-earth, amiable environment — I also review some of the best London pubs.

My Faves: London Restaurants from A to Z

Asia de Cuba

$$$ Piccadilly Circus & Leicester Square   Cuban/Asian

If you're dying to check out the scene at one of London's ultracool hot spots, pack your chic black clothes and call now to reserve a place at Asia de Cuba in Ian Schrager's new St. Martin's Lane hotel. The Asia de Cuba in New York City was so popular that they exported it to London. For starters, try the Cuban black-bean dumplings or the Chinese five-spice foie gras. Then on to Szechuan peppercorn-crusted tuna or Chino Latino spiced baby chicken. At places like this, one always feels more comfortable receiving at least one call on a cellular phone while dining.

45 St. Martin's Lane, WC2 (in the St. Martin's Lane hotel). ☎ *020-7300-5501. Tube: Leicester Sq. (then a 2-minute walk east on St. Martin's Court to St. Martin's Lane). Reservations are essential at least 2 to 3 weeks in advance. Main courses: £14.50–£34 ($24–$56). AE, DC, MC, V. Open: Daily 11:30 a.m.–2:30 p.m. and 6–11 p.m.*

Aubergine

$$$$ Chelsea   French

This top-name restaurant has only 14 tables, and you compete with its rich-and-famous clientele of celebrities, royalty, and commoners for the privilege of dining there. But it's well worth the try. If you do get in, make sure you look reasonably chic (this isn't the place for tourist togs). Every dish, from the fish and lighter Mediterranean-style choices to the Bresse pigeon with wild-mushroom ravioli and the venison filet with braised baby turnips, is a culinary achievement of the highest order, winning two Michelin stars. And the celebrated cappuccino of white beans with grated truffle makes a perfect ending to a superb dining experience.

11 Park Walk, SW10. ☎ *020-7352-3449. Tube: Sloane Sq. (then a 10-minute walk southwest on King's Rd. to Park Walk; or bus 11, 19, 22, or 211 southwest on King's Rd from the tube station). Reservations are essential 2 months in advance. Fixed-price menus: lunch £16 ($26) for 2 courses, £19.50 ($32) for 3 courses; dinner £42.50 ($71) for 3 courses. AE, DC, MC, V. Open: Monday–Friday noon–2:15 p.m., Monday–Saturday 7–10:30 p.m.*

Bluebird

$$$ Chelsea Modern European

This establishment is definitely upscale but still comfortable and refreshingly unpretentious. Formerly a car-repair garage, this sleek white-and-blue place with a gleaming chrome bar, central skylights, and an open kitchen with a wood-burning stove was the creation of Sir Terence Conran. The menu emphasizes hearty, cooked-to-the-minute cuisine, and highlights include fish and fresh shellfish (oysters, clams) and crustaceans (lobster, crab), as well as grilled meats (veal, lamb, pigeon, and organic chicken). On my last visit, the white gazpacho was overly olive-oiled but the roast pork was delicious. A cafe and food store are on the first floor.

350 King's Rd., SW3. ☎ 020-7559-1000. Reservations recommended. Tube: Sloane Sq. (then a 10-minute walk south on King's Rd.; or bus 19, 22 or 49 from the tube station). Main courses: £9.75–£30 ($16–$50). Fixed-price menus: lunch (12:30–3 p.m.), pretheater (6–7 p.m.) £12.75–£15.75 ($21–$26). AE, DC, MC, V. Open: Monday–Friday noon–3:30 p.m. and 6–11:30 p.m., Saturday 11 a.m.–3:30 p.m. and 6–11:30 p.m., Sunday 11 a.m.–3:30 p.m. and 6–10:30 p.m.

Brasserie St. Quentin

$$ South Kensington French

London's most authentic-looking French brasserie, St. Quentin attracts many people in the city's French community (a positive sign for a French restaurant outside of France). Mirrors and crystal chandeliers add a touch of elegance. You can dine on grilled tuna with tomato and pepper salsa, stuffed leg of rabbit, breast of Barbary duck, and corn-fed chicken with leeks, morels, and chablis sauce. Cornish crab with crème fraîche and terrine of duck liver with walnut dressing are among hors d'oeuvres you'll enjoy trying.

243 Brompton Rd., SW3. ☎ 020-7581-5131. Tube: South Kensington (then a 5-minute walk east on Brompton Rd.). Reservations required. Main courses: £11.95–£24 ($19–$40). Fixed-price menus: 2-course lunch £11.50 ($19); 2-course dinner (6:30–7:30pm) £11.50 ($19). AE, DC, MC, V. Open: Monday–Saturday noon–3pm and 6:30–11 p.m., Sunday noon–3:30 p.m. and 6:30–10:30 p.m.

Café Spice Namaste

$$ The City Indian

This establishment's homemade chutneys alone are worth the trip. Despite fierce competition among London's Indian restaurants, this one remains a perennial favorite for the consistently high quality of its food. It's housed in a landmark Victorian hall near Tower Bridge, and its kitchen concentrates on spicy Indian dishes that have a strong Portuguese influence, such as Goa's signature dish, *sorpotel* (diced kidney, liver, and pork slow-cooked and served in an oniony stew). Superb chicken, duck, lamb, and fish dishes are available served mild to spicy-hot. All dishes are accompanied by fresh vegetables and Indian bread.

16 Prescot St., E1. ☎ *020-7488-9242. Tube: Tower Hill (then a 5-minute walk north on Minories St. and east on Goodman's Yard, which becomes Prescot St. after you cross Mansell St.). Reservations are required. Main courses: £8–£10 ($13–$17). AE, DC, MC, V. Open: Monday–Friday noon–3 p.m. and 6–10:30 p.m., Saturday 6–10:30 p.m.*

Café Suze

$$ Marylebone   Pacific Rim/International

At this intimate wine bar a couple of blocks from Madame Tussaud's, ingredients from the Pacific Rim are served in all kinds of deliciously inventive ways. The menu changes every 2 or 3 weeks, but you can find delicacies such as huge New Zealand greenshell mussels, Australian beef medallions on spiced pumpkin mash, and Australian swordfish with cashew butter. The wine list is heavily accented with vintages from Australia and New Zealand. After 10 years, Café Suze has been so successful that it's opened another bistro, at 41 North Audley St., W1 (☎ **020-7491-3237**).

1 Glentworth St., NW1. ☎ *020-7486-8216. Tube: Baker St. (then a 2-minute walk west on Marylebone Rd.). Reservations are recommended. Main courses: £8.50–£9.50 ($14–$16). AE, DC, MC, V. Open: Monday–Friday 11 a.m.–11 p.m.*

Chelsea Kitchen

$ Chelsea   International

A London institution, Chelsea Kitchen has been feeding locals and drop-ins since 1961. At this simple place with a diner-like atmosphere, both the plates and the crowds move fast. Menu staples include leek-and-potato soup, chicken Kiev, chicken parmigiana, burgers, and steaks.

98 King's Rd. (off Sloane Sq.), SW3. ☎ *020-7589-1330. Tube: Sloane Sq. (the restaurant is at the beginning of King's Rd. just west of the square). Reservations are recommended. Main courses: £3–£5.50 ($5–$9). Fixed-price menu: 2-course lunch or dinner £6 ($10). No credit cards. Open: Daily 8 a.m.–11:45 p.m.*

Chiang Mai

$$ Soho   Thai

Chiang Mai is next door to Ronnie Scott's, the most famous jazz club in England, so it's a good stop for an early dinner before a night on the town. Named after the ancient northern capital of Thailand (known for its rich, spicy foods), this unpretentious but pleasant place is good for hot-and-sour beef and chicken dishes, pad thai noodles with various toppings, and vegetarian meals. I suggest that you order a couple of different courses and share. Children's specials are available.

48 Frith St. (off Soho Sq.), W1. ☎ *020-7437-7444. Tube: Tottenham Court Rd. (then a 5-minute walk west on Oxford St. and south on Soho St.; Frith St. is at the southwest corner of Soho Sq.). Main courses: £6–£9 ($10–$15). AE, MC, V. Open: Monday–Saturday noon–3 p.m. and 6–11 p.m., Sunday 6–10:30 p.m.*

Restaurants in and Around The City

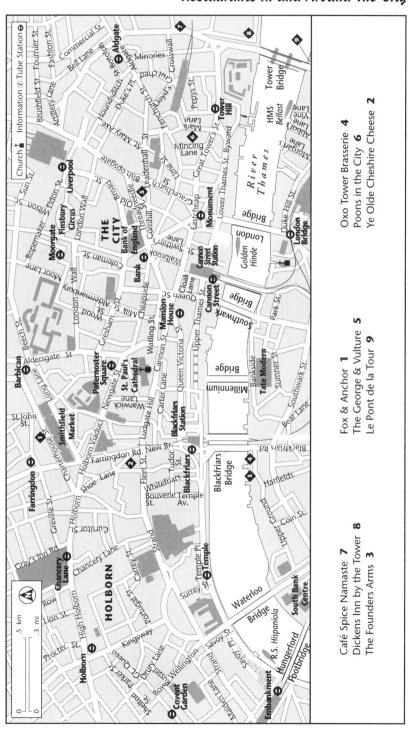

Oxo Tower Brasserie **4**
Poons in the City **6**
Ye Olde Cheshire Cheese **2**

Fox & Anchor **1**
The George & Vulture **5**
Le Pont de la Tour **9**

Café Spice Namaste **7**
Dickens Inn by the Tower **8**
The Founders Arms **3**

Westminster and Victoria Restaurants

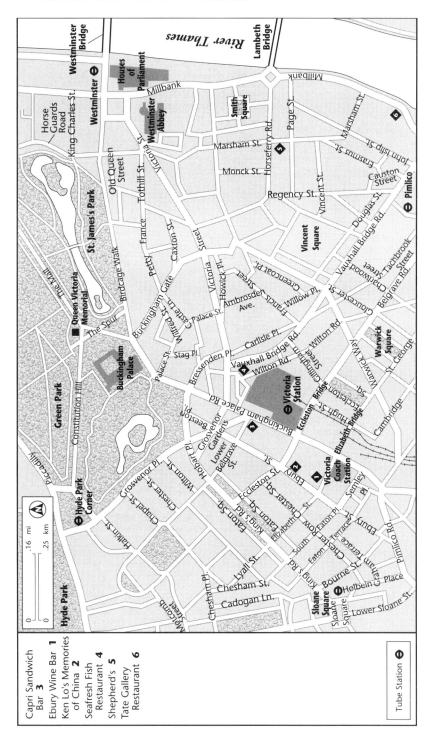

Capri Sandwich Bar **3**
Ebury Wine Bar **1**
Ken Lo's Memories of China **2**
Seafresh Fish Restaurant **4**
Shepherd's **5**
Tate Gallery Restaurant **6**

Tube Station ⊖

Clarke's

$$$ Notting Hill Modern European

This bright modern restaurant owned by chef Sally Clarke is among the hottest in town. Its fixed-price menu offers no choices, but you won't mind when you taste the food. The menu changes daily but emphasizes Mediterranean-style charcoal-grilled foods with herbs and vegetables. A typical meal might include an appetizer of poached cod with anchovy-and-basil mayonnaise; grilled chicken breast with black truffle, crisp polenta, and arugula; and warm pear-and-raisin puff pastry with maple-syrup ice cream.

124 Kensington Church St., W8. ☎ *020-7221-9225. Tube: Notting Hill Gate (then a 5-minute walk south on Kensington Church St.). Reservations are recommended. Fixed-price menus: 2-course lunch £8.50–£14 ($14–$23); 4-course dinner £44 ($73). AE, DC, MC, V. Open: Monday–Friday 12:30–2 p.m. and 7–10 p.m.*

Crank's In London

$ Soho Vegetarian

The wood-and-wicker decor of this restaurant is appropriate for its all-natural cuisine. Just off Carnaby Street, this is the headquarters of a chain of self-service vegetarian restaurants with seven other branches in London. Organic-white and stone-ground flour is used for breads and rolls. The raw vegetable salad is especially good, and a hot stew of savory vegetables served with a salad is always a good choice. Homemade honey cake, cheesecake, tarts, and crumbles are featured.

8 Marshall St., W1 ☎ *020-7437-9431. Tube: Oxford Circus (then a 5-minute walk south on Regent St. and east on Foubert's Pl. to Marshall St.). Main courses: £5–£6.45 ($8–$11). AE, DC, MC, V. Open: Monday–Friday 8:30 a.m.–7 p.m., Saturday 9:30 a.m.–7 p.m.*

Devonshire Arms

$ Kensington Traditional British

This mid-19th-century pub is a good place to stop when shopping on Kensington High Street. It's large enough that you can always get a seat, and the food is above average. You can get a quick bite from the servery that has daily specials or can order from the menu and have your meal served at your table. Pub staples include beef-and-onion pie, fish-and-chips, and steak-and-kidney pudding. Two good choices are the club sandwich and the vegetarian lasagne verdi.

37 Marloes Rd., W8. ☎ *020-7937-0710. Tube: High St. Kensington (then a 5-minute walk west on Kensington High St. and south on Wright's Lane to Marloes Rd.). Main courses: £4.95–£6.50 ($8–$11). AE, MC, V. Open: Monday–Saturday 11 a.m.–11 p.m., Sunday noon–10:30 p.m. (food served noon–3 p.m.).*

Restaurants from Knightsbridge to Earl's Court

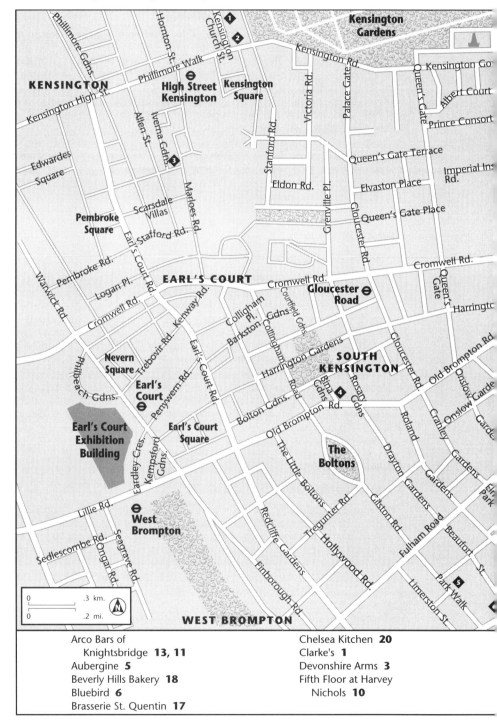

Arco Bars of Knightsbridge **13, 11**	Chelsea Kitchen **20**
Aubergine **5**	Clarke's **1**
Beverly Hills Bakery **18**	Devonshire Arms **3**
Bluebird **6**	Fifth Floor at Harvey
Brasserie St. Quentin **17**	Nichols **10**

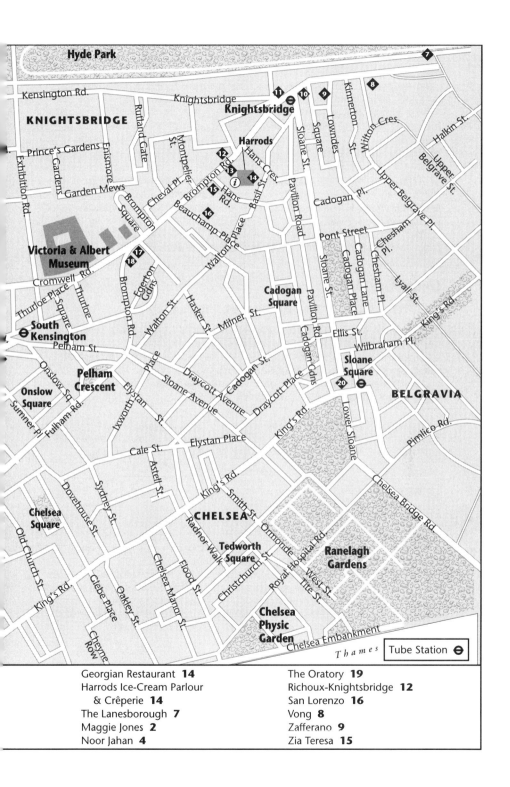

Dickens Inn by the Tower

$ The City   Traditional British

This former spice warehouse is now a 3-story restaurant with sweeping Thames and Tower Bridge views. The ground-floor Tavern Room serves lasagne, soup, sandwiches, and chili. Pizza on the Dock, a floor above, offers four sizes of pizzas. Wheeler's, on the top floor, is a relatively formal (geared more toward adults) dining room serving Modern British cuisine; specials include steaks, charcoal-grilled brochette of wild mushrooms, and baked cod filet.

St. Katharine's Way (near the Tower of London), E1. ☎ *020-7488-2208. Tube: Tower Hill (then a 10-minute walk east on Tower Hill East and south on St. Katherine's St. to St. Katherine's Way). Reservations are recommended. Main courses: Wheeler's, £11.95–£18.95 ($20–$31); Tavern Room, £3.95–£6.50 ($6–$11); Pizza on the Dock, £5.75–£23 ($9–$38). AE, DC, MC, V. Open: Wheeler's, daily noon–3 p.m. and 6:30–10:30 p.m.; Tavern Room, daily 11 a.m.–3 p.m.; Pizza on the Dock, daily noon–10 p.m.*

Ebury Wine Bar

$$ Westminster & Victoria   British/International

You'll think that you're in a Paris bistro because of this restaurant's narrow, woodsy attractive interior. Besides steaks, the oft-changing menu features traditional dishes such as Cumberland sausages, meatloaf, and roast pork, but you may find something with a Pacific Rim influence as well (such as Thai fish balls). This popular wine bar offers a surprisingly good and varied menu and excellent wines.

139 Ebury St., SW1. ☎ *020-7730-5447. Tube: Victoria (then a 10-minute walk west on Belgrave St. and south on Ebury St.). Reservations are recommended. Main courses: £10–£17 ($17–$28). AE, DC, MC, V. Open: Daily 11 a.m.–11 p.m.*

Ed's Easy Diner

$ Soho North   American

It may seem strange to go to London to visit this replica of an old American diner, where customers perch on stools at a wraparound counter and listen to old songs blaring from the jukebox, but it's a safe bet for the kids. A bit more authentic than the version at the Pepsi Trocadero in Piccadilly Circus, this Ed's still attracts a fair share of teens. If you've a yen for the cholesterol-laden chow you're supposed to avoid, chow down with Ed's big burgers with fries or onion rings, giant Kosher weenies slathered with cheddar cheese, chili, tuna melts, and grilled cheese.

12 Moor St. (off Cambridge Circus), W1. ☎ *020-7439-1955. Tube: Leicester Sq. (then a 5-minute walk north on Charing Cross Rd. and west on Moor St.). Main courses: £4.50–£5.50 ($7–$9). MC, V. Open: Monday–Thursday 11:30 a.m.–midnight, Friday 11:30 a.m.–1 a.m., Saturday 9 a.m.–1 a.m., Sunday 9 a.m.–11 p.m.*

Food For Thought

$ Covent Garden Vegetarian

Covent Garden offers a plethora of expensive restaurants for meat-eaters, so this basement hole-in-the-wall with cafeteria-style service is a pleasant and welcome alternative. The menu changes constantly, but the daily soup is always a treat (such as carrot and fresh coriander) and the main courses can include a sweet and tangy Jamaican curry, Italian bean casserole, and cannelloni ripieni (stuffed with eggplant), as well as daily quiche and salad specials. The desserts generally include simple fare such as apple-and-rhubarb crumble and fruit with yogurt.

31 Neal St., WC2. ☎ 020-7836-0239. Tube: Covent Garden (then a 2-minute walk north on Neal St.). Reservations not accepted. Main courses: £3.50–£5.70 ($6–$9). No credit cards. Open: Monday–Saturday noon–3:30 p.m. and 5:30 p.m.–8:15 p.m., Sunday noon–4 p.m.

Fortnum & Mason

$$ St. James's Traditional British

Fortnum & Mason offers three restaurants in addition to its legendary posh London store that's a "purveyor to the Queen" and famous for its food section (see Chapter 19). You can choose the mezzanine-level Patio for lunch and tea. The Patio's lunch menu offers an assortment of pricey sandwiches and main courses, especially hot and cold pies (steak and kidney, curried fish and banana, chicken, and game) and Welsh rarebit prepared with Guinness stout. The lower-level Fountain offers breakfast, lunch, tea, and dinner. The fourth-floor St. James's serves lunch and afternoon tea. The more well heeled dine at St. James's, where the menu is even more traditionally British: For starters, try the kipper mousse or potato and Stilton brûlée; main courses include pies and roast rib of Scottish beef. Though crowded with tourists, these three establishments remain pleasant places where you can get a good meal and a glimpse of the fading empire.

181 Piccadilly, W1. ☎ 020-7734-8040. Tube: Piccadilly Circus (then a 5-minute walk west on Piccadilly). Reservations accepted for St. James's only. Main courses: £7.50–£15.95 ($12–$26). AE, DC, MC, V. Open: St. James's and the Patio, Monday–Saturday 9:30 a.m.–5:30 p.m.; the Fountain, Monday–Saturday 9 a.m.–8 p.m.

The Founders Arms

$ South Bank Modern British

There's nothing like the view of a flowing river. And this modern pub/restaurant sits right on the Thames, a few minutes walk east from the South Bank Centre or west from the new Tate Modern and Shakespeare's Globe. You can sit inside or out by the water. Though some British pub favorites — such as smoked sausage and mash, pork/stuffing/apricot pie, and lamb's liver and bacon on bubble and squeak — are available, other dishes are more ambitious. Pasta, fresh fish, and other daily specials are listed on a chalkboard.

52 Hopton St., SE1. ☎ *020-7928-1899. Tube: Waterloo (then a 10-minute walk north along the Thames Path in front of the National Theatre). Main courses: £4.95–£9.95 ($8–$16). AE, MC, V. Open: Monday–Saturday noon–8:30 p.m., Sunday noon–8 p.m.*

Fox & Anchor

$ The City   Traditional British

This unique pub is just the ticket for starting your day like a real Brit. Butchers from the nearby Smithfield meat market, and nurses coming off their night shifts, City clerks, and tycoons have been eating enormous breakfasts here since 1898. The full house breakfast plate comes with at least eight items, including sausage, bacon, kidneys, eggs, beans, black pudding, and a fried slice of bread, along with unlimited tea or coffee, toast, and jam. If you're feeling festive, order a Black Velvet (champagne with Guinness) or a *Bucks* fizz (orange juice and champagne — what Americans call a mimosa). You can order breakfast until 3 p.m., and breakfast is the meal to go for. If you'd rather have lunch, try a steak or the steak-and-kidney pie. Meat is what the Fox & Anchor does best.

115 Charterhouse St., EC1. ☎ *020-7253-4838. Tube: Barbican (then a 5-minute walk north on Aldersgate and west on Charterhouse St.). Reservations are recommended. Breakfasts: full house £7 ($11); steak £4.50–£9.80 ($7–$16). Lunch: £5–£15 ($8–$22). AE, DC, MC, V. Open: Monday–Friday 7 a.m.–9 p.m., meals served 7 a.m.–3 p.m.*

The Gay Hussar

$$$$ Soho   Hungarian

The Gay Hussar is thought to be the best Hungarian restaurant outside of Hungary. Gay in the cheery old ha-ha sense of the word, the restaurant serves undeniably authentic Hungarian cuisine: chilled wild-cherry soup, caraway potatoes, cabbage stuffed with minced veal and rice, tender chicken served in mild paprika sauce with cucumber salad and noodles, and of course veal goulash with egg dumplings. The portions are immoderately large, but try and save room for the poppyseed strudel or the walnut pancakes for dessert.

2 Greek St. (off Soho Sq.), W1. ☎ *020-7437-0973. Tube: Tottenham Court (then a 2-minute walk west on Oxford St. and south on Soho St.; Greek St. is at the southeast corner of Soho Sq.). Reservations recommended. Main courses: £20–£25 ($33–$41). Fixed-price menus: lunch £15 ($25) for 2 courses, £18 ($30) for 3 courses. AE, DC, MC, V. Open: Monday–Saturday 12:15–2:30 p.m. and 5:30–10:45 p.m.*

The George

$ The Strand   Traditional British

Beware: A headless cavalier is rumored to haunt these premises, evidently looking for his head *and* a drink. A favorite pub for barristers, the George is opposite the Royal Courts of Justice and dates back to 1723, with much of the original structure still standing. Hot and cold platters, including bangers and mash (sausages and mashed potatoes), fish-and-chips, and steak-and-kidney pieare served from a counter at the back. (You can also get lasagna if you need a break from British food.) Additional seating is available in the basement.

213 The Strand, WC2. ☎ 020-7427-0941. Tube: Temple (then a 5-minute walk north on Arundel St. and east on The Strand). Main courses: £3–£6.30 ($5-$10). AE, DC, V. Open: Monday–Friday 11 a.m.-11 p.m., Saturday noon–3 p.m. (food served Monday–Friday 11:30 a.m.–2:30 p.m., Saturday noon–2:30 p.m.).

The George & Vulture

$$ The City   Traditional British

This historic City pub, dating from 1660, serves English lunches on its three floors. When you arrive, give your name and then retire to the Jamaican pub opposite for a drink; the staff will let you know when your table is ready. The pub offers daily specials and a regular menu that includes a mixed grill, a loin chop, and fried Dover sole filets. Potatoes and buttered cabbage are the standard vegetables, and the apple tart is always reliable. After you eat, you can explore the maze of pubs, shops, wine houses, and other old buildings nearby.

3 Castle Court, Cornhill, EC3. ☎ 020-7626-9710. Tube: Bank (then a 5-minute walk east on Cornhill). Reservations accepted if you agree to arrive by 12:45 p.m. Main courses: £6.65–£14.80 ($11–$24). AE, DC, MC, V. Open: Monday–Friday noon–2:30 p.m.

Gourmet Pizza Company

$ St. James's   Pizza/Pasta

This large, bright eatery, frequented by workers in the area's shops and offices, makes an economical place to stop when you're in the West End. You can choose from 20 varieties of pizza — everything from a B.L.T. to one with Cajun chicken and prawns. About half the choices are vegetarian. The crusts are light and crispy and the toppings fresh and flavorful. If you don't want pizza, try the wild mushroom tortellini with chopped basil, tomato, and olive oil. Delicioso!

7–9 Swallow Walk (off Piccadilly), W1. ☎ 020-7734-5182. Tube: Piccadilly Circus (then a 5-minute walk west on Piccadilly and north on Swallow St.). Pizzas: £4.80–£8.45 ($8–$14). Pastas: £6.60–£8.45 ($11–$14). AE, DC, MC, V. Open: Monday–Saturday noon–3 p.m. and 5–10:30 p.m.

The Granary

$ Piccadilly Circus & Leicester Square   Traditional British

This country-style restaurant serves flavorful home-cooked dishes, listed daily on a chalkboard, including such favorites as lamb casserole with mint and lemon, pan-fried cod, or avocado stuffed with prawns, spinach, and cheese. Common vegetarian meals are meatless versions of paella, lasagne, and korma (curried vegetables with Greek yogurt). Having the same owners and many of the same staff for more than 25 years, this reliable restaurant also offers such traditional but tempting desserts as bread-and-butter pudding and brown Betty (both served hot). Large portions guarantee that you'll be well filled.

39 Albemarle St., W1. ☎ *020-7493-2978. Tube: Green Park (then a 5-minute walk east on Piccadilly to Albermarle) or Piccadilly Circus (then a 5-minute walk west on Piccadilly). Main courses: £7.90-£8.90 ($12-$14). MC, V. Open: Monday–Friday 11:30 a.m. –7:30 p.m., Saturday–Sunday 11:30 a.m.–4 p.m.*

Hard Rock Café

$$ **Mayfair   North American**

This is one of a worldwide chain of rock-and-roll/American-roadside-diner-themed restaurants. Teens enjoy the rock memorabilia and loud music as well as the great burgers and shakes. Tasty vegetarian dishes are available, too. The portions are generous, and main dishes include salad and fries or baked potato. Consider the homemade apple pie if you've room for dessert. Be prepared to stand in line in the evenings.

150 Old Park Lane, W1. ☎ *020-7629-0382. Tube: Hyde Park Corner (take the Park Lane exit; Old Park Lane is just to the east of Park Lane). Main courses: £8.50–£15 ($14–$25). AE, MC, V. Open: Sunday–Thursday 11:30 a.m.–12:30 a.m., Friday–Saturday 11:30 a.m.–1 a.m.*

The Ivy

$$ **Soho   British/French**

Are you looking for a hip place to dine after enjoying the theater? The Ivy, with its 1930s look, tiny bar, glamour-scene crowd, and later-than-usual hours fits the bill. The cooking features skillful preparations of fresh ingredients, with such popular dishes as white asparagus with sea kale and truffle butter and seared scallops with spinach, sorrel, and bacon. You can also enjoy Mediterranean fish soup, a great mixed grill, and traditional English desserts such as sticky toffee and caramelized bread-and-butter pudding.

1–5 West St., WC2. ☎ *020-7836-4751. Tube: Leicester Sq. (then a 5-minute walk north on Charing Cross Rd.;West St. is at the southeastern end of Cambridge Circus). Reservations are required. Main courses: £8.75–£21.75 ($14–$36). Fixed-price menu: Saturday–Sunday lunch £15.50 ($26). AE, DC, MC, V. Open: Daily noon– 3 p.m. and 5:30 p.m.–midnight.*

Joe Allen

$$ **Covent Garden   North American**

Joe Allen is a low-profile place on a back street in Covent Garden. Its crowded dining room with checkered tablecloths is the sort of place where actors like to come after a performance to scarf down chili con carne or gnaw on barbecued ribs. The dependable food includes American classics with some international twists, and the set menu is a real value: After a starter (maybe smoked haddock vichyssoise), you can choose main courses such as pan-fried parmesan-crusted lemon sole,

Cajun chicken breast, and grilled spicy Italian sausages. If you're a tad homesick, try a burger, a brownie, and a Coke for consolation. Come before the show for the best prices, come after for potential star-gazing.

13 Exeter St., WC2. ☎ *020-7836-0651. Tube: Covent Garden (then a 5-minute walk south past the Market to Burleigh St. on the southeast corner of the Piazza and west on Exeter St.). Reservations advised. Main courses: £8.50–£14.50 ($14–$24). Fixed-price menus: lunch Monday–Friday £12–£14 ($19–$23); pretheater dinner £13–£15 ($21–$24); Sunday brunch £14.50–£16.50 ($23–$27). AE, MC, V. Open: Monday–Friday noon–12:45 a.m., Saturday 11:30 a.m.–12:45 a.m., Sunday 11:30 a.m.–11:30 p.m.*

Ken Lo's Memories of China

$$$$ **Westminster & Victoria   Chinese**

The late Ken Lo, author of more than 30 cookbooks and once the host of a TV cooking show, founded this establishment, with its appealing but minimalist decor and impeccable service. Spanning broadly divergent regions of China, this is one of the better (and certainly one of the more expensive) pan-Chinese restaurants in London. Its ambitious menu features Cantonese quick-fried beef in oyster sauce, "Bang Bang chicken" (a Szechuan dish), pomegranate prawn balls, and lobster with handmade noodles, among many others.

67–69 Ebury St. (near Victoria Station), SW1. ☎ *020-7730-7734. Tube: Victoria Station (then a 10-minute walk west on Belgrave St. and south on Ebury St.). Reservations recommended. Main courses: £10–£30 ($17–$50). Fixed-price menus: 3-course lunch £19.50–£22 ($32–$36); dinner £27.50 ($45) for 3 courses, £30 ($50) for 5 courses; after-theater 3-course dinner £24.50 ($40). AE, DC, MC, V. Open: Monday–Saturday noon–2:30 p.m.; daily 7–11:15 p.m.*

Langan's Bistro

$$ **Marylebone   British/French**

The menu for this bistro is English with an underplayed (some may say underdeveloped) French influence. Behind a brightly colored storefront, the dining room is covered with clusters of Japanese parasols, rococo mirrors, paintings, and old photographs. Depending on the season, the fixed-price menu may start with a chicken-and-leek terrine or a pepper-and-brie tartlet and move on to brochette of lamb, grilled trout fillets, braised rabbit with mustard sauce, or baked cod. The dessert extravaganza known as "Mrs. Langan's chocolate pudding" is a must for chocoholics.

26 Devonshire St., W1. ☎ *020-7935-4531. Tube: Regent's Park (then a 5-minute walk south on Portland Pl. and west on Devonshire St.). Reservations recommended 3 days in advance. Fixed-price menus: lunch or dinner £17.50 ($29) for 2 courses, £19.50 ($32) for 3 courses. AE, DC, MC, V. Open: Monday–Friday 12:30–2:30 p.m. and 6:30–11:30 p.m., Saturday 6:30–11 p.m.*

West End Restaurants

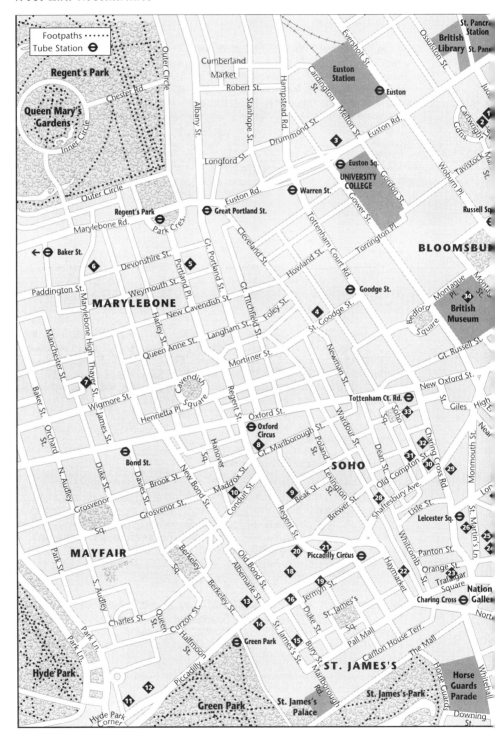

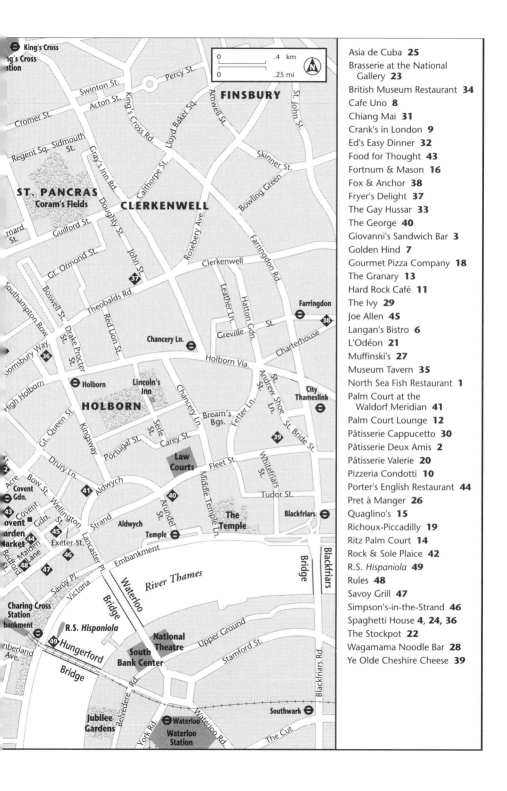

L'Odeon

$$$$ **Piccadilly Circus & Leicester Square   French/International**

L'Odeon had everyone talking when it opened. The interest had to do with its size and sophisticated interior as well as its food. Located in Nash Terrace, the huge second-floor dining room has semicircular windows overlooking the bustle of Regent Street and Piccadilly Circus. The service is efficient, although rather impersonal, but the food is always fresh and beautifully presented. For starters, try the layered foie gras and Serrano ham terrine or mussel saffron mousse. Main courses may include poached salmon with orange zest, roast chicken with parmesan, calf's liver with braised cabbage, or braised lamb.

65 Regent St. (entrance in Air St.), W1. ☎ *020-7287-1400. Tube: Piccadilly Circus (Air St. is the first turning on the south side of Regent St.). Reservations are recommended. Main courses: £14–£25 ($23–$41). Fixed-price menus: lunch and pretheater £15.50–£19.50 ($26–$32). AE, DC, MC, V. Open: Monday–Saturday noon–2:45 p.m. and 5:30–11:30 p.m.*

Le Pont de la Tour

$$$$ **South Bank   International**

If you want a splendid view of the Thames and Tower Bridge, visit this upscale wine-and-dine emporium set within a mid-19th-century warehouse. Amid the brash hubbub of the Bar and Grill, you can order a terrine of ham and foie gras or a half-lobster with roast peppers, olives, and fennel, among other fine dishes. The menu in the larger and more formal The Restaurant offers such elegant foods as roast squab pigeon with morel-and-truffle sauce, braised lamb shank with rosemary *jus* and carrot-and-parsnip purée, and an excellent Dover sole, which you can order grilled or meunière. Sir Terence Conran is the force behind these posh establishments.

36D Shad Thames, Butler's Wharf, SE1. ☎ *020-7403-8403. Tube: London Bridge (then a 10-minute walk east on Tooley St. and north on Lafon St. to Shad Thames). Reservations are not accepted in the Bar and Grill, but are essential in the restaurant. Main courses: Bar and Grill £9–£18 ($15–$30); Restaurant £16–£24 ($26–$40). Fixed-price menu: both venues, 3-course lunch Monday–Friday £28.50 ($47). AE, DC, MC, V. Open: Restaurant Monday–Friday noon–3 p.m.; Monday–Saturday 6–11:30 p.m., Sunday noon–3 p.m. and 6–11 p.m.; Bar and Grill daily 11:30 a.m.–11:30 p.m.*

Maggie Jones

$$ **Kensington   Traditional British**

At this trilevel restaurant with pine tables, you can enjoy British cuisine . . . or British cuisine. As you may have guessed, the menu is all British, including such traditional favorites as grilled leg of lamb chop with rosemary, grilled trout with almonds, and Maggie's famous fish pie. For dessert, try the treacle tart. Everything tastes good and is reliably cooked, but don't expect anything exceptional. By the way, the place is named after Princess Margaret, who used to eat here.

6 Old Court Place (off Kensington Church St.), W8. ☎ *020-7937-6462. Tube: High St. Kensington (then a 5-minute walk east on Kensington High St., north on Kensington Church St., and east on Old Court Pl.). Reservations are required. Main courses: £5–£20 ($8–$33). AE, DC, MC, V. Open: Daily 12:30–2:30 p.m. and 6:30–11 p.m.*

The Museum Tavern

$ Bloomsbury   Traditional British

Across from the British Museum's front entrance, this ornate Victorian pub is a convenient spot for a hearty lunch after perusing the Parthenon sculptures. It's self-service: You order food at the servery and drinks at the bar and bring them to your table. Most of the main courses are traditional pub staples: meat pies (chicken and ham; steak and kidney; cottage), bangers and mash, fish-and-chips, lamb-and-rosemary hot pot, quiche, salads, and lasagna. It is a pub, remember, so expect some cigarette smoke.

49 Great Russell St., WC1. ☎ *020-7242-8987. Tube: Russell Sq. (then a 5-minute walk south on Mondaytgomery St., along the west side of Russel Sq., to Great Russell St.). Main courses: £5.45–£6.95 ($9–$11). AE, MC, V. Open: Monday–Saturday 11 a.m.–11 p.m., Sunday 11 a.m.–10:30 p.m. (food served to half an hour before closing).*

Noor Jahan

$$ South Kensington   Indian

Noor Jahan is a neighborhood favorite in South Ken. The restaurant is small and unpretentious. The food is Indian and reliably good, such as the moist and flavorful marinated chicken and lamb dishes cooked Tandoori style in a clay oven. If you want to try one of their tasty specialties, consider chicken tikka, a staple of northern India, or the biriani dishes — where chicken, lamb, or prawns are mixed with basmati rice, fried in ghee, and served with a mixed vegetable curry. If you're unfamiliar with Indian food, the waiters will gladly explain the dishes.

2A Bina Gardens (off Old Brompton Rd.). ☎ *020-7373-6522. Tube: Gloucester Rd. (then a 5-minute walk south on Gloucester Rd., west on Brompton Rd., north on Bina Gardens). Reservations are recommended. Main courses: £7–£15.50 ($11–$26). Fixed-price menu: £18.50 ($31). AE, DC, MC, V. Open: Daily noon–2:45 p.m. and 6–11:45 p.m.*

North Sea Fish Restaurant

$$ Bloomsbury   Seafood

When they go to London, many people want to experience *real* fish-and-chips — not the generic frozen stuff that often passes for this traditional dish. Definitely try this unassuming chippie where the fish is *always* fresh. With its sepia prints and red velvet seats, the place itself is pleasant and comfortable (and generally crowded). You may want to start with grilled fresh sardines or a fish cake before digging into a main course of cod or haddock. The fish is most often served battered and deep-fried, but you can also order it grilled. The chips are almost as good as the fish.

7–8 Leigh St.(off Cartwright Gardens), WC1. ☎ *020-7387-5892. Tube: Russell Sq. (then a 10-minute walk north Marchmont Place and east on Leigh St.). Reservations recommended. Main courses: £6.95–£15.95 ($12–$26). AE, DC, MC, V. Open: Monday–Saturday noon–2 p.m. and 5:30–10 p.m.*

The Oratory

$$ Knightsbridge Modern British

Named for the nearby Brompton Oratory and close to the Victoria & Albert Museum and Knightsbridge shopping, this funky bistro serves some of the best and least expensive food in tony South Ken. The high-ceilinged room is decorated in what I call Modern Rococo, with enormous glass chandeliers, patterned walls and ceiling, and wooden tables with wrought-iron chairs. Note the daily specials on the chalkboard, especially any pasta dishes. The homemade fish cakes, stir-fried prawns with noodles, and breast of chicken stuffed with Parma ham and fontina cheese are all noteworthy. For dessert, the sticky toffee pudding with ice cream is a melt-in-the-mouth delight.

232 Brompton Rd., SW3. ☎ *020-7584-3493. Tube: South Kensington (then a 5-minute walk north on Brompton Rd.). Main courses: £7–£13.50 ($12–$22). Fixed-price menu: 2-course lunch £8.50 ($14). MC, V. Open: Daily noon–11 p.m.*

Oxo Tower Brasserie

$$$ South Bank French

This stylish brasserie sits atop the landmark Oxo Tower on the South Bank. Although the brasserie is less elegant than the adjacent Oxo Tower Restaurant, its food is marvelous and costs about half of what you pay to dine on tablecloths. The superlative river-and-city views are just as sublime, so book well in advance and insist on a window table. Order such tasty bits as the tender and tart roast poussin (that's French for rabbit) with rocket (that's English for arugula), French beans, and a lemon and green olive butter or the equally fine seared salmon with a spring onion mash and a Meaux mustard beurre blanc.

Oxo Tower Wharf, Barge House St., SE1. ☎ *020-7803-3888. Tube: Waterloo (the easiest foot route is to head north to the South Bank Centre and then follow the Thames pathway east to the Oxo Tower, about a 10-minute walk). Reservations are essential at least 1 or 2 weeks in advance. Main courses: £13–£19.50 ($21–$32). Fixed-price menu: 3-course lunch £27.50 ($45). AE, DC, MC, V. Open: Daily noon–3 p.m. and 5:30–11 p.m.*

Pizzeria Condotti

$ Mayfair Pizza/Pasta

You can take your family to this lovely haven, with its fresh flowers and art-covered walls. The light, crisp pizzas arrive bubbling hot. Choices range from a simple margherita with mozzarella and tomato to the King Edward with potato, four cheeses, and tomato or the "American hot" with mozzarella, pepperoni, sausages, and hot peppers. Plenty of fresh salads and pastas are available, as well as a reasonably priced wine list. End your meal with a scoop of creamy tartufo ice cream made with chocolate liqueur.

4 Mill St. (just off Regent St.), W1. ☎ *020-7499-1308. Tube: Oxford Circus (then a 5-minute walk south on Regent St., west on Conduit St. and north on Mill St.). Reservations are not required. Pizzas: £5–£7 ($8–$12). Pastas: £6.30 ($10). AE, DC, MC, V. Open: Monday–Saturday 11:30 a.m.–midnight, Sunday noon–11 p.m.*

Poons in the City

$$$ The City   Chinese

Poons is famous for Cantonese specialties such as *lap yuk soom* (similar to tacos, with finely chopped wind-dried bacon) and braised honeycomb (a Chinese version of Yorkshire pudding and gravy). Pan-fried dumplings and deep-fried scallops make excellent starters. Other dishes feature crispy duck, prawns with cashews, and barbecued pork. The restaurant is on the ground floor of an office block less than a 5-minute walk from the Tower of London. At the end of the L-shaped restaurant is a simpler and less expensive 80-seat express cafe serving stir-fries and snacks.

2 Minster Pavement, Minster Court, Mincing Lane, EC3. ☎ *020-7626-0126. Tube: Monument (then a 5-minute walk east on Eastcheap and Great Tower St. and north on Mincing Lane). Reservations are recommended for lunch. Main courses: £5–£9 ($8–$15). Fixed-price menus: lunch and dinner £22.50–£32 ($37–$53); express cafe lunch £5.50–£16.50 ($9–$27) per person (minimum of 2). AE, DC, MC, V. Open: Monday–Friday noon–10:30 p.m.*

Porter's English Restaurant

$$ Covent Garden   Traditional British

This comfortably informal restaurant specializes in English pies, including Old English fish pie; lamb and apricot; and ham, leek, and cheese. Forgo appetizers because the main courses, accompanied by vegetables and side dishes, are generous. If pie isn't your thing, try the bangers and mash, grilled sirloin, lamb steak, or pork chops. The puddings, including bread-and-butter pudding and steamed syrup sponge, are real puddings (in the American sense); they're served hot or cold, with whipped cream or custard.

17 Henrietta St., WC2. ☎ *020-7836-6466. Tube: Covent Garden (then a 5-minute walk south on James St.; Henrietta St. is at the southwest corner behind Covent Garden Market). Reservations are recommended. Main courses: £8–£22 ($13–$36). Fixed-price menu: £16.50 ($27). AE, DC, MC, V. Open: Monday–Saturday noon–11:30 p.m, Sunday noon–10:30 p.m.*

Restaurants from Marylebone to Notting Hill

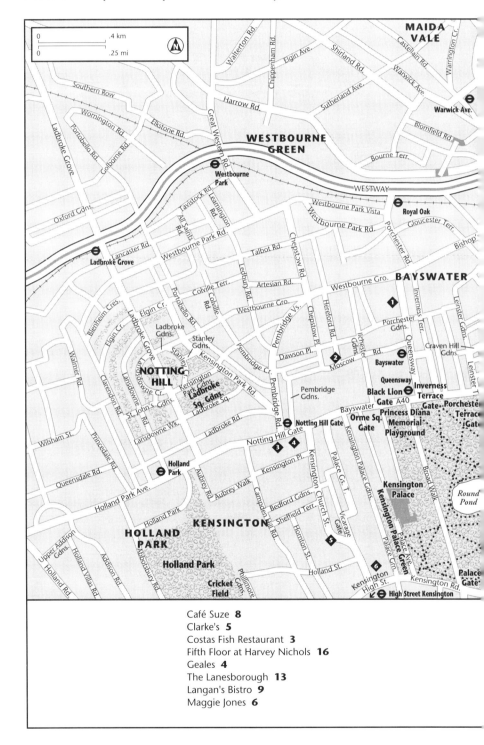

Café Suze **8**
Clarke's **5**
Costas Fish Restaurant **3**
Fifth Floor at Harvey Nichols **16**
Geales **4**
The Lanesborough **13**
Langan's Bistro **9**
Maggie Jones **6**

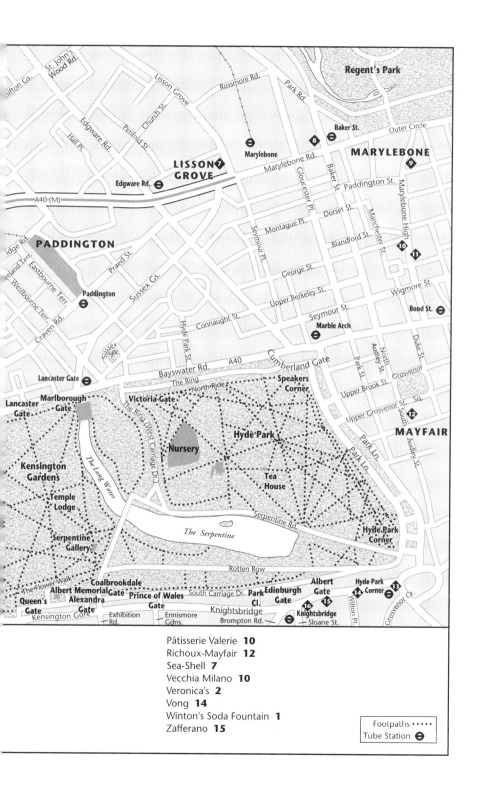

Pâtisserie Valerie **10**
Richoux-Mayfair **12**
Sea-Shell **7**
Vecchia Milano **10**
Veronica's **2**
Vong **14**
Winton's Soda Fountain **1**
Zafferano **15**

Footpaths •••••
Tube Station ⊖

Quaglino's

$$$$ St. James's Modern European

This power-charged mega-eatery is *the* place for food and fun, with a huge sunken dining room that reminds you of an ocean liner's. The shellfish are always excellent, but other menu items are unreliable, as is the service. The menu changes often; choices may include goat cheese and caramelized onion tart, gnocchi with tomato-and-herb sauce, crab tartlet with saffron, or roasted cod and ox cheek with charcoal-grilled vegetables. Be sure to try the puddings (vanilla mascarpone tart and pannacotta with fresh figs), which are wonderfully delectable.

16 Bury St., SW1. ☎ *020-7930-6767. Fax: 020-7839-2866. Tube: Green Park (then a 10-minute walk northeast on Piccadilly, southeast on St. James's St., and east on King St. to Bury St.). Reservations are essential at least 1 or 2 weeks in advance. Main courses: £10.50–£19.50 ($17–$32). Fixed-price menu: (Monday–Thursday at lunch and at pretheater dinner 5:30–6:30pm) £12.50–£15 ($21–$25). AE, DC, MC, V. Open: Daily noon–3 p.m. and 5:30–11:30 p.m.*

R.S. Hispaniola

$$$ The Strand British/French

This former passenger boat is permanently moored in the Thames and provides good food and spectacular views of the river traffic. The menu changes often, with a variety of sturdy and generally well-prepared dishes, such as flambéed Mediterranean prawns with garlic, poached halibut on a bed of creamed spinach, rack of lamb flavored with rosemary and shallots, and a number of vegetarian dishes. The place can be fun and romantic — live music is played most nights — if a bit touristy.

River Thames, Victoria Embankment, Charing Cross, WC2. ☎ *020-7839-3011. Tube: Embankment (the restaurant a few steps from the station). Reservations are recommended. Main courses: £9.50–£16.50 ($16–$27); £15 ($25) minimum per person. AE, DC, MC, V. Open: Monday–Friday noon–2:30 p.m. and 6:30–11 p.m.; Saturday 6–11:30 p.m. Closed December 24–January 4.*

Rules

$$$ Covent Garden Traditional British

If you want to eat classic British cuisine in a memorable (nay, venerable) setting, put on something reasonably dressy and head for Maiden Lane. Founded in 1798, Rules is London's oldest restaurant, numbering two centuries worth of prints, cartoons, and paintings among its decor. If you're game for game, go for it because that's what Rules is famous for. Ptarmigan, widgeon, partridge, and snipe — game birds shot at the restaurant's hunting seat — are roasted to order September through February. In recent years, they've added fish and a few vegetarian dishes, such as the wild mushroom lasagna in basil cream sauce.

35 Maiden Lane, WC2. ☎ *020-7836-5314. Tube: Covent Garden (then a 5-minute walk south on James St. to Southampton St. behind Covent Garden Market and west on Maiden Lane). Reservations are essential. Main courses: £15–£18 ($25–$30). Fixed-price menu: pretheater Monday–Friday 3–5 p.m. £15.95 ($26). AE, DC, MC, V. Open: Daily noon–midnight.*

San Lorenzo

$$$ Knightsbridge   Italian

This fashionable restaurant was once a favorite of Princess Diana. Italian cuisine from all the regions of Italy, with a special nod toward Tuscany and the Piedmont, is the specialty. Seasonal fish, game, and vegetables appear in such dishes as risotto with fresh asparagus, partridge in white-wine sauce, and *tagliate di bue* (filet steak with arugula and balsamic vinegar). The fettuccine, gnocchi, and penne are all homemade. The food is reliably good, but some diners complain that too much attitude accompanies it.

22 Beauchamp Place, SW3. ☎ *020-7584-1074. Tube: Knightsbridge (then a 5-minute walk southwest on Brompton Rd. and south on Beauchamp Place). Reservations are required. Main courses: £14.50–£20 ($24–$33). No credit cards are accepted. Open: Monday–Saturday 12:30–3 p.m. and 7:30–11:30 p.m.*

Savoy Grill

$$$$ The Strand   Traditional British

Like the hotel that houses it, the Savoy Grill caters to the rich, the powerful, the prestigious, and anyone else who can dress up and put together enough to afford the price of a meal. Service is impeccable, and the dining room is spacious but low-key, with yew-paneled walls that give it a warm woody blush. If you like old-fashioned meat dishes, choose the daily special from the trolley: beef Wellington, roast sirloin, saddle of lamb, or pot-roasted guinea hen with horseradish crust. Other traditional dishes get some unusual pairings from the chef, such as roast duck with caramelized oranges, asparagus and pancetta, pan-fried salmon with mushroom risotto, and fish cakes with roasted tomato-and-fennel compote.

In the Savoy Hotel, Strand, WC2. ☎ *020-7240-6040. Tube: Charing Cross (then a 5-minute walk east along The Strand). Reservations are essential. Main courses: £15–£37 ($25–$61). AE, DC, MC, V. Open: Monday–Friday 12:30–2:30 p.m.; Monday–Saturday 6–11:15 p.m.*

Shepherd's

$$$ Westminster & Victoria   Traditional British

This popular restaurant sits between Tate Britain and Parliament. Regulars include a loyal crowd of barristers and MPs (a bell rings in the dining room to let them know it's time to go back to the House of Commons for a vote). Amid a nook-and-cranny setting of leather banquettes, sober 19th-century accessories, and English portraits and landscapes, you can dine on rib of

Scottish beef with Yorkshire pudding, cream of watercress, hot salmon and potato salad with dill dressing, filet of lemon sole, and roast leg of lamb with mint sauce. You choose everything from a fixed-price menu but are given an impressive number of options.

Marsham Court, Marsham St. (at the corner of Page St.), SW1. ☎ 020-7834-9552. Tube: Westminster (then a 10-minute walk south on St. Margaret Place and Millbank and west on Westminster St. to Page and Marsham streets; or Pimlico, then north on Bessboro St., John Islip St., and Marsham St.). Reservations are recommended. Fixed-price menus: £23.50 ($39) for 2 courses, £25.50 ($42) for 3 courses. AE, DC, MC, V. Open: Monday–Friday 12:30–2:45 p.m. and 6:30–11 p.m.

Simpson's-in-the-Strand

$$$ **The Strand**   **Traditional British**

Open since 1828, Simpson's boasts an array of the best roasts in London—sirloin of beef, saddle of mutton with red-currant jelly, and Aylesbury duckling—served by a veritable army of formal waiters. (Remember to tip the tailcoated carver.) For a pudding, try the treacle roll and custard or Stilton with vintage port. That's downstairs, where the atmosphere is formal and dressy. They've now opened a more relaxed, brighter, lighter dining area on the second floor that's actually (gasp) nouvelle. This is also a great place to come for a real English breakfast.

100 The Strand (next to the Savoy Hotel), WC2. ☎ 020-7836-9112. Tube: Charing Cross (then a 5-minute walk east along The Strand). Reservations are required. Main courses: downstairs, £9.50–£22.95 ($16–$38); upstairs, £9.70–£15.50 ($16–$26). Fixed-price menus: both upstairs and downstairs, 2-course lunch and pretheater dinner £14.50 ($24); breakfast £13.50 ($22). AE, DC, MC, V. Open: Monday–Friday 7:15–10:30 a.m., 12:15–2:30 p.m. and 5–11 p.m.; Saturday–Sunday noon–2:30 p.m. and 5–11 p.m.

The Stockpot

$ **Piccadilly Circus & Leicester Square**   **British/Continental**

Now here's a dining bargain! This simple bilevel restaurant in the heart of the West End doesn't offer refined cooking, but the food is filling and satisfying and the price right. You can find such fare as minestrone soup, spaghetti bolognese (the eternal favorite), braised lamb, and apple crumble on the fixed-price daily menu. (During peak dining hours, you may have to share the table with other guests.)

38 Panton St. (off Haymarket, opposite the Comedy Theatre), SW1. ☎ 020-7839-5142. Tube: Piccadilly Circus (then a 5-minute walk south on Haymarket and east on Panton St.). Reservations are accepted for dinner. Main courses: £2.60–£6.50 ($4–$11). Fixed-price menus: 2-course lunch £3.70 ($6); 3-course dinner £6.20 ($10). No credit cards. Open: Monday–Saturday 7 a.m.–11:30 p.m., Sunday 7 a.m.–10 p.m.

Veronica's

$$ **Bayswater** **Traditional British**

Veronica's is a celebration of historical and regional cuisine of the British Isles. It offers some dishes based on medieval and Tudor recipes, but all are given a creative, modern twist. One month the chef may focus on Victorian foods, the next month on foods of Scotland, and the month after that on Wales or Ireland. Your appetizer may be an Elizabethan salad called salmagundy, made with crunchy pickled vegetables, or Tweed Kettle, a 19th-century recipe to improve the taste of salmon. Many dishes are vegetarian, and everything tastes better when followed with a British farmhouse cheese or a pudding. The restaurant is brightly and attractively decorated and the service warm and efficient.

3 Hereford Rd., W2. ☎ *020-7229-5079. Tube: Bayswater (then a 5-minute walk west on Moscow Rd. and north on Hereford Rd.). Reservations are required. Main courses: £10.50–£17.50 ($17–$29). Fixed-price menus: £12.50–£16.50 ($21–$27). AE, DC, MC, V. Open: Monday–Friday noon–3 p.m. and 6:30–11:30 p.m., Saturday 6:30–11:30 p.m.*

Vong

$$$ **Knightsbridge** **French/Thai**

This artily minimalist restaurant is a chic hangout for food groupies who can't get enough of chef/owner Jean-Georges Vongerichten's food. The cooking is subtle, innovative, and inspired. (Try the "black plate" sampler of six starters for a distinctly palatable taste tour.) You can dine on perfectly roasted halibut or sublime lobster-and-daikon roll with rosemary-and-ginger sauce. Other temptations include the crab spring roll with vinegary tamarind dipping sauce and sautéed foie gras with ginger and mango, which literally melts in your mouth. The exotic desserts include a salad of banana and passion fruit with white-pepper ice cream. You may get a same-day table if you dine early; the place starts filling up after 8 p.m.

In the Berkeley Hotel, Wilton Place, SW1. ☎ *020-7235-1010. Tube: Knightsbridge (then a 3-minute walk east on Knightsbridge and south on Wilton Pl.). Reservations are required 7 days in advance. Main courses: £13.75–£29.75 ($23–$49). Fixed-price menus: tasting £49 ($81); lunch £20 ($33); pre- and post-theater dinner £19.50 ($32). AE, DC, MC, V. Open: Monday–Saturday noon–2:30 p.m. and 6–11:30 p.m.*

Wagamama Noodle Bar

$ **Soho** **Japanese**

Try this trendsetting noodle bar modeled after the ramen shops of Japan if you're exploring Soho and want a delicious, nutritious meal uncontaminated by cigarette smoke, You enter along a stark, glowing hall with a busy open kitchen and descend to a large open room with communal tables. The specialties are ramen, Chinese-style thread noodles served in soups with various toppings, and the fat white noodles called *udon.* You can also order various rice dishes, vegetarian dishes, dumplings, vegetable and chicken skewers, and tempura. Your order is sent via radio signal to the kitchen and arrives the moment it's ready, which means that not everyone in a group will be served at the same time. You may have to stand in line to get in, but it's worth the wait.

10A Lexington St., W1. ☎ 020-7292-0990. Tube: Piccadilly Circus (then a 5-minute walk north on Shaftesbury Ave. and Windmill St., which becomes Lexington St.). Reservations are not accepted. Main courses: £4.70–7.25 ($8–$12). MC, V. Open: Monday–Saturday noon–11 p.m., Sunday 12:30–10 p.m.

Ye Olde Cheshire Cheese

$$ The City   Traditional British

Opened in 1667 and a one-time haunt of Samuel Johnson, Charles Dickens, and Fleet Street newspaper scandalmongers, Ye Olde Cheshire Cheese is London's most famous chophouse. The place contains six bars and two dining rooms and is perennially popular with families and tourists looking for some Olde London atmosphere. The house specialties include "ye famous pudding" (steak, kidney, mushrooms, and game), Scottish roast beef with Yorkshire pudding and horseradish sauce, and Dover sole. If those choices repulse the kids, they can choose sandwiches and salads.

Wine Office Court, 145 Fleet St., EC4. ☎ 020-7353-6170. Tube: Blackfriars (then a 10-minute walk north on New Bridge St. and west on Fleet St.). Main courses: £7–£15 ($12–$25). AE, DC, MC, V. Open: Daily noon–11 p.m.; Sunday noon–3:30 p.m.; drinks and bar snacks daily 11:30 a.m.–11 p.m.

Zafferano

$$$$ Knightsbridge   Italian

When you visit Zafferano, you've found the best Italian food in London, served in a quietly elegant, attitude-free restaurant. You may not find a table, though, unless you reserve in advance. The semolina pastas are perfectly cooked and come with various additions, such as sausage and fennel seeds, pheasant parcels with rosemary, sweet chili garlic and crab, or meat and black truffle. The main courses, such as roast rabbit with Parma ham and polenta, charcoal-grilled chicken, and tuna with rocket (arugula) and tomato salad, are deliciously simple and tender. For dessert, try the sublime lemon-and-marscapone tart.

15 Lowndes St., SW1. ☎ 020-7235-5800. Tube: Knightsbridge (then a 5-minute walk south on Lowndes St., 2 streets east of Sloane St.). Reservations are essential. Fixed-price menus: 2-course lunch £18.50 ($31), 3-course lunch £21.50 ($35); 2-course dinner £29.50 ($49), 3-course dinner £35.50 ($59). AE, MC, V. Open: Daily noon–2:30 p.m. and 7–11 p.m.

Chapter 15

Light Bites: Snacking and Eating on the Go

In This Chapter

▶ Grabbing a quick bite at sandwich shops, department stores, and "chippies"

▶ Finding the best spots for a spot of tea

*L*ondoners have a much less casual attitude toward food than Americans have. You won't see adults in London eating pretzels on the street or having a bite while traveling the tube. And you don't find street vendors peddling hot dogs and other foods from carts (though you may see a fast-food van or two near major attractions).

Even the most frenetic Londoner likes to eat a proper, civilized "sit down" meal. So what's a too-rushed tourist to do?

Well, you could take in the All-American fast-food restaurants sprouting up all over Central London, including **Burger King, KFC, Pizza Hut,** and **McDonald's.** They're familiar, and your kids may clamor for them. But you're in London, after all; to help you enjoy snacks and light meals the London way, this chapter offers some interesting alternatives.

Refer to the maps in Chapter 14 to find the locations of the eateries in this chapter.

Cut off the Crust: Sandwich Bars

Sandwiches are an English invention (supposedly of the earl of Sandwich), and sandwich bars are a faster and cheaper alternative to sit-down restaurants and pubs. Most open early for breakfast and close in the afternoon. You can usually eat at a counter or in booths, or you can take your sandwich and go to the nearest park for an alfresco lunch. Coffee, tea, and nonalcoholic beverages are sold.

Americans are sometimes confused by the way the English style their sandwiches. In general, the Brits use the word *mayonnaise* the way Americans use *salad. Tuna mayonnaise* or *egg mayonnaise* simply means "tuna salad" or "egg salad." The word *salad* is used in Britain to denote that lettuce and tomato have been added to a sandwich, as in "chicken with salad." At a sandwich bar, make sure that the sandwiches are *freshly cut* — meaning that they haven't been sitting around in the display case for hours.

The following sandwich bars are worth a bite:

- ✔ If you've dropped a bundle at Harrods and suddenly want to be frugal, just across the street is **Arco Bars of Knightsbridge** (46 Hans Crescent, SW1; ☎ 020-7584-6454; Tube: Knightsbridge); a smaller location is just around the corner from the Knightsbridge Tube station (16 Brompton Arcade; ☎ 020-7584-3136). Both are open Monday through Friday 7 a.m. to 6 p.m. and Saturday 8 a.m. to 6 p.m.

- ✔ Near Victoria Station, an imaginative variety of sandwiches is served at the **Capri Sandwich Bar** (16 Belgrave Rd., NW1; ☎ 020-7834-1989; Tube: Victoria), open daily 7:30 a.m. to 3:30 p.m.

- ✔ If you're in the vicinity of Euston Station, try the unpretentious but cheerful **Giovanni's Sandwich Bar** (152 North Gower St., at Euston Road; ☎ 020-7383-0531; Tube: Euston), open daily 6:30 a.m. to 4 p.m.

In addition, the **Pret à Manger** chain, found throughout Central London, offers reliably fresh, inventive sandwiches and fast counter service. The best one is at 77–78 St. Martin's Lane, WC2; ☎ 020-7379-5335; Tube: Leicester Sq.. It's open Monday through Thursday 7:30 a.m. to 9 p.m., Friday 7:30 a.m. to 11 p.m., Saturday 9 a.m. to 11 p.m., and Sunday 9 a.m. to 9 p.m.

Eat Hearty with Fish-and-Chips

In England a fish-and-chips place is called a *chippie*. At some chippies the food is wonderful, at others it's hideous. At the good places (the only ones I recommend), the fish (usually cod, haddock, or plaice) is fresh, the batter crisp, and the fries (chips) hand-cut. You can get tartar sauce, but the British also like to splash their fish-and-chips with malt vinegar. The following restaurants all have sit-down and takeaway service and welcome families with kids.

- ✔ **North Sea Fish Restaurant** (7–8 Leigh St., WC1; ☎ 020-7387-5892; Tube: Russell Sq.) is a restaurant (see Chapter 14), but it also offers takeaway service Monday through Saturday noon to 2:30 p.m. and 5:30 to 11:30 p.m. If the weather is good, take your meal over to Russell Square in the heart of Bloomsbury.

✔ **Rock & Sole Plaice** (47 Endell St., WC2; ☎ **020-7836-3785;** Tube: Covent Garden) offers all-day takeaway service as well as a place to sit down and eat amid the bustle of the Covent Garden Piazza (tables are available on the lower level). Because of its location, this chippie is the most expensive of the lot, so prepare to pay at least £8 ($13) for a meal. It's open Monday through Saturday 11:30 a.m. to 11:30 p.m. and Sunday 11:30 a.m. to 10 p.m.

✔ **Fryer's Delight** (19 Theobald's Rd., WC1; ☎ **020-7405-4114;** Tube: Chancery Lane or Holborn) is across from the Holborn Police Station. A plate of cod and chips is £4.25 ($7) if you eat in or £3.80 ($6) for takeout; takeaway is available the same hours that the restaurant is open, Monday through Saturday noon to 11 p.m.

✔ **Golden Hind** (73 Marylebone Lane, W1; ☎ **020-7486-3644;** Tube: Baker St. or Bond St.) is a few blocks south of Madame Tussaud's. It is another bargain chippie where an average meal costs £5 ($8); it's open Monday through Saturday noon to 3 p.m. and 6 to 10 p.m.

✔ **Sea-Shell** (49–51 Lisson Grove, NW1; ☎ **020-7723-8703;** Tube: Marylebone) is within easy walking distance west of Madame Tussaud's and is considered one of the best chippies in London. It's open Monday through Friday noon to 2 p.m. and 5:15 to 10:30 p.m.; it's open Saturday noon to 10:30 p.m., and Sunday noon to 2:30 p.m.

✔ **Seafresh Fish Restaurant** (80–81 Wilton Rd., SW1; (☎ **020-7828-0747;** Tube: Victoria), offers a good cod fillet and great chips for about £8 ($13). It's open Monday through Saturday noon to 10:30 p.m.

✔ **Costas Fish Restaurant** (18 Hillgate St., W8; ☎ **020-7727-4310;** Tube: Notting Hill Gate) is open Tuesday through Saturday noon to 2:30 p.m. and 5:30 to 10:30 p.m.

✔ **Geales** (2 Farmer St., W8; ☎ **020-7727-7969;** Tube: Notting Hill Gate) is open Tuesday through Saturday noon to 3 p.m. and 6 to 11 p.m.

The **Costas Fish Restaurant** and **Geales** are both good if you've been poking around the antiques and what-not stands along Portobello Road.

Chomp Where You Shop: Department Store Restaurants

London is a great city for shopping, and you may not want to tear yourself away from the stores in order to get a bite to eat. The answer is to grab a bite at a department store restaurant. These eateries are convenient, but they aren't cheap. Here are a few of the most noteworthy:

- ✔ **Fortnum & Mason** (181 Piccadilly, W1; ☎ **020-7734-8040;** Tube: Piccadilly) has three restaurants to choose from, the **Fountain** being the least expensive (see Chapter 14).

- ✔ **Harrods** (87–135 Brompton Rd., SW1; ☎ **020-7730-1234;** Tube: Knightsbridge), in addition to its ice-cream parlor and awe-inspiring Food Hall, offers its **Famous Deli Counter,** where you can perch on stools (no reservations) and pay too much for what's called "traditional Jewish food" but often isn't. It's open Monday through Saturday 10 a.m. to 6 p.m.

- ✔ **Harvey Nichols** (109–125 Knightsbridge, SW7; ☎ **020-7235-5250;** Tube: Knightsbridge) is another Knightsbridge emporium with a restaurant, the **Fifth Floor at Harvey Nichols.** It's open Monday through Friday noon to 3 p.m. and dinner 5:30 to 10 p.m., but eating there is pretty expensive. A better bet is the cafe, also on the fifth floor, where you can get a cup of tea and a salad or light meal; it's open Monday through Saturday 10 a.m. to 11 p.m. and Sunday 10 a.m. to 6 p.m. Like Harrods, Harvey Nichols has a fabulous food emporium where you can buy now and eat later.

Take a Spot of Tea

The stereotype is true in this case; Brits do drink tea. In fact, they drink 171 million cups per day (give or take a cup). Tea may be served fast-food style in paper cups, home-style in mugs, or more elegantly in bone china.

Taking tea at tea rooms and pâtisseries

In the following comfortable neighborhood tea rooms and pâtisseries, you can get a good cup of tea along with a scone or other pastry or a plate of tea sandwiches for about £3 to £10 ($5 to $17):

- ✔ **Beverly Hills Bakery** (3 Egerton Terrace, SW3; ☎ **020-7584-4401;** Tube: Knightsbridge) is noted for its muffins and serves light lunches from noon on. It's open Monday through Saturday 7:30 a.m. to 6 p.m. and Sunday 8 a.m. to 5:30 p.m.

- ✔ **Muffinski's** (5 King St., WC2; ☎ **020-7379-1525;** Tube: Leicester Sq.) offers a great lowfat, homemade, and vegetarian muffin. It's open Monday through Friday 8 a.m. to 7 p.m., Saturday 9 a.m. to 7 p.m., and Sunday 10 a.m. to 6 p.m.

- ✔ **Pâtisserie Cappucetto** (8 Moor St., W1; ☎ **020-7437-9472;** Tube: Leicester Sq.) serves breakfast, sandwiches, soups, and superb desserts daily 7:30 a.m. to 11:30 p.m.

- ✔ **Pâtisserie Deux Amis** (63 Judd St., WC1; ☎ **020-7383-7029;** Tube: Russell Sq.) is a good choice for a quick bite. It's open Monday through Friday 9 a.m. to 5:30 p.m. and Saturday and Sunday 9 a.m. to 1:30 p.m.

✔ **Pâtisserie Valerie** (44 Old Compton St., W1; ☎ **020-7437-3466;** Tube: Leicester Sq. or Tottenham Court Rd.) has been around since 1926 and serves a mouthwatering array of pastries, but expect to stand in line night or day. It's open Monday through Friday 8 a.m. to 8 p.m., Saturday 8 a.m. to 7 p.m., and Sunday 9:30 a.m. to 6 p.m.

Pâtisserie Valerie has two branches in Marylebone (one at 105 Marylebone High St., W1; ☎ **020-7935-6240;** Tube: Bond St. or Baker St., and the other near Regent's Park at 66 Portland Place, W1; ☎ **020-7631-0467;** Tube: Regent's Park). Both are open Monday through Friday 7:30 a.m. to 7 p.m., Saturday 8 a.m. to 7 p.m. and Sunday 9 a.m. to 6 p.m.

✔ **Richoux** has three old-fashioned tearooms situated in choice London locations. They serve food all day long, and they're kind to your budget: **Richoux-Knightsbridge,** (215 Brompton Rd., SW3; ☎ **020-7823-9971;** Tube: Knightsbridge); **Richoux-Mayfair,** (41a South Audley St., W1; ☎ **020-7629-5228;** Tube: Bond St. or Green Park); **Richoux-Piccadilly,** (172 Piccadilly, W1; ☎ **020-7493-2204;** Tube: Piccadilly Circus).

Enjoying a lavish high tea

A traditional afternoon English tea, which has cakes, sandwiches, and scones with clotted cream and jam, and which is "taken" in a high-toned hotel or restaurant, can be an afternoon affair or a nice alternative to lunch or dinner.

So what exactly, you ask, is the difference between afternoon tea and high tea?

✔ **Afternoon tea** is tea with cakes and/or sandwiches, served between 3 and 5 p.m.

✔ **High tea,** served from about 5 to 6 p.m., is a more elaborate affair: It's a light supper with a hot dish, followed by dessert and tea.

These rather lavish affairs are expensive. You're paying for the location, the food, and the service. But at any one of the following places, you can get a very proper traditional tea without busting the bank or breaking a tooth:

✔ The **Palm Court Lounge,** in the Park Lane Hotel (Piccadilly, W1; ☎ **020-7499-6321;** Tube: Hyde Park Corner or Green Park), requires that you make reservations. Teatime is daily 3:30 to 6:30 p.m., and afternoon tea runs £16 ($26).

✔ **Ritz Palm Court,** in the Ritz Hotel (Piccadilly, W1; ☎ **020-7493-8181;** Tube: Green Park), requires reservations at least 8 weeks in advance. Men must wear jackets and ties. Teatime is daily 2 to 6 p.m., and afternoon tea is £27 ($45).

✔ **Fortnum & Mason** (181 Piccadilly, W1; ☎ **020-7734-8040;** Tube: Piccadilly Circus) offers two venues for tea. **St. James's** serves tea Monday through Saturday 3 to 5:30 p.m. at a cost of £16.50 ($27); the **Fountain** serves tea Monday through Saturday 3 to 6 p.m. for £12.95 ($21).

✔ **Palm Court** at the Waldorf Meridien Hotel (Aldwych, WC2; ☎ **020-7836-2400;** Tube: Covent Garden) serves afternoon tea Monday through Friday 3 to 5:30 p.m., and holds tea dances (live music) on Saturdays 2:30 to 5:30 p.m. and Sundays 4 to 6:30 p.m. You must make reservations. If you want to attend the tea dance, men must wear jackets and ties. Afternoon tea runs £18 to £21 ($30 to $35), and the tea dance £25 to £28 ($41 to $46).

✔ **Georgian Restaurant,** on the fourth floor of Harrods (87–135 Brompton Rd., SW1; ☎ **020-7225-6800;** Tube: Knightsbridge), serves high tea Monday through Saturday 3:45 to 5:30 p.m. (last order). It runs £18 ($30) per person.

✔ **Lanesborough** hotel (Hyde Park Corner, SW1; ☎ **020-7259-5599;** Tube: Hyde Park Corner) requires reservations for high tea daily 3:30 to 5:30 p.m. (last order). It runs £20.50 ($34); the price goes up to £26.50 ($44) if you add strawberries and champagne.

Slurp Up Spaghetti and Other Pasta

If you're backpacking around London on a budget or you just want to save some dough, visit a pasta parlor for a plate of spaghetti or cannelloni. These places are open for lunch and dinner, and you can get a set-price meal for about £10 ($17).

Spaghetti House has several locations in Central London:

✔ 20 Sicilian Ave., WC1; ☎ **020-7405-5215;** Tube: Holborn

✔ 30 St. Martin's Lane, WC2; ☎ **020-7836-1626;** Tube: Leicester Sq.

✔ Called **Vecchia Milano,** 74 Welbeck St., W1; ☎ **020-7935-2371;** Tube: Bond St.

✔ Called **Zia Teresa,** 6 Hans Rd., SW3; ☎ **020-7589-7634;** Tube Knightsbridge

✔ 15 Goodge St., W1; ☎ **020-7636-6582;** Tube: Goodge St.

Children are welcome at all of the preceding locations; they have high chairs and reduced-price kids' portions.

Another big pasta chain, **Cafe Uno,** with more than 20 branches, also provides these items for kids. The most popular is at 5 Argyll St., W1; ☎ **020-7437-2503;** Tube: Oxford Circus.

Enjoying a long tradition: Meat pies and jellied eels

When Simple Simon met that pieman going to the fair, chances are the pieman was selling meat (and fish) pies along with jellied eels (who'd buy from a jellied eelman?). The eels in gelatin are served with mashed potatoes (*mash*) and a salty, parsley-based green gravy called *liquor.* The Brits have been enjoying this workers' fast food for centuries.

Unfortunately, many of the old *pie shops* in Central London have gone the way of the dinosaur; jellied eels are getting hard to find. But near the Tower of London, not far from London Bridge, is **Manze's** (87 Tower Bridge Rd., SE1; ☎ **020-7407-2985;** Tube: London Bridge), which keeps the old tradition alive. It's open Monday 11 a.m. to 2 p.m., Tuesday through Thursday 10:30 a.m. to 2 p.m., Friday 10 a.m. to 2:15 p.m., and Saturday 10 a.m. to 2:45 p.m.

Nip in for a Taste of Ice Cream

Nearly everybody likes ice cream, and **Häagen-Dazs** has several well-placed branches in tourist-heavy sections of London:

- 14 Leicester Sq.; ☎ **0207287-9577;** Tube: Leicester Sq.

- Unit 6, Covent Garden Piazza; ☎ **020-7240-0436;** Tube: Covent Garden

- 83 Gloucester Rd., SW7; ☎ **020-7373-9988;** Tube: Gloucester Rd

The preceding are no-smoking places that welcome kids, provide high chairs, and offer children's portions. They're open daily 10 a.m. to 11 p.m. (sometimes to midnight in summer).

More upscale (and overpriced) is **Harrods Ice-Cream Parlour & Crêperie** (87 Brompton Rd., SW1; ☎ **020-7225-6628;** Tube: Knightsbridge), on the fourth floor of Harrods department store. It's open Monday, Tuesday, and Saturday 10 a.m. to 5:30 p.m. and Wednesday through Friday 10 a.m. to 6:30 p.m.

Farther west in Bayswater, you can find **Winton's Soda Fountain** on the second floor of Whiteley's Shopping Centre (151 Queensway, W2; ☎ **020-7229-8489;** Tube: Bayswater or Queensway). It's open Monday through Thursday and Sunday 11 a.m. to 10 p.m. and Friday and Saturday 11 a.m. to 11 p.m.

Regent Milk Bar (362 Edgware Rd., W9; ☎ **020-7723-8669;** Tube: Edgware Rd.) is a classic 1950s milk bar offering about a dozen flavors of ice cream. You can also get sandwiches and snacks. Popular with families, it's open daily 7:30 a.m. to 5:30 p.m.

Take Advantage of a Nice Day: Eat Alfresco

London may not be the perfect city for picnics. Rain can quickly put a damper on a picnic hamper, and nothing is quite as unappetizing as a wet sandwich. But on days when the weather cooperates, you may enjoy packing up some sandwiches and heading to a green spot to eat.

Delis and sandwich shops or expensive **Fortnum & Mason** or **Harrods,** whose Food Halls are legendary (see Chapter 19), can provide all the necessary picnic provisions, if you're in the West End. In neighborhoods outside of the West End (South Kensington or Marylebone, for example), you can go into any supermarket and generally find packaged sandwiches, crisps (potato chips), fresh fruit, and drinks.

In the West End, the **Embankment Gardens** is a pretty picnic spot, looking out on the Thames. This flower-filled strip of green is next to the Embankment tube station, below the Savoy Hotel. You'll have to sit on benches instead of the grass and the traffic noise along the Embankment can be annoying, but it's still a nice place to know about.

Kensington Gardens (see Chapter 16) offers vast green lawns, frolicsome fountains, Kensington Palace, and the famous statue of Peter Pan. This spot is a favorite with children of all ages. The Princess Diana Memorial Playground, under construction at press time, should be open by the time this book is published. The park is close to all the great museums in South Ken. Adjacent **Hyde Park** is another lovely picnic site, particularly along the shores of Serpentine Lake. You can buy sandwiches and snacks at the **Dell Restaurant** (see Chapter 16) at the east end of the lake. In summer, bandstand concerts are given in the park.

The *royal parks* — **Green Park** and **St. James's Park** — are more sedate. You can choose to picnic on a lovely knoll and gaze upon Buckingham Palace.

Looking for an urban space good for people-watching and with great views across the river? Picnic on the South Bank of the Thames, along the riverside promenade close to Royal Festival Hall and the National Theatre. Beside the busy Thames are trees and flowers — but no lawns for stretching out.

Part V
Exploring London

"Hurry, Michael! The maids are about to perform the changing-of-the-towels."

In this part . . .

After you arrive at your hotel, unpack, freshen up, and maybe grab a bite to eat, the real fun begins: It's time to consult your worksheet of must-sees, examine a street map and an Underground map, and prepare for your first taste of all that London has to offer. This is always a magical moment, even if you're so jet-lagged you can't see straight.

Where to begin when there's so much to see and do? If you're traveling with children, have limited time, or are a bit nervous about exploring on your own, you'll find Chapter 18's list of guided tours helpful. Given London's size and complexity, a guided tour can be fun and relaxing even if you're a traveler who normally craves complete independence. On the other hand, if you're raring to see the top sights on your own, you'll find them — along with directions, open hours, and admission prices — in Chapter 16. One of the great things about London sightseeing, though, is that it can be as general or as specialized as you want. Browsing through Chapter 17's rundown of other intriguing museums and sights (not the most popular, but definitely worth considering), you'll see just how varied your choices are.

Check out Chapter 19 for some great tips on how to make the most of your shopping in London, as well as for specific stores to visit. In Chapter 20, you'll find some suggested London itineraries, sightseeing strategies that'll help you to see the top sights and enjoy the city on a *realistic* schedule. Finally, in Chapter 21, I wave you off at the train station and send you on your way to some fascinating places you can explore on a day trip. I think you'll love each and every one of them.

Chapter 16

Seeing the Best Sights

*H*ere's the big question: What do you want to see and enjoy while you're in London? The possibilities are endless: fabulous museums, important historic sites, beautiful parks and gardens, and grand churches. Advance planning will ease your stress and save time when you reach the great city. In this chapter, I give you the information you need to make your itinerary fit your interests, time, and energy level.

To help you find your way around London, I recommend that you augment my directions in this chapter with a *London A to Z* map. If you do get turned around, ask someone who's likely to know the area, such as a shop owner. Londoners are usually polite and helpful.

Because London is a city with 150 museums, 600 art galleries, and countless places of historic interest, you need to plan considerably for sightseeing. In this chapter, I index the best attractions by neighborhood and type.

I've arranged the sights of London in alphabetical order and added cross-references when necessary (also see the handy map "London's Top Sights"). I include a Kid Friendly icon next to attractions that children may enjoy.

If you're a disabled visitor on wheels, you can still visit every sight I mention in this chapter. Churches and museums provide wheelchair access, but it's a good idea to call first because you may need to use a special entrance. The paths in the royal parks are generally flat and paved.

The sights in this chapter are my roster of the most important, but they represent only the tip of the iceberg. Chapter 17 offers plenty more to choose from. To help in your planning, use the *Must-See Attractions* worksheet at the end of this guide. For useful information about planning workable itineraries based on the length of time you have, turn to Chapter 20 and the itinerary worksheet at the end of this book.

London's Top Sights

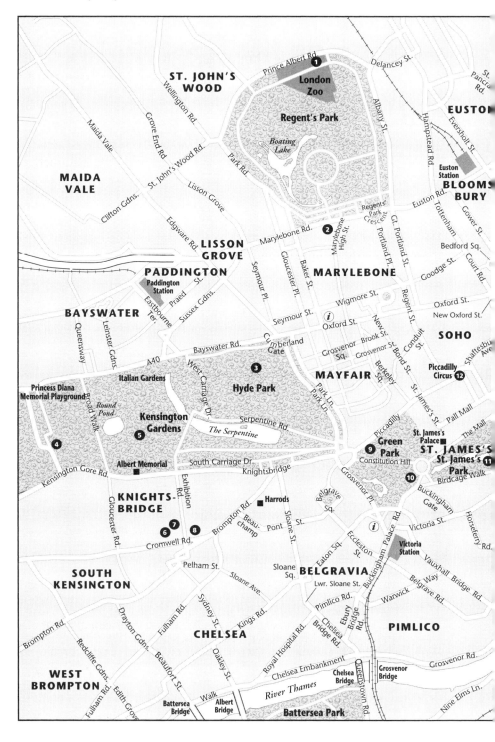

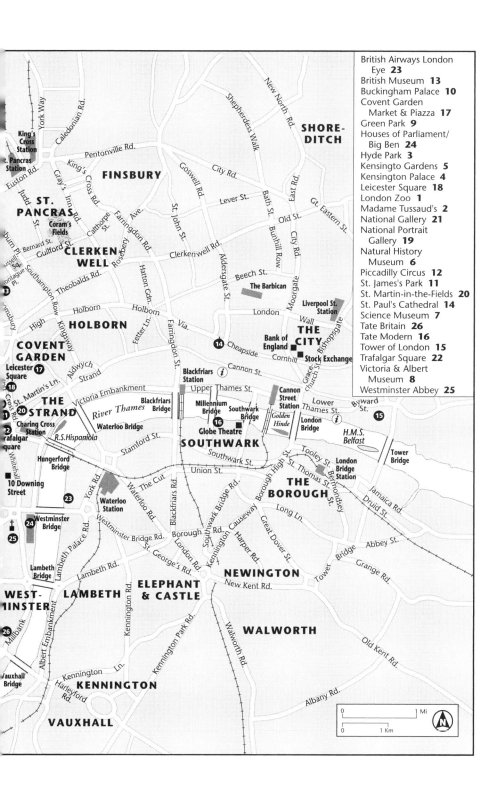

British Airways London
  Eye **23**
British Museum **13**
Buckingham Palace **10**
Covent Garden
  Market & Piazza **17**
Green Park **9**
Houses of Parliament/
  Big Ben **24**
Hyde Park **3**
Kensingto Gardens **5**
Kensington Palace **4**
Leicester Square **18**
London Zoo **1**
Madame Tussaud's **2**
National Gallery **21**
National Portrait
  Gallery **19**
Natural History
  Museum **6**
Piccadilly Circus **12**
St. James's Park **11**
St. Martin-in-the-Fields **20**
St. Paul's Cathedral **14**
Science Museum **7**
Tate Britain **26**
Tate Modern **16**
Tower of London **15**
Trafalgar Square **22**
Victoria & Albert
  Museum **8**
Westminster Abbey **25**

Index of Attractions by Neighborhood

Bloomsbury

British Museum
City of London
St. Paul's Cathedral
Tower of London

Covent Garden

Covent Garden Market
    and Piazza

Kensington and South Kensington

Kensington Gardens
Kensington Palace
Natural History Museum
Science Museum
Victoria & Albert Museum

Marylebone

London Zoo
Madame Tussaud's

Piccadilly Circus and Leicester Square

Piccadilly Circus
Leicester Square

Pimlico

Tate Britain

South Bank

British Airways London Eye
Tate Modern

St. James's

Buckingham Palace
National Gallery
National Portrait Gallery
St. James's Park and Green
    Park
Trafalgar Square

Westminster

Houses of Parliament and
    Big Ben
Hyde Park
Westminster Abbey

Index of Attractions by Type

Churches

St. Paul's Cathedral
Westminster Abbey

Museums

British Museum
Madame Tussaud's
National Gallery
National Portrait Gallery
Natural History Museum
Science Museum
Tate Britain
Tate Modern
Victoria & Albert Museum

Palaces and Other Historic Buildings

Buckingham Palace
Houses of Parliament and
    Big Ben
Kensington Palace
Tower of London

Parks, Gardens, and the Zoo

Hyde Park
Kensington Gardens
London Zoo
St. James's Park and Green
    Park

Squares	Viewpoints
Covent Garden Market and Piazza	British Airways London Eye
Leicester Square	
Piccadilly Circus	
Trafalgar Square	

The Top Attractions from A to Z

British Airways London Eye

South Bank

As a piece of fast-track engineering, the 400-foot-high London Eye millennium observation wheel is impressive. Having ridden on it, I know that the observation pod feels safe. Each glass-sided elliptical module holds about 25 passengers, with enough space so you can move about freely. Although most people stand the entire time, you can sit on the available bench if you prefer. Lasting about 30 minutes (equivalent to one rotation), the ride (or *flight* as they call it) is remarkably smooth — even on windy days riders don't feel any nerve-twittering shakes. Providing that the weather is good, the wheel provides unrivaled views of London. It's scheduled to remain in operation until at least 2003.

For the London Eye, I recommend that you reserve your place (with a specific entry time) before you arrive; if you're ticketless, you can line up for a ticket at the office right behind the wheel, but you may have to wait an hour or two.

Bridge Rd., SE1 (beside Westminster Bridge). ☎ *0870-500-0600 (advance credit-card booking; 50p/$1 booking fee added). Tube: Westminster (then a 5-minute walk south across Westminster Bridge; or Waterloo, then a 3-minute walk west along the riverside promenade). Admission: £7.95 ($13) adults, £6.45 ($11) seniors, £5.45 ($9) children under 16. Open: April–October daily 9 a.m.–10 p.m.; November–March daily 10 a.m.–6 p.m.*

British Museum

Bloomsbury

The British Museum ranks as the most visited attraction in London, with a splendid, wide-ranging collection of treasures from around the world.

Wandering through the museum's 94 galleries (see the map, "The British Museum"), you can't help but be struck by humanity's enduring spirit and creativity. Permanent displays of antiquities from Egypt, Western Asia, Greece, and Rome are on view, as well as prehistoric and Romano-British, Medieval, Renaissance, Modern, and Oriental collections.

The British Museum

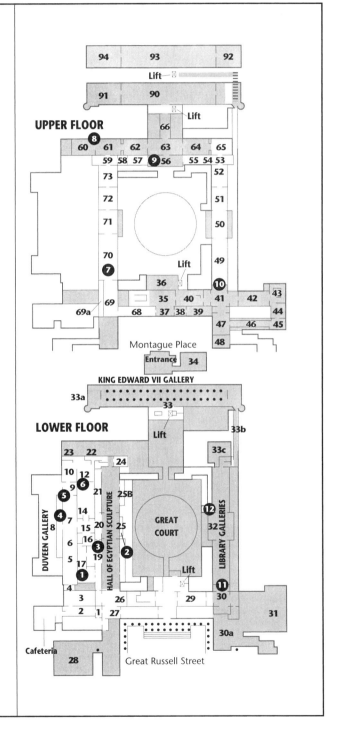

Highlights

Assyrian Transept **1**

Black Obelisk of
   Shalmaneser III **3**

Caryatid from the
   Erechtheum **5**

Library Galleries **12**

Manuscript Room **11**

Mausoleum of
   Halicarnassus **6**

Mummies **8**

Parthenon Sculptures
   (formerly called the
   Elgin Marbles) **4**

Portland Vase **7**

Rosetta Stone **2**

Standard of Ur **9**

Sutton-Hoo
   treasure hoard **10**

The most famous of the countless treasures are the superb **Parthenon Sculptures** (known in less politically correct times as the Elgin Marbles, brought to England in the 1801 by the seventh Lord Elgin) that once adorned the Parthenon in Athens (and which Greece desperately wants returned); the **Rosetta Stone** (which enabled archaeologists to decipher Egyptian hieroglyphics); the **Sutton Hoo Treasure,** an Anglo-Saxon burial ship, believed to be the tomb of a 7th-century East Anglian king; and **Lindow Man,** a well-preserved ancient corpse found in a bog.

The museum's ethnography collections are filled with marvelous curiosities: everything from a pair of polar-bear slacks worn by Eskimos to a Hawaiian god with a Mohawk haircut, found by Captain Cook and shipped back to London. In November 2000, the museum's Great Court reopened with a glass-and-steel roof designed by Lord Norman Foster. I suggest you give yourself at least 3 unhurried hours here: A restaurant (see Chapter 15) is open if you get hungry along the way. Weekday mornings are the best times to go and avoid big crowds.

To enhance your enjoyment and understanding of the **Parthenon Sculptures** (formerly known as the Elgin Marbles), pick up one of the sound guides available right outside Room 8, on the first floor, where the sculptures are exhibited. Payment is by contribution.

The incredible literary cache that was once housed in the British Museum (including its rare copy of the Magna Carta, the charter of liberties that was a forerunner to modern constitutions) has been moved to a remarkable new space in North London. For details, see the entry for the **British Library Exhibition Galleries** in Chapter 17.

If you have only limited time for the British Museum, consider taking one of the 90-minute highlight tours offered Monday through Saturday at 10:30 a.m. and 1 p.m. and Sunday at 12:30, 1:30, 2:30, and 4 p.m.; the cost is £7 ($12). The 60-minute focus tour covers some of the most important objects in the museum's collections Monday through Saturday at 3:15 p.m. and Sunday at 4:30 p.m.; the cost is £5 ($8). Tickets and information for both tours are available at the information desk.

Great Russell St., WC1, between Bloomsbury St. and Montgomery St. ☎ 020-7636-1555. Tube: Russell Sq. (then a 5-minute walk south on Montgomery St., along the west side of Russell Sq., to the museum entrance on Great Russell St.). Admission: Free. Most of the museum has wheelchair access via elevators; call for entrance information. Open: Monday–Saturday 10 a.m. –5 p.m., Sunday noon–6 p.m. Closed January 1, Good Friday, December 24–26.

Buckingham Palace

St. James's Park & Green Park

Since Victoria ascended the throne in 1837, Buckingham Palace has been the home of the British monarch and has hidden all the majesty, scandal, intrigue, triumph, tragedy, power, wealth, and tradition associated with the British monarchy.

An impressive early-18th-century pile, the palace was rebuilt in 1825 and further modified in 1913. Late July or early August (the dates change yearly) to September, when the royal family isn't in residence, you can buy a ticket to get a glimpse of the impressive staterooms used by Elizabeth II and the other royals. You don't get a guided palace tour; you can wander at your own speed through 18 rooms, most of them baroque, filled with some of the world's finest artworks. In these rooms the Queen receives guests on official occasions. You leave via the gardens where the Queen's famous garden parties are held each summer. Budget about 2 hours for your visit.

On Monday through Thursday throughout the year, you can visit the **Royal Mews,** one of the finest working stables in existence, where the magnificent Gold State Coach, used in every coronation since 1831, and other royal conveyances are housed (and horses stabled). The **Queen's Gallery,** which features changing exhibits of works from the Royal Collection, has been closed for refurbishment and will reopen in time for the Queen's Golden Jubilee in 2002.

Things came to a head for the scandal-ridden House of Windsor after Princess Diana's death, when national polls showed that the British public viewed the monarchy as aloof, out of touch, and something of a waste of taxpayers' money. The Queen was so shocked at the findings (so out of touch) that in February 1998, she hired a Washington-style spin doctor to boost the family's sagging ratings. By the way, did you know the Windsors are really the Saxe-Coburg-Gothas? They wisely changed their German name at the onset of World War I. And they have their own official Royal Web site: www.royal.gov.uk.

You can charge tickets for Buckingham Palace tours by calling the Visitor Office at ☎ **020-7321-2233.** Green Park also houses a ticket office, open daily July 29–October 1; it opens at 9 a.m. and closes at 4 p.m. or when the last ticket has been sold. Keep in mind that every visitor is allocated a specific time for entry into the palace, which is why phoning ahead for tickets is smart. You save yourself the time and bother of queuing for tickets outside the palace and then having to return hours later to get in. All phone-charged tickets are £10.50 ($17); at the ticket booth special rates are available for seniors, kids under 17, and families.

Buckingham Palace Rd., SW1. Palace Visitor Office and Royal Mews ☎ 020-7839-1377 (9:30 a.m.–5:30 p.m.) or 020-7799-2331 (24-hour recorded info). Tube: St. James's Park (then a 10-minute walk north on Queen Anne's Gate and west on Birdcage Walk to Buckingham Gate); or Green Park (walk directly south through the park). Admission: Palace, £10.50 ($17) adults, £8 ($13) seniors, £5 ($8) children under 17, £25.50 ($42) families (2 adults/2 children under 17). Royal Mews, £4.30 ($7) adults, £3.30 ($5) seniors, £2.10 ($4) children. Visitors with disabilities must prebook for palace visits; Royal Mews is wheelchair accessible. Open: Palace, July 29–October 1 (these are the dates for 2000; dates may change in 2001) daily 9:30 a.m.–4:30 p.m. Royal Mews, October–July Monday–Thursday noon–4 p.m.; August–September Monday–Thursday 10:30 a.m.–4:30 a.m.

Buckingham Palace's Changing of the Guard

St. James's Park

The ritual of the Changing of the Guard is carried out by the Foot Guards of the Household Division of the Army, the Queen's personal guard. The Old Guard forms in the palace forecourt before going off duty and handing everything over to the New Guard, which leaves Wellington Barracks at 11:27 a.m. precisely and marches to the palace via Birdcage Walk, usually accompanied by a band. The Guard consists of three officers and 40 men but is reduced when the Queen is away. The entire ceremony takes around 40 minutes. If you can't find a spot at the front of the railings of Buckingham Palace, you can see pretty well from the Victoria Memorial in front of the palace.

*The pageantry of the **Changing of the Guard** is no longer a daily occurrence. It takes place at 11:30 a.m. daily from April 1–early June and on alternate days thereafter. To avoid disappointment, call ☎ **020-7799-2331** to find out whether it's taking place on the day of your visit.*

If you miss the Changing of the Guard or it's not on the day you're there, you can still get an eyeful of London pageantry by attending the **Mounted Guard Changing Ceremony** at the Horse Guards Building in Whitehall.

*The **Mounted Guard Changing Ceremony** takes place daily Monday–Saturday at 11 a.m. and Sunday at 10 a.m. No ticket is required, but arrive early for a good view. To get there, take the tube to Charing Cross and walk south from Trafalgar Square along Whitehall (about a 5-minute walk); the Horse Guards Building will be on your right.*

Covent Garden Market and Piazza

Covent Garden, the West End

In 1970, the old market — the noisy, bustling public market where vendors hawked everything under the sun — moved out of Covent Garden and the area became the site of one of London's earliest and most successful urban recycling efforts. The market buildings now house dozens of enticing shops and eating and drinking places. The wrought-iron stalls in the former Flower Market are loaded with vendors. The piazza in front may be the most popular public gathering place outside of Trafalgar Square; it's always "heaving," as the Brits say. Covent Garden is also the home of the **Royal Opera House** (see Chapter 23) and two excellent museums: the **Transport Museum** and the **Theatre Museum** (see Chapter 17 for descriptions of both).

Tube: Covent Garden (when you come out of the tube stop you're in Covent Garden; the Market and piazza is a 1-minute walk south in a pedestrian-only zone).

Houses of Parliament and Big Ben

Westminster

Big Ben is synonymous with the city of London. The **Houses of Parliament,** situated along the Thames, house the landmark clock tower containing **Big Ben.** Designed by Sir Charles Barry and A.W.N. Pugin, the impressive Victorian buildings were completed in 1857. Covering approximately 8 acres, they occupy the site of an 11th-century palace of Edward the Confessor.

At one end (Old Palace Yard) is the **Jewel House,** built in 1366 and once the treasury house of Edward III, who reigned from 1327 to 1377. The best view is from Westminster Bridge, but if you prefer, you can sit in the **Stranger's Gallery** to hear Parliament debate.

Alas, overseas visitors can't tour the Houses of Parliament without going through an elaborate procedure weeks before the planned visit. If you're interested, find the details on the Web at www.parliament.uk.

Bridge St, and Parliament Sq, SW1. ☎ *020-7219-3000. Tube: Westminster (you can see the clock tower with Big Ben directly across Bridge St. when you exit the tube). Open: Stranger's Gallery, Monday–Wednesday 2:30–8:30 p.m., Thursday 11:30 a.m.–7:30 p.m., most Friday 9:30 a.m.–3 p.m. Parliament isn't in session late July to mid-October or on weekends. Admission: Free. For tickets, join the line at St. Stephen's entrance. Call the information Office at* ☎ *020-7219-4272 to find out whether the House will be in session and ask about the current topics for debate.*

Hyde Park

Westminster

With adjoining Kensington Gardens, Hyde Park offers 630 acres of lushly landscaped lawns, magnificent flower beds, avenues of trees, and a 41-acre lake known as the **Serpentine,** where you can row and sail model boats. **Rotten Row,** the park's famous 300-year-old riding track, was the country's first public road to be lit at night. At the northeastern tip, near Marble Arch, is **Speakers' Corner,** a famous Sunday-morning venting spot foranyone who wants to climb up on a soapbox. Hyde Park was once the private hunting domain of the royals, including Henry VIII, but now it's open to everyone and is one of the largest urban free parks in the world.

Big Ben tolls for thee

Big Ben is not the name of the clock tower or its clock. It's the name of the largest bell you hear booming in that famous hourly chime. Some believe that the bell was named after Sir Benjamin Hall, the commissioner of works when the bell was hung in 1859. Others maintain that Big Ben was named for a champion prizefighter of the time, Ben Gaunt.

The 5-ton clock mechanism housed in the 316-foot tower kept ticking until 1976, when it succumbed to "metal fatigue" and had to be repaired. At night, new energy-efficient lighting now gives the illuminated clock faces a greenish tinge. The light at the very top is lit when Parliament is in session.

Trivia buffs will be interested to know that the minute hand on each of the tower's four clocks is as large as a double-decker bus.

Free band concerts are held in the park's bandshell on Sundays and Bank Holidays May to August, and the Dell Restaurant (☎ **020-7706-0464**) at the east end of the Serpentine offers cafeteria-style food and drinks Monday through Friday 10 a.m. to 4 p.m. in winter (to 5 p.m. on weekends) and 10 a.m. to 6 p.m. in summer (to 7 p.m. on weekends). The park is a pleasant place for an hour's stroll, but staying longer is tempting.

Bounded by Knightsbridge to the south, Bayswater Rd. to the north, and Park Lane to the east. ☎ 020-7298-2100. Tube: Marble Arch or Lancaster Gate on the north side (the park is directly across Bayswater Rd.) or Hyde Park Corner in the southeast corner of the park. Open: Daily dawn–midnight.

Kensington Gardens

Kensington

Kensington Gardens adjoins Hyde Park west of the Serpentine. Children especially love the famous bronze statue of **Peter Pan,** located north of the Serpentine Bridge. Commissioned in 1912 by Peter Pan's creator, J. M. Barrie, the statue marks the spot where Peter Pan in the book *Peter Pan in Kensington Gardens* entered the gardens to get to his home on Serpentine island.

The park is also home to the **Albert Memorial,** an ornate neo-Gothic memorial honoring Queen Victoria's husband, Prince Albert; the lovely **Italian Gardens;** and the free **Serpentine Gallery** (☎ **020-7402-6075l**), which is gaining a reputation for showing cutting-edge art and is open daily (except December 24 to 27 and January 1) 10 a.m. to 6 p.m. The **Princess Diana Memorial Playground,** which should be open when you get to London, is in the northwestern corner of the park. If the weather is fine, give yourself enough time for a leisurely stroll — at least a couple of hours.

Bounded by Kensington Palace Gardens and Palace Green on the west, Bayswater Rd. on the north, Kensington Rd. and Kensington Gore on the south. ☎ 020-7298-2100. Tube: High Street Kensington (then a 10-minute walk east on Kensington High St.) or Queensway (which is directly across from the northwest corner of the park). Open: Daily dawn–midnight.

Kensington Palace

Kensington Gardens

Kensington Palace was used as a royal residence until 1760. Victoria was born in the palace and it was here, in 1837, that she was informed she was the new Queen of England (and could move to the grander Buckingham Palace). One wing of Kensington Palace was Princess Diana's London home after her divorce from Prince Charles.

The palace is home to Princess Margaret and the duke and duchess of Kent, so portions of it are closed off to visitors. But you can see the **State Apartments** and the **Royal Ceremonial Dress Collection**'s "Dressing for Royalty" exhibit, which takes visitors through the process of being presented at court, from the first visit to the tailor/dressmaker to the final bow or curtsy. Dresses worn by Queen Elizabeth II and Princess Diana are on display. The freshly restored **King's Apartment** features a magnificent collection of Old Masters. Give yourself about 1½ hours to view the palace.

For a pleasant and not-too-expensive tea or snack after visiting Kensington Palace, stop in at **The Orangery** (☎ **020-7376-0239**) in the gardens adjacent to the palace. It's open daily: March through October 10 a.m. to 6 p.m. and November through March 10 a.m. to 4 p.m.

The Broad Walk, Kensington Gardens, W8. ☎ 020-7937-7079. Tube: Queensway on the north side (then a 10-minute walk south through the park) or High Street Kensington on the southwest side (then a 10-minute walk through the park). Open: April–October daily 10 a.m.–6 p.m.; November–March Wednesday–Saturday 10 a.m.–6 p.m. Admission: £9.50 ($16) adults, £7.10 ($12) seniors/children 5 and older. There are some stairs, but it's still accessible for the disabled; call first.

Leicester Square

Soho

In the center of Leicester Square, surrounded by movie theaters and restaurants, is **Leicester Square Gardens,** with four corner gates named for William Hogarth, Sir Joshua Reynolds, John Hunter, and Sir Isaac Newton, all of whom once lived or worked in the area. There are also statues of **William Shakespeare** and **Charlie Chaplin,** a bow to theater and cinema. Leicester (pronounced *Lester*) Square is now a pedestrian zone (although it was once a dueling ground), and it's the heart of West End entertainment. A half-price ticket booth (no phone) for theater, opera, and dance is at the south end of the square (see Chapter 23). **Leicester Square** is a crowded place with a big-city buzz. Mimes, singers, and street entertainers of all kinds vie for the attention of passersby. You probably won't want to linger long, but it can be fun just walking by. If you're traveling with kids, this is one place with a rest room (coin-operated).

Tube: Leicester Sq. (take the Leicester Sq. exit and you're in the pedestrian-only zone that leads to the square).

London Zoo

Regent's Park, Marylebone

The 36-acre London Zoo is Britain's largest, with about 8,000 animals in various species-specific houses. The best attractions are the **Insect House** (bird-eating spiders); the **Reptile House** (huge monitor lizards and a 15-foot python); the **Sobell Pavilion for Apes and Monkeys;** and the **Lion Terraces.** In the **Moonlight World,** special lighting effects simulate night for the nocturnal creatures so you can see them in action. The newest exhibit, **Web of Life,** in the Millennium Conservatory, brings together special animal displays with interactive activities to show the interconnectedness and diversity of different life forms. The **Children's Zoo,** with interactive exhibits placed at low height, is designed for 4- to 8-year-olds. Many families budget almost an entire day for the zoo, I recommend that you give it at least 3 hours.

A fun way to arrive at the London Zoo is by water. The **London Waterbus Co.** (☎ 020-7482-2550) operates single and return trips in snug converted canalboats along the Regent's Canal from Warwick Crescent in Little Venice to Camden Lock Market. Take the tube to Warwick Avenue and walk south across Regent's Canal, and then you can see the moorings. Trips from both locks depart daily 10 a.m. to 5 p.m. The round-trip fare is £4 ($7).

At the north end of Regent's Park, NW1. ☎ 020-7722-3333. Tube: Regent's Park (then bus C2 north on Albany St. to Delaney St., 10 minutes, or a half-hour walk north through the park) or Camden Town (then a 12-minute walk south on Parkway, following the signs). Open: March–September daily 10 a.m.–5:30 p.m.; October–February daily 10 a.m. –4 p.m. Admission: £9 ($15) adults, £7.50 ($12) seniors/students/disabled, £7 ($12) children 4–14, families (2 adults/2 children) £26 ($43). Closed December 25.

Madame Tussaud's

Marylebone

People either love it or they hate it, but Madame Tussaud's wax museum is a world-famous tourist attraction. The question is: Do you want to pay the admission and devote the time to see the hauntingly lifelike figures? (Once in, you need at least 1½ hours to see everything.) The original moldings of members of the French court, to whom Mme. Tussaud had direct access (literally, because she made molds of their heads after they were guillotined during the French Revolution), are undeniably fascinating. And animatronic gadgetry makes the **Spirit of London** theme ride fun. But the **Chamber of Horrors** is definitely for the ghoulish. This is where you can see one of Jack the Ripper's victims lying in a pool of (wax?) blood and likenesses of mass murderers such as Gary Gilmore and Charles Manson. The **planetarium** (see Chapter 17) next door offers some better stars.

When it was announced that the Prince and Princess of Wales were separating, their mannequins at Madame Tussaud's were moved slightly apart. When they were divorced, Diana was moved to the end of the royal line, but since her death she has been brought down from the royal enclosure so people can get closer to her (or it, I should say).

Go early to beat the crowds; better still, reserve tickets 1 day in advance, then go straight to the head of the line. You can order tickets with a credit card by calling ☎ **020-7935-6861**.

Marylebone Rd., NW1. ☎ 020-7935-6861. Tube: Baker St. (then a 2-minute walk east on Marylebone Rd). Admission: £10.50 ($17) adults, £8 ($13) seniors, £7 ($11) children under 16; children under 4 not admitted. Combination tickets (including the planetarium): £12.75 ($21) adults, £8.50 ($14) children under 16. Open: June–August 9 a.m.–5:30 p.m. daily ; September–May 10 a.m.–5:30 p.m. Monday–Friday, Saturday–Sunday 9:20 a.m. –5:30 p.m. It's wheelchair accessible via elevators, but call first because only three chair-users are allowed in at a time.

National Gallery

Trafalgar Square, St. James's

If great art is your passion, then you'll think that the National Gallery is paradise. It houses one of the world's most comprehensive collections of British and European paintings. All the major schools from the 13th to the 20th century are represented, but the Italians get the bulk of the wall space, displaying the works of artists such as Leonardo da Vinci, Botticelli, and Raphael. The French Impressionist and post-Impressionist works by Monet, Manet, Seurat, Cézanne, Degas, and van Gogh are splendid. And since you're on English soil, check out at least a few of Turner's stunning seascapes, Constable's landscapes, and Reynolds' society portraits. And you won't want to miss the Rembrandts. Budget at least 2 hours to enjoy the gallery. A good restaurant for lunch, tea, or snacks is on the second floor.

Use the free computer information center to make the most of your time at the gallery. The center allows you to design a tour based on your preferences (a maximum of 10 paintings from the 2,200 entries) and prints out a customized tour map. You can also rent a portable audio tour guide for £3 ($5). Every painting has a reference number. Punch in the appropriate number to hear information about any work that interests you.

Trafalgar Sq., WC2. ☎ 020-7747-2885. Tube: Charing Cross (then a 2-minute walk north across Trafalgar Sq.). Admission: Free, but special exhibits may require paying a fee, usually around £5 ($8). Open: Monday–Tuesday and Thursday –Sunday 10 a.m.–6 p.m., Wednesday 10 a.m.–9 p.m. Closed January 1, Good Friday, December 24–26. The entire museum is wheelchair accessible.

National Portrait Gallery

Trafalgar Square, St. James's

What do these people all have in common: Sir Walter Raleigh, Shakespeare (wearing a gold earring), Queen Elizabeth I, the Brontë sisters, Winston Churchill, Oscar Wilde, Noël Coward, Mick Jagger, and Princess Di? You can find lifelike portraits of them, as well as nearly every other famous English face, at the National Portrait Gallery. The portraits are arranged in chronological order. The earliest portraits are in the **Tudor Gallery;** portraits from the 1960s to the 1980s are displayed in the **Balcony Gallery.** The rooftop cafe provides great West End views. Plan on spending at least 2 hours here; it's easy to get sidetracked.

St. Martin's Place (off Trafalgar Sq. behind the National Gallery), WC2. ☎ 020-7306-0055. Tube: Leiceister Sq. (then a 2-minute walk south on Charing Cross Rd.). Admission: Free; audio tour £3 ($5). Open: Monday 11 a.m.–6 p.m., Tuesday–Saturday 10 a.m. –6 p.m., Sunday noon–6 p.m. All but the landing galleries are wheelchair accessible; call first for entry instructions.

Natural History Museum

South Kensington

Is it plant, animal, or mineral? You'll know at the Natural History Museum, the home of the national collections of living and fossil plants, animals, and minerals. You can find magnificent specimens and exciting displays relating to natural history. The most popular attraction in this enormous Victorian-era museum is the huge dinosaur exhibit, which includes 14 complete skeletons and a trio of full-size robotic Deinonychus lunching on a freshly killed Tenontosaurus. **Creepy Crawlies** is another popular kid pleaser. The sparkling gems and crystrals in the **Mineral Gallery** are dazzling, and in the **Meteorite Pavilion** you can see fragments of rock that have crashed into the earth from the farthest reaches of the galaxy. There's enough here to keep you occupied for at least 2 hours.

Cromwell Rd., SW7. ☎ *020-7942-5000. Tube: South Kensington (the tube station is on the corner of Cromwell Road and Exhibition Rd., at the corner of the museum). Admission: £6.50 ($11) adults; £3.20 ($5) seniors/students, £16 ($26) families (2 adults/4 children). Free admission Monday–Friday after 4:30 p.m. and Saturday–Sunday after 5 p.m. Open: Monday–Saturday 10 a.m.–5:50 p.m., Sunday 11 a.m.–5:50 p.m. Nearly all the galleries are flat or ramped for wheelchair users; call for instructions on entering the building.*

Piccadilly Circus

The West End

Nearly everyone who visits London wants to see Piccadilly Circus, which lies at the beginning of the West End. Piccadilly Circus, along with neighboring Leicester Square, is London's equivalent to New York's Times Square. Around the landmark statue of Eros, jostling crowds pack the pavements and an international contingent of teens heads for the **Pepsi Trocadero,** the area's mega-entertainment center (see Chapter 17). Regent Street at the west side of the circus and Piccadilly at the south end are major shopping streets (see Chapter 19). Piccadilly, traditionally the western road out of town, was named for the "picadil," a ruffled collar created by a 17th-century tailor named Robert Baker.

Tube: Piccadilly Circus.

Science Museum

South Kensington

The Science Museum is a popular tourist attraction that covers the history and development of science, medicine, and technology. The state-of-the-art interactive displays are brain-tickling and fun for 7- to 12-year-olds, and the **Garden Galleries** provide construction areas, sound-and-light shows, and games for younger kids. The fascinating displays include the

Apollo 10 space module, an 1813 steam locomotive, Fox Talbot's first camera, and Edison'original phonograph. The **Wellcome Wing,** which opened in summer 2000, is devoted to contemporary science and has an IMAX 3-D film theater. Give yourself at least 2 hours, more if you're going to see the film.

Exhibition Rd., London SW7. ☎ *020-7942-4454. Tube: South Kensington (a sign-posted exit in the Underground station goes directly to the museum). Admission: £6.50 ($11) adults; children under 16 free. Free admission after 4:30 p.m. Open: Daily 10 a.m.–6 p.m. Closed December 24–26. All galleries are wheelchair accessible.*

St. James's Park and Green Park

Westminster

These two adjoining royal parks were acquired by Henry VIII in the early 16th century. St James's Park, the prettier of the two, was landscaped in 1827 by John Nash in a picturesque English style with an ornamental lake and promenades. **The Mall,** the processional route between Buckingham Palace and Whitehall and Horse Guards Parade, is the route used for major ceremonial occasions. Prince Charles and his sons live at **St. James's Palace,** and **Clarence House,** next door, is the residence of the Queen Mum. The residences — neither of which is open to visitors — are between The Mall and **Pall Mall** (pronounced *Pell Mell*), a broad avenue running from Trafalgar Square to St. James's Palace.

Green Park is called Green Park because it's the only royal park without any flower beds. Why? A popular story has it that one day, as Charles II was walking through the park with his entourage, he announced he wa s going to pick a flower and give it to the most beautiful lady present. This happened to be a milkmaid and not Queen Catherine, his wife. The queen was livid and ordered that all flowers be removed from the park (a horticultural version of "Off with their heads!").

Bounded by Piccadilly to the north, Regent St. to the east, Birdcage Walk and Buckingham Palace Rd. to the south, and Grosvenor Place to the west. ☎ *020-7930-1793. Tube: Green Park (the tube station is right at the northeast corner of Green Park) or St. James's Park (then a 5-minute walk north on Queen Anne's Gate to Birdcage Walk, the southern perimeter of St. James's Park). Open: Daily dawn–dusk.*

St. Paul's Cathedral

The City of London

Many will want to see St. Paul's simply because it was here that Lady Diana Spencer wed Prince Charles in what was billed as "the fairy-tale wedding of the century." You can see the entire cathedral in an hour or less. (See the map "St. Paul's Cathedral.") By the time you get to London, St. Paul's will be linked to the Tate Modern by the pedestrian-only **Millennium Bridge,** designed by Lord Norman Foster.

St. Paul's Cathedral

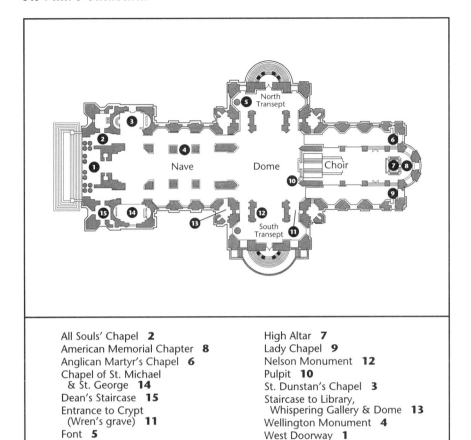

All Souls' Chapel **2**	High Altar **7**
American Memorial Chapter **8**	Lady Chapel **9**
Anglican Martyr's Chapel **6**	Nelson Monument **12**
Chapel of St. Michael	Pulpit **10**
& St. George **14**	St. Dunstan's Chapel **3**
Dean's Staircase **15**	Staircase to Library,
Entrance to Crypt	Whispering Gallery & Dome **13**
(Wren's grave) **11**	Wellington Monument **4**
Font **5**	West Doorway **1**

The great architect Christopher Wren was called on to design St. Paul's, a huge and harmonious Renaissance-leaning-toward-baroque building, after the Great Fire of 1666 destroyed the city's old cathedral. Nazi bombing raids wiped out the surrounding area, so Wren's masterpiece, capped by the most famous dome in London, rises majestically above a crowded sea of undistinguished office buildings. The exceptionally beautiful choir stalls carved by Grinling Gibbons are the only impressive art inside.

Christopher Wren is buried in the crypt, and his epitaph, on the floor below the dome, reads "LECTOR, SI MONUMENTUM REQUIRIS, CIRCUM-SPICE" (Reader, if you seek his monument, look around you). His companions in the crypt include Britain's famed heroes, the duke of Wellington, who defeated Napoleon at Waterloo, and Admiral Lord Nelson, who took down the French at Trafalgar during the same war.

You can climb up to the **Whispering Gallery** for a bit of acoustical fun or gasp your way up to the very top for a breathtaking view of London.

St. Paul's Churchyard, Ludgate Hill, EC4. ☎ 020-7246-8348. Tube: St. Paul's (then a 5-minute walk west on Ludgate to cathedral entrance on St. Paul's Churchyard). Admission: £5 ($8) adults, £4 ($6.50) seniors/students, £2.50 ($4) children. Tours: Guided tours £2.50 ($4) adults, £2 ($3) seniors, £1 ($1.65) children under 10. Audio tours £3 ($5) adults, £2.50 ($4) seniors, £7 ($12) families. Open: Monday–Saturday 8:30 a.m.–4 p.m.; galleries Monday–Saturday 9:30 a.m.–4 p.m.; no sightseeing on Sunday (services only). It's wheelchair accessible by service entrance near the South Transept; ring the bell for assistance.

Tate Britain

Pimlico

The Tate Gallery took this name to distinguish it from its new counterpart, Tate Modern, which opened in May 2000. Tate Britain retains the older (pre-20th century) collections of exclusively British art. Among the masterpieces on display are dreamy works by the British pre-Raphaelites, the celestial visions of William Blake, bawdy satirical works by William Hogarth, genteel portraits by Sir Joshua Reynolds, bucolic landscapes by John Constable, and the shimmering seascapes of J.M.W. Turner. Plan on spending at least 2 hours here. A restaurant and a café are on the lower level.

Millbank, Pimlico SW1. ☎ 020-7887-8000. Tube: Pimlico (then a 10-minute walk south on Vauxhall Bridge Rd. to the river and north on Millbank to the museum entrance). Bus: For a more scenic route, take bus 77A, which runs south along The Strand and Whitehall to the museum entrance on Millbank. Admission: Free; varying admission fees for special exhibits (for advance ticket sales call ☎ 020-7420-0055); audio tours £3 ($5). Open: Daily 10 a.m.–5:50 p.m. Most of the galleries are wheelchair accessible, but call first for details on entry.

Tate Modern

Bankside

The former Bankside Power Station is the setting for the fabulous Tate Modern, which opened in May 2000. Considered one of the three or four top modern art museums in the world, it houses the Tate's collection of international 20th-century art, displaying major works by some of the most influential artists of this century: Picasso, Matisse, Dalí, Duchamp, Moore, and Bacon among them. A gallery for the 21st-century collection exhibits new art as it's created. For fans of contemporary art and architecture, this new star on the London art scene isn't to be missed. Plan on spending at least 2 hours. By the time you get to London, the museum will be linked to St. Paul's Cathedral by the pedestrian-only **Millennium Bridge,** designed by Lord Norman Foster.

25 Sumner St., SE1. ☎ 020-7887-8000. Tube: Southwark (then a 10-minute walk north along Blackfriars Rd. and east along the riverside promenade) or Blackfriars (then a10-minute walk south across Blackfriars Bridge). Admission: Free; special exhibits may require paying a fee. Open: Monday–Thursday 10 a.m.–6 p.m.; Friday–Saturday 10 a.m.–10 p.m.

That's the way the bridge bounces

Lord Norman Foster's $28-million **Millennium Bridge** linking Tate Modern to St. Paul's got off to a very wobbly start when it opened on June 10, 2000. There was only one slight problem with this much-publicized, highly visible, high-tech pedestrian span: It swayed and bounced so much that people couldn't walk on it. Seems that the "untraditional" suspension system of aluminum and stainless steel wasn't doing in real life what it had done on paper. The bridge had to be closed immediately to determine whether major repairs were needed; however, it should be open and less bouncy when you get to London. Acerbic Londoners immediately compared the bridge fiasco to another major millennial dud: the Dome, which didn't open on time and has had dismal attendance.

Tower of London

The City of London

The Tower of London offers enough to keep you captivated for a good 3 to 4 hours, but *make sure* that you save time for the **Crown Jewels,** which include the largest diamond in the world (the 530-carat Star of Africa) and other breathtaking gems set into royal robes, swords, sceptres, and crowns. No trip to London would be complete without a viewing of this exhibit.

The Tower of London (see the map, "Tower of London") is the city's best-known and oldest historic site. It was built by William the Conqueror in 1066 and served as his fortress and later as a prison, holding famous captives such as Sir Walter Raleigh and Princess Elizabeth I. Ann Boleyn and Catherine Howard (two of the eight wives of Henry VIII), the 9-day queen Lady Jane Grey, and Sir Thomas More were among those who got their heads chopped off on **Tower Green.** According to Shakespeare, the two little princes (the sons of Edward IV) were murdered in the **Bloody Tower** by henchmen of Richard III — but the story is controversial among modern historians.

You can attend the nightly **Ceremony of the Keys,** the ceremonial locking-up of the Tower by the Yeoman Warders. For free tickets, write to the Ceremony of the Keys, Waterloo Block, Tower of London, London EC3N 4AB, and request a specific date but also list alternate dates. At least 6 weeks' notice is required. All requests must be accompanied by a self-addressed stamped envelope (British stamps only) or two International Reply Coupons. If you have a ticket, a Yeoman Warder will admit you at 9:35 p.m.

Tower of London

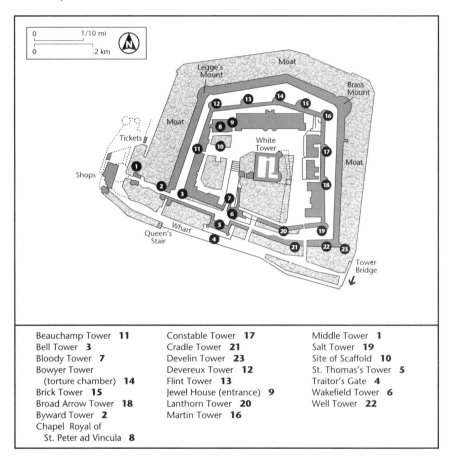

Beauchamp Tower **11**	Constable Tower **17**	Middle Tower **1**
Bell Tower **3**	Cradle Tower **21**	Salt Tower **19**
Bloody Tower **7**	Develin Tower **23**	Site of Scaffold **10**
Bowyer Tower	Devereux Tower **12**	St. Thomas's Tower **5**
(torture chamber) **14**	Flint Tower **13**	Traitor's Gate **4**
Brick Tower **15**	Jewel House (entrance) **9**	Wakefield Tower **6**
Broad Arrow Tower **18**	Lanthorn Tower **20**	Well Tower **22**
Byward Tower **2**	Martin Tower **16**	
Chapel Royal of		
St. Peter ad Vincula **8**		

Huge black ravens hop around the grounds of the Tower of London. An old legend says that the world will end when the ravens leave the tower. Their wings have been clipped as a precaution.

Tower Hill, EC3. ☎ *020-7709-0765. Tube: Tower Hill (then a 5-minute walk west and south on Tower Hill). Bus: You can take the eastbound bus 25 from Marble Arch, Oxford Circus, or St. Paul's; it stops at Tower Hill, north of the entrance. Admission: £11 ($18) adults, £8.30 ($14) seniors/students, £7.30 ($12) children 5–15, £33 ($55) families (no more than 2 adults). Tours: Free 1-hour guided tours of the entire compound are given by the Yeoman Warders (also known as "Beefeaters") every half hour, starting at 9:30 a.m. (Sunday 10 a.m.) from the Middle Tower near the main entrance. The last guided walk starts about 3:30 p.m. in summer or 2:30 p.m. in winter; weather permitting. Open: March–October Monday–Saturday 9 a.m.–5 p.m., Sunday 10 a.m.–4 p.m.; November–February Tuesday–Saturday 9 a.m.–4 p.m., Sunday 10 a.m.–4 p.m. Closed January 1 and December 24–26. Wheelchair access onto the grounds is available, but many of the historic buildings can't accommodate wheelchairs.*

In the bad old days, important prisoners often arrived at the tower by boat. You can, too. **Catamaran Cruises (☎ 020-7987-1185)** *provides daily ferry service between Embankment Pier (Tube: Embankment) and Tower Pier. A round-trip ticket is £6.10 ($10) adults and £3.70 ($6) children under 16. See Chapter 18 for more options.*

Trafalgar Square

St. James's

Trafalgar Square is a roaringly busy traffic interchange surrounded by historic buildings, such as St. Martin-in-the-Fields church and the National Gallery. Besides being a major tourist attraction, Trafalgar Square is the site of many large gatherings, such as political demonstrations and holiday celebrations. The square honors military hero Horatio, Viscount Nelson (1758–1805), who lost his life at the Battle of Trafalgar. **Nelson's Column,** with fountains and four bronze lions at its base, rises 145 feet above the square. At the top, a 14-foot-high statue of Nelson (5 feet 4 inches tall in real life) looks commandingly toward **Admiralty Arch,** passed through by state and royal processions between Buckingham Palace and St. Paul's Cathedral.

You don't need more than a few minutes to take in the square; the National Gallery across the street and the National Portrait Gallery behind it will take up more of your time. The neoclassical church on the northeast corner of Trafalgar Square was the precursor for dozens of similar-looking churches throughout colonial New England. Designed by James Gibbs, a disciple of Christopher Wren, **St. Martin-in-the-Fields** (**☎ 020-7930-0089**) was completed in 1726; the 185-foot spire was added about 100 years later. The **Academy of St. Martin-in-the-Fields,** a famous ensemble, frequently performs here. Lunchtime concerts are held on Monday, Tuesday, and Friday at 1 p.m., and evening concerts are held Thursday through Saturday at 7:30 p.m. Concert tickets are £6 to £15 ($10 to $24). For reservations by credit card, call **☎ 020-7839-8362.** The church is open Monday through Saturday 10 a.m. to 6 p.m. and Sunday noon to 6 p.m.; admission is free.

Café-in-the-Crypt (☎ 020-7839-4342), one of the West End's most pleasant restaurants, is in the crypt of St. Martin-in-the-Fields and serves up helpings of traditional English home cooking daily 10 a.m. to 8 p.m. The busy crypt also contains the **London Brass Rubbing Centre (☎ 020-7437-6023),** which provides paper, metallic waxes, and instructions on how to rub your own replica of historic brasses. Prices range from £2 to £15 ($3 to $24). This is great diversion for kids 10 and up. It's open Monday through Saturday 10a.m. to 6 p.m. and Sunday noon to 6.p.m.

Bounded on the north by Trafalgar, on the west by Cockspur St., and on the east by Whitehall. Tube: Charing Cross (there's an exit from the Underground station to the square).

Victoria & Albert Museum

South Kensington

The Victoria & Albert (known as the V&A) is the national museum of art and design. In the 145 galleries filled with fine and decorative arts from around the world, you can find superbly decorated period rooms, a fashion collection spanning 400 years of European designs, Raphael cartoons (designs for tapestries in the Sistine Chapel), the Silver Galleries, and the largest assemblage of Renaissance sculpture outside Italy and Indian art outside India. The museum's newest addition, the Canon Photography Gallery, shows work by celebrated photographers. Allow at least 2 hours just to cover the basics.

Cromwell Rd., SW7. ☎ ***020-7942-2000****. Tube: South Kensington (the museum is across from the Underground station). Admission: £5 ($8) adults, £3 ($5) seniors; free for students with ID and children under 18. Open: Daily 10 a.m.–5:45 p.m. Closed December 24–26. It's wheelchair accessible (about 95 percent of the exhibits are step free).*

Westminster Abbey

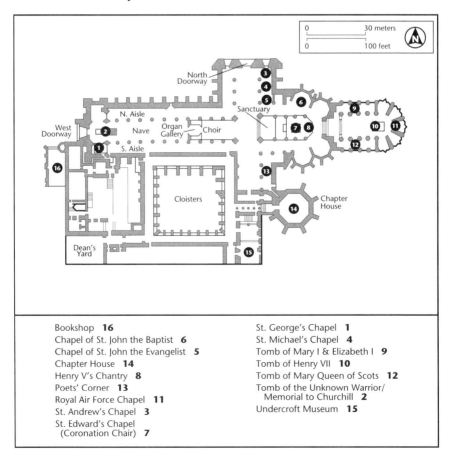

Bookshop **16**
Chapel of St. John the Baptist **6**
Chapel of St. John the Evangelist **5**
Chapter House **14**
Henry V's Chantry **8**
Poets' Corner **13**
Royal Air Force Chapel **11**
St. Andrew's Chapel **3**
St. Edward's Chapel
  (Coronation Chair) **7**

St. George's Chapel **1**
St. Michael's Chapel **4**
Tomb of Mary I & Elizabeth I **9**
Tomb of Henry VII **10**
Tomb of Mary Queen of Scots **12**
Tomb of the Unknown Warrior/
  Memorial to Churchill **2**
Undercroft Museum **15**

Westminster Abbey

Westminster

The Gothic and grand Westminster Abbey is one of London's most important historic sites. (See the map, "Westminster Abbey.") It's within walking distance of the Houses of Parliament. The present abbey dates mostly from the 13th and 14th centuries, but there's been a church on this site for over a thousand years. Since 1066, when William the Conquerer became the first English monarch to be crowned here, every successive British sovereign except for two (Edward V and Edward VIII) has sat on the **Coronation Chair** to receive the crown and sceptre.In the **Royal Chapels,** you can see the **chapel of Henry VII,** with its delicate fan vaulting, and the **tomb of Queen Elizabeth I,** who was buried in the same vault as her Catholic half-sister, Mary I, and not far from her rival Mary Queen of Scots. In **Poets' Corner,** some of England's greatest writers (including Chaucer, Dickens, and Thomas Hardy) are interred or memorialized. You may remember that in September 1997, the abbey was the site of Princess Diana's funeral.

In 1995, 100 years after his release from Reading Gaol (where he was imprisoned after his trial for "gross indecency"), the immortal genius of **Oscar Wilde** was finally recognized by the Church of England with an abstract-design blue memorial window at Westminster Abbey. But since his name is nowhere to be seen, it's the kind of dubious honor that would no doubt provoke a witty quip from the great playwright. Maybe something like, "Clear glass wasn't good enough for me; it had to be stained."

Broad Sanctuary, SW1. ☎ 020-7222-5152. Tube: Westminster (then a 3-minute walk west following Parliament Sq. to Broad Sanctuary). Bus: The 77A going south along The Strand, Whitehall, and Millbank stops near the Houses of Parliament, near the Abbey. Admission: Abbey and Royal Chapels, £5 ($8) adults, £3 ($5) seniors/students, £2 ($3.25) children 11–16, families (2 adults, 2 children) £10 ($17). Chapter House, Pyx Chamber and Museum, free with Super Tour (see following information on guided tours) or £2.50 ($4) adults, £1.30 ($2) children. Guided tours: Led by an Abbey Verger £8 ($13); guided Super Tours £3 ($5); call for times; tickets for tours at Enquiry Desk in the Abbey. Open: Cathedral, Monday–Friday 9 a.m.–4:45 p.m. (last admission 3:45 p.m.), Saturday 9 a.m.–2:45 p.m., late opening Wednesday 6 p.m.–7:45 p.m.; no sightseeing on Sunday (services only). Cloisters, daily 10 a.m.–6 p.m. Chapter House, Pyx Chamber, and Museum, daily 10:30 a.m.–4 p.m. College Garden, Tuesday and Thursday 10 a.m.–6 p.m. Ramped wheelchair access is available via the Cloisters; ring the bell for assistance.

Chapter 17

More Cool Things to See and Do

*1*f you think you've "done" London because you've been to see the Queen (or her house, anyway), watched the Changing of the Guard, imagined yourself a wronged royal in the Tower of London, feasted your eyes on the Parthenon Sculptures and other great works of art in the British Museum, and wandered through Westminster Abbey and St. Paul's Cathedral, you may need to think again. London is a treasure trove of masterpieces, large and small: glorious gardens, magnificent mansions, singular museums, ancient corners, historic churches, and many themed attractions that fill you in on the history and flavor of majestic London Town. This chapter highlights only a few of the many activities you can find to tickle your fancy and make the most of your visit. (See the map "More London Sights.")

I also cover four major attractions not in Central London but near it and easily accessible by tube or train — **Hampstead Heath, Hampton Court Palace, Kew Gardens, and Windsor Castle.** You can spend the better part of a day visiting them, but the sights are well worth the time spent, and you can easily get back to Central London in time for a play or concert in the evening.

If you're the "see everything" type, consider purchasing the *London Go See Card,* a money-saving pass that gets you in to 17 museums and galleries. Adult cards cost £16 ($26) for 3 days or £26 ($43) for 7 days; a family pass (up to two adults and four children 16 or under) is £32 ($53) for 3 days or £50 ($82) for 7 days. The cards are sold at the Britain Visitor Centre, 1 Regent St., SW1 (Tube: Piccadilly Circus); the Tourist Information Centre in the forecourt of Victoria Station (Tube: Victoria); and the London Visitor Centre at Waterloo International (Tube: Waterloo). You can also buy them at all the participating museums and galleries, including the Victoria & Albert Museum, Museum of London, London Transport Museum, Design Museum, Imperial War Museum, Hayward Gallery, and Natural History Museum.

More London Sights

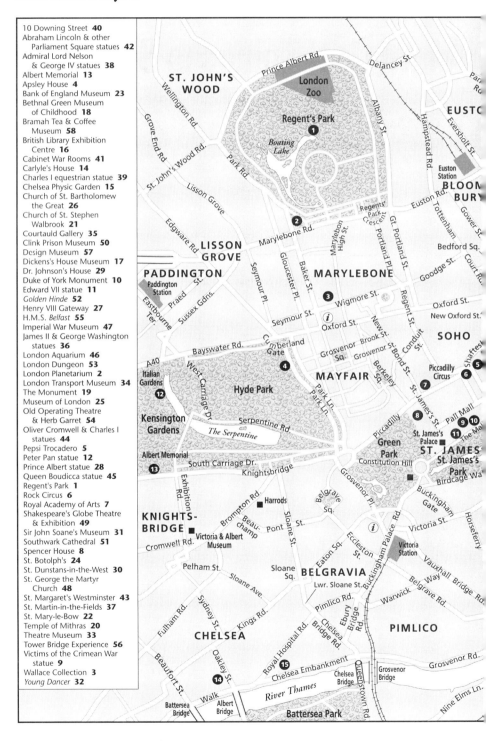

10 Downing Street **40**
Abraham Lincoln & other
  Parliament Square statues **42**
Admiral Lord Nelson
  & George IV statues **38**
Albert Memorial **13**
Apsley House **4**
Bank of England Museum **23**
Bethnal Green Museum
  of Childhood **18**
Bramah Tea & Coffee
  Museum **58**
British Library Exhibition
  Centre **16**
Cabinet War Rooms **41**
Carlyle's House **14**
Charles I equestrian statue **39**
Chelsea Physic Garden **15**
Church of St. Bartholomew
  the Great **26**
Church of St. Stephen
  Walbrook **21**
Courtauld Gallery **35**
Clink Prison Museum **50**
Design Museum **57**
Dickens's House Museum **17**
Dr. Johnson's House **29**
Duke of York Monument **10**
Edward VII statue **11**
Golden Hinde **52**
Henry VIII Gateway **27**
H.M.S. *Belfast* **55**
Imperial War Museum **47**
James II & George Washington
  statues **36**
London Aquarium **46**
London Dungeon **53**
London Planetarium **2**
London Transport Museum **34**
The Monument **19**
Museum of London **25**
Old Operating Theatre
  & Herb Garret **54**
Oliver Cromwell & Charles I
  statues **44**
Pepsi Trocadero **5**
Peter Pan statue **12**
Prince Albert statue **28**
Queen Boudicca statue **45**
Regent's Park **1**
Rock Circus **6**
Royal Academy of Arts **7**
Shakespeare's Globe Theatre
  & Exhibition **49**
Sir John Soane's Museum **31**
Southwark Cathedral **51**
Spencer House **8**
St. Botolph's **24**
St. Dunstans-in-the-West **30**
St. George the Martyr
  Church **48**
St. Margaret's Westminster **43**
St. Martin-in-the-Fields **37**
St. Mary-le-Bow **22**
Temple of Mithras **20**
Theatre Museum **33**
Tower Bridge Experience **56**
Victims of the Crimean War
  statue **9**
Wallace Collection **3**
Young Dancer **32**

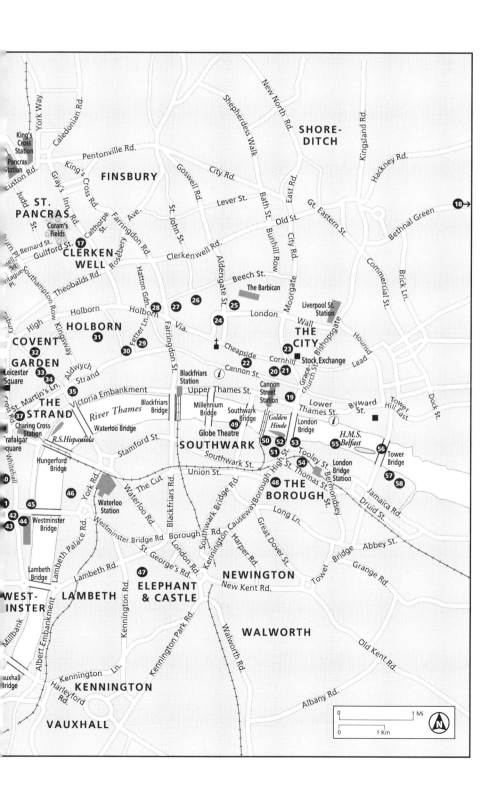

The following sights are fully or partially wheelchair accessible; visitors with disabilities should call the attraction to find out about special entrances, ramps, and elevator locations:

- Bank of England Museum
- Bethnal Green Museum of Childhood
- Bramah Tea & Coffee Museum
- British Library Exhibition Galleries
- Chelsea Physic Garden
- Courtauld Gallery
- Design Museum
- Hampton Court
- Imperial War Museum
- London Aquarium

- London Dungeon
- London Planetarium
- London Transport Museum
- Museum of London
- Regent's Park
- Rock Circus
- Royal Academy of Art
- Royal Botanic Gardens (Kew Gardens)
- Theatre Museum
- Tower Bridge Experience
- Wallace Collection

Sights for History Buffs

Cabinet War Rooms

In a 21-room underground bunker, Prime Minister Winston Churchill and his War Cabinet planned out the military campaigns of World War II. The site has been meticulously preserved, right down to the nightshirt and cigar waiting by Churchill's bed. Give yourself an hour to explore the site; you can almost hear the air-raid sirens.

Clive Steps, King Charles St. (Westminster), SW1. ☎ *020-7930-6961. Tube: Westminster (then a 10-minute walk west, staying on the north side of the street, to Parliament St., turn right to reach King Charles St.). Admission: £4.80 ($8) adults, £3.50 ($6) seniors/students, children under 16 free; a free self-guided audio tour comes with your ticket. Open: Daily 10 a.m.–6 p.m. (last admission 5:15 p.m.).*

Imperial War Museum

The former insane asylum known as Bedlam is now devoted to the insanity of war. You can see a wide range of weapons and equipment, including a Battle of Britain Spitfire, a German one-man submarine, a Mark V tank, and a rifle once carried by Lawrence of Arabia. Other exhibits include coded messages, forged documents, espionage equipment from World War I to the present, and multimedia presentations about the Blitz and trench warfare. The Holocaust Gallery documents one of history's darkest episodes through film, photos, and artifacts, many shown for the first time. Enough history is on display to keep you occupied for a couple of hours.

Lambeth Rd. (Lambeth), SE1. ☎ 020-7416-5320. Tube: Lambeth North (then a 10-minute walk south on Kennington, south of Westminster Bridge Rd., and east on Lambeth Rd.). Admission: £5.20 ($9) adults, £4.20 ($7) seniors/students, children under 16 free; admittance for everyone free after 4:30 p.m. Open: Daily 10 a.m.–6 p.m.

Museum of London

The Museum of London may be the most comprehensive city museum anywhere in the world. Located in the original square-mile Londinium of the Romans and overlooking the city's Roman and medieval walls, the museum includes archaeological finds; paintings and prints; social, industrial, and historical artifacts; and costumes, maps, and models to recount the city's history from prehistoric times to today.

150 London Wall (in the Barbican district near St. Paul's Cathedral), EC2. ☎ 020-7600-3699. Tube: St. Paul's (then a 10-minute walk north on St. Martin Le Grand and Aldersgate). Open: Monday–Saturday 10 a.m.–5:50 p.m., Sunday noon–5:50 p.m. Admission: £5 ($8) adults, £3 ($5) children/students/seniors; £12 ($20) families (2 adults/3 children); admission free after 4:30 p.m. Closed December 24–26 and January 1.

10 Downing Street

The prime minister's residence is a place on many visitors' "must see" lists, so I'm sorry to tell you that there's nothing to see except a heavily guarded gate. By peering through the gate you can get a glimpse, on the right side, of No. 10, the official residence of the British PM since 1732. The Chancellor of the Exchequer resides next door at No. 11, and No. 12 serves as the office of the chief government whip, responsible for maintaining discipline and cooperation in the vociferous House of Commons. These three small brick terrace houses, built on a cul-de-sac in 1680, stand in sharp contrast to the enormous 19th-century offices lining Whitehall, the government quarter around Downing Street.

Of course, London gossip swirls around 10 Downing Street, just as it does around Buckingham Palace. In 1999, Cherie Blair, wife of poll-sensitive Prime Minister Tony Blair, announced that she was pregnant with the couple's fourth child. Mrs. Blair, a high-powered lawyer specializing in employment law, made it known (when she was 7 months pregnant) that she thought her husband should take advantage of the paternity leave policy his Labour government has incorporated into law. (Since 1999, new fathers in Britain have the right to take up to 13 unpaid weeks off work during the first 5 years of their children's lives.) Mr. Blair, a seasoned spinmeister, was uncharacteristically tongue-tied by his wife's suggestion. It obviously wasn't a question of financial hardship if he took unpaid leave. Cherie Blair, QC (Queen's Counsel), the first prime minister's wife to hold a full-time job, reputedly earns three times the $175,000 annual salary of her prime minister husband. In the end, Prime Minister Blair took a week off when his wife gave birth to a son, Leo. Gossip swirled again in July 2000, when the Blair's 16-year-old son, Euan, was arrested in Leicester Square for drunkenness.

10 Downing St., SW1. Tube: Westminster (then a 5-minute walk north on Parliament St. and Whitehall).

Attractions for Art Lovers

Courtauld Gallery

If you like paintings by the impressionists, visit the Courtauld Gallery, which boasts one of the greatest collections outside Paris. Masterpieces by all the great names — Degas, Renoir, Cézanne, Manet, Monet, and Gauguin — are all on view in this suprisingly little-known museum. Give yourself at least an hour, preferably two.

Somerset House, The Strand, WC2. ☎ *020-7873-2526. Tube: Temple (then a 5-minute. walk north on Arundel St. and west on The Strand). Admission: £4 ($7) adults, £2 ($3) students, free for children under 18. Open: Monday–Saturday 10 a.m.–6 p.m., Sunday noon–6 p.m.*

Royal Academy of Arts

Housed in 18th-century Burlington House, the site of Britain's first art school, the Royal Academy presents major exhibits throughout the year and mounts a renowned (and usually jam-packed) Summer Exhibition of juried works from around the United Kingdom. Reconsider taking any young children because none of the exhibits is interactive. Give yourself about 90 minutes.

Burlington House, Piccadilly (St. James's), W1. ☎ ***020-7300-8000.*** *Tube: Piccadilly Circus (then a 5-minute walk down Piccadilly; the Academy is on the north side of the street just before the Burlington Arcade). Admission: Varies according to exhibit but usually £7 ($12) adults. £4.50 ($8) seniors, £2.50 ($4) children 11 to 18, £1 ($2) children under 11. Open: Daily 10 a.m.–6 p.m. (last admission 5:30 p.m.).*

Wallace Collection

The palatial town house of the late Lady Wallace is the setting for a spectacular collection of art and armaments. You can enjoy outstanding French works by the likes of Watteau and Fragonard, as well as masterpieces from the Dutch (Frans Hals and Rembrandt), English, Spanish, and Italian schools. Decorative art and ornaments from 18th-century France and European and Asian armaments may also claim your eye. Give yourself at least an hour to give everything a quick glance.

Hertford House, Manchester Sq. (Marylebone), W1. ☎ ***020-7935-0687.*** *Tube: Baker St. (then a 10-minute walk south on Baker St. to the museum entrance on the north side of Manchester Sq.). Admission: Free. Open: Monday–Saturday 10 a.m.–5 p.m., Sunday 2–5 p.m.*

Literary Landmarks

British Library Exhibition Centre

Opened in 1998, this literary offshoot of the British Museum (see Chapter 16) houses some of the world's most famous books, maps, manuscripts, and documents, including a copy of the Magna Carta, the illustrated *Lindisfarne Gospel* from Ireland, *The Diamond Sutra* (the world's earliest-dated printed book), Shakespeare's first folio, and handwritten manuscripts by authors such as Jane Austen and Thomas Hardy. Multimedia exhibits and a "Workshop of Words, Sounds and Images" trace the story of book production. Give this sight at least an hour; allow more time if you love literature or literary history.

Euston Rd. (Marylebone), NW1. ☎ 020-7412-7332. Tube: King's Cross/St. Pancras (then a 5-minute walk west on Euston; the museum entrance is just beyond Midland Rd.). Admission: Free. Open: Monday and Wednesday–Friday 9:30 a.m.–6 p.m., Tues 9:30 a.m.–8 p.m., Saturday 9:30 a.m.–5 p.m., Sunday 11 a.m.–5 p.m.

Carlyle's House

The pretty 1708 Queen Anne terrace house where Thomas Carlyle (author *of The French Revolution*) and his wife, Jane (a wit and noted letter writer), lived from 1834 to 1881 is located in Chelsea. The house is furnished as it was during their residence and is an accurate representation of Victorian domestic life. Carlyle's "soundproof" study in the skylit attic is filled with memorabilia — his books, a letter from Benjamin Disraeli, personal effects, a writing chair, and even his death mask. You can browse through in about a half an hour.

24 Cheyne Row (Chelsea), SW3. ☎ 020-7352-7087. Tube: Sloane Sq. (then a 20-minute walk south on Lower Sloane St. and Hospital Rd. to Cheyne Walk and north on Cheyne Row; or from Sloane Sq. take bus 11, 19, or 22). Admission: £3.20 ($5) adults, £1.60 ($3) children. Open: April–November Wednesday–Sunday 11 a.m.–4:30 p.m.

Dickens's House Museum

Charles Dickens lived in many places, but he and his family called the this Bloomsbury house home from 1837 to 1839. Here the great author penned *The Pickwick Papers, Oliver Twist,* and *Nicholas Nickleby,* the poignant and now-famous portrayals of Victorian England. The museum contains the world's most comprehensive Dickens library, portraits, illustrations, and rooms furnished exactly as they were in Dickens's time.

48 Doughty St. (Bloomsbury), WC1. ☎ 020-7405-2127. Tube: Russell Sq. (then a 10-minute walk up Guilford St. and turn right on Doughty St.; the museum is on the east side of the street). Admission: £3.50 ($6) adults, £2.50 ($4) seniors, £1.50 ($2) for children. Open: Monday–Friday 9:45 a.m.–5 p.m., Saturday 10 a.m.–5 p.m.

Dr. Johnson's House

Hidden away in a tiny square north of Fleet Street is the Queen Anne house where Dr. Samuel Johnson, best known as the lexicographer who compiled one of the first dictionaries of the English language, lived (quite humbly) from 1748 to 1759. A copy of the original dictionary is on display, along with Johnson memorabilia. The restored 17th-century house is close to Ye Olde Cheshire Cheese pub (see Chapter 14), a favorite haunt of the good doctor, who was celebrated as a raconteur of the first order.

17 Gough Sq., EC4. ☎ 020-7353-3745. Tube: Temple (then a 10-minute walk north on Arundel St. to Fleet St. and east on Fleet St. to Dunstan's Court; Gough Sq. is to one side of Dunstan's Court). Admission: £3 ($5) adults, £2 ($3) seniors/students.Open: April–September Monday–Saturday 11 a.m.–5:30 p.m., October–March Monday– Saturday 11 a.m.–5 p.m.

Intriguing Museums of All Shapes, Sorts, and Sizes

Bank of England Museum

The devoted capitalist will enjoy the Bank of England Museum, housed in the enormous Bank of England building. The museum chronicles changes in the banking industry since the Bank of England's beginnings in 1694, when funds were needed to finance the war against France's Louis XIV. On display are documents from famous customers (including George Washington), gold bullion, banknotes (forged and real), and coins. Interactive video displays present information about today's high-tech world of finance and a reconstructed 18th-century Banking Hall. You can see it all in less than an hour.

Bartholomew Lane (City of London), EC2. ☎ 020-7601-5545. Tube: Bank (then a 5- minute walk east on Threadneedle St., turn left on Bartholomew's Lane for the museum entrance). Open: Monday–Friday 10 a.m.–5 p.m.

Old Operating Theatre &Herb Garret

The Old Operating Theatre is not for the faint of heart. The roof garret of the church of St. Thomas, once attached to St. Thomas's Hospital, con- tains Britain's oldest operating theater (from 1822), where students could witness surgical procedures on poor (literally and figuratively) patients. You'll shudder over the collection of mid-19th-century "state-of-the-art" medical instruments, including amputation saws. The theater was in use long before the advent of anesthesia in 1846. Prior to that time, if a patient had a limb amputated, only a blindfold and a bottle of liquor could provide any relief.The herb garret was used for the storage and curing of medicinal herbs.

9A St. Thomas St. (Southwark), SE1. ☎ 020-7955-4791. Tube: London Bridge (then a 5-minute walk east on St. Thomas St.). Admission: £3.25 ($5) adults, £2.25 ($4) seniors, £1.60 ($3) children. Open: Daily 10:30 a.m.–5 p.m.; closed December 20–January 5.

Bramah Tea & Coffee Museum

Tea and coffee play an integral role in the history and daily lives of the people of London — and the United States. Set among the old tea warehouses of Butlers Wharf, this museum explores the history and traditions of these two important beverages. It illustrates how tea was brought into Europe by the Dutch in the 17th century, studies the 8th-century London phenomena of "Tea and Leisure Gardens," examines the reasons why tea became so popular in England, and discusses the reasons behind the Boston Tea Party. A cafe on the premises serves the real thing.

Maguire St., Butlers Wharf (South Bank), SE1. ☎ 020-7378-0222. Tube: London Bridge (then a 10-minute walk east along the riverside path to Shad Thames and right on Maguire St.). Admission: £3.50 ($6) adults, £2 ($3.30) seniors. Open: Daily 10 a.m.–6 p.m.

Design Museum

This museum houses the kind of collection that makes visitors say, "I remember those." If you're a design enthusiast — or want to see how commercial design affects our everyday lives — be sure to check out this museum. Classical, kitsch, modern, surreal and innovative — from Corbusier chairs to the Coke bottle — it's all chronicled here. Plus the river views are great.

Butlers Wharf, Shad Thames (South Bank), SE1. ☎ 020-7403-6933. Tube: Tower Hill (then a 10-minute walk across Tower Bridge to Butler's Wharf east of the bridge on the South Bank; or London Bridge, then a 10-minute walk east along The Queen's Walk beside the Thames). Admission: £5.50 ($9) adults, £4 ($6) for seniors/children; £10 ($16.50) families. Open: Monday–Friday 11:30 a.m.–6 p.m., Saturday–Sunday 11:30 a.m.–6 p.m.

Sir John Soane's Museum

If you have strange dreams filled with symbolic imagery, you may feel right at home in this museum. The house of Sir John Soane (1753–1837), architect of the Bank of England, is an eccentric treasure trove of ancient sculpture, artifacts, and art mixed in with odd architectural perspectives, fool-the-eye mirrors, flying arches, and domes. This captivating Holborn attraction is rarely crowded, which makes spending an hour even more of a treat. The oldest piece in the house is the 3,300-year-old sarcophagus of Pharaoh Seti I. Top prize in the picture gallery goes to William Hogarth's satirical and sometimes bawdy series from *The Rake's Progress.*

13 Lincoln's Inn Fields (Holborn), WC2. ☎ 020-7405-2107. Tube: Holborn (then a 5-minute walk south on Kingsway to Lincoln's Inn Fields; the museum entrance is on the north side of the street). Admission: Free. Open: Tuesday–Saturday 10 a.m.–5 p.m., first Tuesday of every month 6–9 p.m.

Theatre Museum

The National Collections of the Performing Arts are housed at this branch of the Victoria & Albert (see Chapter 16). Spend an hour or so checking out the collections related to British theater, ballet, opera, music-hall pantomime, puppets, circus, and rock and pop music (both past and present). Kids will enjoy the daily stage make-up demonstrations. The costume workshops use costumes from the Royal Shakespeare Company and the Royal National Theatre.

Russell St. (Covent Garden), WC2. ☎ *020-7836-8791. Tube: Covent Garden (then a 3-minute walk south to Russell St. on the east side of Covent Garden Piazza). Admission: £4.50 ($8) adults, £2.50 ($4) seniors/students, free for children under 16. Open: Tuesday–Sunday 10 a.m.–6 p.m.*

Activities for Teens

London Dungeon

Don't bring young children unless you want to pay for therapy, but teens seem to love the grisly re-creations of medieval torture and executions presented at this house of horrors. There's a scream (literally) around every corner. Amid the tolling bells, dripping water, and caged rats, you can face Jack the Ripper or witness a simulated burning at the stake. If you're hungry after all the murder and mayhem, you're in luck: A Pizza Hut is on the premises.

28–34 Tooley St. (South Bank), SE1. ☎ *020-7403-7221. Tube: London Bridge (the exhibit is across from the station). Admission: £9.95 ($16) adults, £8.50 ($14) students, £6.50 ($11) seniors/children under 15. Children 14 and under must be accompanied by an adult. Not recommended for young children. Open: April–September daily 10 a.m.–6:30 p.m. (last admission 5:30 p.m.); October–March daily 10 a.m.–5:30 p.m. (last admission 4:30 p.m.).*

Pepsi Trocadero

This "total entertainment complex" is right on Piccadilly Circus. The lead attraction is **Segaworld,** which offers varous rides, including Max Drop, the world's first indoor freefall ride (don't eat for at least an hour before), and 400 ear-splitting, eye-popping video games and simulators. The United Kingdom's first IMAX 3-D cinema (☎ **020-7494-4153**) is another big draw, as is Rock Circus. Theme restaurants include **Planet Hollywood,** the ersatz **Rainforest Café** (which doesn't pretend its proceeds go to support the rain forests), and the 1950s-style **Ed's Easy.** Plan to spend some time, because the Pepsi Trocadero is cleverly designed and packaged so that once you're in, finding your way out again is a long process.

Piccadilly Circus. ☎ *0891-881-100. Tube: Piccadilly Circus (then a 2-minute walk to the northeast side). Admission: IMAX theater, £6.95 ($11) adults, £5.50 ($9) children. Segaworld, free, games and rides 20p–£3 (50¢–$5). Open: Sunday–Thursday 10 a.m.–midnight, Friday–Saturday 10 a.m.–1 a.m.*

Rock Circus

This popular outpost of Madame Tussaud's (see Chapter 16) presents the history of rock and pop music. The audio-animatronic performers move and sing golden oldies and more recent chart toppers. You and your kids can enjoy plenty of memorabilia and a sensory overload of videos and personal stereo sound. Of course, it's always disconcerting for adults to hear the songs they grew up with called "oldies."

Pepsi Trocadero, Piccadilly Circus, W1. ☎ *020-7734-7203. Tube: Piccadilly Circus (it's on the north side). Admission: £8.25 ($13) adults, £7.25 ($12) seniors/students, £6.25 ($11) children under 16. Open: Wednesday–Monday 10 a.m.–5:30 p.m., Tuesday 11 a.m.–5:30 p.m.*

Places That Please Kids

Bethnal Green Museum of Childhood

A branch of the Victoria & Albert (see Chapter 16), this museum specializes in toys from the past and present. You can find a staggering collection of dolls, many with elaborate period costumes, and fully furnished dollhouses ranging from simple cottages to miniature mansions. Optical toys, marionettes, puppets, tin soldiers, war toys, toy trains and aircraft, and a display of clothing and furniture relating to the social history of childhood make this an enchanting place to invest a couple of hours.

Cambridge Heath Rd. (Bethnal Green), E2. ☎ *020-8980-2415. Tube: Bethnal Green (then a 5-minute walk north on Cambridge Heath Rd. to the museum entrance on the east side of the street). Admission: Free. Open: Monday–Thursday and Saturday–Sunday 10 a.m.–5:50 p.m.*

London Aquarium

London's subterranean aquarium, located right beside the London Eye observation wheel, may be a bit disappointing if you've been to any of the great aquariums in the United States. Nevertheless, children always enjoy observing the antics of its more than 350 species of fish and aquatic invertebrates, including sharks, graceful stingrays, man-eating piranha, and sea scorpions. Exhibits, a couple with floor-to-ceiling tanks, re-create marine habitats from around the world. Plan on spending at least 1½ hours — more if you can't pull the kids away.

Bridge Rd. (South Bank, beside Westminster Bridge), SE1. ☎ *020-7967-8000. Tube: Waterloo (then a 5-minute walk west along the river). Admission: £8 ($13) adults, £6.50 ($11) seniors, £5 ($8) children, £22 ($36) families. Open: Daily 10 a.m.–6 p.m. (last admission 5 p.m.).*

London Planetarium

Do you want to accompany a spaceship of travelers forced to desert their planet and travel through the solar system, visiting its major landmarks and witnessing spectacular cosmic activity? Partnered with Madame Tussaud's (see Chapter 16), this planetarium takes you on a journey to very different stars from the ones cast in wax next door. It offers many kid-friendly hands-on exhibits (including one that lets you see what shape or weight you'd be on other planets). You can also hear Stephen Hawking talk about mysterious black holes. Give this sight at least a couple of hours.

Marylebone Rd. (Marylebone), NW1. ☎ **020-7935-6861.** *Tube: Baker St. (then a 1-minute walk east on Marylebone Rd.). Admission: £6 ($10) adults, £4.60 ($8) seniors, £4 ($6) children under 16. Children under 5 not admitted. Combination ticket: For Planetarium and Madame Tussaud's, £12.75 ($21) adults, £8.50 ($14) children. Open: Daily 9 a.m.–5:30 p.m. Half-hour shows begin at 12:20 p.m. Monday–Friday and at 10:20 a.m. Saturday–Sunday.*

London Transport Museum

Housed in a splendid Victorian building (once the Flower Market at Covent Garden), this museum chronicles the development of the city's famous Underground and double-decker red bus system. A fabulous collection of historic vehicles, including an 1829 omnibus, a horse-drawn bus, and London's first trolley bus, are on display. Several KidZones offer interactive exhibits that enable younger visitors to operate the controls of a tube train, get their tickets punched, and play with touch-screen technology. After two hours, you may have to drag them away.

The Piazza, Covent Garden, WC2. ☎ **020-7379-6344.** *Tube: Covent Garden (then a 2-minute walk west to the Piazza; the museum is in the southeast corner). Admission: £5.50 ($9) adults, £2.95 ($5) children, £13.95 ($23) families. Open: Saturday–Thursday 10 a.m.–6 p.m., Friday 11 a.m.–6 p.m. (last admission at 5:15 p.m.).*

To See or Not to See: Shakespeare Sights

Shakespeare's Globe Theatre & Exhibition

At this full-size replica of Shakespeare's Globe Theatre, just east of its original site, you can take guided tours through the theater and its workshops. Be prepared for a taste of life in the days of Shakespeare and Elizabethan theater: what audiences were like, the rivalry among the theaters, the cruel bear-baiting shows, and the notorious Southwark Stews (a nearby area where prostitutes plied their trade). Watching a Shakespeare play from one of the benches in this roofless "wooden O" is a memorable experience, though the hard benches can torture the backside. See Chapter 22 for details on obtaining tickets for one of the performances presented May through September.

If you plan to see a Shakespeare play at the Globe, you can have a snack, tea, or a full meal in the theater itself. No reservations are required at **The Globe Café;** it's open daily: May through September 10 a.m. to 11 p.m. and October through April 10 a.m. to 6 p.m. Make reservations ahead for lunch or dinner at **The Globe Restaurant ☎ 020-7928-9444**), open daily noon to 2:30 p.m. and 5:30 to 11 p.m.

New Globe Walk (South Bank, just west of Southwark Bridge), SE1. ☎ 020-7902-1500. Tube: Mansion House (then a 10-minute walk across Southwark Bridge; the theater is visible on the west side along the river). Tours: £7.50 ($12) adults, £6 ($10) seniors/ students, £5 ($8.25) children. Open: October–April daily 10 a.m.–5 p.m., May– September (performance season) daily 9 a.m.–noon.

Southwark Cathedral

Chaucer and Shakespeare both worshiped at Southwark Cathedral. London's second-oldest church after Westminster Abbey, Southwark (pronounced *Suthick*) Cathedral is in what was London's first theater district (as well as a church-sanctioned center of prostitution). Although it was partially rebuilt in 1890, a great deal of history is associated with this 15th-century church. In under 30 minutes, you can see the entire site, including the Shakespeare memorial window and a 13th-century wooden effigy of a knight. Lunchtime concerts are regularly given on Monday and Tuesday; call for exact times and schedules.

Montague Close (South Bank, just west of London Bridge) SE1. ☎ 020-7367-6700. Tube: London Bridge (then a 5-minute walk across London Bridge Rd. to Cathedral St.). Admission: Free, but a £2 ($3) donation is suggested. Open: Daily 8 a.m.–6 p.m.

Ships Ahoy! Nautical London

 ### *H.M.S.* Belfast

The *Belfast,* a huge Royal Navy cruiser built in 1938 and used in World War II, is now moored in the Thames near London Bridge opposite the Tower of London. Tours of this floating 10,500-ton museum allow visitors to see all seven decks. On-ship exhibits are devoted to the history of the ship and the Royal Navy. You and your kids can witness a re-created surface battle. Plan to spend about 90 minutes.

Morgan's Lane, Tooley St. (South Bank, between Tower Bridge and London Bridge), SE1. ☎ 020-7940-6300. Tube: London Bridge (then a 10-minute walk north across Tooley St. and north on Hays Lane toward the entrance on the river). Admission: £4.70 ($8) adults, £3.60 ($6) seniors/students, children under 16 free. Open: November–February daily 10 a.m.–5 p.m.; March–October daily 10 a.m.–6 p.m. (last admission 45 minutes before closing).

 ### Golden Hinde

A full-scale reconstruction of Sir Francis Drake's 16th-century flagship, complete with a crew dressed in Tudor costumes, the *Golden Hinde* was built in Devon but launched in San Francisco in 1973 to commemorate Drake's claiming of California for Queen Elizabeth I. Like the original, it circumnavigated the globe, sailing over 140,000 miles before becoming a permanent floating museum in 1996. A self-guided tour of the fully rigged ship, once the home to 20 officers and gentlemen and between 40 to 60 crew members, takes about a half hour.

St. Mary Overie Dock, Cathedral St. (South Bank, west of London Bridge), SE1. ☎ *020-7403-0123. Tube: London Bridge (then a 5-minute walk west on Bedale and Cathedral streets). Admission: £2.50 ($4) adults, £2.10 ($3.50) seniors, £1.75 ($3) children, £6.50 ($11) families. Open: Monday–Friday 10 a.m.–5:30 p.m., some weekends (call first).*

Architectural Highlights and Stately Homes

Apsley House

Once known as Number One London because it was the first house past the toll-gate into London, this magnificent neoclassical mansion designed by Robert Adam and built between 1771 and 1778 was the London residence of the first duke of Wellington. It's the last great London townhouse and contains original collections that are mostly intact. After his phenomenal military career, which included defeating Napoléon at Waterloo in 1815, the duke was one of the most popular men in England. Apsley House, with its sumptuous interiors and treasure trove of paintings, china, swords, and military honors, reflects the first duke's position as the most powerful commander in Europe. A handy free sound guide explains it all on a self-guided tour that last about an hour. Its family is still in residence (though you'll never see them).

Hyde Park Corner, W1. ☎ *020-7499-5676. Tube: Hyde Park Corner (Exit 3 brings you up next to the house). Admission: £4.50 ($7) adults, £3 ($5) seniors, children under 18 free. Open: Tuesday–Sunday 11 a.m.–5 p.m.*

The Monument

This 202-foot-high Doric column was designed by Sir Christopher Wren and commemorates the Great Fire of 1662, which allegedly began in nearby Pudding Lane and swept through London. The Monument is the tallest isolated stone column in the world — you'll know just how tall if you climb the 311 steps to the viewing platform at the top.

Monument St. (just north of London Bridge), EC3. ☎ *020-7626-2717. Tube: Monument (you get out right across the street). Admission: £1.50 ($2.50) adults, 50p (80¢) children. Open: Daily 10 a.m.–5:40 p.m.*

Spencer House

The late Princess Diana is probably the most famous member of the Spencer family, but she never lived in her family's ancestral London home. The house, one of London's most beautiful private palaces, hasn't been a private residence since 1927. It was built in 1766 for the first Earl Spencer. Brilliantly restored and opened as a museum in 1990, its rooms are filled with period furniture and art loans from Queen Elizabeth, the Tate Gallery, and the Victoria & Albert. Guided tours (the only way to see the place) take about an hour.

27 St. James's Place (St. James's), SW1. ☎ 020-7499-8620. Tube: Green Park (then a 5-minute walk south on Queen's Walk to St. James's Place on your left). Admission: £6 ($10) adults, £5 ($8) children 10–16. Children under 10 not admitted. Open: Sunday 10:30 a.m.–4:45 p.m. Closed January and August.

Tower Bridge Experience

The "experience" lets you get inside one of the world's most famous bridges to find out why, how, and when it was built. "Harry," a Victorian bridge worker brought to life by animatronics, tells you the story of this famous drawbridge with its pinnacled towers and how the mechanism for raising the bridge for ship traffic actually works. You can also meet the architect's ghost and visit a miniature music hall. The experience takes about 90 minutes. The spectacular views up and down the Thames from the bridge's glass-enclosed walkways double the value of this attraction.

North Pier, Tower Bridge, SE1. ☎ 020-7378-1928. Tube: Tower Hill (then a 10-minute walk south to the north pier of Tower Bridge). Admission: £6.15 ($10) adults, £4.15 ($7) seniors/students/children 5–15. Open: April–October daily 9:30 a.m.–6:30 p.m.; November–March daily 9:30 a.m.–6 p.m. (last admission 75 minutes before closing).

For fans of Princess Di

If you're a true Princess Diana fan, note that she's buried on a picturesque island on the Oval Lake at **Althorp,** the Spencer family estate in Northamptonshire. The grounds are open for a limited time each year in July and August, but you can view the island only across the lake.

Admission is £10 ($17) adults, £7.50 ($12) seniors, and £5 ($8) children. The charge includes admission to the Diana Museum set up by her brother, Earl Spencer. It contains an exhibit celebrating Diana's childhood, her royal wedding (including her famous wedding gown), and her charitable works. You must book tickets long in advance by calling ☎ **01604-592-020** or writing Althorp Admissions, c/o Wayhead, The Hollows, St. James's Street, Nottingham, NG1 6FJ. You can get the most up-to-date information from the Web site at `www.althorp.com`.

Parks and Gardens

Chelsea Physic Garden

This garden is a paradise of over 7,000 exotic herbs, shrubs, trees, and flowers, plus England's earliest rock garden. Protected behind high brick walls, the Chelsea Physic Garden is the second-oldest surviving botanical garden in England and one of London's most beautiful places. The garden was founded in 1673 by the Worshipful Society of Apothecaries to develop medicinal and commercial plant species. Cotton seeds from this garden launched an industry in the new colony of Georgia. It's small enough (3½ acres) to wander through in an hour, but budget some more time if you love plants.

Swan Walk, 66 Royal Hospital Rd. (Chelsea), SW3. ☎ 020-7352-5646. Tube: Sloane Sq. (then a 15-minute walk south on Lower Sloane St. and west to the end of Royal Hospital Rd.). Bus: Southbound bus 11, 19, or 22 from Sloane Sq. Admission: £3.50 ($5) adults, £1.80 ($3) students/children 5–15. Open: April–October Wednesday 2–5 p.m., Sunday 2–6 p.m.; daily 2–5 p.m. during the Chelsea Flower Show in May.

Regent's Park

Regent's Park spans 400 acres of green, mostly open parkland fringed by imposing Regency terraces. It's the home of the **London Zoo** (see Chapter 16). People come here to play soccer, cricket, tennis, and softball; boat in the lake; visit **Queen Mary's Rose Garden** (which includes an outdoor theater — see Chapter 22); and let their kids have fun in the many playgrounds. The sight offers summer lunch and evening bandstand concerts as well as puppet shows and other children's activities on weekdays throughout August. The northernmost section of the park rises to the summit of **Primrose Hill,** which provides fine views of Westminster and the City. The restrooms by Chester Gate, on the east side of the park, offer facilities for persons with disabilities.

Just north of Marylebone Rd. and surrounded by the Outer Circle road. ☎ 020-7486-7905. Advance booking for Open Air Theatre (operating late May to early September) ☎ 020-7486 2431. Tube: Regent's Park or Baker St. (then a 5-minute walk north to the south end of the park. Open: Daily 5 a.m.–dusk.

Royal Botanic Gardens (Kew Gardens)

Located 9 miles southwest of Central London, the **Royal Botanic Gardens** at Kew — more familiarly known as Kew Gardens — are a gift to garden lovers. A trip to Kew will take the better part of a day to allow for travel time and garden strolling, but the enjoyment you'll receive is well worth the time investment. On display in the 300-acre gardens is a marvelous array of specimens first planted in the 17th and 18th centuries. Orchids and palms are nurtured in the Victorian glass pavilion hothouse. The sight boasts a lake, aquatic gardens, a Chinese pagoda, and even a royal palace. **Kew Palace,** the smallest and most lovely of the former royal compounds, is where King George III went insane. **Queen Charlotte's Cottage** (closed for restoration until 2001) was the mad king's summer retreat.

Tired of the tube? Why not take a boat to Kew Gardens? April to late September, vessels operated by the **Westminster Passenger Service Association** (☎ **020-7930-4721**) leave from Westminster Pier daily 10:15 a.m. to 2 p.m. Round-trip fares for the 90-minute journey are £10 ($16.50) adults, £8 ($13) seniors, and £5 ($8) children. The last boat from Kew usually departs around 5.30 p.m. (depending on the tide).

Kew. ☎ 020-8332-5000. Tube: Kew Gardens (then a 10-minute walk west on Broomfield St. to Victoria Gate entrance on Kew Rd.). Admission: £5 ($8) adults, £3.50 ($6) seniors, £2.50 ($4) children 5–16, £13 ($21) families. Tours: March–November 1-hour tours daily at 11 a.m. and 2 p.m.; tickets £1 ($2) at Information Desk; call ☎ 0181-332-5640 for info. Open: Gardens, daily 9:30 a.m.–dusk; glasshouse closes 1 hour before gardens. Kew Palace, April–October Saturday–Sunday 11 a.m.–5:30 p.m.

A Quaint Village Just a Tube Ride Away

The London you see today was once a series of separate villages. The nearby village of Hampstead, with its adjacent heathland, still retains its bucolic charm and makes for an excellent excursion.

Hampstead and Hampstead Heath

Although it's only 15 minutes by tube from Central London, **Hampstead** maintains its old-world charm. (See the map "Hampstead.") It's filled with Regency and Georgian houses (many set in lovely gardens) favored by artists and writers from Keats to John Le Carré. **Flask Walk,** the village's pedestrian mall, provides an eclectic assemblage of historic pubs, shops, and chic boutiques. The village itself has lots of old alleys, steps, courts, and groves just begging to be explored.

Adjacent **Hampstead Heath** is 800 acres of high parkland offering an opportunity for picnicking, swimming, and fishing. On a clear day you can see St. Paul's Cathedral and even the hills of Kent. An excursion here will take up at least half a day or more.

Tube: Hampstead (the tube stop is a minute from Flask Walk) or Hampstead Heath (Parliament Hill, right behind the tube stop, leads up into to the park itself).

Kenwood Lake villa

This lovely neoclassical villa sits on the shore of Kenwood Lake in the northern section of Hampstead Heath. The villa was remodeled in the 1760s by Robert Adam. Inside is a small but impressive collection of paintings (with works by Rembrandt, Vermeer, Gainsborough, Turner, and Reynolds) and jewelry. A cafeteria is in the former coach house. For a remarkable summer outdoor concert experience, visit the Kenwood Lakeside concert (see Chapter 23 for information).

Hampstead

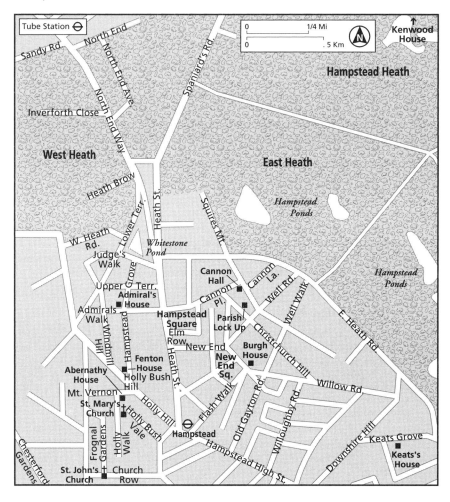

Hampstead Lane (Hampstead), NW3. ☎ *020-8348-1286. Tube: Archway (then bus 210 west along Highgate and Hampstead Lane). Admission: Free. Open: April–October daily 10 a.m.–6 p.m.; November–March daily 10 a.m.–4 p.m.*

Royal Castles and Palaces

Everyone wants to see Buckingham Palace, the Queen's London residence. But there's another royal residence, accessible year-round, at nearby Windsor. Just as memorable is Hampton Court, another great royal compound from the time of Henry VIII.

Hampton Court Palace

In 1514, Cardinal Wolsey began building the splendid Tudor Hampton Court in East Moseley, Surrey, 13 miles west of London on the north side of the Thames. Henry VIII nabbed Hampton Court for himself and made it a royal residence, which it remained until 1760. Some people claim that one of Henry VIII's six wives, Anne Boleyn (mother of Elizabeth I), haunts the place even today. The **Anne Boleyn Gate,** with its 16th-century astronomical clock, and the **Great Hall,** with its hammer-beam ceiling, are remnants from Hampton Court's Tudor days. Later, it was much altered by Sir Christopher Wren for William and Mary. Wren also designed the famous **Maze,** where visitors can wander in dizzy confusion. Inside the enormous palace are various state apartments and private rooms, including the **King's Dressing Room,** the Tudor kitchens, wooden carvings by Grinling Gibbons, Italian paintings, and guides dressed in period costumes. The manicured Thames-side gardens are lovely. A cafe and restaurant are on the grounds. You need a full day for this excursion.

Want to live on a royal scale for a while? Then stay at Hampton Court. Two self-contained, self-catering locations are available in the palace for 4- and 7-day rentals. Reserve through _**Landmark Trust**_ (Shottesbrooke, Maidenhead, Berks, SL6 3SW; ☎ _**01628-825-925;**_ Internet www.landmarktrust.co.uk). See Chapter 8 for more information.

Hampton Court, East Moseley, Surrey. ☎ _020-8781-9500. Train: Frequent trains from Waterloo Station make the half-hour trip to Hampton Court Station; a round-trip fare costs £4.30 ($7). Admission: £10.50 ($17) adult, £8 ($13) seniors/students, £7 ($12) children. Open: Mid-March–mid-October Tuesday–Sunday 9:30 a.m.–6 p.m., Monday 10:15 a.m.–6 p.m.; mid-October–mid-March, Tuesday–Sunday 9:30 a.m.–4:30 p.m., Monday 10:15 a.m.–4:30 p.m. Closed December 24–26, January 1._

Windsor Castle

Windsor is one of the queen's official residences. The castle, with its imposing skyline of towers and battlements rising from the center of the 4,800-acre Great Park, is located in Windsor, Berkshire, 20 miles from the center of London. It has been used as a royal residence since its construction by William the Conquerer approximately 900 years ago. The **State Apartments** that are open to visitors range from the intimate chambers of Charles II to the enormous Waterloo Chamber, built to commemorate the victory over Napoléon in 1815. All are furnished with important works of art from the Royal Collection. **Queen Mary's Dollhouse,** designed by Sir Edwin Lutyens as a present for Queen Mary in 1921, is a marvelous palace in miniature.

April through June, the **Changing of the Guard** takes place at 11 p.m. Monday through Saturday (on alternate days the rest of the year). From the ramparts of Windsor you can look down on the playing fields of **Eton College,** where aristocrats have been sending their boys for generations. All the royals attend the famous school in the charming town of **Eton** across the Thames Bridge.

Give yourself a full day for this excursion.

☎ **01753-831-118.** *Train: Trains leave every half-hour from Waterloo Station for the 50-minute trip (the stop is Windsor & Eton); the round-trip fare is £5.90 ($10). Admission: £10.50 ($17) adults, £8 ($13) seniors/students, £5 ($8) children 17 and under, £25.50 ($42) families. Open: November–February daily 10 a.m.–4 p.m. (last admission 3 p.m.); March–October daily 10 a.m.–5:30 p.m. (last admission 4 p.m.). Closed March 28, June 16, December 25–26, January 1.*

Greenwich: The Center of Time and Space

Time is of the essence in Greenwich, a town and borough of Greater London, about 4 miles east of The City. The world's clocks are set according to Greenwich Mean Time, and visitors from around the globe flock here to stand on the **Prime Meridian,** the line from which the world's longitude is measured. As the site of the **Millennium Dome,** a futuristic theme-expo decommissioned at the end of 2000, Greenwich served as the focal point for England's 21st-century millennium celebrations. Because its historic grouping of buildings on the Thames is considered to be the finest and most dramatically sited architectural and landscape ensemble in the British Isles, the buildings comprising "Maritime Greenwich" have been designated a World Heritage Site by UNESCO. Greenwich offers enough to keep you fully occupied for a full day, and it's a great outing for kids.

The easiest and most interesting route to get to Greenwich is by Docklands Light Rail from Tower Hill Gateway, which takes you past Canary Wharf and all the new Docklands development. The one-way fare is £1.60 ($3) or 80p ($1.50) if you have a Travelcard. Take the train to Island Gardens, the last stop, and then walk through the foot tunnel beneath the Thames to Greenwich. You'll come out next to the *Cutty Sark*. The tube stop for the Dome is North Greenwich, but remember that it was decommissioned at the end of 2000.

All the attractions in Greenwich are clearly signposted, and you can see them on foot. The Greenwich Tourist Information Centre (46 Greenwich Church St.; ☎ **020-8858-6376**) is open daily 10 a.m. to 5 p.m. It offers 1½ to 2-hour walking tours (at 12:15 and 2:15 p.m.) of the town's major sights for £4 ($6). Reservations aren't necessary, but it's a good idea to call first to make certain that the schedule hasn't changed. If you take the walking tour, you get 20 percent off admission to the **National Maritime Museum** and **Old Royal Observatory.**

If you're looking for a nice spot for lunch, try the **Green Village Restaurant** (11–13 Greenwich Church St.; ☎ **020-8858-2348**). It serves several kinds of fresh fish (try the fish pie if it's available), American-style burgers, salads, and omelets. It's open daily 11 a.m. to midnight.

The Greenwich Passport will save you money if you're planning to visit the major attractions. It provides admission to the *Cutty Sark*, the National Maritime Museum, and the Royal Observatory (see the following entries). The cost is £12 ($20) adults and £9.60 ($16) seniors and students. You can obtain the Passport at the Tourist Information Centre or at any of the three attractions it covers.

Cutty Sark

The majestic *Cutty Sark*, berthed on the Thames River, is the last of the tea-clipper sailing ships. It was launched in 1869 and first used for the lucrative China Sea tea trade. Later, it carried wool from Australia and after that (up until the end of World War II) served as a training ship. Today, the hold contains a rich collection of nautical instruments and paraphernalia. You can visit the ship on a self-guided tour and see everything in under an hour.

King William Walk. ☎ *020-8858-3445. Admission: £3.50 ($6) adults, £2.50 ($4) children, £8.50 ($14) families. Open: Daily 10 a.m.–5 p.m.*

National Maritime Museum

The paintings of ships tend to be boring, but the National Maritime Museum also displays sailing crafts and models. Also available is an extensive exhibit on Lord Nelson, which includes approximately 600 of his personal artifacts (including the coat he was wearing when he was shot at the Battle of Trafalgar). You can see everything in about half an hour.

In Greenwich Park. ☎ *020-8312-6608. Admission: £7.50 ($12) adults, £6 ($10) seniors/ students, free for children 16 and under. Open: Daily 10 a.m.–5 p.m.*

Old Royal Observatory

After leaving Queen's House (see the next entry), you can huff your way up the hill in the park to explore the center of time and space, the **Prime Meridian** (longitude 0 degrees). Of particular interest inside the observatory is the collection of original 18th-century chronometers (marked H1, H2, H3, and H4), beautiful instruments that were developed to help mariners chart longitude by time instead of by the stars.

In Greenwich Park. ☎ *020-8312-6608. Admission: £6 ($10) adults, £4.80 ($8) seniors/ students, free to children under 16. Open: Daily 10 a.m.–5 p.m.*

Queen's House

Adjacent to the National Maritime Museum is the splendidly restored Queen's House, designed by Inigo Jones in 1616 and later used as a model for the White House. The museum was the first classical building in England. It was commissioned by Anne of Denmark, the wife of James I, and completed in 1635 (with later modifications). You can visit the royal apartments on a self-guided tour that takes about half an hour. Special exhibits are also held here.

In Greenwich Park. ☎ *020-8312-6608. Admission: £7.50 ($12) adults, £6 ($10) seniors/students, £3.75 ($6) children. Open: Daily 10 a.m.–5 p.m.*

Royal Naval College

Near the *Cutty Sark* , the Royal Naval College occupies the site of Greenwich Palace, which stood here from 1422 to 1620 and was the birthplace of Henry VIII, Mary I, and Elizabeth I. Badly damaged by Cromwell's troops during the English Civil War, the palace was later torn down and in 1696 a naval hospital for retired seamen was erected in its place. The Thames-side buildings, designed by Sir Christopher Wren, became the Naval College in 1873 and are today a UNESCO-designated World Heritage Site. The only rooms open to visitors are the chapel and the imposing **Great Hall** with its dazzling painted ceiling. The body of Lord Nelson lay in state here in 1805.

King William Walk. ☎ *020-8858-2154. Admission: Free. Open: Daily 2:30–4:45 p.m.*

Chapter 18

And on Your Left, Buckingham Palace: Taking a Guided Tour

*L*ondon is a vast metropolis with centuries of history. The city offers something for everyone. Whether you love history, gardens, the arts, or royalty, you can find sights and events of interest. But how do you know where to begin discovering London? Ideally, you can examine the lists of sights in Chapters 16 and 17 and make some wise choices based on your preferences. Then you can use public transportation to visit your selections and spend as much time as you have available for each site. However, some people may find a general city overview to be helpful. And some travelers have only a couple of days to cover the most popular sights, such as Buckingham Palace and Westminster Abbey. Some visitors to London may not be able to comfortably use the Underground subway system or walk long distances. In these cases, a guided tour may be just the ticket. This chapter gives you the details on this option.

Ways to Go: Touring by Bus, Boat, or Foot

Everyone has seen the stereotype of the unsophisticated tourist on a whirlwind city tour listening to the monotone narration of a bored tour guide. Guided tours are often dismissed as an unfulfilling way to sight-see, chosen only by tourists who lack travel experience and creativity. However, that's not the case in London. Guided tours can free you from the anxiety of finding your way around the city and can introduce you to the specific sights that you most want to see.

This chapter provides information on all kinds of tours; you can travel on a motorcoach, a boat, or your own shoe leather.

The best way to fully experience any city is to get out and explore on your own. But sometimes exploring on your own is easier after you've gone on a tour and gotten your bearings.

The lay of the land: Getting oriented by bus

The general sightseeing companies offer variations of two basic half-day orientation tours:

- ✔ An excursion that covers sights in the West End, including a visit to Westminster Abbey and a chance to see the Changing of the Guard at Buckingham Palace (however, see the following paragraph).

- ✔ An excursion that heads east into The City, with stops at St. Paul's Cathedral and the Tower of London.

Many folks take tours that include **Buckingham Palace** because they think a tour is the easiest way to see the **Changing of the Guard.** Keep in mind that the Changing of the Guard is no longer a daily occurrence; it takes places every *other* day August 1 through March 31 (see Chapter 16 for details). If it's not scheduled to occur the day you take your tour, you'll probably visit the Household Cavalry in Whitehall instead. It's less impressive but still noteworthy.

The following sections describe the main sightseeing tours that travel by bus. Evan Evans (see the later section "River Views: Cruising Down the Thames") operates a daily coach tour as well.

London Pride Sightseeing

If you prefer to pick and choose where you want to stop and spend more time on your sightseeing excursion, you can call London Pride Sightseeing. This company maintains a fleet of double-decker buses (many of them open on top), and offers hop-on/hop-off service at 100 boarding points around the city (look for London Pride bus stop signs; they're everywhere). You can choose from a variety of tours.

London Pride Sightseeing has a time-saving *Fast Track ticket service* for many London attractions. On the bus, for no additional charge, you can buy tickets for the Tower of London, museums, and other places that are on your itinerary. When you arrive, you don't have to stand in line for tickets.

☎ *01708-631-122. The Grand Tour lasts 90 minutes and passes every major sight in Central London and the South Bank; it starts from Piccadilly Circus (Tube: Piccadilly Circus) outside the Trocadero in Coventry Street and departs every 15 minutes daily 9 a.m.–6 p.m. (to 9 p.m. in summer). You don't have to book in advance for any of the London Pride tours and can pay on the bus. A ticket good for 24 hours on all routes costs £15 ($25) for adults and £6 ($10) for children under 16.*

Original London Sightseeing Tours

Original London Sightseeing Tours is another all-purpose sightseeing company that uses open-topped double-decker buses (ideal for photo ops).

Jews Row, London SW18; ☎ ***020-8877-1722****. Pickups are at Victoria Coach Station (Tube: Victoria), Marble Arch (Tube: Marble Arch), Haymarket (Tube: Piccadilly Circus), and Baker Street (Tube: Baker St.). Tours cost £15 ($25) for adults and £6 ($10) for children under 16.*

Visitors Sightseeing Tours

Visitors Sightseeing Tours provides tours that are more individualized than those of competitors. However, these excursions are also more pricey. Tours, available daily, are conducted on luxury buses with certified guides; tour prices vary according to the itinerary.

On Wednesday, Friday, and Sunday at 6:50 p.m., Visitors Sightseeing Tours offers a macabre tour called *Ghosts, Ghouls & Ancient Taverns* that explores sights associated with Jack the Ripper and the medieval plague and stops in at a couple of pubs along the way. The cost is £16 ($26); the tour isn't recommended for children under 14.

Departure Lounge, Royal National Hotel, Bedford Way; ☎ ***020-7636-7175****; Tube: Russell Sq.*

Golden Tours

Another tour company with many guided excursions to choose from is Golden Tours. The comfortable buses are equipped with rest rooms, and the certified guides have certifiable senses of humor. The daily *Historic & Modern London* tour is a full-day outing that includes the West End, Westminster Abbey, the Changing of the Guard, the City of London, St. Paul's Cathedral, the Tower of London, and a cruise from the Tower down to Charing Cross Pier; the fee includes a pub lunch, a tea aboard ship, and all admission prices, so this tour is a good value. The cost is £51.50 ($85) for adults and £46 ($76) for kids under 16.

4 Fountain Square, 123–151 Buckingham Palace Rd.; ☎ ***800-456-6303*** *in the United States or 020-7233-7030; Internet:* www.goldentours.co.uk. *Tours depart from the office at Buckingham Palace Road (Tube: Victoria) and other points in Central London. Courtesy pick-up service is available from several hotels. You can book your tickets directly or online, or you can ask your hotel concierge to do it 2 days in advance.*

River views: Cruising down the Thames

For many people, a boat trip down the Thames is one of the grand highlights of a trip to London. Children especially enjoy these trips on the water. Sightseeing boats regularly ply the river between Westminster and the Tower of London; some continue downstream to Greenwich (site of the Prime Meridian, *Cutty Sark*, and Old Royal Observatory) and upstream to Kew Gardens and Hampton Court (see

Chapter 17 for details). As you float past, you can view many of London's great monuments: the Houses of Parliament, Westminster Abbey, St. Paul's Cathedral, and the Tower and Tower Bridge. The main departure points along the Thames are at Westminster Pier (Tube: Westminster), Waterloo Pier (Tube: Waterloo), Embankment Pier (Tube: Embankment), Tower Pier (Tube: Tower Hill), and Greenwich Pier (Tube: Greenwich). For recorded information on these tours, call ☎ 0839-123-432.

You'll enjoy the river tours that the following companies provide:

✔ **Evan Evans** (☎ 020-7950-1777; www.evanevans.co.uk), in addition to daily coach tours of London, offers three river cruises. A daily lunch cruise aboard the *Silver Bonito* is £17 ($28) per person. Another daily offering starts with a guided bus tour of The City and continues down the Thames aboard a chartered vessel; the price is £18.50 ($31) for adults and £16 ($26) for children ages 3 to 16. A daily full-day tour takes in Westminster Abbey, continues through Westminster to Buckingham Palace for the Changing of the Guard, includes a lunch cruise on the Thames, and returns by bus to St. Paul's and the Tower of London. The price is £49.50 ($82) for adults and £44.50 ($74) for children.

✔ **Catamaran Cruisers** (☎ 020-7987-1185) runs a year-round fleet of boats on the Thames. A round-trip ticket from Embankment Pier to Greenwich is £7.50 ($12) for adults, £5.65 ($9) for seniors, and £4.10 ($7) for children. From March to October, it offers a nightly (6:30, 7:30, and 10:30 p.m.) 50-minute circular cruise from Embankment Pier that passes most of London's major floodlit monuments. All the boats provide live commentary and have a fully licensed bar. The cost is £6.70 ($11) for adults and £4.70 ($8) for children.

✔ **Westminster Passenger Services** (☎ 020-7930-4097) operates boats year-round from Westminster Pier, across from the Houses of Parliament, and Tower Pier, just below the Tower of London. If you want a half-hour trip on the river from Westminster to the Tower of London or the other way around, this is the place to try. A one-way ticket in either direction is £4.60 ($8) for adults and £2.30 ($4) for children.

And don't forget Golden Tours' *Historic & Modern London* tour (see the previous section), which includes a cruise from the Tower down to Charing Cross Pier.

Splendid scenery, great food: Dining on the river

If you just want a romantic river dining experience, **Bateaux London** (☎ 020-7925-2215) offers a nightly dinner cruise that leaves Embankment Pier (Tube: Embankment) at 7:15 p.m. and returns at 9:45 p.m. The cruise, which includes a four-course dinner with live music and after-dinner dancing, costs £56 ($93) per person.

A 1-hour lunch cruise with a three-course set menu and live commentary is offered Monday through Saturday at £20 ($34) per person; it departs from Embankment Pier at 12:15 p.m. A 2-hour (three-course) Sunday lunch cruise departs from Embankment Pier at 12:15 p.m and costs £27.50 ($45) per person. Advance reservations are required for all of these, and a "smart casual" dress code (no sweat pants or running shoes) is in effect.

Walk this way: Taking a walking tour

Nothing beats walking as a means of getting acquainted with a city. And walking tours give you the additional benefit of a knowledgeable guide providing reliable information. This form of exploration is great for people with special interests (such as architecture, history, or literature). And older children usually enjoy walking tours as well. The weekly events listed in *Time Out* magazine, available at every newsagent in London, include dozens of intriguing walks; a walk goes on every day.

If you want to follow detailed strolls on your own, check out the 11 tours offered in *Frommer's Memorable Walks in London* (published by IDG Books Worldwide, Inc.). The following companies offer enjoyable guided walking tours:

✔ **London Walks** (P.O. Box 1708, London NW6 4LW; ☎ **020-7624-3978;** Internet: www.london.walks.com) is the oldest walking tour company in London. It offers a terrific array of tours, including *Jack the Ripper's London, Christopher Wren's London, Oscar Wilde's London,* and *The Beatles' Magical Mystery Tour.* Different walks are available for every day of the week, rain or shine; they last about 2 hours and end near an Underground station. You don't need to reserve in advance. A London Walk costs £5 ($8) for adults and £4 ($6) for students with ID; kids are free if accompanied by a parent. Write, call, or check out the Web site for more information.

✔ **Stepping Out** (32 Elvendon Rd.; ☎ **020-8881-2933;** Internet: www.walklon.ndirect.co.uk) offers guided walking tours of several London neighborhoods, including Southwark on the South Bank. One offbeat theme walk called *Brothels, Bishops and the Bard* explores the **Clink** (the oldest prison in London), Shakespeare's memorial window in **Southwark Cathedral,** and the site of the original **Globe Theatre.** The cost is £5 ($8) for adults and £3.50 ($6) for seniors/students.

✔ **London Pub Walks** (☎ **020-8445-9191**) combines a walking tour with a pub crawl. For £4 ($7), as you visit old pubs you learn the history of English beer. Walks depart from Temple tube stop every Friday at 7:30 p.m. You don't need to book in advance.

Gays and lesbians may be interested in the weekly 2-hour *Walking Tour of Gay & Lesbian Soho — Past and Present,* which leaves from the steps of **St. Martin-in-the-Fields Church** at Trafalgar Square (Tube: Charing Cross) every Sunday at 3 p.m. and costs £5 ($8). For more information, call ☎ **020-7437-6063.**

Smell the Roses: Enjoying London Garden Tours

Brits are well known for their fabulous gardens. If flowers are your thing or you just want to savor gorgeous garden views, check out:

✔ **Expo Garden Tours** (33 Fox Crossing, Litchfield, CT 06759; ☎ 800-448-2685; e-mail: info@expgardentours.com; Internet: www.expogardentours.com) offers tours of public and private gardens in the countryside, plus a visit to London's Chelsea Flower Show in May.

✔ **Select Travel Service** (99 Bauer Dr., Oakland, NJ 07436; ☎ 800-752-6787; e-mail: info@selectTravel.com; Internet: www.SelectTravel.com) provides tours of the springtime extravaganza in Chelsea.

Both must be booked before you leave home for London.

Chapter 19

Shopping in Paradise: London's Stores and Markets

*L*ondon is one of the world's great shopping meccas. If shopping is on your agenda, you'll find any item you're looking for. But you won't find many bargains, except during the department stores' big sales in January and July (see the sidebar "Saving on the London sales," later in this chapter).

The best values are goods manufactured in England. Items from The Body Shop, Filofax, or Dr. Martens cost less than they do in the United States. Other potentially good values include woolens and cashmeres, English brands of bone china, English toiletries, antiques, used silver, old maps and engravings, and rare books. You can also do well with French products; the prices are almost as good as Paris offers.

You may be surprised — and perhaps disappointed — at the number of big U.S. chains that have opened stores in London. But in addition to the familiar chains and megastores, London is still the home of hundreds of small, unique specialty shops and boutiques to delight the eye and empty the wallet.

British retailers now have the option to charge more for goods and services bought by credit card, though they're obliged to display a clear indication that differentiated pricing applies. Normal shopping hours are Monday through Saturday 10 a.m. to 5:30 p.m., with a late closing (7 or 8 p.m.) on Wednesday or Thursday. The law allows stores to be open for 6 hours on Sunday, usually 11 a.m. to 5 p.m.

Getting the VAT Tax Back

The *VAT (value-added tax)* in London and throughout the United Kingdom is 17.5 percent. It's added on to the price on every price tag. Anyone who isn't a resident of the European Union can get a VAT refund, but every store requires a minimum purchase to qualify. The exact amount varies from store to store, although the minimum expenditure is £50 ($82). Not every store honors this minimum: It's £100 ($165) at Harrods, for example. But qualifying for a tax refund is far easier in Britain than in almost any other country in the European Union.

To get the refund, you must get a VAT refund form from the retailer, and it must be completed by the retailer at the time of purchase. Don't leave the store without a completed refund form. Don't let any merchant tell you that you can get refund forms at the airport.

VAT isn't charged on goods shipped out of the country, no matter how much you spend. You can avoid VAT and the hassle of lugging large packages back with you by having London stores ship your purchases for you; many are happy to do so. However, shipping charges can *double* the cost of your purchase, and you may also have to pay U.S. duties when the goods arrive. Instead of this costly strategy, consider paying for excess baggage (rates vary with the airline).

You can get back about 15 percent of the 17.5 percent VAT you pay on your purchases. Follow these steps:

1. **Ask the store if it does VAT refunds and how much the minimum purchase is.**

2. **If you've spent the minimum amount, ask for the VAT refund paperwork.**

   The retailer must fill out a portion.

3. **Fill out your portion of the form (name, address).**

4. **Present the form — along with the goods — at the VAT Refunds counter in the airport.**

Remember: You're required to show the goods at your time of departure, so don't pack them in your checked luggage; put them in your carry-on instead. (I say this even though the authorities didn't ask to see anything last time I went through this procedure.)

After the paperwork is stamped, you have two choices:

✔ You can mail in the papers and receive your refund in a British check (no!) or a credit-card refund (yes!).

✔ You can go directly to the Cash VAT Refund desk at the airport and get your refund in cash.

The bad news: If you accept cash other than sterling, you lose money on the conversion rate. Many stores charge a flat fee for processing your refund, so £3 to £5 ($5 to $8) may be automatically deducted from the total refund. Even so, you may still be saving a bundle.

 If you're traveling from London to other countries in the European Union, don't apply for your VAT refund at the London airport. Apply for all your VAT refunds at one time at your final destination, prior to departure from the European Union.

Choosing Wisely at Duty-Free Shops

Many visitors to London and other cities take advantage of the duty-free shopping at the airports. The *duty* they avoid paying in these shops is the local tax on the items (like state sales tax in the United States), not any import duty that may be assessed by the U.S. Customs office. Duty-free shopping is big business at airports. Heathrow Airport's Terminal 4 resembles a shopping mall, and the other terminals also offer a good bit of shopping and not much crossover between brands.

Before you decide to spend your preboarding time shopping, consider this fact: Not every item is a duty-free area is a bargain. Airport prices for souvenirs and candy bars, for example, are higher than elsewhere in London. Duty-free prices on luxury goods are usually fair but not bargain basement. Liquor and cigarettes, on the other hand, are often much less expensive than in the United States. If you do find yourself shopping in the airport stores, watch for special promotions and coupons that will save you some pounds at the time of purchase.

 Don't postpone your shopping until you get to the airport. And if you do intend to shop the duty-free stores, familiarize yourself with London prices beforehand so you know what is a good value and what isn't. And understand that buying items at a duty-free shop before flying home does *not* exempt them from counting toward your U.S. Customs limits (monetary or otherwise).

Getting Your Goodies Through Customs

The Customs authority doesn't impose limits on how much loot U.S. citizens can bring home from a trip abroad, but it does put limits on how much you can bring back for free. You may bring home $400 worth of goods duty-free, providing you've been out of the country at least 48 hours and haven't used the exemption in the past 30 days. Here's some additional information about the limit and Customs law:

- ✔ It includes not more than 1 liter of an alcoholic beverage (you must be over 21).
- ✔ It includes not more than 200 cigarettes and 100 cigars.

✔ Antiques over 100 years old and works of art are exempt from the $400 limit, as is anything you mail home from abroad.

✔ You may mail up to $200 worth of goods to yourself (marked "For Personal Use") and up to $100 worth to others (marked "Unsolicited Gift") once each day, as long as the package doesn't include alcohol or tobacco products.

✔ You must pay an import duty on anything over these limits, a flat rate of 10 percent duty on the next $1,000 worth of purchases.

Be sure to have your receipts with you. For more specific guidance, write to the U.S. Customs Service (P.O. Box 7407, Washington, D.C. 20044 ☎ **202-927-6724**), requesting the free pamphlet *Know Before You Go*. Or check out the details on the Customs Department Web site at www.customs.ustreas.gov. Table 19-1 lists size conversions so you get the right fit and won't need to worry about returning anything.

Table 19-1	The Right Fit: Size Conversions		
U.S.	**U.K.**	**U.S.**	**U.K.**
Women's Clothes		**Women's Shoes**	
8	10	4½	3
10	12	5½	4
12	14	6½	5
Women's Clothes		**Women's Shoes**	
14	16	7½	6
16	18	8½	7
18	20	9½	8
Men's Clothes/Shirts		**Men's Shoes**	
Sizes are the same		7	6
		8	7
		9	8
		10	9
		11	10
		12	11

Returning Canadian citizens are allowed a $300 exemption and can bring back, free of duty, 200 cigarettes, 2.2 pounds of tobacco, 40 imperial ounces (1.2 quart.) of liquor, and 50 cigars. All valuables you're taking with you to the United Kingdom, such as expensive cameras, should be declared on the Y-38 Form before departure from Canada. For a clear summary of Canadian rules, write for the booklet *I Declare*, issued by Revenue Canada (2265 St. Laurent Blvd., Ottawa K1G 4KE; ☎ **800-461-9999** or 613-993-0534).

The duty-free allowance for returning Australian citizens is A$400 (A$200 for those under 18). Citizens can bring home, free of duty, 250 cigarettes or 250 grams of loose tobacco, and 1.125 liters of alcohol. Australian citizens who'll be returning home with valuable goods they already own (for example, foreign-made cameras) should file form B263 before leaving. For more information, contact Australian Customs Services (GPO Box 8, Sydney NSW 2001; ☎ **02-9213-2000**).

The duty-free allowance for New Zealand citizens is NZ$700. Citizens over 17 can bring in 200 cigarettes, or 50 cigars, or 250 grams of tobacco, or a mix of all three if the combined weight doesn't exceed 250 grams; plus 4.5 liters of beer and wine, or 1.125 liters of liquor. To avoid paying duty on goods you already own (cameras and the like), fill out a certificate of export before you leave, listing the valuables you are taking out of the country. For more information, contact New Zealand Customs (50 Anzac Ave., P.O. Box 29, Auckland; ☎ **09-359-6655**).

Shopping the Big Names: London Department Stores

Harrods

Harrods may be the most famous department store in the world. Carrying one of the coveted green plastic Harrods bags that you'll get with your purchase can provide you with a sense of accomplishment. The store's 300 departments offer merchandise that's breathtaking in its range, variety, and quality. Best of all are the Food Halls, stocked with a huge variety of foods and several cafes.

The London gossip columns were ablaze early in 2000 when Prince Philip withdrew his royal warrant (official royal patronage) from Harrods, claiming that the royal household just didn't use the store as much as it used to. Harrods just happens to be owned by Mohamed Al Fayed, father of Dodi Al Fayed, who was killed with Princess Diana in that famous car crash. The elder Mr. Al Fayed, an Egyptian who's been denied U.K. citizenship, has made some startling allegations against the House of Windsor, claiming that the deaths of Diana and his son were not accidental.

87–135 Brompton Rd., SW1; ☎ *020-7730-1234; Tube: Knightsbridge. Open: Monday, Tuesday, and Saturday 10a.m. – 6 p.m. and Wednesday–Friday 10 a.m.–7 p.m.*

Saving on the London sales

The tradition is for the London stores to hold sales in January and July. In recent times, the July sales have begun in June or earlier. The January sale is the main event, and it generally starts after the first week (when round-trip airfares are low).

The January sale at Harrods is the most world famous, but nearly every other store, except Boots, has a big sale at the same time. Discounts are usually from 25 to 50 percent at the major stores, such as Harrods and Selfridges. At Harrods, the best buys are on the store's logo souvenirs, English china, and English designer brands such as Jaeger.

Harvey Nichols

Harvey Nichols, the late Princess Diana's favorite store, has its own gourmet food hall and fancy restaurant, the **Fifth Floor,** and is crammed with designer home furnishings, gifts, and fashions. Women's clothing is the largest segment of its business, a familiar fact to those who were fans of the TV series *Absolutely Fabulous.* Harvey Nicks, as it's called, doesn't compete with Harrods because it features a much more upmarket, fashionable image.

109–125 Knightsbridge, SW1; ☎ *020-7235-5000; Tube: Knightsbridge. Open: Monday, Tuesday, and Saturday from 10 a.m.–7 p.m., Wednesday–Friday 10 a.m.–8 p.m., and Sunday noon–6 p.m.*

Fortnum & Mason

Fortnum & Mason, down the street from the Ritz hotel, holds two royal warrants (a royal warrant is a form of official patronage the store can use in its advertising) and is the Queen's London grocer (but don't expect to see Her Majesty in the store). Amid a setting of deep-red carpets and crystal chandeliers, you can find everything from pâté de foie gras to Campbell's soup. The grocery department carries the finest foods from around the world, and on the other floors are bone china, crystal, leather, antiques, and stationery departments, Dining choices include the **Patio, St. James's,** and **The Fountain** (see Chapter 14).

181 Piccadilly, W1; ☎ *020-7734-8040; Tube: Piccadilly Circus. Open: Monday– Saturday 9:30 a.m.–6 p.m.*

Liberty

Liberty provides six floors of fashion, china, and home furnishings, upholstery fabrics, scarves, ties, luggage, and gifts. The store is best known for its Liberty Prints — finest quality fabrics, typically in floral patterns. These distinctive fabrics are highly sought after by interior decorators because they add an unmistakable touch of England to any room decor.

214–220 Regent St., W1; ☎ 020-7734-1234; Tube: Oxford Circus. Open: Monday–Wednesday 10 a.m.–6:30 p.m, Thursday 10 a.m.–8 p.m., and Friday 10 a.m –7 p.m.

Fenwick of Bond Street

Fenwick of Bond Street, a short walk west from Liberty, is a high-style women's fashion store. Fenwick (pronounced "*Fen*-ick") was founded in 1891, and offers an impressive collection of designer womenswear, ranging from moderately priced ready-to-wear items to more expensive designer fashions. A wide range of lingerie in all price ranges is also sold.

63 New Bond St., W1; ☎ 020-7629-9161; Tube: Bond St. Open: Monday–Wednesday and Thursday–Saturday 10 a.m.–6:30 p.m. and Wednesday 10 a.m.–8 p.m.

Selfridges

From Liberty or Fenwick, you can walk north to Selfridges, one of the largest department stores in Europe. The store has been redone to attract upscale customers, but the vast size of the store provides room for less expensive mass-marketed lines as well. Over 500 divisions sell everything from artificial flowers to groceries. The Miss Selfridge boutique, on one side of the store near the cosmetics department, features teen fashions, hotshot clothes, accessories, makeup, and moderately priced cutting-edge fashions. While on this side of the store, you can visit the café.

400 Oxford St., W1; ☎ 020-7629-1234; Tube: Bond St. or Marble Arch. Open: Monday–Wednesday 10 a.m.–7 p.m., Thursday and Friday 10 a.m. –8 p.m., Saturday 9:30 a.m.–8 pm., and Sunday 11:30 a.m.–6 p.m.

Marks & Spencer

Marks & Spencer is a private-label department store that offers basics of all kinds. The merchandise at both locations is high quality, if a bit conservative.

458 Oxford St., W1; ☎ 020-7935-7954; Tube: Marble Arch; and 173 Oxford St., W1 ☎ 020-7437-7722; Tube: Oxford Circus. Open: Monday–Friday 9 a.m.–8 p.m., Saturday 9 a.m.–to 7:30 p.m., and Sunday noon–6 p.m.

Doing Your Best Shopping at Knightsbridge and the West End

All of the department stores in the previous section "Shopping the Big Names: London Department Stores," are located in London's two major shopping areas: Knightsbridge and the West End. You can find some of London's most famous and most impressive stores along several key streets in these two neighborhoods.

West End Shopping

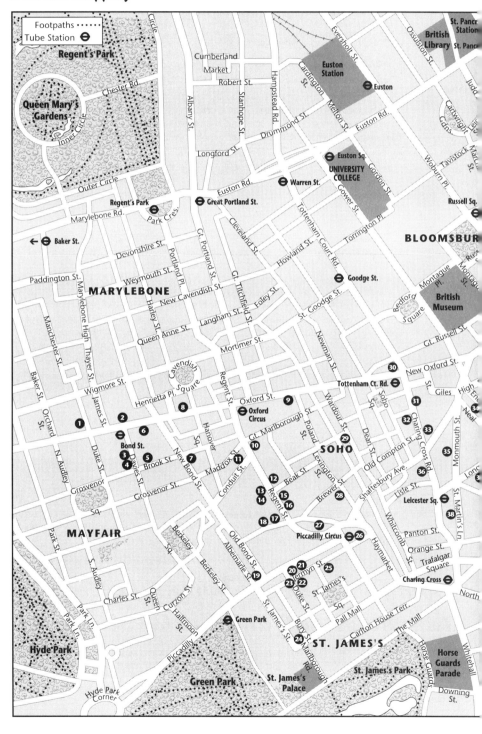

Footpaths ······
Tube Station ⊖

Regent's Park

Queen Mary's Gardens

Chester Rd.

Inner Circle

Outer Circle

Cumberland Market

Robert St.

Longford St.

Albany St.

Stanhope St.

Hampstead Rd.

Drummond St.

Cardington St.

Melton St.

Euston Station

⊖ Euston

Euston Rd.

Eversholt St.

Ossulston St.

St. Pancr Station

British Library

St. Pancr

Judd

Cartwright Gdns.

Euston Rd.

⊖ Euston Sq.

UNIVERSITY COLLEGE

Gordon St.

Gower St.

Woburn Pl.

Tavistock Squa

Marc

Russell Sq.

Regent's Park ⊖

Marylebone Rd.

Park Cres.

⊖ Warren St.

⊖ Great Portland St.

Tottenham Court Rd.

Torrington Pl.

BLOOMSBUR

Ruse

← ⊖ Baker St.

Devonshire St.

Paddington St.

MARYLEBONE

Weymouth St.

Harley St.

Portland Pl.

Gt. Portland St.

New Cavendish St.

Cleveland St.

Howland St.

Montague Pl.

Montague

Bedford Square

British Museum

Baker St.

Manchester St.

Thayer St.

Marylebone High St.

Wigmore St.

Queen Anne St.

Langham St.

Gt. Titchfield St.

Foley St.

Mortimer St.

St. Goodge St.

⊖ Goodge St.

Gt. Russell St

Henrietta Pl.

Cavendish Square

Regent St.

Oxford St.

Newman St.

Tottenham Ct. Rd. ⊖

New Oxford St.

Soho Sq.

St. Giles High

New

Orchard St.

N. Audley

James St.

Duke St.

Davies St.

Brook St.

New Bond St.

Hanover Sq.

⊖ Oxford Circus

Gt. Marlborough St.

Poland St.

Waddour St.

Dean St.

Old Compton St.

SOHO

Charing Cross Rd.

Monmouth St.

St. Giles

Neal

Bond St. ⊖

Maddox St.

Conduit St.

Beak St.

Lexington St.

Brewer St.

Shaftesbury Ave.

Lisle St.

Leicester Sq.

St. Martin's Ln.

Lon

Grosvenor Sq.

Grosvenor St.

Old Bond St.

Regent St.

Piccadilly Circus ⊖

Whitcomb St.

Panton St.

MAYFAIR

Berkeley Sq.

Berkeley St.

Albemarle St.

Haymarket

Orange St.

Trafalgar Square

Charing Cross ⊖

S. Audley

Park St.

Charles St.

Queen St.

Curzon St.

Halfmoon St.

Jermyn St.

Duke St.

St. James's Sq.

Pall Mall

Carlton House Terr.

North

Hyde Park

Piccadilly

Green Park ⊖

St. James's St.

Bury St.

Marlborough Rd.

St. James's Palace

St. JAMES'S

St. James's Park

Horse Guards Parade

Whiteha

Horse Guards

Hyde Park Corner

Green Park

Hyde Park

ST. JAMES'S

Downing St.

The Mall

1 2 3 4 5 6 7 8 9 10 11 12 13 14 15 16 17 18 19 20 21 22 23 24 25 26 27 28 29 30 31 32 33 34 35 36 38

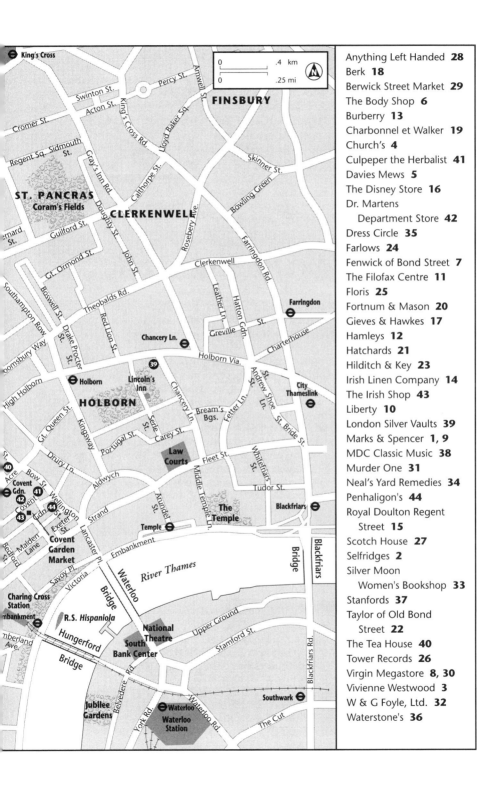

Finding a drugstore

In England, a drugstore is called a *chemists' shop.* All over London, you can find **Boots the Chemist** stores. In terms of size and convenience, the best one is just across from Harrods (at 72 Brompton Rd., SW3; ☎ **020-7589-6557;** Tube: Knightsbridge). In addition to medicine, it sells film, pantyhose (called tights), sandwiches, and all of life's little necessities. The store is open Monday through Friday 8:30 a.m. to 7 p.m. and Saturday 9 a.m. to 7 p.m. One of the most centrally located chemists is **Bliss the Chemist** (5 Marble Arch, W1; ☎ **020-7723-6116;** Tube: Marble Arch), open daily 9 a.m. to midnight. **Zafash Pharmacy** (233–235 Old Brompton Rd., SW5; ☎ **020-7373-2798;** Tube: Earl's Court) is London's only 24-hour pharmacy.

Knightsbridge: Home of Harrods

The home of Harrods and Harvey Nichols (see the previous section "Shopping the Big Names: London Department Stores"), Knightsbridge is the second-most famous of London's retail districts (see the map "Knightsbridge and Chelsea Shopping").

Brompton Road (home to Harrods) runs southwest from the Knightsbridge tube stop. Beauchamp Place (pronounced "Beecham"), one of the streets running south from Brompton Road, is only one block long, but it's full of the kinds of trendy, upscale shops where young British aristocrats buy their clothing for "the season." In the 1980s, the future Princess Diana and other young blue-bloods and yuppies were dubbed "the Sloane Rangers" because this area near Sloane Square was their favorite shopping grounds (and Range Rovers were their favorite cars). Cheval Place, running parallel to Brompton Road to the north, is lined with designer resale shops. Sloane Street, where you can find plenty of fashion boutiques, runs south from the Knightsbridge tube stop to Sloane Square and the beginning of Chelsea.

Map House (54 Beauchamp Place, SW3; ☎ **020-7589-4325;** Tube: Knightsbridge) is an ideal place to find an offbeat souvenir, maybe an antique map, an engraving, or an old print of London; a century-old original engraving can cost as little as £10 ($17).

Chelsea: The young and the antique

Chelsea is famous for King's Road (Tube: Sloane Sq.). It's the area's main street and, along with Carnaby Street, is branded in Londoner's minds (those over 40, that is) as the street of the Swinging Sixties. About one-third of King's Road is devoted to antiques markets and *multistores,* large or small groups of indoor stands, stalls, and booths within one enclosure; another third houses design trade showrooms and stores of household wares, and the remaining third is faithful to the area's teenybopper roots. King's Road begins on the west side of the Sloane Square tube stop.

Shopping in Knightsbridge and Chelsea

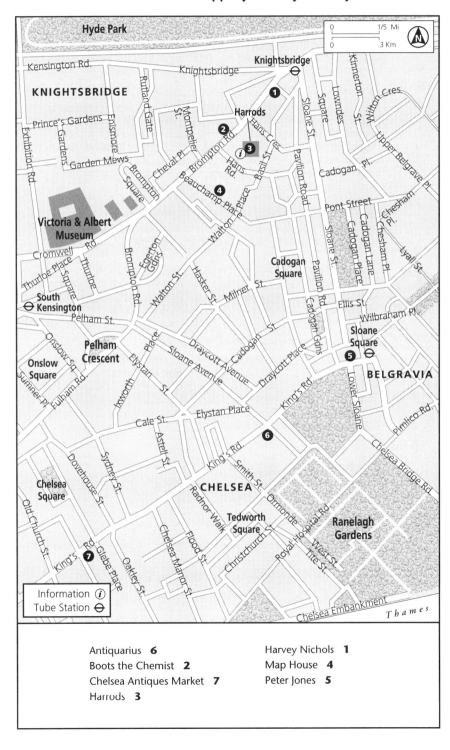

Antiquarius **6**

Boots the Chemist **2**

Chelsea Antiques Market **7**

Harrods **3**

Harvey Nichols **1**

Map House **4**

Peter Jones **5**

A Chelsea emporium founded in 1877, **Peter Jones** (Sloane Sq., SW1; ☎ 020-7730-3434; Tube: Sloane Sq.) is known for household goods, household fabrics and trims, china, glass, soft furnishings, and linens. The linen department is one of the best in London. You may also want to check out the **Chelsea Antiques Market** and **Antiquarius** (see the section "Hitting Portobello and Other Markets" later in this chapter).

Kensington: Street chic

You can reach Kensington, west of Knightsbridge, by taking the tube to High Street Kensington, the area's preeminent shopping street. Many of this neighborhood's retail shops cater to street chic teens. Although this strip offers a few staples of basic British fashion, most of the stores feature items that stretch and are very, very short or very, very long; very, very tight; and very, very black. And, of course, they sell the clunky shoes that go with these ensembles.

Kensington Church Street, running north to Notting Hill, is one of the city's main shopping avenues for antiques, selling everything from antique furniture to impressionist paintings.

The **Children's Book Centre** (237 Kensington High St., W8; ☎ 020-7937-7497; Tube: High Street Kensington) is the best place in London to go for children's books. Fiction is arranged according to age, up to 16. The center also sells videos and toys for kids.

Holborn: Heigh-ho, Silver!

Don't let the slightly out-of-the-way Holborn location, or the facade's lack of charm, put you off from visiting the **London Silver Vaults** (Chancery House, 53–63 Chancery Lane, WC2; ☎ 020-7242-3844; Tube: Chancery Lane). Downstairs are the real vaults — 40 in all — filled with a staggering collection of old and new silver and silverplate, plus a collection of jewelry.

The West End

The key areas in the West End are

- ✔ **Oxford Street** for affordable shopping
- ✔ **Regent Street** for fancier shops and more upscale department stores and specialty dealers
- ✔ **Piccadilly** for older established department stores
- ✔ **Jermyn Street** for traditional English luxury goods
- ✔ **Bond Street** for chic upscale fashion boutiques
- ✔ **Covent Garden** for all-purpose shopping, often with a hipper edge
- ✔ **St. Martin's Court (between Charing Cross Road and St. Martin's Lane)** for prints, posters, and books

Around Piccadilly Circus: A bit of everything

Many people consider Piccadilly Circus to be the center of London. However, for the best shopping, head south from the Piccadilly tube stop along Piccadilly (the street) or northwest along Regent Street. The following represent some of the most renowned Piccadilly Circus stores:

- ✔ **Burberry** (18–22 Haymarket, SW1; ☎ **020-7930-3343**; Tube: Piccadilly Circus) sells those famous raincoats, plus top-quality men's shirts, sportswear, knitwear, and accessories.

- ✔ **Hatchards** (187 Piccadilly, W1; ☎ **020-7439-9921**; Tube: Piccadilly Circus) was established in 1797 and is London's most historic and atmospheric bookstore.

- ✔ **Tower Records** (1 Piccadilly Circus, W1; ☎ **020-7439-2500**; Tube: Piccadilly Circus) is one of the largest tape and CD stores in Europe. It's practically a tourist attraction in its own right.

Jermyn Street: Traditional luxury

Two-block-long Jermyn Street lies a block south of Piccadilly between St. James's Street and Duke Street. Many of the posh men's haberdashers and toiletry shops along this street have been doing business for centuries and cater to the royals. They include the following:

- ✔ **Farlows** (5 Pall Mall, SW1; ☎ **020-7839-2423**; Tube: Piccadilly Circus) is famous for fishing and shooting equipment and classic country clothing.

- ✔ **Floris** (89 Jermyn St., SW1; ☎ **020-7930-2885**; Tube: Piccadilly Circus) is a small mahogany-clad store that's been selling its own line of soaps and perfumes since 1851.

- ✔ **Hilditch & Key** (73 Jermyn St., SW1; ☎ **020-7930-5336**; Tube: Piccadilly Circus) has been selling perhaps the finest men's shirts in the world for over a century. These quality goods are 100% cotton, cut by hand, and sport buttons fashioned from real shell.

- ✔ **Taylor of Old Bond Street** (74 Jermyn St., SW1; ☎ **020-7930-5544**; Tube: Piccadilly Circus) was established in 1954 and is devoted to the shaving and personal hygiene needs of men. The store offers the world's finest collection of shaving brushes, razors, and combs, plus soaps and hair lotions.

Regent Street: Upscale specialties

Regent Street begins in a grand sweeping curve on the west side of Piccadilly Circus and heads north to intersect with Oxford Street. This majestic street is lined with upscale department stores and specialty boutiques. The **Burlington Arcade** is a must-see if you're in this area. This famous glass-roofed Regency passage, running from Regent Street to Savile Row, is lit by wrought-iron lamps and decorated with clusters of ferns and flowers. It is lined with intriguing shops and boutiques.

Savile Row, synonymous with hand-tailored men's suits, lies a block west of Regent Street. Its once-countercultural counterpart — in the early Beatles' years — is **Carnaby Street,** now a sad tourist attraction trying to trade in on a vanished past; it's a block east of Regent Street. **Royal Doulton Regent Street** (154 Regent St., W1; ☎ 020-7734-3184; Tube: Piccadilly Circus or Oxford Circus) carries English bone china, including Royal Doulton, Minton, and Royal Crown Derby. (The January and July sales are excellent.) **Scotch House** (84–86 Regent St., W1; ☎ 020-7734-0203; Piccadilly Circus) is known globally for its selection of cashmere and wool knitwear for men, women, and children; it also sells tartan garments and accessories, as well as Scottish tweed classics.

If you're left-handed, you're in luck at **Anything Left Handed** (57 Brewer St., off Regent St., W1; ☎ 020-7437-3910; Tube: Piccadilly Circus). This unique store sells practical items — everything from scissors to corkscrews — for the southpaws in the world.

Do I need to tell you what you'll find at **The Disney Store,** 140 Regent St., W1 (☎ 020-7287-6558; Tube: Piccadilly Circus), which you'll see as you walk farther north toward Oxford Street? If you're looking for non-Disney toys, you couldn't do any better than **Hamleys** (188–196 Regent St., W1; ☎ 020-7494-2000; Tube: Piccadilly Circus) is the finest toy shop in the world, and stocks more than 35,000 toys and games on seven floors of fun and magic. You can get everything from cuddly stuffed animals and dolls to radio-controlled cars, train sets, model kits, board games, outdoor toys, and computer games.

Oxford Street: Affordable big names

Instead of beginning your shopping adventure on Regent Street, you may want to visit Oxford Street first, getting out at the Oxford Circus, Bond Street, or Tottenham Court Road tube stop. Oxford Street is more affordable than Regent Street — not as tony, but offering a good variety and quantity of merchandise.

If you are a chronic organizer who can't live without your Filofax, head immediately for **The Filofax Centre** (21 Conduit St., W1; ☎ 020-7499-0457; Tube: Oxford Circus). At this store on Conduit Street, which leads west from Regency Street, you can find the entire range of inserts and books at prices that are about half of what they are in the States. **The Body Shop** stores are based in the U.K but are now all over the States; however, prices at the London branches are much lower. You can stock up on their politically and environmentally correct beauty, bath, and aromatherapy products at **The Body Shop** (375 Oxford St., W1; ☎ 020-7409-7868; Tube: Bond St.). You can find other branches in every shopping zone in London.

The **Virgin Megastore** has two Oxford Street locations. The larger is at 14–16 Oxford St., W1; ☎ 020-7631-1234; Tube: Tottenham Court Rd.; the other is at 527 Oxford St., W1; ☎ 020-7491-8582; Tube: Oxford Circus). Thousands of current CDs in every genre are sold, and you can hear the release on headphones at listening stations before making a purchase.

Bond Street: Designer chic

Bond Street, running parallel to Regent Street on the west and connecting Piccadilly with Oxford Street, is home to all the hot international designers and is London's answer to New York's Fifth Avenue. It is divided into New (northern section) and Old (southern portion). Very expensive fashion boutiques line Bond Street and the adjacent streets. **Davies Street,** running south from outside the Bond Street tube station, is just one of the area's choicer streets; **Davies Mews** is an upscale shopping zone noted for its antiques dealers. You can access the area from the north by the Bond Street tube stop and from the south by Green Park.

Vivienne Westwood (6 Davies St., W1; ☎ **020-7629-3757;** Tube: Bond St.) is one of the hottest British designers for women. This flagship store carries a full range of jackets, skirts, trousers, blouses, dresses, and evening dresses. **Church's** (133 New Bond St., W1; ☎ **020-7493-1474;** Tube: Bond St.) sells classy shoes easily recognized by the fashion elite. Chocolate connoisseurs should visit **Charbonnel et Walker** (1 The Royal Arcade, 28 Old Bond St., W1; ☎ **020-7491-0939;** Tube: Green Park), famous for its hot chocolate (buy it by the tin) and strawberries-and-cream chocolates.

Around Leicester Square: Music and memorabilia

Leicester Square itself boasts only giant movie palaces and touristy restaurants (and the reduced-price ticket booth). But the streets around Leicester Square are filled with shops selling rare books, prints, and posters, some relating to the performing arts.

The Leicester Square shops include

- ✔ **Dress Circle** (57–59 Monmouth St., WC2; ☎ **020-7240-2227;** Tube: Leicester Sq.) specializes in show-business memorabilia for all West End and Broadway shows.

- ✔ **MDC Classic Music** (31–32 St. Martin's Lane, WC2; ☎ **020-7240-0270;** Tube: Leicester Sq.), sitting right next to the English National Opera, specializes in opera recordings; you can receive expert knowledge and personal service.

- ✔ **Stanfords** (12–14 Long Acre, WC2; ☎ **020-7836-1321;** Tube: Leicester Sq.) was established in 1852, and is the world's largest map shop (many of its maps, which include worldwide touring and survey maps, are unavailable elsewhere). It's also London's best travel bookstore.

Charing Cross Road: A Book lovers' delight

Charing Cross Road is a book lover's paradise because of its vast number of bookstores, selling both new and old volumes. Many of these places sell maps and guides, too, including the tourist's necessity, *London A to Z.* Some of the most fascinating bookstores include the following:

- ✔ **Murder One** (71–73 Charing Cross Rd., WC2; ☎ **020-7734-3485;** Tube: Leicester Sq.) specializes in crime, romance, science fiction, and horror books. Crime and science-fiction magazines, some obscure, are also available.

✔ **Silver Moon Women's Bookshop** (64–68 Charing Cross Rd.; ☎ 020-7836-7906; Tube: Tottenham Court Rd.) stocks thousands of titles by and about women, including a large selection of les-bian-related books. Plus the shop offers videos and jewelry.

✔ **Waterstone's** (121 Charing Cross Rd.; ☎ 020-7434-4291; Tube: Tottenham Court Rd.) is a U.K. chain with branches all over London. You can find the latest releases and well-stocked sections of books currently in print.

✔ **W & G Foyle, Ltd.** (113–119 Charing Cross Rd., WC2; ☎ 020-7440-3225; Tube: Tottenham Court Rd.) claims to be the world's largest bookstore, with an impressive array of hardcovers and paper-backs, as well as travel maps, records, videotapes, and sheet music.

Covent Garden: Something for everyone

Try to save some of your shopping energy for Covent Garden, home of what may be the most famous "market" in all of England: the **Covent Garden Market** (see the next section "Hitting Portobello and Other Markets").

Excellent English soaps, toiletries, and aromatherapy goods, as well as herbal goods, are available throughout the market and surrounding streets, including at the following shops:

✔ **Culpeper the Herbalist** (8 The Market, Covent Garden, WC2; ☎ 020-7379-6698; Tube: Covent Garden) sells food, bath, and aro-matherapy products as well as dream pillows, candles, sachets, and that popular favorite: the battery-operated aromatherapy fan.

✔ **Neal's Yard Remedies** (15 Neal's Yard, off Shorts Garden, WC2; ☎ 020-7379-7222; Tube: Covent Garden) is noted the world over for its all-natural, herbal-based bath, beauty, and aromatherapy products in cobalt-blue bottles.

✔ **Penhaligon's** (41 Wellington St., WC2; ☎ 020-7836-2150; Tube: Covent Garden) is an exclusive-line Victorian perfumery dedicated to good grooming. Choose from a large selection of perfumes, after-shaves, soaps, candles, and bath oils for women and men.

Also in Covent Garden you can find **Dr. Martens Department Store** (1–4 King St., WC2; ☎ 020-7497-1460; Tube: Covent Garden), the flag-ship for internationally famous "Doc Marts" shoes. Prices are far better here than they are in the States.

Farther along, at 14 King St., is **The Irish Shop** (☎ 020-7379-3625; Tube: Covent Garden), which sells a wide variety of articles shipped directly from Ireland, including colorful knitwear, traditional Irish linens, hand-knitted Aran fisherman's sweaters, and Celtic jewelry.

And you can finish off at **The Tea House** (15A Neal St., WC2; ☎ 020-7240-7539; Tube: Covent Garden), which sells everything associated with tea, tea drinking, and teatime.

Hitting Portobello and Other Markets

Kensington Church Street dead-ends at the Notting Hill Gate tube station, which is the jumping-off point for **Portobello Market,** the famous London street market along Portobello Road, about 2 blocks north of the tube stop. Portobello (market and road) is a magnet for collectors of virtually anything from precious junk to precious antiques. The Market is mainly open Saturday 6 a.m. to 5 p.m. You may find that perfect Regency commode you've always been looking for. But mixed in with the good things is a lot of overpriced junk, so you have to wade through to find anything worthwhile. Now that everything's been discovered and designated *collectible,* the prices are often too high.

My best advice is simply to treat Portobello Road on Saturday as a browsing event. Approximately 90 antiques and art shops along Portobello Road are open during the week when the street market is closed. Weekdays are actually a better time for serious collectors to shop, because they get more attention from dealers and aren't distracted by the throngs of shoppers.

The Portobello Market on a busy Saturday is prime pickpocketing territory. Keep an eye or a hand on your wallet or purse.

Covent Garden and Jubilee

The **Covent Garden Market** (☎ 020-7836-9136; Tube: Covent Garden) includes many different markets and is open daily 9 a.m. to 5 p.m. Traders sell all kinds of goods at the busy **Apple Market.** Much of the merchandise is what the English call *collectible nostalgia,* which includes glassware and ceramics, leather goods, toys, clothes, hats, and jewelry. Antiques dealers predominate on Mondays. Some of London's best shopping is available at the restored hall on The Piazza and at specialty shops in the area (see "The West End," earlier in this chapter).

On the back side is the **Jubilee Market** (☎ 020-7836-2139), a fancy hippie market offering cheap clothes and books.

Chelsea and Antiquarius

In a rambling old building, the **Chelsea Antiques Market** (245A–253 King's Rd., SW3; ☎ 020-7352w-5686; Tube: Sloane Sq.) offers endless bric-a-brac browsing possibilities. It's definitely a good place to search out old or rare books. You're likely to run across Staffordshire dogs, shaving mugs, Edwardian buckles and clasps, ivory-handled razors, old velours, lace gowns, wooden tea caddies; and that's just the beginning. It's closed on Sunday.

Another good market is **Antiquarius** (131–141 King's Rd., SW3; ☎ 020-7351-5353; Tube: Sloane Sq.), where more than 120 dealers offer specialized merchandise — usually of the small, domestic variety, such as antique and period jewelry, porcelain, silver, first-edition books, boxes, clocks, prints, and paintings.

Chapter 20

Planning Your Itinerary

• •

In This Chapter

▶ Seeing London on a reasonable schedule

▶ Planning fun itineraries for trips lasting from 3 to 7 days

▶ Organizing time and saving your energy

• •

*T*here's one problem every London visitor must face: how to see as much as possible in a limited amount of time. Lucky you if you have an entire week or even more. But what if you have only 3 or 5 days at your disposal? How can you sort out what's really worth seeing and fit it into a do-able day? That's what this chapter is all about. If you budget your time wisely and choose your sights carefully, even a short trip will be more enjoyable.

Start with two basic premises. The first is that you won't have as much time as you'd like, so you need to be selective because you simply can't see everything. The second is that you want to see the highlights of London without turning your trip into a test run for the London Marathon; to avoid racing about requires some advance planning because London is a huge place.

Many of London's major sights are concentrated in specific areas, so walking is the best way to see several sights in a short period of time. And transportation by Underground is fast and convenient (see Chapter 11).

Over the years, my feet have logged hundreds of miles exploring this endlessly fascinating city. I still get lost, but even that can be fun, if you look on London as an adventure waiting to happen. (And it's always a good idea to have a copy of *London A to Z* with you.)

This chapter offers three easy-to-do suggested daily itineraries. They're intended for the first-timer but include places that returning visitors (such as myself) always want to see again. The first 3 days are devoted to the big sights. After that, the itineraries become a little more adventurous. Each day's itinerary is a mix of sights and experiences. I don't believe in sending you to three museums in one day; the result is sensory overload and you would end up not seeing anything.

I believe that the street life of London — its unadulterated urban pulse — is just as valuable and interesting as historic palaces and the master-pieces you can find in museums. So I encourage you to walk in London's parks and through its crowded West End streets and squares. That is as much a part of the London experience as viewing its famous and fabulous monuments.

For fuller descriptions of the sights, plus exact street addresses, open-ing hours, and admission prices, see Chapters 16 and 17.

London in 3 Days

Three days doesn't seem like a very long time. But in that short period, you can hit most of the key sights in London and enjoy a memorable trip.

Day 1

Start your trip on **Day 1** with a visit to majestic **Westminster Abbey,** visiting the Royal Tombs and Poets' Corner. Afterward, because they're right next door, stroll around the **Houses of Parliament.** Unless you queue up to hear a debate, you won't be able to get inside, but you can enjoy a great riverside view from Westminster Bridge. On the opposite side of the Thames is the **British Airways London Eye,** a new 450-foot-high observation wheel. Reserve in advance for the trip up and over London, otherwise you may spend at least a half hour in line for a ticket and another hour before your scheduled "flight." You're not far from **Tate Britain,** so if you're in the mood to look at great English art, head over to Pimlico. Renting a self-guided audio tour will add to your enjoyment. Later in the afternoon, explore **Piccadilly Circus,** the teem-ing epicenter of London's West End. There's great shopping on Regent Street, Piccadilly, and Jermyn Street. If you haven't already reserved a seat for a **West End show,** you may want to stop by the half-price ticket booth in **Leicester Square** to see what's available. Have dinner in Soho before the show.

Day 2

Greet **Day 2** with a walk through **Green Park.** You're on your way to **Buckingham Palace** to witness the pageantry of the **Changing of the Guard** (check beforehand to make certain that it's taking place that day). For details on touring the State Rooms of Buckingham Palace during August and September, see Chapter 16. Reserve tickets in advance so you'll know your specific entry time, otherwise you may have to wait in line for an hour or more to get in. If you're not touring the palace itself, visit the **Royal Mews.** From Buckingham Palace you can stroll down The Mall, through **St. James's Park,** passing **Clarence House,** home of the Queen Mother, and **St. James's Palace,** London home of Prince Charles and his two sons.

Trafalgar Square, London's grandest and certainly most famous plaza, is your next stop. You can have lunch or tea at the **National Gallery's**

restaurant or in the **restaurant in the crypt** of St. Martin-in-the-Fields church on the east side of the square (see Chapter 16). Spend your afternoon viewing the treasures of the **National Gallery.** Renting one of the self-guided audio tours will help you to hone in on the most important paintings in the collection. After **dinner** in the Covent Garden area or on the Thames (see Chapter 18), cruise on to one of the **bars, pubs,** or **clubs** I describe in Chapter 24.

Day 3

On **Day 3,** arrive as early as you can at the **Tower of London** and immediately hook up with one of the 1-hour guided tours led by the Beefeaters. Later, you can explore the precincts on your own, making certain you allot enough time to see the **Crown Jewels.** From the Tower, head over to nearby **St. Paul's Cathedral,** which you can see in about half an hour.

The **British Museum,** your next stop, has enough to keep you occupied for several days; if you want to see only the highlights, allow yourself a minimum of 2 hours. Finish off your afternoon in Knightsbridge at **Harrods,** the most famous department store in London, and perhaps the world. Knightsbridge and adjacent South Kensington offer innumerable dining options (see Chapter 14).

London in 5 Days

This section assumes that you've already followed the suggested itineraries (see the preceding section) for your first 3 days.

Day 4

Day 4 begins at the **National Portrait Gallery,** where you can find the likeness of just about every famous British person you've ever heard of. Renting one of the self-guided audio tours is a good idea. From the portrait gallery you can easily walk to **Covent Garden Market.** Scores of interesting shops are in and around the market, and Covent Garden Piazza is a lively hub filled with restaurants, so it's a perfect spot for lunch. Spend your afternoon strolling in **Kensington Gardens** and visiting **Kensington Palace,** once the London home of Princess Diana. Then go for a traditional English dinner at **Rules,** London's oldest restaurant, or **Simpson's-in-the-Strand.** Are you up for a play or a concert tonight?

Day 5

Day 5 begins with a museum morning. The choice of museum is your call. Choosing among the three major South Kensington museums — the **Natural History Museum,** the **Science Museum,** and the **Victoria & Albert** — is entirely a matter of taste. If you like modern art, the newly opened **Tate Modern** on the South Bank is the place to spend your morning. (See Chapter 16 for a description of all the museums.) In the afternoon, expand your horizon with a short trip outside the city. Chapter 17 offers descriptions of the **Royal Botanic Gardens** at Kew, **Hampton Court, Windsor Palace, Hampstead Heath,** and **Greenwich.** None of these places is terribly far away; it'll take you anywhere from 20 minutes to an hour to reach them. You can be back in time for dinner and that show you've been wanting to see.

London in 7 Days

How time flies! By now, if you've followed the suggested itineraries for the last 5 days (see the preceding two sections), you've seen most of the major sights in London.

Day 6

On **Day 6,** you're ready for a day trip. It's terrific fun to ride in one of Britain's sleek new trains. The only problem is that you have to decide where you want to go. In Chapter 21, I give you the lowdown on six places, each remarkable in its own way. Do you want to see Shakespeare's birthplace in **Stratford-upon-Avon** or the famous prehistoric stone circle called **Stonehenge?** Do you want to spend a day by the seaside in **Brighton** or strolling around ancient **Canterbury** with its mighty cathedral? Or perhaps head to **Bath** to discover its splendid Georgian crescents. You can reach most of these places in 90 minutes or less.

Day 7

Day 7 is your last day in London and you'll want it to be special. In the morning, visit **Madame Tussaud's** or one of the museums you haven't yet seen. Afterward, stroll through **Hyde Park** and stop at **Apsley House,** the London home of the first duke of Wellington. This will give you a glimpse of what life was like inside one of London's great private palaces. If it's Sunday, you may instead want to visit **Spencer House,** the family home of the late Princess Diana. You can do some last-minute shopping, if you want to. Check out London's various shopping neighborhoods in Chapter 19, then make your way to the major shopping arteries: Knightsbridge, Oxford Street, Bond Street, King's Road in Chelsea, or Regent Street. A traditional afternoon tea at one of London's great hotels (see Chapter 15) is a delightful way to end the afternoon. After that? You've booked theater tickets, haven't you?

More Tips to Organize Your Time

Even a life-long Londoner can't hope to see everything the city has to offer. But you, with limited time, can see more if you organize your days efficiently and with common sense. Disorganized travelers waste a lot of time, show up at the museum on the day it's closed, and end up in the nether regions of Tooting Bec because they hopped the wrong

Underground line. Don't assume that every museum or site is open every day, all day. Take a moment to look at the details I provide for each attraction in Chapters 16 and 17. And carry a copy of *London A to Z* with you.

I know that for many of you this will be the first and perhaps only time you'll be in London, meaning that you'll want to cram in as much as possible, so I wrote the itineraries in this chapter with that reasoning in mind. Use them to help budget and organize your time so you can get the most out of your stay in London.

You probably have a list of places you want to see no matter what (fill out the worksheet at the back of the book to help you remember). The "must-sees" (see Chapter 16) are at the top of most lists of priorities, so I include them in the suggested daily itineraries. The itineraries are commonsense, limited-time suggestions only, however. You may want to spend your days doing something else entirely. Maybe it's more important for you to spend all day rather than a couple of hours in the British Museum. Maybe shopping in Chelsea and cafe hopping in Soho is more appealing to you than watching the Changing of the Guard at Buckingham Palace. Go for it! London can be enjoyed in countless ways that have nothing to do with traditional sightseeing.

A word of advice: Try to hit the very top sites on your list early in the day, preferably when they open or late in the afternoon. Visit the places that are really important to you when you're feeling fresh and when they're less crowded. I mean, in particular, Buckingham Palace (when it's open to the public during August and September), the Tower of London, Westminster Abbey, and Madame Tussaud's. Westminster Abbey, to cite just one example, can receive upward of 15,000 visitors per day!

An average top sight takes about 2 hours to visit, after you're actually inside. Some (Buckingham Palace and the Royal Mews) take more, others (Westminster Abbey and Kensington Palace) take less. But other variables enter in: whether or not you're taking a guided tour (usually about an hour to 90 minutes, no matter where), if you have kids in tow, or if lines move slowly due to the crowds of visitors. It's difficult to allot a certain amount of time to great institutions such as the British Museum and the National Gallery, loaded with so many treasures you could easily spend a full day or more. But as a general rule, you can "do" about three or four sights in a day if you're pushing yourself, fewer if you're not.

Nightlife Goals

A certain magic descends on London — especially in the West End — when night falls The street and neon lights begin to glow, and people head for restaurants, theaters, and pubs. Unless you have adrenaline to spare, try to unwind a little before you begin your round of after-dark diversions. You'll probably need some down time between the end of your sightseeing day and the beginning of your evening activities, so I suggest that you head back to your hotel to take a shower or bath and curl up with a novel or the evening paper for an hour or maybe catch a quick snooze to recharge your batteries. This plan allows you to think about your nightlife goals as a separate mini-itinerary — you'll hit the town refreshed and ready for action.

Keep geography and transportation time in mind so you don't find yourself finishing up your day at a pub in South Kensington with only half an hour before you have to get to a West End theater. Remember to leave time not only for resting, showering, changing, and dressing, but for that other pleasure of London: the fortuitous and unexpected things that happen when you finally *slow down*.

Chapter 21

Exploring Beyond London: Five Great Day Trips

In This Chapter

▶ Taking the best day trips from London

▶ Getting there and back

▶ Deciding what to see and do after you arrive

*I*n comparison to the United States, England is a small country. You may be delighted to find that practically every site in England is a day side trip from London.

In Chapter 17, I describe the easiest side trips from London: **Kew Gardens, Hampton Court Palace, Windsor Palace,** and **Greenwich.** In this chapter, I venture out to some of England's most popular, impressive, and famous places: Bath, Brighton, Canterbury, Stratford-upon-Avon, and Stonehenge. All these sites are within a few hours from London (see the map "Side Trips from London").

By Train or by Car: Weighing the Options

Because of England's small size and easy-access train and road networks, this country is a joy to explore.

From London you can reach Bath, Brighton, and Canterbury, in 90 minutes or less by train and in about 2 hours by car. The train trip to Stratford-upon-Avon or to Salisbury (the closest large town to Stonehenge) is about 2 hours; it'll take you about 3 hours by car. If you get an early start you can explore any one of these places, have lunch, and still be back in London in time for dinner.

The following sections help you decide whether train travel or automotion is for you.

Side Trips from London

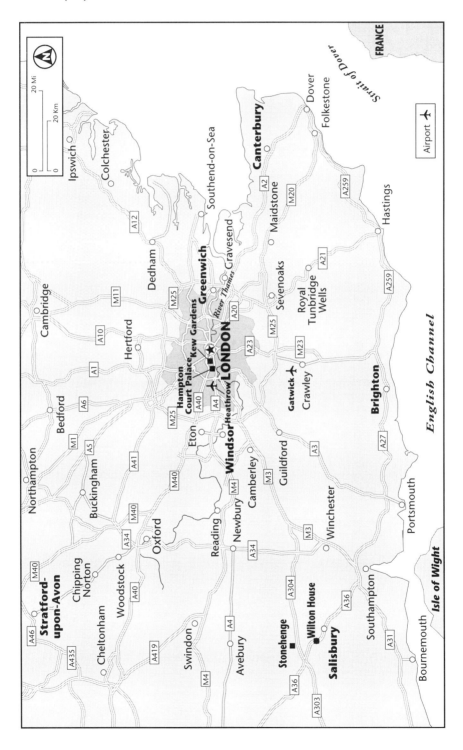

Taking the B train

If you plan to travel around England by train, get a BritRail pass before you arrive (see Chapter 3 for more informtaion). The BritRail Southeast Pass will get you to three of the towns in this chapter (but not to Bath or Stratford-upon-Avon). The cost for first-class travel for any 3 days in an 8-day period is $94 adults and $27 children (5 to 15 years); second-class is $69 adults and $18 children. Also available are 4-day and 7-day Southeast Passes.

Taking a car: Driving on the left, passing on the right

I always suggest that people travel by train instead of driving. Much of your car trip will be on motorways without much scenery, so what's the point? But some people want to drive, no matter what. If you're one of those people, this section is for you.

Before you even consider renting a car, ask yourself if you're comfortable driving with a steering wheel on the right-hand side of the vehicle while shifting with your left hand (you can get an automatic, but it'll cost considerably more). Remember, you must drive on the left and pass on the right.

Though the car-rental market in Britain is highly competitive, renting a car here costs more than in the United States — unless, that is, you can find a special promotional offer from an airline or a car-rental agency. Most U.K. car-rental agencies accept U.S. driver's licenses. In most cases you must be 23 years old (21 in some instances), no older than 70, and have had your U.S. license for more than a year.

You can often get a discount on car-rental rates if you reserve 48 hours in advance through the toll-free reservations offices. Weekly rentals are almost always less expensive than daily rates. And the rate, of course, depends on the size of the vehicle.

When you make your reservation, ask if the quoted price includes the 17.5 percent VAT and unlimited mileage. Then find out whether personal accident insurance (PAI), collision-damage waiver (CDW), and any other insurance options are included. If they aren't a part of the deal, which is usually the case, be sure to ask how much they cost. When you drive in any foreign country (or anywhere, for that matter), arrange for as much coverage as possible.

The collision-damage waiver and some other types of insurance are sometimes offered free by credit-card companies if you use that card to pay for the rental. If you're planning to rent a car, check with your credit-card company to see what's covered or you may end up paying for coverage you already have.

Bath

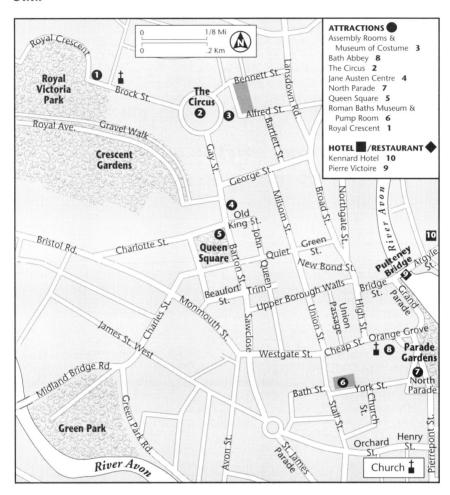

ATTRACTIONS ●

Assembly Rooms &
  Museum of Costume **3**
Bath Abbey **8**
The Circus **2**
Jane Austen Centre **4**
North Parade **7**
Queen Square **5**
Roman Baths Museum &
  Pump Room **6**
Royal Crescent **1**

HOTEL ■/RESTAURANT ◆

Kennard Hotel **10**
Pierre Victoire **9**

Bath: Hot Mineral Springs and Cool Georgian Magnificence

Bath, 115 miles west of London, is a beautiful spa town on the Avon
River. Since the days of the ancient Celts — and later the Romans —
Bath has been famous for its hot mineral springs. In 1702, Queen Anne
frequented the soothing, sulphurous waters and transformed Bath into
a spa for the elite. Aristocrats, socialites, social climbers, and flamboyant dandies such as Beau Nash have added to the spa's eclectic history. The great author Jane Austen used Bath as an upwardly genteel
setting for her class-conscious plots.

Today, the spa is a grand legacy from the Georgian era, boasting beautiful curving crescents and classically inspired buildings of honey-colored stone. Must-sees are the **Roman Baths Museum** and adjoining **Pump Room** (where visitors can continue the long tradition of sipping water while listening to music), the adjacent **Abbey,** and the **Assembly Rooms** (once used for balls and gaming).

Getting there

Trains for Bath leave from London's Paddington Station every half hour; the trip takes about 90 minutes. The off-peak (after 9 a.m.) round-trip fare is £30 ($49) except on Fridays, when it's £38.50 ($63).

By car, take the M4 to Junction 18, and then drive a few miles south on A46. (See the map "Bath.")

Getting visitor information and taking a tour

The free guided walks provided by Bath's Tourist Information Centre (☎ 01225-477-761), in the center of town on the square in front of Bath Abbey, are a great value. The tours leave from outside the **Pump Room** Monday through Friday at 10:30 a.m. and 2:30 p.m., Saturday at 10:30 a.m., and Sunday at 10:30 a.m. and 2:30 p.m. Additional walks are offered at 7 p.m. on Tuesday, Friday, and Saturday from May through October. From May through September, the information center is open Monday through Saturday 9:30 a.m. to 6 p.m. and Sunday 10 a.m. to 4 p.m. The rest of the year, it's open Monday through Saturday 9:30 a.m. to 5 p.m. and Sunday 10 a.m. to 4 p.m.

Seeing the sights

The Romans — who arrived in A.D. 75 — built the huge complex at the center of the **Roman Baths Museum (☎ 01225-477-785),** beside Bath Abbey. When visitors enter, they receive a portable self-guided audio tour keyed to everything on display, including the original Roman baths and heating system; it's fun, informative, and very well done. Admission is £6.90 ($12). The museum is open daily: October through March 9:30 a.m. to 5 p.m., April through September 9 a.m. to 6 p.m., and August 9 a.m. to 9 p.m.

Overlooking the Roman baths is the late-18th-century **Pump Room (☎ 01225-477-7785),** where the fashionable assembled to sip the vile-tasting but reputedly health-promoting water. Your ticket gains you entrance and you're welcome to taste it for yourself, if you dare. In the Pump Room, you can enjoy *elevenses* (morning tea), lunch, or after-noon tea to a background of live music. Main courses cost £9 to £10 ($15 to $17), a fixed-price lunch menu is £11.50 to £12.95 ($19 to $21), and afternoon tea is £5.75 to £8 ($9 to $13). The Pump Room is open Monday through Saturday 9:30 a.m. to 4:40 p.m. and Sunday 10:30 a.m. to 4:30 p.m.

Step inside **Bath Abbey** and view the graceful fan vaulting, the great East Window, and the ironically simple memorial to Beau Nash, the most flamboyant of the dandies who frequented Bath in its heyday. April through October, it's open Monday through Saturday 9 a.m. to 6 p.m. (to 4:30 p.m. November through March); year-round, it's open Sunday 1 to 2:30 p.m. and 4:30 to 5:30 p.m. Admission is by donation.

Another classic building worth visiting is the **Assembly Rooms** (Bennett Street; ☎ 01225-477-789), the site of all the grand balls and social climbing in 18th-century Bath. Admission is free unless you want to visit the excellent **Museum of Costume** that's part of the complex (£4/$7). Both are open daily 10 a.m. to 5 p.m.

Bath's newest attraction, the **Jane Austen Centre** (40 Gay St.; ☎ 01225-443-000) is located in a Georgian town house on an elegant street where Austen once lived. Exhibits and a video convey a sense of what life was like in Bath during the Regency period. The center is open Monday through Saturday 10 a.m. to 5 p.m. and Sunday 10:30 a.m. to 5:30 p.m. Admission is £4 ($7).

Bath is a wonderful walking town, filled with beautiful squares and sweeping residential crescents. Stroll along the North Parade and the South Parade, Queen Square, and The Circus and be sure to have a look at the **Royal Crescent,** a magnificent curving row of 30 town houses designed in 1767 by John Wood the Younger. Regarded as the epitome of Palladian style in England, the Royal Crescent is now designated a World Heritage site. **No. 1 Royal Crescent (☎ 01225-428-126)** is a gorgeously restored 18th-century house with period furnishings. It's open Tuesday through Sunday: mid-February to October 10:30 a.m. to 5 p.m. and November 10:30 a.m. to 4 p.m. Admission is £4 ($7).

Finding a place to stay

If you want to spend the night in Bath, try the **Kennard Hotel** (11 Henrietta St., Bath BA2 6LL; ☎ 01225-310-472; Fax: 01225-460-054; e-mail: kennard@dircon.co.uk; Internet: www.kennard.co.uk). On the east side of Pulteney Bridge, within walking distance of everything in Bath, this elegant hotel with 13 guest rooms occupies a beautifully restored 1794 Georgian town house. The rates are £78 to £98 ($129 to $162) double, breakfast included. American Express, MasterCard, and Visa are accepted.

Deciding where to dine

Pulteney Bridge was built in 1770 and spans the Avon a few blocks south of the Assembly Rooms. It's one of the few bridges in Europe lined with shops and restaurants, including the picturesque and popular eatery **Pierre Victoire** (16 Argyle St.; ☎ 01225-334-334). The Modern French/British menu changes daily, with a fixed-price two-course lunch at £7.95 ($13); main courses run about £9 to £15 ($15 to

$25). It accepts MasterCard and Visa and is open Monday through Friday 11a m. to 11 p.m, Saturday 1:30 a.m. to 11 p.m., and Sunday 10:30 a.m. to 10:30 p.m. Book in advance on weekends.

Brighton: Fun beside the Seaside

On the Sussex coast, a mere 50 miles south of London, Brighton is England's most famous, and probably most popular, seaside town. It was a small fishing village until the Prince Regent, who would become George IV, became enamored of the place and had the incredible Royal Pavilion built. Where royalty moves, fashion follows, and Brighton eventually became one of Europe's most fashionable towns. The lovely Georgian terraces you see everywhere date from this period. Later in the 19th century, when breathing ozone-laden sea air was considered healthy, the Victorians descended in hordes. Today, Brighton is a commuter suburb of London and a popular place for conventions and romantic weekend getaways. Gays and lesbians are very much a part of the local and visitor scene.

Getting there

Connex South Central has over 40 trains a day from London's Victoria Station. The trip takes about an hour. If you travel off-peak (after 9 a.m.), a round-trip ticket is £14.60 ($24).

If you're driving, the M23 from central London leads to Brighton. The drive should take about an hour, but if roads are clogged it'll take twice that time.

Getting visitor information

Brighton is a compact town, and the easiest way to get around is on foot. Forget about that frantic need for sightseeing and relax. That's what Brighton is all about. It's a place for leisurely strolling, either in the town or along the seaside promenades. The town is small enough so you won't get lost and large enough to offer some good cultural diversions. (See the map "Brighton.")

Brighton's **Tourist Information Centre** (10 Bartholomew Sq.; ☎ 01273-292-599) is opposite the town hall, about a 10-minute walk south from the train station. It's a good place to pick up info on current events and a Gay Information Sheet listing gay guesthouses, pubs, and clubs. If you fall in love with Brighton and decide to stay overnight, you can reserve a room at the information center. It's open Monday through Friday 9 a.m. to 6 p.m. (to 5 p.m. September through May), Saturday 10 a.m. to 5 p.m. (to 6 p.m. May through September), and Sunday 10 a.m. to 4 p.m. (to 6 p.m. May through September); it's closed Sundays December through February.

Brighton

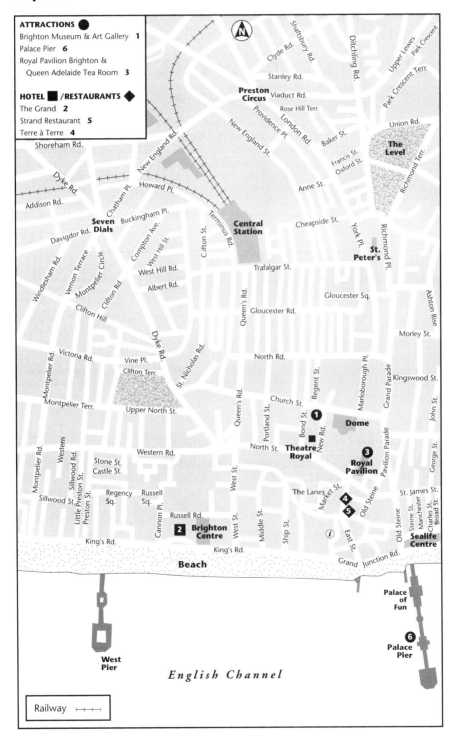

ATTRACTIONS ●
Brighton Museum & Art Gallery **1**
Palace Pier **6**
Royal Pavilion Brighton &
    Queen Adelaide Tea Room **3**

HOTEL ■ /RESTAURANTS ◆
The Grand **2**
Strand Restaurant **5**
Terre à Terre **4**

Shoreham Rd.
Clyde Rd.
Shaftsbury Rd.
Ditchling Rd.
Upper Lewes
Park Crescent
Park Crescent Terr.
Stanley Rd.
Preston Circus
Viaduct Rd.
Rose Hill Terr.
Providence Pl.
London Rd.
Baker St.
Union Rd.
New England St.
New England Rd.
Francis St.
Oxford St.
The Level
Richmond Terr.
Anne St.
Dyke Rd.
Howard Pl.
Chatham Pl.
Addison Rd.
Seven Dials
Buckingham Pl.
Davigdor Rd.
Compton Ave.
Clifton St.
Terminus Rd.
Central Station
Cheapside St.
York Pl.
Richmond Pl.
St. Peter's
West Hill St.
West Hill Rd.
Windlesham Rd.
Vernon Terrace
Montpelier Circle
Clifton Rd.
Albert Rd.
Trafalgar St.
Gloucester Sq.
Ashton Rise
Clifton Hill
Queen's Rd.
Gloucester Rd.
Dyke Rd.
Morley St.
Victoria Rd.
Montpelier Rd.
Vine Pl.
Clifton Terr.
St. Nicholas Rd.
North Rd.
Regent St.
Marloborough Pl.
Grand Parade
Kingswood St.
Montpelier Terr.
Upper North St.
Queen's Rd.
Church St.
John St.
Western Rd.
Portland St.
Bond St.
New Rd.
Dome
Montpelier Rd.
Western
Stone St.
Castle St.
North St.
Theatre Royal
Royal Pavilion
Pavilion Parade
George St.
Sillwood Rd.
Little Preston St.
Preston St.
Regency Sq.
Russell Sq.
Cannon Pl.
Russell Rd.
The Lanes
Market St.
Old Steine
St. James St.
Steine St.
Manchester St.
Charles St.
Broad St.
Sillwood St.
Brighton Centre
West St.
Middle St.
Ship St.
East St.
Old Steine
Sealife Centre
King's Rd.
King's Rd.
Beach
Grand Junction Rd.

West Pier

Palace of Fun

Palace Pier

English Channel

Railway ┝━┿━┥

Seeing the sights

Brighton's one must-see attraction is the **Royal Pavilion (☎ 01273-290-900),** set in a small landscaped park bounded by North Street, Church Street, Olde Steine, and New Road. It's one of the most extraordinary palaces in Europe. John Nash redesigned the original farmhouse and villa on this site for George IV (when the king was still Prince Regent), who lived here with his mistress, Lady Conyngham, until 1827.

The exterior, as crazily wonderful as anything King Ludwig of Bavaria dreamed up, is an Indian fantasy of turrets and minarets. The interior, decorated in the Chinese style, is sumptuous and fantastically extravagant. The pavilion was later used by the king's brother, William IV, and Queen Victoria. Admission is £4.50 ($7) adults. The pavilion is open daily: October to May 10 a.m. to 5 p.m. and June to September 10 a.m. to 6 p.m. Guided tours, given daily at 11:30 a.m. and 2:30 p.m., cost an extra £1 ($1.65).

Before you leave the pavilion, consider having lunch or a cream tea in the superbly restored **Queen Adelaide Tea Room (☎ 01723-292-736),** open daily 10:30 a.m. to 4:30 p.m. (to 5 p.m. in summer). Queen Adelaide, who used this suite in 1830, didn't appreciate the epicurean tastes of her husband, George IV. Dismissing his renowned French chefs, she reverted back to British cuisine so dreary that Lord Dudley complained "you now get cold pâté and hot champagne." The lunch selections range from £2 to £5 ($3 to $9) and cream teas from £4 to £6 ($7 to $10).

Close to the Royal Pavilion, on Church Street, is the small **Brighton Museum & Art Gallery (☎ 01273-290-900),** with some interesting art nouveau and art deco collections of furniture, glass, and ceramics, plus a Fashion Gallery. It's a good place to wile away an hour or two on a rainy day when you can't go to the beach. Admission is free, and it's open Monday and Tuesday and Thursday through Saturday 10 a.m. to 5 p.m. and Sunday 2 to 5 p.m.

The town's famous amusement area, **Palace Pier,** jutting out into the sea just south of the Royal Pavilion, was built in the late 19th century. Today it's rather tacky but worth visiting nonetheless. At night, all lit up with twinkling lights, it's almost cheerily irresistible. Spend half an hour but don't expect to find much more than junk food and arcade games.

The entire seafront is a pebbly public beach used for swimming and sunning. If you're into sunbathing *au naturel,* Brighton has the only nude beach in England, about a mile west of Brighton Pier. You'll recognize it when you get there.

Finding a place to stay

The grandest place to stay is **The Grand** (King's Road, Brighton, Sussex BN1 2FW; ☎ **01273-321-188;** Fax: 01273-202-694; E-mail: grandbrighton.co.uk). This huge 1864 seaside resort hotel, dazzlingly white, is five-star luxury throughout. The 200 guest rooms are spacious and predictably gorgeous, done mostly in blues and yellows, with big tile baths. The most expensive have sea-facing balconies and floor-to-ceiling double-glazed windows. The special weekend and Leisure rates can cut the rack rate almost in half. Rack rates are £210 to £250 ($346 to $412) double, full English breakfast included. American Express, Diners Club, MasterCard, and Visa are accepted.

Deciding where to dine

One of the hippest (and friendliest) places for dining is the bow-fronted **Strand Restaurant** (6 East St.; ☎ **01273-747-096**), which serves Modern British cuisine. The ever-changing fixed-price menu is an extremely good value. Herby homemade vegetable soup, pâté, or mussels cooked with fresh cream, wine, and garlic may be followed by chicken breast with leeks and blue cheese sauce, artichoke-and-pesto lasagne, or lamb chops with gravy and a dessert. Main courses are £8 to £15 ($13 to $25), and the three-course fixed-price menu is £9.95 ($17). It's open daily 12:30 to 10 p.m. (to 10:30pm on weekends). American Express, Diners Club, MasterCard, and Visa are accepted.

For a new outlook on vegetarian food, try **Terre à Terre** (71 East St.; ☎ **01273-729-051**). Considered the best vegetarian restaurant in England, perhaps in all Europe, it elevates meatless cuisine into the art it should be but rarely is. The food is impeccably fresh and beautifully presented. You can eat your way through the menu with the Terre à Tapas, a superb selection of all their best dishes, big enough for two. Main courses are £9.50 to £10.50 ($16 to $17). It's open Tuesday through Saturday noon to 10:30 p.m., Sunday 10 a.m. to 10:30 p.m. (brunch 10 a.m. to 1 p.m.), and Monday 6 to 10:30 p.m. Reservations are essential. Diners Club, MasterCard, and Visa are accepted.

Canterbury: Tales from the Great Cathedral

Magnificent **Canterbury Cathedral** is one of the glories of England. It was here that Chaucer's pilgrims made their way, spinning the yarns found in *The Canterbury Tales.* For nearly 400 years, the devout, in search of miracles and salvation, trekked to the cathedral's shrine of Thomas à Becket, archbishop of Canterbury, who was murdered in 1170 by henchmen of Henry II. (The pilgrims didn't stop coming until Henry VIII had the shrine destroyed in 1538.) Modern pilgrims, today called "day-trippers," continue to pour into the Kentish city of Canterbury, on the river Stour, 56 miles southeast of London. They come to see the cathedral, of course, but also to visit the host of small museums and to enjoy the picturesque semi-medieval town surrounding it.

Getting there

Waterloo Station provides frequent train service. For schedules and information, call ☎ **0345-484-950.** The journey takes 1½ hours. To drive from London, take the A2 and then the M2; Canterbury is signposted all the way. The city center is closed to cars, but several parking areas are close to the cathedral.

Getting visitor information and taking a tour

At the **Visitors Information Centre** (34 St. Margaret's St.; ☎ **01227-766567**), near St. Margaret's Church, you can buy tickets for daily guided-tour walks of the city and cathedral. The walks leave from here at 11:30 a.m. (July 1 through August) and 2 p.m. (April 11 through October). The cost is £3.50 ($6) adults, £3 ($5) seniors/students/children under 14, and £8.50 ($14) families. April through October, the center is open daily 9:30 a.m. to 5:30 p.m. (to 5 p.m. November through March, to 6 p.m. July and August).

On the Stour, just below the 15th-century Weavers House, **Weavers River Trip** (Weavers House, 1 St. Peter's St.; ☎ **01227-464660**) offers half-hour boat trips with a commentary on the history of the buildings the tour passes. April through September, boats depart each half hour from 1 p.m. through sunset. Tickets are £3.50 ($6) adults and £2.50 ($4) children. Umbrellas are available in case of rain.

Seeing the sights

Make your first stop **Canterbury Cathedral** (11 The Precincts; ☎ **01227-762862**), an imposingly magnificent structure that was the first major expression of the Gothic style in England. The crypt dates from about 1100 and the cathedral itself (rebuilt after a fire) from the 13th century, with a bell tower added in the 15th century. (See the map "Canterbury.")

Though Henry VIII destroyed Becket's shrine, its site is still honored in the Trinity Chapel, near the high altar. Noteworthy features of the cathedral are a number of panels of rare stained glass and the medieval royal tombs of Henry IV and Edward the Black Prince. Admission is £2.50 ($4) adults and £1.50 ($3) children/students/seniors. Guided tours (based on demand) cost £3 ($5) adults, £2 ($3) students/seniors, and £1.50 ($3) children. The cathedral is open daily: Easter through September 8:45 a.m. to 7 p.m. and October through the day before Easter 8:45 a.m. to 5 p.m. As you stroll the cathedral grounds, you may encounter flocks of well-behaved boys and girls wearing blazers and ties: They attend **King's School,** the oldest public school in England, housed in several fine medieval buildings north of the cathedral.

Canterbury

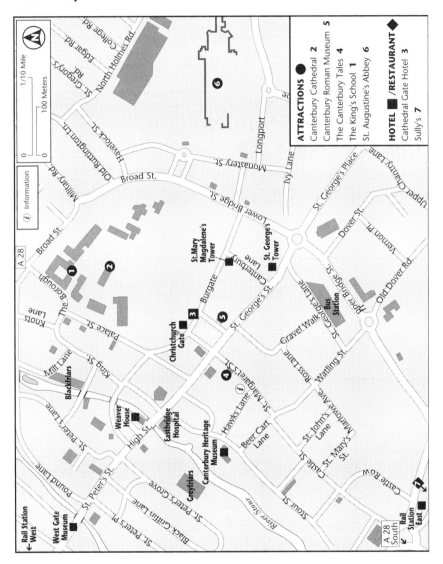

Off High Street, near the cathedral, is the entertaining museum/exhibition known as **The Canterbury Tales** (23 St. Margaret's St.; ☎ **01227-454888**), where medieval tableaux re-create the pilgrimages of Chaucerian England. On audio headsets you can hear five of Chaucer's *Canterbury Tales* and the story of the murder of St. Thomas à Becket. Give yourself 45 minutes to an hour to see/hear the entire show. Admission is £5 ($8) adults, £4.25 ($7) seniors/students, and £4 ($6) children 5 to 16. It's open daily 9:30 a.m. to 5:30 p.m.

Two millennia ago, the conquering Romans were living in Canterbury, which they called Cantuaria. Their daily lives are chronicled in the small but fascinating **Canterbury Roman Museum (☎ 01227-785-575)**, in the excavated Roman levels of the city between the cathedral and High Street on Butchery Lane. Admission is £2.20 ($4) adults, £1.45 ($2.40) seniors/students, and £1.10 ($1.80) children. The museum is open Monday through Saturday 10 a.m. to 5 p.m. (Sunday 1:30 to 5 p.m. from June through October).

Although the cathedral gets the lion's share of attention in Canterbury, another Christian site predates it by about 600 years. Set in a spacious park, about a 10-minute walk east from the center of town, are the atmospheric ruins of **St. Augustine's Abbey** (Longport; ☎ 01227-673-345), founded in 598 and one of the oldest Anglo-Saxon monastic sites in the country. This World Heritage site offers interactive audio tours. Admission is £2.50 ($4) adults and £1.90 ($3.15) seniors/students. The site is open daily 10 a.m. to 6 p.m. Trek another 5 minutes east to visit the oldest parish church in England. **St. Martin's Church** (North Holmes Road; **(☎ 01227-459-482),** founded by Queen Bertha (the French wife of Saxon King Ethelbert), was already in existence when Augustine arrived from Rome to convert the natives in 597. Admission is free, and the church is open daily 9 a.m. to 5 p.m.

Finding a place to stay

If you're planning an overnight in Canterbury and want, like the pilgrims of yore, to stay near the cathedral, you can't get any closer than the **Cathedral Gate Hotel** (36 Burgate, Canterbury, Kent CT1 2HA; ☎ **01227-464381**; Fax: 01227-462800; E-mail: cgate@cgate.demon.co.uk). Dating from 1438, the 27-room hotel adjoins Christchurch Gate and overlooks the Buttermarket. The guest rooms are comfortable and modestly furnished, with sloping floors, massive oak beams, and winding corridors — what else would you expect from a hotel built over 500 years ago? Rates are £75 ($120) double, continental breakfast is included. American Express, Diners Club, MasterCard, and Visa are accepted.

Deciding where to dine

One of the best restaurants in Canterbury is **Sully's,** in the County Hotel (High Street; ☎ **01227-766266**). You can choose from a selection of traditional English dishes or try one of the more imaginatively conceived platters or seasonal specialties. Reservations are recommended. A fixed-price lunch is £17 ($27) for 2 courses or £16 ($26) for 3 courses; a fixed-price dinner goes for £23 to £27.50 ($37 to $45). American Express, Diners Club, MasterCard, and Visa are accepted, and it's open daily 12:30 to 2:20 p.m. and 7 to 10 p.m.

Stratford-upon-Avon: Where Shakespeare Walked

Stratford-upon-Avon is a shrine to the world's greatest playwright, William Shakespeare, who was born, lived much of his life, and is buried in this market town on the Avon River, 91 miles northwest of London.

Stratford boasts many Elizabethan and Jacobean buildings, and the charms of its once-bucolic setting haven't been totally lost, but you may have trouble finding a quiet spot to enjoy them. In summer, crowds of international tourists overrun the town, which aggressively hustles its Shakespeare connection. Besides the literary pilgrimage sights, the top draw in Stratford is the **Royal Shakespeare Theatre,** where Britain's foremost actors perform. If you visit the shrines and see a play, you can quickly move on to another of England's attractions, confident that you haven't missed anything in Stratford.

Getting there

Direct trains leave frequently from London's Paddington Station; the journey takes about 2 hours at a cost of ₤22.50 ($37) for an off-peak (after 9:30 a.m.) or weekend round-trip ticket. Call ☎ **0345-484-950** for information and schedules. To drive from London, take the M40 toward Oxford and continue to Stratford-upon-Avon on the A34.

Getting visitor information and taking a tour

Stratford's **Tourist Information Centre** (Bridgefoot; ☎ **01789-293-127**) provides information and maps of the town and its major sites. Easter through October, it's open Monday through Saturday 9 a.m. to 6 p.m. and Sunday 11 a.m. to 5 p.m.; November through February, it's open Monday through Saturday 9 a.m. to 5 p.m. Guided tours of Stratford leave from outside the tourist office. Open-top double-decker buses depart every 15 minutes daily 9:30 a.m. to 5:30 p.m. in summer. Tour tickets are valid all day, and you can take a 1-hour ride without stops or can get off and on at any or all of the town's five Shakespeare properties (see the following section). Tours cost ₤8 ($13) adults, ₤6.50 ($11) seniors/students, ₤2.50 ($4) children under 12, and ₤18.50 ($31) families (2 adults and up to 4 children).

Stratford-upon-Avon

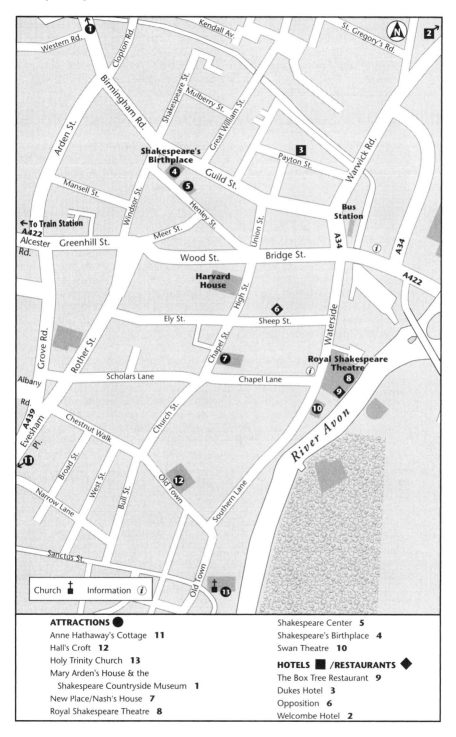

Church ✝   Information (i)

ATTRACTIONS ●
Anne Hathaway's Cottage **11**
Hall's Croft **12**
Holy Trinity Church **13**
Mary Arden's House & the
   Shakespeare Countryside Museum **1**
New Place/Nash's House **7**
Royal Shakespeare Theatre **8**

Shakespeare Center **5**
Shakespeare's Birthplace **4**
Swan Theatre **10**

HOTELS ■ **/RESTAURANTS** ◆
The Box Tree Restaurant **9**
Dukes Hotel **3**
Opposition **6**
Welcombe Hotel **2**

Seeing the sights

A combination ticket that you can buy at your first stop gets you into the five sites administered by the Shakespeare Birthplace Trust: **Shakespeare's Birthplace, Anne Hathaway's Cottage, New Place/Nash's House, Mary Arden's House,** and **Hall's Croft.** The ticket costs £11 ($18) adults, £10 ($17) seniors/students, £5.50 ($9) children, and £26 ($42) families (2 adults, 3 children).

You can start your tour where Shakespeare did: at **Shakespeare's Birthplace** (Henley Street; ☎ 01789-204-016), where the Bard was born on April 23, 1564. Today, the two 16th-century half-timbered houses joined together (his father's glove and leather shop on one side and the family residence on the other) are filled with Shakespeare memorabilia. After visiting the bedroom where wee Willie winked into the world, the Elizabethan kitchen, and the Shakespeare Museum illustrating his life and times, you can walk through the garden. The modern **Shakespeare Centre** next door is a library, exhibition space, and study center. Both the Birthplace and the Centre are open daily: March 20 through October 19, 9 a.m. to 5 p.m. (from 9:30 a.m. on Sunday) and off-season 9:30 a.m. to 4 p.m. (from 10 a.m. on Sunday). It's closed December 24 through 26. Admission is £4.90 ($8) adults and £2.20 ($4) children. Anne Hathaway was married to William Shakespeare. Her family members were yeomen farmers, and they all lived in a lovely thatched cottage before she married 18-year-old Shakespeare (a May-September marriage in reverse: Anne was much older than Will).

To visit **Anne Hathaway's Cottage** (Cottage Lane, Shottery; ☎ 01789-292-100; about a mile south of Stratford), take a bus from Bridge Street or, better still, walk there along the well-marked country path from Evesham Place. Many original 16th-century furnishings, including the courting settle, are preserved inside the house, which was occupied by Anne's ancestors until 1892. Before leaving, be sure to stroll through the beautiful garden and orchard. It's open daily: March 20 through October 19 from 9:30 a.m. to 5 p.m. and off-season 9:30 a.m. to 4 p.m. (from 10 a.m. on Sunday). It's closed January 1, Good Friday, and December 24 through 26. Admission is £3.90 ($7) adults, £1.60 ($3) children, and £9 ($15) families.

Shakespeare retired in 1610 to **New Place** (Chapel Street; ☎ 01789-204-016). By that time, he was a relatively prosperous man whose plays had been seen by Queen Elizabeth; New Place was a Stratford house that he'd purchased a few years earlier and where he was to die in 1616. The house was later torn down and, today, only the gardens remain. To reach the site from his birthplace, walk east on Henley Street and south on High Street, which becomes Chapel Street. Visitors enter through **Nash's House,** which belonged to Thomas Nash, husband of Shakespeare's granddaughter. The house contains 16th-century period rooms and an exhibit illustrating the history of Stratford. Adjoining the house is a **Knott Garden** landscaped in an Elizabethan style. The house is open daily: March 20 through October 19 9:30 a.m. to 5 p.m. (from 10 a.m. on Sunday) and off-season 10 a.m. to 4 p.m. (from 10:30 a.m. on Sunday). It opens at 1:30 p.m. on January 1 and Good Friday; it's closed December 24 through 26. Admission is £3.30 ($5) adults, £1.60 ($3) children, and £7.50 ($12) families.

Shakespeare's daughter, Susanna, probably lived with her husband, Dr. John Hall, in **Hall's Croft** (Old Town; ☎ **01789-292-107**), a magnificent Tudor house with a walled garden. From New Place, continue south on Chapel and Church streets and turn east on Old Town to reach Hall's Croft. The house is furnished in the style of a middle-class 17th-century home. On view are exhibits illustrating the theory and practice of medicine in Dr. Hall's time. Opening times and admissions are the same as for Nash's House (see the preceding paragraph).

Shakespeare died on his birthday, aged 52, and is buried in **Holy Trinity Church** (Old Town; ☎ **01789-266-316**), a beautiful parish church in an attractive setting near the Avon River. Apparently, Shakespeare didn't want to leave Stratford, even in death. The inscription on his tomb reads "and curst be he who moves my bones." March through October, you can visit the church Monday through Saturday 8:30 a.m. to 6 p.m. (to 4 p.m. the rest of the year); year-round, it's open Sunday 2 to 5 p.m. Admission to the church is free, but a small donation is requested to see Shakespeare's tomb.

A Tudor farmstead, with its old stone dovecote and outbuildings, is the last of the five Shakespeare shrines and was reputedly the girlhood home of Shakespeare's mother. About 3½ miles north of Stratford on the A34 (Birmingham) is **Mary Arden's House** and the **Shakespeare Countryside Museum** (Wilmcote; ☎ **01789-204-016**). The house contains country furniture and domestic utensils; in the barns, stable, cowshed, and the farmyard is an extensive collection of farming implements illustrating life and work in the local countryside from Shakespeare's time to the present. The house and museum are open daily: March 20 through October 19 9:30 a.m. to 5 p.m. (from 10 a.m. on Sunday) and off-season 10 a.m. to 4 p.m. (from 10:30 a.m. on Sunday). It opens at 1:30 p.m. on January 1 and Good Friday; it's closed December 24 through 26. Admission is £4.40 ($7) adults, £2.20 ($4) children, and £11 ($18) families.

Seeing Hamlet or Twelfth Night As You Like It

The **Royal Shakespeare Theatre** (Waterside, Stratford-upon-Avon CV37 6BB; ☎ **01789-295-623**) is the home of the **Royal Shakespeare Company,** which typically stages five Shakespeare plays during a season running November through September. You can reserve seats through a North American or an English travel or ticket agent (see Chapters 9 and 22). A few tickets are always held for sale on the day of a performance; but if you wait until you arrive in Stratford, you may not be able to get a good seat. The box office is open Monday through Saturday 9 a.m. to 8 p.m. but closes at 6 p.m. on days when no performances are on the schedule. Ticket prices are £6 to £46 ($10 to $74).

Finding a place to stay

During the long theater season, reserve in advance if you're planning to sleep, perchance to dream, in Stratford. However, the **Tourist Information Centre** (Bridgefoot; ☎ **01789-293-127**) can help you find accommodations.

If you want to stay in the lap of luxury, try the **Welcombe Hotel** (Warwick Road, Stratford-upon-Avon, Warwickshire CV37 0NR; ☎ **01789-295-252;** Fax: 01789-414-666; Internet: www.welcombe.co.uk). Located 1½ miles northeast of the town center, this top-of-the-line, full-service hotel is in one of the country's great Jacobean houses. The largest of the 68 guest rooms are big enough for tennis matches; in the smaller rooms you'd have to content yourself with table tennis. You can enjoy an 18-hole golf course and 157 acres of grounds. Rates are £150 to £175 ($248 to $280) double, English breakfast included. Diners Club, MasterCard, and Visa are accepted.

Dukes (Payton Street, Stratford-upon-Avon, Warwickshire CV37 6UA; ☎ **01789-269-300;** Fax: 01789-414700; Internet: www.astanet.com/get/dukeshtl) is a charming choice for the budget-conscious. The hotel was formed from two Georgian townhouses and is located in Stratford's center, near Shakespeare's birthplace. The nicely restored public areas and 22 guest rooms are attractive. Many amenities are available that are usually found in more expensive hotels. The hotel's restaurant serves good English and continental cuisine. No children under 12 are accepted. Rooms go for £70 to £115 ($116 to $190) double, English breakfast included. American Express, MasterCard, and Visa are accepted.

Deciding where to dine

Take your camera to snap some pictures of the river Avon and its gliding white swans when you visit **The Box Tree Restaurant** (Waterside; ☎ **01789-293-226**) in the Royal Shakespeare Theatre. The menu offers French, Italian, and English cuisine, and you can dine by candlelight after a performance. Reservations are required (a special phone for reservations is available in the theater lobby). The matinee lunch is £16 ($26). Three-course fixed-price dinners cost £25.50 ($42) on Monday through Thursday and £26.50 ($44) on Friday and Saturday. American Express, MasterCard, and Visa are accepted. The restaurant is open noon to 2:30 p.m. on matinee days and Monday through Saturday 5:45 p.m. to midnight.

The **Opposition** (13 Sheep St.; ☎ **01789-269-980**), housed in a 16th-century building in the heart of Stratford, offers a historic setting but moderate prices. Lunch and dinner choices are a mix of traditional and Modern British cuisine. Reservations are recommended, and main courses are £6.25 to £15 ($10 to $24). The restaurant accepts MasterCard and Visa and is open daily noon to 2 p.m. and 5 to 11 p.m.

Salisbury

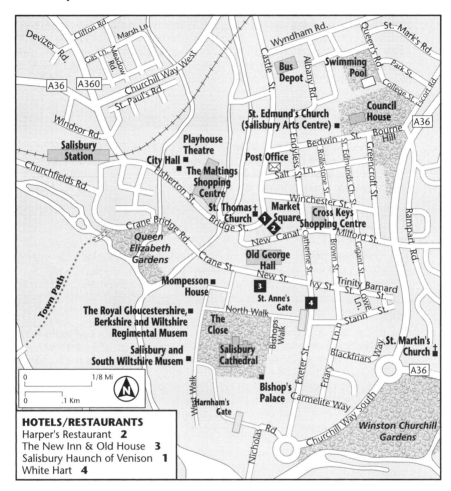

HOTELS/RESTAURANTS
Harper's Restaurant **2**
The New Inn & Old House **3**
Salisbury Haunch of Venison **1**
White Hart **4**

Salisbury and Stonehenge: Gothic Splendor and Prehistoric Mysteries

The tall slender spire of Salisbury Cathedral rises up from the plains of Wiltshire and marks the lovely old market town of **Salisbury,** or New Sarum, as it was once called. The town lies in the valley of the Avon River, 90 miles southwest of London and is the picturesque site of Tudor inns and tearooms, all dominated by the beautiful cathedral. The ancient pillars of **Stonehenge** are about 9 miles away.

Getting there

Hourly **Network Express trains** leave Waterloo Station and travel to Salisbury. The journey takes 2 hours and costs £21.90 ($36) for an off-peak (after 9:30 a.m.) round-trip ticket. For information and schedules, call ☎ **0345-484-950.** If you're driving from London, head west on the M3 to the end of the run, continuing the rest of the way on the A30.

Getting visitor information

Salisbury's **Tourist Information Centre** is on Fish Row (☎ **01722-334-956).** October through April, it's open Monday through Saturday 9:30 a.m. to 5 p.m. (to 6 p.m. June and September, to 7 p.m. July and August); May to September, it's also open Sunday 10:30 a.m. to 4:30 p.m.

Seeing the sights

The lovely old market town of Salisbury is often overlooked by visitors eager to see Stonehenge, but I suggest that you try to spend a bit of time wandering through Salisbury Cathedral. (See the map "Salisbury.")

Salisbury

Despite an ill-conceived renovation in the 18th century, the **Salisbury Cathedral's** (The Close; ☎ **01722-323-279**) 13th-century structure remains the best example of the Early English, or Perpendicular, style in all England. The 404-feet spire is the tallest in the country. The beautiful 13th-century octagonal chapter house possesses one of the four surviving original texts of the Magna Carta. Adding to the serene beauty of the cathedral are the cloisters and an exceptionally large **close,** comprising about 75 buildings. May through August, the cathedral is open daily 8:30 am. to 8:30 p.m. (to 6:30 p.m. September through April). The suggested donation for admission is £2.50 ($4) for the cathedral and 30p (50 cents) for the chapter house.

Shakespeare's troupe entertained there. General Eisenhower and his advisors formulated plans for the D-Day landings at Normandy on the same site. Where is this place of such historic diversity? In the town of Wilton, 3 miles west of Salisbury on the A30, is **Wilton House** (☎ **01722-746-729),** the home of the earls of Pembroke. The 21-acre grounds include rose and water gardens, riverside and woodland walks, and a huge adventure playground for children.

The house is noted for its 17th-century staterooms by the celebrated architect Inigo Jones (who designed the Queen's House at Greenwich). It's filled with beautifully maintained furnishings and world-class art, including paintings by Van Dyck, Rubens, Brueghel, and Reynolds. You can visit a reconstructed Tudor kitchen and Victorian laundry, plus the Wareham Bears, a collection of approximately 200 miniature dressed teddy bears. Easter through October, the house is open daily 11 a.m. to 6 p.m. (last admission 5 p.m.). Admission is £6.75 ($11) adults and £4

($7) children 5 to 15. If you're without wheels, take the bus that stops on New Canal, just north of the Salisbury train station; check with the tourist office for schedules.

Stonehenge

About 9 miles north of Salisbury, at the junction of the A303 and the A344/A360, is one of the world's most renowned prehistoric sites and one of England's most popular attractions, the prehistoric stone circle known as **Stonehenge (☎ 01980-624-715).** If you're not driving, hop on one of the Wilts & Dorset buses that depart from the train station daily between 11 a.m. and 2 p.m.; the trip takes about 40 minutes, and the round-trip fare is £4.80 ($8). The crowds can be overwhelming as the day wears on, so arrive as early as possible.

Stonehenge is a stone circle of megalithic pillars and lintels built on the flat Salisbury Plain. Experts believe that the site is from 3,500 to 5,000 years old. Many visitors to Stonehenge are disappointed to find that the site isn't as enormous as they envisioned, and is now surrounded by a fence that keeps sightseers 50 feet from the stones. Keep in mind, however, that many of the stones, which weigh several tons, were mined and moved from sites as far away as southern Wales in a time before forklifts, trucks, and dynamite.

Obviously, Stonehenge was a shrine and/or ceremonial gathering place of some kind. The old belief that Stonehenge was built by the Druids has been discredited (it's probably older than the Celtic Druids). A popular theory is that the site was an astronomical observatory because it's aligned to the summer equinox and people can accurately predict eclipses based on the placement of the stones. But in an age when experts think they know everything, Stonehenge still keeps its tantalizing mysteries to itself. The site is open daily: March 16 through May and September through October 15, 9:30 a.m. to 6 p.m., June through August 9 a.m. to 7 p.m., and October 16 to March 15, 9:30 a.m. to 4 p.m. Admission is £4 ($7) adults, £3 ($5) students/seniors, and £2 ($3) children.

Finding a place to stay

I recommend the **White Hart** (1 St. John St., Salisbury, Wiltshire SP1 2SD; ☎ 01722-327-476; Fax: 01722-412-761; Internet: www.heritagehotels. com) for anyone who is visiting Salisbury. The 68-room hotel has been a landmark since Georgian times and was totally renovated in 1995. It offers accommodations in the older section of the building or in a new motel-like section in the rear. A good restaurant is on site. Rates are £115 to £140 ($190 to $224) double, and it accepts American Express, MasterCard, and Visa.

If you're looking for an inexpensive but atmospheric (and smoke-free) B&B, try **The New Inn & Old House** (39–47 New St., Salisbury, Wiltshire SP1 2PH; ☎ 01722-327-679). This 15th-century building, with a walled garden backing up to the Cathedral Close Wall, offers seven well-appointed oak-beamed guest rooms. The Inn restaurant serves reasonably priced meals. Rates are £50 to £70 ($83 to $116) double, continental breakfast included. American Express, MasterCard, and Visa are accepted.

Deciding where to dine

Looking for homemade, simple, and healthy food? Go to **Harper's Restaurant** (7–9 Ox Row, Market Square; ☎ 01722-333-118). You can order from two menus, one featuring cost-conscious bistro-style platters and the other a longer menu with all-vegetarian pasta dishes. Reservations are recommended. Main courses are £8.50 to £12.50 ($14 to $21) and fixed-price three-course meals £8 ($13) at lunch and £13 ($21) at dinner. American Express, MasterCard, and Visa are accepted. It's open Monday through Saturday noon to 2 p.m. and 6:30 to 9:30 p.m. and Sunday 6 to 9:30 p.m. (October through May, it's closed on Sunday).

The **Salisbury Haunch of Venison** (1 Minster St.; ☎ 01722-322-024) is a creaky-timbered 1320 chophouse and pub that serves English roasts and grills. The house specialty is roast haunch of venison with bubble and squeak (mashed potatoes and cabbage). Main courses are £9 to £13 ($15 to $21), with pub platters at £4 to £6 ($7 to $10). American Express, MasterCard, and Visa are accepted. The restaurant is open daily noon to 2:30 p.m. and Monday through Saturday 7 to 9:30 p.m. The pub is open Monday through Saturday 11 a.m. to 11 p.m. and Sunday noon to 10:30 p.m. It's closed Christmas through Easter.

Part VI
Living It Up After Sundown

"I know you're all classically trained actors, but I don't think the public's ready for Titus Andronicus performed by the cast of Stomp."

In this part . . .

*L*ondon, for some of us, is synonymous with the performing arts. Year-round, on every evening of the week,
you'll find someone performing something somewhere.
Planning a night out here isn't the problem — choosing
from among all the possibilities is where the difficulty lies.

Because theater is unquestionably the most popular of the
city's cultural choices — for many visitors, a trip to
London wouldn't be complete without seeing at least one
play or musical — I begin this part by giving you the lowdown on the scene in Chapter 22. But if theater isn't your
thing, you won't be lacking for other diversions. In
Chapter 23, I highlight London's other performing arts:
grand opera performed by two companies; symphonic
concerts by London's and the world's leading orchestras,
modern and classical ballet by the top dance companies,
and countless musical recitals by chamber groups and
internationally known artists.

Nightlife in London is certainly not restricted to the "high
arts," however. In Chapter 24, I introduce you to some of
the many places where you can rub elbows with Londoners
and perhaps have a pint or two — pubs, bars, clubs, discos,
cabarets, and jazz spots.

Chapter 22

Experiencing the Grand Tradition: London's Theater Scene

In This Chapter

▶ Getting the inside scoop on London's theater scene

▶ Finding out what's on and where

▶ Getting tickets

▶ Enjoying pre- or post-theater dinner

---

*I*n the United States, people think of New York City as the theater capital. But from a global perspective, London may hold that title, based on the number of offerings and the quality of the performances. Of course, London didn't attain this stature overnight. The city has been building its theatrical reputation since the Elizabethan era, when Shakespeare, Marlowe, and others were staging their plays in a South Bank theater district.

Plays and musicals are staged all over the city in approximately 100 theaters, but the commercial hits are centered in the West End (the site of approximately 50 theaters). **The Barbican** and the South Bank area also provide major theater venues. Just like New York, London is the home of many *fringe* venues (the equivalent of Off or Off Off Broadway theaters).

This chapter gives you the information you need in order to take advantage of London's long theater tradition.

Seeing the Big — and Not So Big — Shows

Before you begin to consider which plays or musicals to attend, you need some basic information. You should know that booking a seat before you leave is the best way to ensure that you'll get to enjoy the performance of your dreams, especially if you want to see one of the hot musicals or a big-name star in a limited-run show. Hit shows such as *The Lion King* can be sold out months in advance.

Do you know what you should wear for your evening at the theater? You certainly don't have to dress to the nines, but if you arrive in a sweatsuit and running shoes you'll be pretty conspicuous. (No one would be rude enough to say anything, of course.) London theater audiences are, on the whole, pretty well dressed. There are no hard and fast rules here, just use common sense and "try to look nice," as my mum used to say.

With those critical details in mind, you can begin to orient yourself to the London theater scene. The following sections provide the basics.

Visiting Theaterland

The West End theater district — also called Theaterland — is concentrated in the area around Piccadilly Circus, Leicester Square, and Covent Garden (see the map "Central London Theaters" on the Cheat Sheet at the front of this book). But the theaters at the **Barbican** and **South Bank Centre** (see the next section) are theatrically considered West End venues as well.

I can't guarantee that you'll like whatever play you see in the West End. But you can expect that the production values and the performances will be of the highest quality. Major British stars with international screen reputations regularly perform in the West End, though you're just as likely to see a show starring someone you've never heard of but who's well known in England. You can also expect to find a few American plays and musicals, because the crossover between London and New York is increasing. And here's some good news: Tickets are considerably cheaper here than in New York. In London, you'll rarely pay more than £35 ($58) for the best seats in the house.

London's theater offerings always include new plays, long-run favorites, and revivals of the classics, as well as Shakespeare. Some of the shows in the West End have been running for years and show no sign of winding down, for example Agatha Christie's *Mousetrap* and Andrew Lloyd Webber's *Phantom of the Opera*. In general, evening performances are Monday through Saturday and, depending on the show, matinees are on Wednesday or Thursday and Saturday. Some shows have added Sunday performances, too. Matinees are a couple of pounds cheaper than evening performances.

Plays in the West End have varying curtain times. Evening performances may begin at 7:30, 8, or 8:30 p.m. and matinees at 1:30, 2, or 2:30 p.m. Check your ticket to be certain because if you're late you won't be admitted until the second act or a suitable pause in the action. (If it's a one-act play, good luck.) Londoners take their theater very seriously (even the comedies), so don't be one of those boorish latecomers who whines that the tube was late. If you come laden with packages, you can check them in the coatroom. Don't tip the usher who shows you to your seat. Talking and noisily unwrapping pieces of candy during the performance will be frowned on — especially if I'm in the audience.

Finding a ticket bargain beyond the West End

I can't list all the theaters in Theaterland, but I need to highlight three stand-out venues. They're geographically outside of London's West End but are still considered part of the West End theater community.

✔ The **Barbican Centre** (Silk Street, EC2; Tube: Barbican), a multi-arts center in The City, is the London home of the prestigious **Royal Shakespeare Company** (☎ **020-7638-8891**), which performs in the 1,156-seat **Barbican Theatre.** Other plays are performed in **The Pit,** a 200-seat studio theater. Also in the complex are bars, cafes, and restaurants. Ticket pries vary from show to show but generally are less than those for commercial hits in the West End; theatergoers under 25 and over 60 qualify for special reductions. The box office is open daily 9 a.m. to 8 p.m. Call ☎ **020-7382-7297** for 24-hour recorded info on all Barbican Centre events, or you can check out the performance calendar on the Web at www.rsc.org.uk.

✔ The **South Bank Arts Centre** (South Bank, SE1; Tube: Waterloo) is home to the **Royal National Theatre** (☎ **020-7452-3000),** which performs in three theaters: the **Olivier** (1,160 seats), **Lyttelton** (890 seats), and **Cottesloe** (a smaller theater-in-the-round). The Royal National performs Shakespeare but is just as likely to offer a new David Hare work or a Tennessee Williams revival. Ticket prices are slightly lower than at the commercial theaters on the other side of the river, generally £10 to £29 ($17 to $48) for evening performances and £9 to £25 ($15 to $41) for matinees. Unsold seats are offered at even lower prices 2 hours before curtain The facility also houses cafes, bars, and a good bookstore. The box office is open Monday through Saturday 10 a.m. to 8 p.m. For information on performances, call ☎ **020-7452-3400** (Monday through Saturday 10 a.m. to 11 p.m.). All performances, and an online booking form, can be found at www.nationaltheatre.org.uk.

✔ **Shakespeare's Globe Theatre** (New Globe Walk, Bankside, SE1; ☎ **020-7401-9919;** Tube: Cannon St. or London Bridge) is the newest addition to the South Bank theater scene. It presents a June-through-September season of the Bard's plays in a reconstructed oak-and-thatch open-air Elizabethan theater (performances may be cancelled because of rain). The benches can be numbing, but the discomfort is worth it to see Shakespeare performed not far from the original theater and right beside the Thames. Check out www.shakespeares-globe.org for current performances.

In London, play programs aren't handed out free of charge to every patron at a West End theater. If you want a program, you must buy it. The cost is usually £2 to £3 ($3 to $5).

Exploring the fringe

In many ways, fringe theater is London's real theatrical heartbeat. The *fringe* is London's equivalent of New York's Off or Off Off Broadway. Now, it's commonly called *Off West End.* (When my own play, *Beardsley*, was produced in London, it was on the fringe.) Groups performing on the fringe don't have the big bucks to mount lavish West End productions, but they often hope that their shows will be critical hits and move to the West End. With the overabundance of acting talent in London, the fringe is where you may see tomorrow's stars acting today and next season's hit in its original bare-bones form. The plays performed on the fringe are sometimes controversial or experimental, but for true theater lovers they can provide a stimulating alternative to the tradition and glamour of the West End. The performance spaces for fringe productions are usually smaller than for West End shows (sometimes tiny, sometimes above a pub) and the ticket prices much lower (rarely more than £10/$17). Fringe theaters and spaces adapted to fringe productions are scattered far and wide, so consult a *London A to Z, Time Out,* or call the theaters directly for directions on how to find them.

Enjoying the outdoor theater

If you don't enjoy the confines of a crowded, stuffy theater, you can sit in the moonlight and watch a good play. The **Regent's Park Open Air Theatre** (Regent's Park, NW1; ☎ **020-7486-2431**; Tube: Baker St.) has a May-to-August season. This large venue offers real theater seats but no roof, so rain may cancel the show. It's on the north side of Queen Mary's Rose Garden. **Shakespeare's Globe** (see the previous section "Beyond the West End") is another venue that's open to the heavens.

Finding Out What's On

You know that you want to attend a play, but how do you find out what's playing where? You can find details for all London shows, concerts, and other performances in the daily London newspapers: the *Daily Telegraph*, the *Evening Standard*, the *Guardian*, the *Independent*, and the *Times*. Another good source is the free booklet *London Planner*, available at the British Travel Centre (1 Regent St.) or by mail from a British Tourist Authority travel office (for addresses, see "Information" in the Appendix). For the most comprehensive listings of London theatrical performances, plus thumbnail synopses of the plots and (usually scathing) critical opinion, buy a copy of the weekly magazine *Time Out,* available at London newstands on Wednesdays for £1.95 ($3), or see its Web site at www.timeout.com. The Web is one of the best places to search in advance for information on plays and performances currently running in London. The following sites may be useful:

✔ www.londontheatre.co.uk

✔ www.keithprowse.com

✔ www.albemarle-london.com

✔ www.timeout.com

✔ www.telegraph.co.uk

✔ www.Sunday-times.co.uk

Getting Tickets

If you have your heart set on seeing a major London theatrical performance, order your tickets in advance — before you leave home — to ensure that you'll have a seat (see Chapter 9). That's my best advice.

But if you're in London and decide then that you want to see a show, you may still be able to get a seat. Even though an announcement has been made that a show is sold out, you can often buy a ticket from the theater's box office, which usually opens at 10 a.m. Ticket cancellations occur, and last-minute house seats go on sale the day of the performance or an hour before. Many London theaters offer standby seats, sold an hour before the performance to students and seniors with proper ID. Matinees are somewhat cheaper than evening performances.

If you don't have time to go to the box office and have a major credit card handy, call the theater directly. The phone numbers are listed in the papers and in *Time Out.* Many London theaters accept telephone credit-card bookings at regular prices (plus a minimal fee of under $2 a ticket). They'll hold your tickets at the box office, where you pick them up any time up to a half-hour before the curtain.

By buying directly from the box office, you don't have to pay the commission fee (up to 30 percent) charged by ticket agencies.

Buying a ticket in "the stalls" doesn't mean that you'll be seated in the ladies' powder room. It means that you may have one of the best seats in the house. *Stalls* is the British term for first-floor orchestra. Most of the West End theaters are fairly old, which means that they may have *boxes* for sale as well. These box seats will be on the sides of the second or third tier.

Using ticket agencies

All over the West End ticket agencies boldly advertise that they have tickets to the sold-out hit shows. Most of these places are legitimate, but their commission fees vary. If you choose to use the services of a ticket agency rather than booking directly with the box office (see the preceding section), I recommend that you call, stop in, or book online at one of the following trustworthy agencies:

✔ **Globaltickets/Edwards & Edwards** maintains a counter at the Britain Visitor Center (1 Regent St., SW1; ☎ **020-7734-4555** or 020-7734-4500; Internet: www.globaltickets.com Tube: Piccadilly Circus). It's open Monday through Friday 10:15 a.m. to 6:15 p.m. and Saturday and Sunday 10 a.m. to 4 p.m. You'll pay a variable commission on top of the ticket price.

✔ The **Albemarle Booking Agency** (74 Mortimer St., London, W1; ☎ **020-7637 9041;** Internet: www.albemarle-london.com; Tube: Oxford Circus or Goodge St.) is another long-established agency, open Monday through Friday 10 a.m. to 6 p.m. and Saturday 10 a.m. to 5 p.m. Its commission fee is 25 percent. Albemarle maintains dedicated theater desks at several of London's ritzier hotels, including the **Savoy,** the **Park Lane Hilton,** the **Dorchester,** and **Claridge's.** Its commission fee of 25 percent on top of the ticket price is what you can expect to pay for just about any theater booking made through a hotel concierge.

Two trustworthy agencies accept credit-card bookings 24 hours and charge a 25 percent commission:

✔ **First Call** (☎ **01293-453-744;** Internet: www.firstcalltickets.com)

✔ **TicketMaster** (☎ **0870-606-9999;** Internet: wwwticketmaster.co.uk)

You can pick up your tickets at the box office.

Before you buy any ticket from any agency, the agent must tell you the face value of the tickets (you can ask to see them). Before you sign the charge receipt, be sure to check the seat numbers, the face value of the tickets, and the agent's booking fee. If you're making a telephone booking, the agent must disclose the face value of the tickets, their locations, and whether you'll have a restricted view.

Beware of unlicensed ticket agencies that charge far more than the face value of the ticket plus a very hefty commission fee. A commission fee should *never* be more than 30 percent of the regular ticket price. Reputable ticket agencies belong to the Society of Ticket Agents and Retailers (STAR) and always advertise this fact.

The **Society of London Theatre** (☎ **020-7836-0971**) operates a half-price ticket booth in the clock tower building by the gardens in Leicester Square (Tube: Leicester Sq.). The booth provides no telephone info line, so you have to show up in person to see what's on sale that day. The booth is open Monday through Saturday noon to 6:30 p.m. and noon to 2 p.m. for matinees (which may be on Wednesday, Thursday, Saturday, or Sunday). Tickets are sold only on the day of performance. This transaction is a cash-only affair; no credit cards or traveler's checks are accepted. You pay exactly half the price plus a nominal fee (under $5). The most popular shows usually won't be available, but you may luck out. Tickets for the English National Opera and other events are sometimes available as well. You may want to stop by in any case to pick up a free copy of *The Official London Theatre Guide*, which lists every show with addresses and phone numbers and includes a map of the West End theater district.

You'll see ticket agencies around Leicester Square advertising half-price or reduced-price tickets. Keep in mind that there's only one official half-price ticket booth. At these other places, you may be sold a reduced-price ticket for a seat that just happens to be in the last row of the balcony or a seat with a restricted view. And wave away those pesky scalpers who hang out in front of mega-hits. They may indeed be selling (for an astronomical price) a valid ticket. But some of these *touts,* as they're called, also forge tickets, which means that you'll be out of cash and out of a show. By law, any tout must disclose the face value of the ticket, so you'll know exactly what the mark-up is. The best advice: Don't deal with them.

Dining Before or After the Performance

After you decide which show to see, you need to figure out whether to eat dinner before or after your theatrical experience. By eating before-hand, you may feel too rushed to make the curtain — and hungry again after the show lets out. Eating late is more fun and relaxed, but hunger pangs may mar your theater enjoyment and not every restaurant is open late.

Many of the restaurants I review in Chapter 14 serve pretheater meals. These places are geared for the theater crowd, so they know your time is limited. Pretheater menus are usually served 5:30 to 7 p.m. Your choices are limited to a set menu, but you'll be out by 7:30 p.m. or earlier. The prices are usually a good value.

The following restaurants are close to West End theaters and have pretheater menus:

- ✔ **The Ivy,** 1–5 West St., Soho, WC2; ☎ **020-7836-4751;** Tube: Leicester Sq.

- ✔ **Joe Allen,** 13 Exeter St., Covent Garden, WC2; ☎ **020-7836-0651;** Tube: Covent Garden

- ✔ **L'Odeon,** 65 Regent St. (entrance on Air Street), Piccadilly Circus, W1; ☎ **020-7287-1400;** Tube: Piccadilly Circus

- ✔ **Quaglino's,** 16 Bury St., St. James's, SW1; ☎ **020-7930-6767;** Tube: Green Park

- ✔ **Rules,** 35 Maiden Lane, Covent Garden, WC2; ☎ **020-7836-5314;** Tube: Covent Garden

- ✔ **Simpson's-in-the-Strand,** 100 The Strand (next to the **Savoy Hotel**), WC2; ☎ **020-7836-9112;** Tube: Charing Cross

Just be certain to book a table beforehand. If you're dining outside of the West End, allot extra time to order, eat, pay the bill, get your coats, and then hop on the tube or hail a taxi to make the curtain.

If you're not fussy about what you eat and you just want to keep your stomach from growling during the performance, fast-food joints are plentiful in Leicester Square and Piccadilly Circus. And if you're going farther afield — to the **Barbican** or **South Bank Centre** — you can ward off impending hunger pangs with a light meal or a sandwich at one of the cafes or restaurants on the premises.

I'm not a big one for late dining, and in the West End the final curtain rarely comes down before 10:30 p.m. (at the opera the performance usually isn't over until 11 p.m.). If you're dining after the show, find out whether the restaurant of your choice is open (the late-night dining custom isn't as established in London as in New York). And if you're using the tube, remember that most lines end service at 11:30 p.m. or midnight at the very latest. You may want to have dinner before the show and dessert and coffee afterward.

Chapter 23

The Performing Arts

In This Chapter

▶ Going to symphony, chamber-music, and rock concerts

▶ Seeing opera, dance performances, and films

▶ Finding out what's playing

▶ Getting tickets

*L*ondon is a mecca of the performing arts. Whether you enjoy symphony or rock concerts, operas or classical ballets, you can feed your need for music or dance. Take your pick from the city's own Royal Opera, Royal Ballet, English National Opera, or London Symphony Orchestra. Or see one of the internationally renowned groups for which London is a tour stopover. This chapter gives you the information you need to plan your trip to include the performing arts.

Finding Out What's Where

London newspapers have Arts or Culture sections in their Sunday editions, and you can access many of them on the Web to see what the city has scheduled in the performing arts. The most comprehensive are the *Times* (www.Sunday-times.co.uk) and the *Telegraph* (www.telegraph.co.uk). For a week-long list of what's happening, check *Time Out,* available at newsstands on Wednesdays and on the Web at www.timeout.com. For a map of London's theatre district, see the Cheat Sheet at the front of this book.

Artsline at ☎ **020-7388-2227** provides advice on disabled accessibility to London arts and entertainment events.

Purchasing Tickets

If you want to attend a musical event or a dance performance, I recommend that you go to the box office to buy tickets or call the venue and order tickets by phone. Buying direct saves you from paying a big commission fee. Generally, by using a credit card, you can order tickets from the box office — or online — before you leave home and pick them up in London.

The following agencies accept credit-card bookings 24 hours a day, all charging at least 25 percent commission:

✔ **Keith Prowse** (☎ **800-669-7469** in the U.S. or 0293/453-744; www.keithprowse.com)

✔ **Albemarle Booking Agency** (☎ **020-7637-9041**; www.albemarle-london.com)

✔ **TicketMaster** (☎ **0870-606-9999**; www.ticketmaster.co.uk)

✔ **Globaltickets** (☎ **020-7734-4555**; www.globaltickets.com)

Enjoying a Night at the Opera

London is home base to two major opera companies. The **Royal Opera** enjoys the most international prestige. It performs operas in the original languages and boasts the most famous international singers. Its home is the **Royal Opera House** (Covent Garden, WC2E; ☎ **020-7304-4000** info line; Tube: Covent Garden), which just reopened after a years-long state-of-the-art refurbishment that added two smaller venues — the **Linbury Studio Theatre** and the **Glore Studio Theatre.** Ticket prices for grand opera run £8 to £150 ($12 to $247). For a summary of the opera (and ballet) season, check the Web site www.royalopera.org. If you have your heart set on seeing an opera at the Royal Opera, book as far ahead as you possibly can — I'm talking months, not days. The season runs September through August.

The **English National Opera** (usually referred to as the ENO) beats the Royal Opera in popularity and inventiveness. It performs at the **London Coliseum** (St. Martin's Lane, WC2N; ☎ **020-7632-8300** for box office, open 24 hours Monday through Saturday for phone bookings, 10 a.m. to 8 p.m. in person; Tube: Leicester Sq.). The operas are all sung in English. Seats run £5 to £55 ($9 to $91); 100 balcony seats at £2.50 ($4) and 37 Dress Circle seats at £27 ($45) go on sale at 10 a.m. on the day of the performance (except for Saturday evenings). The opera season runs September through July. You can see the ENO program and book online by going to its Web site at www.eno.org.

The following two venues also offer the opportunity to see opera during your time in London:

✔ The **Holland Park Theatre** (Holland Park, W8; ☎ **020-7602-7856**; Tube: Holland Park) boasts London's most charming outdoor stage, set in the ruins of a Jacobean mansion and used for a mid-June through August season of opera. Performances are held in a covered auditorium; tickets run £14 to £25 ($23 to $41).

✔ The **D'Oyly Carte Opera Company** performs Gilbert & Sullivan's comic operas at the **Savoy Theatre,** The Strand (☎ **020-7836-8888**; Tube: Charing Cross); tickets are £12.50 to £35 ($21 to $58).

Enjoying Bach, Beethoven, and Brahms

London offers some of the world's finest classical and chamber music. This section describes your choices for enjoying these types of music.

From the Barbican to the Royal Albert

The home base for the **London Symphony Orchestra** (www.lso.co.uk) is the **Barbican Hall** at the Barbican Centre (Silk Street, EC2Y; ☎ 020-7638-8891 for 24-hour recorded info; Tube: Barbican), the concert hall portion of a giant performing-arts complex in The City. You may also catch a performance by the **Royal Philharmonic Orchestra** (www.rpo.co.uk), which plays concerts here and at the Royal Albert Hall, another all-purpose venue for classical music.

The **Royal Albert Hall** (Kensington Gore, SW7; ☎ 020-7589-8212; Tube: High St. Kensington) is an enormous circular domed concert hall that has been a landmark in South Kensington since 1871. The box office is open daily 9 a.m. to 9 p.m.; ticket prices vary by the event.

A summer tradition: Going to the Proms

From mid-July through mid-September, fans of classical and pops concerts attend the wildly popular concert series — featuring musicians from all over Europe — called the *Proms.* These are held at the **Royal Albert Hall** (see the preceding section), where they began in 1895. For Proms concerts, all seats are removed from the orchestra-level stalls. Reserved seats are available, but devotees stand for a close look at the orchestras. Starting in July, you can book seats through the Royal Albert Hall box office at ☎ 020-7589-2141; for standing room, you have to stand in line — usually a long one — on the day of the performance.

The South Bank Centre

The **South Bank Centre** (South Bank, SE1; ☎ 020-7960-4242; Tube: Waterloo) presents approximately 1,200 classical music and dance concerts per year; performances are held year-round in three separate auditoriums: The **Royal Festival Hall** presents symphonic works performed by a variety of orchestras (some British, some international). The **Queen Elizabeth Hall,** a smaller venue, offers chamber music concerts and dance programs. The **Purcell Room,** an intimate setting, is ideal for recitals. You can get tickets and information on all three venues at the box office or online at www.sbc.org.uk; prices vary for each event. For credit-card bookings, call ☎ 020-7960-4242.

Chamber music in Wigmore Hall

Wigmore Hall (36 Wigmore St., W1; ☎ 020-7935-2141; Tube: Bond St.) is an old but renovated concert hall that's the site of chamber-music concerts and recitals.

Chamber-music performances are also held in the **Purcell Room** at the **South Bank Centre** (see the preceding section). Prices vary for every concert.

Romantic concerts by candlelight

Evening candlelit concerts of baroque music are performed every Thursday, Friday, and Saturday at 7:30 p.m. in the lovely church of **St. Martin-in-the-Fields,** Trafalgar Square, W1 (☎ 020-7839-8362 for credit-card bookings; Tube: Charing Cross). Lunch concerts are held on Monday, Tuesday, and Friday at 1 p.m. Tickets run £6 to £15 ($10 to $24).

Music under the stars

A picturesque lakeside estate in Hampstead Heath is the setting for outdoor concerts held at 7:30 p.m. on Saturdays in August and presented by **Kenwood Lakeside Concerts** (Hampstead Lane, NW3; (☎ 020-7413-1443; Tube: East Finchley). A free shuttle bus runs between the East Finchley tube station and the concert bowl. From Central London, you need at least 20 minutes to get to the tube stop, and another 15 minutes for the ride on the shuttle bus. Tickets are £6 to £20 ($10 to $33).

Finding the Dance Venues

The **Royal Ballet** performs at the **Royal Opera House** and the **English National Ballet** and other visiting companies perform at the **London Coliseum** (see the section "Enjoying a Night at the Opera" for details).

Refurbished in 1998, the **Sadler's Wells** (Rosebery Avenue, Islington EC1R; ☎ 020-7863-6000; Tube: Angel) is well known for its contemporary dance, theater, and music productions and as a venue for solo performers. It also manages the **Peacock Theatre** (Portugal Street, WC2; ☎ 020-7863-8222; Tube: Covent Garden), a home for dance in the West End, and the **Lillian Baylis Theatre** (Arlington Way, EC1; ☎ 020-7713-6000; Tube: Farringdon), a smaller venue for dance and performance. Programs for all three theaters are listed on the Web at www.sadlers-wells.com.

The **Place Theatre** (17 Duke's Rd., WC1; ☎ 020-7387-0031; Tube: Euston) is the main venue for contemporary dance in the United Kingdom. **Riverside Studios** (Crisp Road, W6; ☎ 020-8237-1111; Tube: Hammersmith) is an arts center that showcases theater, cinema, and dance.

Braving the Mega Concerts: They Will, They Will Rock You

When the rock and pop stars play London, they need a *huge* arena to hold their shrieking fans. The two biggest venues are **Wembley Stadium** (Empire Way, Wembley, Middlesex; ☎ 020-8902-8833; Tube: Wembley Park) and the **Earl's Court Exhibition Centre** (Warwick Road, SW5; ☎ 020-7373-8141; Tube: Earl's Court).

A much smaller (by that I mean less than 70,000 seats) rock-and-pop venue is the **Brixton Academy** (211 Stockwell Rd., SW9; ☎ 020-7771-2000; Tube: Brixton).

Another big-event hall is **Shepherd's Bush Empire** (Shepherd's Bush Green, W12; ☎ 020-7711-2000; Tube: Shepherd's Bush). And sometimes the old **Royal Albert Hall** (see the previous section "From the Barbican to the Royal Albert") rocks, too.

Chapter 24

Enjoying a Pint: Pubs, Clubs, and Bars

....

In This Chapter

▶ Getting the lowdown on the London pubs

▶ Searching out your kind of music and dancing

▶ Getting a dose of British humor

▶ Enjoying a game of chance

▶ Unwinding over cocktails

▶ Staying up late: The real late-night spots

▶ Gambling London style

▶ Finding gay and lesbian nightclubs and bars

....

*M*aybe your idea of a perfect evening is going to an upscale hotel bar for an elegant cocktail, or sitting back in a historic pub and quaffing a pint of ale. In this chapter, I help you find a comfortable nightspot. And if you need music to make you happy, this chapter can point you in the direction of your kind of beat.

Doing the Pub Crawl

A great way to experience real-life London is to do *a pub crawl,* that is, walk from pub to pub and sample the different brews. If you're accustomed to ordering a typical American beer with a rather conventional name, you may be bowled over by the colorful names and vast assortment of British beers on tap in a pub. You can find Courage Best, Old Speckled Hen, Wadworths 6X, Brakspears, Friary Meux, and Ind Coope Burton, to name just a few. Although you can get a hard drink at both bars and pubs, when you're in a pub you're better off confining yourself to beer. See the sidebar "A beer primer: Are you bitter or stout?" to familiarize yourself with your beer choices. Of course, if you find just the right pub, you can order a pint, get comfortable, and spend the evening.

London Clubs, Pubs, and Bars

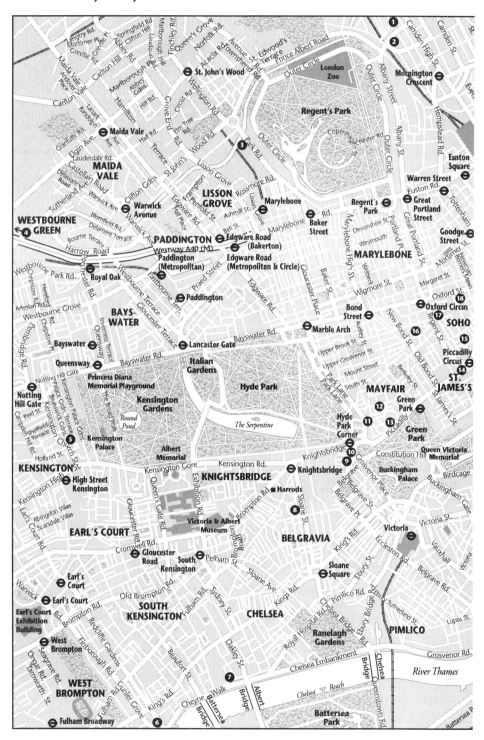

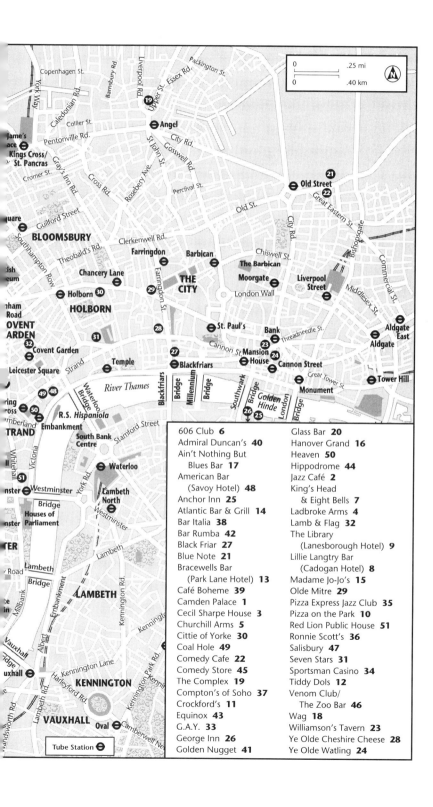

606 Club **6**	Glass Bar **20**
Admiral Duncan's **40**	Hanover Grand **16**
Ain't Nothing But	Heaven **50**
Blues Bar **17**	Hippodrome **44**
American Bar	Jazz Café **2**
(Savoy Hotel) **48**	King's Head
Anchor Inn **25**	& Eight Bells **7**
Atlantic Bar & Grill **14**	Ladbroke Arms **4**
Bar Italia **38**	Lamb & Flag **32**
Bar Rumba **42**	The Library
Black Friar **27**	(Lanesborough Hotel) **9**
Blue Note **21**	Lillie Langtry Bar
Bracewells Bar	(Cadogan Hotel) **8**
(Park Lane Hotel) **13**	Madame Jo-Jo's **15**
Café Boheme **39**	Olde Mitre **29**
Camden Palace **1**	Pizza Express Jazz Club **35**
Cecil Sharpe House **3**	Pizza on the Park **10**
Churchill Arms **5**	Red Lion Public House **51**
Cittie of Yorke **30**	Ronnie Scott's **36**
Coal Hole **49**	Salisbury **47**
Comedy Cafe **22**	Seven Stars **31**
Comedy Store **45**	Sportsman Casino **34**
The Complex **19**	Tiddy Dols **12**
Compton's of Soho **37**	Venom Club/
Crockford's **11**	The Zoo Bar **46**
Equinox **43**	Wag **18**
G.A.Y. **33**	Williamson's Tavern **23**
George Inn **26**	Ye Olde Cheshire Cheese **28**
Golden Nugget **41**	Ye Olde Watling **24**

A beer primer: Are you bitter or stout?

Most of the pubs in London and throughout the United Kingdom are *tied* to a particular brewery and sell only that brewery's beers (an outside sign displays the brewery name). Independent pubs can sell more brands than a *tied pub.* Either way, you still have to choose from what may seem like a bewildering variety of brews. The colorful names of individual brews don't provide much help — you can only wonder what Pigswill, Dogs Bollocks, Hobgoblin, Old Thumper, or Boondoggle taste like. The taste of any beer, whether it's on draught or in a bottle, is crafted by the brewery and depends on all sorts of factors: the water, the hops, the fermentation technique, and so on. You can get a few U.S. and international brands, but imports are more expensive than the homegrown products.

When you order beer in a pub, you need to specify the type, the brand, and the amount (pint or half-pint) you want. It's perfectly okay to ask the bartender to recommend something based on your taste preferences. Just remember that most English beer is served at room temperature. Here are some brief descriptions that'll come in handy in a pub:

- **Bitter** is what most locals drink. It's a clear yellowish traditional beer with a strong flavor of hops.

- **Real ale** is a bitter that's still fermenting (*alive*) when it arrives from the brewery; it's pumped and served immediately.

- **Ale** isn't as strong as bitter and has a slightly sweeter taste. You can order *light* or *pale ale* in a bottle; *export ale* is a stronger variety.

- **Lager,** when it's chilled, is probably closest to an American-style beer. It's available in bottles or on draught.

- **Shandy** is equal parts bitter and lemonade (sometimes limeade or ginger beer); it's for those who like a sweet beverage that's only partially beery.

- **Stout** is a dark, rich, creamy version of ale. Guinness is the most popular brand. A *black and tan* is half lager and half stout.

Most pubs adhere to strict hours governed by Parliament: Monday through Saturday 11 a.m. to 11 p.m. and Sunday noon to 10:30 p.m. Americans take note: No service charge is asked for or expected in a pub, and you never tip the bartender; the best you can do is offer to buy him or her a drink. Ten minutes before closing a bell rings, signaling that it's time to order your last round.

A movement is afoot to abolish the strict pub hours throughout the United Kingdom. The laws restricting pub hours were passed during World War I so that munitions workers and others involved in the war effort couldn't spend too much time drinking at their "local." It requires an Act of Parliament to deregulate pub hours, but the drinkers who want pubs to remain open 'til the wee hours have a great deal of support.

When you're in The City, try these pubs:

- ✔ **Cittie of Yorke** (22 High Holborn, WC1; ☎ 020-7242-7670; Tube: Holborn or Chancery Lane) has the longest bar in Britain and looks like a great medieval hall — that appearance is appropriate because a pub has existed at this location since 1430.

- ✔ **Seven Stars** (53 Carey St., WC2; ☎ 020-7242-8521; Tube: Holborn) is tiny and modest except for its collection of Toby mugs and law-related art. It's located at the back of the law courts, so lots of barristers drink here—it's a great place to pick up some British legal jargon.

- ✔ **Olde Mitre** (Ely Place, EC1; ☎ 020-7405-4751; Tube: Chancery Lane), named after an inn built on this site in 1547, is a small pub with an eccentric assortment of customers.

- ✔ **Black Friar** (174 Queen Victoria St., EC4; ☎ 020-7236-5650; Tube: Blackfriars) is an Edwardian wonder made of marble and bronze art nouveau. It features bas-reliefs of mad monks, a low-vaulted mosaic ceiling, and seating carved out of gold marble recesses.

When you're in West London, try the following pubs:

- ✔ **Churchill Arms** (119 Kensington Church St., W8; ☎ 020-7727-4242; Tube: Notting Hill Gate or High St. Kensington) is loaded with, of course, Churchhill memorabilia. The pub hosts an entire week of celebration leading up to Winston's birthday on November 30. Visitors are often welcomed like regulars here, and the overall ambience is down-to-earth and homey.

- ✔ **Ladbroke Arms** (54 Ladbroke Rd., W11; ☎ 020-7727-6648; Tube: Holland Park) strays a bit from a traditional pub environment with its jazz in the background and rotating art prints, but it makes for a pleasant stop and a good meal. This pub's changing menu may include such items as chicken breast stuffed with avocado and garlic steak in pink peppercorn sauce.

If you want to try a truly historic pub, check out my suggestions in Chapter 28. Remember that pubs are almost always full of cigarette smoke.

Feeling the Beat: Music and Dancing

London has much more musical diversity to offer than simply authentic, traditional English music. Whether you want to cool down to some cool jazz or boogie to a big beat, this section can help you find the right nightspot for you.

Jazzing up the night

Small, smoky jazz clubs are common in London. In Soho, **Ronnie Scott's** (47 Frith St., W1; ☎ 020-7439-0747; Tube: Tottenham Court Rd.) has been London's preeminent jazz club for years, with dependably high-caliber performances. Bring a full wallet, because you have to order food (meals or snacks) on top of the £5 to £20 ($8 to $33) admission. For a trendier, less touristy experience, try Islington's **Blue Note** (1 Hoxton Sq., N1; ☎ 020-7729-8440; Tube: Old St.) for its innovative and wide-ranging musical program. Cover ranges from £3 to £10 ($5 to $17).

In Earl's Court, the **606 Club** (90 Lots Rd., SW10; ☎ 020-7352-5953; Tube: Earl's Court or Fulham Broadway) is a basement club where young British jazz musicians play. The good news is that you don't have to pay a cover charge to get in, but you do have to order food. And to pay the musicians, the establishment adds to your bill an additional charge of £5 ($8) Monday through Thursday and Sunday and about $1 more on Friday and Saturday. You can find good food and diverse music (Afro-Latin jazz to rap) at the **Jazz Café** (5 Parkway, NW1; ☎ 020-7916-6060; Tube: Camden Town). Admission is £6 to £18 ($10 to $30).

In Soho, try the **Pizza Express Jazz Club** (10 Dean St., W1; ☎ 020-7439-8722; Tube: Tottenham Court Rd.). Big names from the American jazz scene regularly perform in this intimate venue, and you can enjoy pizza, too. It's open daily 7:45 p.m. to midnight, and the admission is £10 to £20 ($17 to $33). In Knightsbridge, you can also order pizza at **Pizza on the Park** (11 Knightsbridge, SW1; ☎ 020-7235-5273; Tube: Hyde Park Corner), where mainstream jazz is performed in the basement Jazz Room. It's open daily from 7:30 p.m., with sets at 9:15 and 11:15 p.m.; admission is £20 ($33). The cover charges at both pubs don't include food.

London's only authentic blues venue is the **Ain't Nothing But Blues Bar** (20 Kingly St., W1; ☎ 020-7287-0514; Tube: Oxford Circus). It features local acts and touring American bands. Expect long lines on weekends. The cover charge is £3 to £5 ($5 to $8) on Friday and Saturday; you get in free before 9:30 p.m.

Singing with your supper, catching a cabaret, or laughing at the comics

Performers entertain diners with madrigals, Noël Coward ditties, Gilbert & Sullivan tunes, vaudeville acts, and music-hall songs at **Tiddy Dols** (55 Shepherd Market, Mayfair, W1; ☎ 020-7499-2357; Tube: Green Park), which is housed in nine small Georgian townhouses. Main courses are £12 to £15.25 ($20 to $25) and set dinners £22 ($37). It's open Monday through Saturday 6 to 11:30 p.m. and Sunday 6 to 11 p.m. There's no cover charge.

Both gays and straights enjoy the drag/cabaret scene at **Madame Jo-Jo's** (8–10 Brewer St., Soho, W1; ☎ 020-7734-2473; Tube: Leicester Sq.). The shows produced in its plush theater/bar are a campy and fun tradition. It's open daily 10 p.m. to 4 a.m., and tickets cost £5 to £10 ($9 to $14).

The **Comedy Store** (1A Oxendon St., off Piccadilly Circus, SW1; ☎ 020-7344-0234; Tube: Piccadilly Circus) is London's best showcase for established and rising comic talent. Visitors must be 18 or older, and the cover is £12 ($20); doors open at 6:30 p.m., and shows start at 8 p.m. The **Comedy Cafe** (66 Rivington St., EC2; ☎ 020-7739-5706; Tube: Old St.) is another good place to sample stand-up London style. The cover is £8 to £12 ($13 to $20); doors open at 7 p.m. and shows start at 8:30 p.m.

Shaking your groove thang at the clubs

London is a large, cosmopolitan city that's home to many cultures, and its music scene reflects its diversity. In the London clubs, you can listen to drum 'n' bass, indie, Asian underground (or tabla 'n' bass, as it's called), chemical beats (don't ask), breakbeats, techno, trance, psychedelic, and many others.

 I must warn you: The London club scene is overwhelmingly a youth scene. If you're a woman under 30 and can squeeze into a leather miniskirt and a sleeveless zip-up top, or a man under 30 who wears Doc Martens and an earring, you'll probably fit in.

The following two dance clubs frequently book live bands; the action doesn't really get hot until around midnight (for more options, check out the Music and Clubs listings in *Time Out*):

- ✔ **The Complex**, in Islington (1–5 Parkfield St., N1; ☎ 020-7288-1986; Tube: Angel), has four floors with different dance vibes on each. It's open Friday and Saturday 10 p.m. to 7 a.m.; admission is £10 to £12 ($17 to $20).

- ✔ **Wag** (35 Wardour St., W1; ☎ 20-7437-5534; Tube: Leicester Sq. or Piccadilly Circus) is a split-level affair that's one of the more stylish live-music places in town. The downstairs stage usually attracts cutting-edge rock bands, and a DJ spins dance records upstairs. The door policy can be selective. Admission ranges from £4 to £10 ($7 to $17), and it's open Tuesday through Sunday 10 p.m. to 3 a.m.

The **Equinox** (Leicester Square, WC2; ☎ 020-7437-1446; Tube: Leicester Sq.) boasts London's largest dance floor and one of the largest lighting rigs in Europe. A diverse crowd dances to equally diverse music, including dance hall, pop, rock, and Latin. The cover is £5 to £12 ($8 to $19), and it's open Monday through Saturday 9 p.m. to 3 a.m.

The **Hippodrome** (at the corner of Cranbourn Street and Charing Cross Road, WC2; ☎ 020-7437-4311; Tube: Leicester Sq.) is a cavernous place with a great sound system and lights to match. It was once a favorite of Princess Diana (during her early club-hopping days); now it's tacky, touristy, and packed on weekends. The cover is £4 to £12 ($6 to $20), and it's open Monday through Saturday 9 p.m. to 3 a.m.

A trendy Euro-androgynous crowd and music so loud you have to use sign language are featured at **Venom Club/The Zoo Bar** (13–17 Bear St., WC2; ☎ 020-7839-4188; Tube: Leicester Sq.). It boasts the slickest, flashiest, most psychedelic decor in London, and even 35-year-olds come here. The cover is £3 to £5 ($5 to $8) after 10 p.m., and it's open daily 9 p.m. to 3 a.m.

Bar Rumba (36 Shaftesbury Ave., W1; ☎ 020-7287-2715; Tube: Piccadilly Circus) is all over the map musically; every night this club features a different type of music, including jazz fusion, phat funk, hip hop, drum 'n' bass, soul, R&B, and swing. The minimum age for admittance is 21 on Saturday and Sunday and 18 on Monday through Friday. The cover is £3 to £12 ($5 to $20); hours are Monday through Thursday 10 p.m. to 3 a.m., Friday 10 p.m. to 4 a.m., Saturday 9 p.m. to 6 a.m., and Sunday 8 p.m. to 1 a.m.

The **Hanover Grand** (6 Hanover St., W1; ☎ 020-7499-7977; Tube: Oxford Circus) is funky and down and dirty on Thursday but otherwise cutting-edge and always crowded. Age and gender are not always easy to distinguish here. The cover £5 to £15 ($8 to $24), and it's open Monday through Saturday 10 p.m. to 4 a.m.

Housed in a former theater, the **Camden Palace** (1A Camden High St., NW1; ☎ 020-7387-0428; Tube: Camden Town) draws a young all-night crowd addicted to trendy downtown costumes. The music varies from night to night, so call in advance. The cover is £5 ($8) on Tuesday and Wednesday and £7 to £20 ($11 to $32) on Friday and Saturday. It's open Tuesday and Wednesday 9 p.m. to 2 a.m., Friday 10 p.m. to 6 a.m., and Saturday 10 p.m. to 8 a.m.

Unwinding in Elegance

Maybe you just want a quiet, romantic spot where you and your significant other can enjoy a cocktail and actually talk to one another for a change. Or perhaps you're looking for a sophisticated place to enjoy a pre- or post-theater drink. The following establishments are just the ticket. They're located in grand hotels and offer a bit of privacy from the crowds. Jackets and ties are required for gents at the American Bar; a "smart casual" dress code is in effect at the others.

What bartender is known for his special concoctions, the Savoy Affair and the Prince of Wales, as well as what's reputedly the best martini in town? He's in the employ of the **American Bar** (in the Savoy Hotel, The Strand, WC2; ☎ 020-7836-4343; Tube: Charing Cross Rd. or Embankment), one of London's most sophisticated gathering places

Bracewells Bar (in the Park Lane Hotel, Piccadilly, W1; ☎ 020-7499-6321; Tube: Green Park or Hyde Park) is chic and nostalgic, with a plush decor of Chinese lacquer, comfortable sofas, and soft lighting.

Looking for high ceilings, leather chesterfields, oil paintings, grand windows, and old-world charm? Visit **The Library** (in the Lanesborough Hotel, 1 Lanesborough Place, SW1; ☎ 020-7259-5599; Tube: Hyde Park Corner), one of London's poshest drinking retreats. Its collection of ancient cognacs is unparalleled in town.

At the **Lillie Langtry Bar** (in the Cadogan Hotel, Sloane Street, SW1; ☎ 020-7235-7141; Tube: Sloane Sq. or Knightsbridge), you can go back in time to the charm and elegance of the Edwardian era, when Lillie Langtry, an actress and a society beauty (and a mistress of Edward VII), lived here. Writer Oscar Wilde — often a guest in Lillie's home and in this hotel — is honored on the drinks menu by his favorite libation, the Hock and Seltzer (see Chapter 8 for a description of the hotel).

Seeking Spots for Night Owls

Except for the die-hards in the all-night discos, Londoners retire to bed fairly early. Restaurants and bars routinely close before midnight. A few places in restless, nightclub-heavy Soho stay open late to accommodate night owls:

- **Bar Italia** (22 Frith St., W1; ☎ 020-7437-4520; Tube: Tottenham Court Rd.) is open 24 hours for coffee and serves a limited snack menu.

- **Atlantic Bar & Grill** (20 Glasshouse St., W1; ☎ 020-7734-4888; Tube: Piccadilly Circus) is open for drinks Monday through Saturday to 3 a.m. You may have wait in line for a place to sit.

- **Café Boheme** (13–17 Old Compton St., W1; ☎ 020-7734-0623; Tube: Tottenham Court Rd. or Leicester Sq.) offers a chance to get a drink until 3 a.m. Monday through Wednesday, until 11:30 p.m. Sunday, and 24 hours Thursday through Saturday.

Taking a Turn at the Tables

Before Queen Victoria forbade her loyal subjects from participating in all games of chance, London was quite a gambling town. After a long dry spell, gambling was again permitted (only in bona fide gaming clubs) in 1960. However, U.S. citizens will recognize that London gaming differs significantly from Las Vegas gambling. At a London gambling club, you must first become a member and then wait 24 hours before you can play at the tables. Games are cash only and commonly include roulette, blackjack, punto banco, and baccarat. Men must wear jackets and ties in all the following establishments; hours for each club are daily 2 p.m. to 4 a.m.:

- **Crockford's** (30 Curzon St., W1; ☎ 020-7493-7777; Tube: Green Park) is a 150-year-old club with an impressive number of international clients. It offers American roulette, punto banco, and blackjack.

- **Golden Nugget** (22 Shaftesbury Ave., W1; ☎ 020-7439-0099; Tube: Piccadilly Circus) is where gamblers go to play blackjack, punto banco, and roulette.

- **Sportsman Casino** (3 Tottenham Court Rd., W1; ☎ 020-7414-0061; Tube: Tottenham Court Rd.) offers a dice table along with American roulette, blackjack, and punto banco.

Finding Gay Clubs and Discos

To be where it's happenin', stroll along Old Compton Street in Soho (Tube: Leicester Sq.). You may want to duck into **Admiral Duncan's** (54 Old Compton St., W1; ☎ **020-7437-5300**) or the two-floor **Compton's of Soho** (53–55 Old Compton St., W1; ☎ **020-7479-7961**). Both of these gay bar/pubs are Soho institutions, open Monday through Saturday noon to 11 p.m. and Sunday noon to 10:30 p.m.

The city's largest women-only bar is the bilevel **Glass Bar** (West Lodge, Euston Square Gardens, 190 Euston Rd., NW10; ☎ **020-7387-6184;** Tube: Euston). It has a "smart casual" dress code and is open Tuesday through Friday 5 p.m. until "late," Saturday 6 p.m. until "late," and Sunday 2 to 7 p.m.; there's no admittance after 11:30 p.m. Monday through Saturday.

In terms of size, central location, and continued popularity, the best gay (and everyone else) disco in London is **Heaven** (Under the Arches, Craven Street, WC2; ☎ **020-7930-2020;** Tube: Charing Cross or Embankment). It's open Monday and Wednesday 10:30 p.m. to 3 a.m., Friday 10:30 p.m. to 6 a.m., and Saturday 10:30 p.m. to 5 a.m. Admission varies from £3 to £10 ($5 to $17).

G.A.Y. (London Astoria, 157 Charing Cross Rd., Soho, WC2; ☎ **0906-100-016** Tube: Tottenham Court Rd.) is the biggest gay dance venue in Europe. It's open Saturday 10:30 p.m. to 5 a.m., and charges a £10 ($17) admission.

Check the gay listings in *Time Out* for nightclubs that have dedicated gay nights, as well as *Frommer's Gay & Lesbian Europe* (published by IDG Books Worldwide, Inc.), which has extensive coverage of London's gay scene.

Part VII
The Part of Tens

The 5th Wave   By Rich Tennant

The new soccer team from the UK, "The London Fog," has just scored the winning goal, and in celebration, the team members are ripping off their double-breasted trench coats, and tossing them into the stands!

In this part . . .

This part contains lots of "extra" fun. You can have a wonderful time in London without reading a word of it or can use it to enhance your trip. If you've been to London once or twice already and are now ready to expand your explorations, the chapters in this part can give you a few good ideas.

Though this is The Part of Tens, in Chapter 25 I give you more than ten reasons to visit London's often unexplored South Bank. I unveil the stories behind ten famous London statues in Chapter 26. In Chapter 27, I describe ten historic London churches, and in Chapter 28 I tell you about ten extra-special London pubs.

Chapter 25

Ten+ Reasons to Visit the South Bank

In This Chapter

▶ Going under and over the South Bank: The Waterloo International Terminal and the London Eye Observation Wheel

▶ Visiting the South Bank's theaters and museums

▶ Finding the historic inns

▶ Exploring South Bank bridges and ships

*M*any visitors to London cross over the Thames to hear a concert or to see a play at the South Bank Centre (see Chapters 22 and 23), but for most, Southwark (pronounced *Suth*-ick), the surrounding area to the east along the river (and 5 miles south), remains *terra incognita*. This is a shame, because Southwark is one of London's most historic boroughs, filled with fascinating remnants and re-creations of the borough's theatrical, seafaring, literary, and industrial past. Interwoven with the old fabric are modern developments that are transforming the area into a trendy new residential hot spot. Two new attractions, the **London Eye Observation Wheel** and **Tate Modern** art gallery (Chapter 16 describes both), may bring you over to the South Bank.

If you have the time and the inclination, I recommend that you explore the area in more detail. This chapter describes a walk that follows a 3-mile path, most of it alongside the river (no car traffic on this side), and passes all sorts of fascinating sights, old and new. (No, I couldn't squeeze them all into a list of ten.)

A convenient place to start your South Bank tour is Waterloo Station (for the exact locations of these sights, see the "More London Sights" map in Chapter 17). From the Waterloo Underground station, follow the signs up to the main train station to have a look at the new **Waterloo International Terminal.**

Waterloo International Terminal

The **Waterloo International Terminal,** Nicholas Grimshaw's sinuously curved glass-roofed terminal for the Eurostar trains that zip beneath the English Channel (through the Channel Tunnel, also known as the Chunnel) to Paris in just 3 hours. The first link between Britain and the Continent since the Ice Age, the $15-billion Chunnel is one of the great engineering feats of all time. Queen Elizabeth II and late French president François Mitterrand officially opened the Chunnel in 1994, the same year Eurostar Express trains began arriving and departing from this distinctive new terminal.

Walk down the riverside promenade south of Waterloo Station and beside **Westminster Bridge** you can see the new 40-story London Eye Observation Wheel.

London Eye Observation Wheel

The **London Eye Observation Wheel** dominates the area (see Chapter 16). It was built to celebrate the millennium and will remain in operation until at least 2003. A few yards from the wheel is the **London Aquarium** (see Chapter 17), located in the former London County Hall.

Follow the riverside promenade north of Waterloo Station and you come to the complex of buildings known as the **South Bank Centre.**

South Bank Centre

The **South Bank Centre** was built in 1951 as part of the Festival of Britain, which was meant to be a "Tonic to the Nation" following the ravages of World War II. The 2,900-seat **Royal Festival Hall** (see Chapter 23) and its adjacent river-facing buildings sit on land formerly occupied by derelict warehouses and factories. The hall's foyers, with cafes and restaurants, are open daily 10 a.m. to 10 p.m. and host art exhibits and free music events. Concerts by the world's finest orchestras as well as rock, jazz, ballet, and world music events are performed in the acoustically outstanding auditorium, whose outer walls are faced with 150-million-year-old fossilized limestone from Derbyshire. The South Bank Centre also includes the **Queen Elizabeth Hall,** opened by Queen Elizabeth II in 1967, and the **Hayward Gallery,** opened by the Queen in 1968. This modern-art gallery is a classic example of 1960's "brutalist" architecture (as ugly as it sounds); the neon strips of yellow, magenta, red, green, and blue on its roof are controlled by the changes in the strength and direction of the wind.

Used-book sellers usually have stalls and tables set up beneath Waterloo Bridge. As you continue, you find the next large building facing the river is the **Royal National Theatre.**

Royal National Theatre

The **Royal National Theatre** is the nation's flagship theater — or theaters, I should say, because three are under one roof. The National presents an enormous variety of plays, classic to contemporary, from the entire repertoire of world drama. Sir Laurence Olivier was the first director of the Royal National, which began in 1963 and moved into this building in 1976 (see Chapter 22 for ticket information).

From the theater, follow the riverside path east, enjoying the views of the north bank. The path jogs alongside the landmark **Oxo Tower,** whose top floor contains one of London's best river-view restaurants, the **Oxo Tower Brasserie** (see Chapter 14). Stay on the riverside path until you come to the unmistakably mammoth **Bankside Power Station,** which was converted and reopened in May 2000 as Tate Modern.

Tate Modern

Tate Modern is the work of the Swiss architectural firm of Herzog & de Meuron, which was responsible for the striking remodel of the power station (the original architect was Sir Giles Gilbert Scott). See Chapter 16 for details on the museum, which contains the Tate Gallery's collection of international modern art. Lord Norman Foster, one of Britain's most currently revered architects, designed the sleek new **Millennium Bridge** that now connects Tate Modern to St. Paul's Cathedral across the river.

Just east of Tate Modern, the riverside path becomes Bankside, which was beyond the strict jurisdiction of The City across the river. It used to be the entertainment center of London — home to brothels, bear- and bull-baiting amphitheaters, and four theaters, the most important being the Globe. William Shakespeare, a shareholder in the Globe, wrote *Hamlet, Othello, Macbeth,* and *King Lear* to be performed there. Continuing east along Bankside, you come to a row of 18th-century buildings and a half-timbered structure that looks curiously old and new at the same time. This is **Shakespeare's Globe Theatre & Exhibition.**

Shakespeare's Globe Theatre & Exhibition

The original Globe burned down in 1613 after an ember from a cannon fired during a performance of *Henry VIII* set the thatched roof alight. A second Globe was built in 1614 and survived until 1642, when Cromwell's Puritan ban on places of public entertainment forced it to close; it was demolished in 1644. Its construction spearheaded by late American actor/director Sam Wanamaker, **Shakespeare's Globe**

Theatre & Exhibition is a replica built using original techniques — it was the first thatched building to be allowed in London since the Great Fire of 1666. To maintain authenticity, the structure has no roof and no stage lighting, so performances can take place only during daylight in summer and only during clement weather (see Chapter 22 for ticket information and Chapter 17 for a description of the exhibition).

Continue east on Bankside, beneath **Southwark Bridge,** into an area of looming old warehouses. At the corner of Bankside and Park Street you may want to take a break at the **Anchor Inn**.

Anchor Inn

The **Anchor Inn,** on Park Street (☎ **020-7407-1577**) was frequented by Samuel Johnson (1709–1784), who produced the monumental *Dictionary of the English Language*; playwright Oliver Goldsmith (1728–1774), whose best-known work is *She Stoops to Conquer;* and painter Sir Joshua Reynolds (1723–1792), first president of the Royal Academy. It's not exactly a literary salon today, but you can have a drink in the pub or on its riverside terrace.

Continue east along Bankside, which becomes Clink Street. The use of the word *clink* to mean "prison" comes from the Clink Prison, once located here. Because Southwark was a rowdy, bawdy, and sometimes murderous area that was frequented by prostitutes and desperate, debt-ridden actors, the Clink got a great deal of use. This area is also the site of the remains of the **Palace of the Bishops of Winchester.** The Clink was under the jurisdiction of the powerful Bishops of Winchester, who basically owned this area from the Middle Ages up to the reign of Henry VIII. Today, all that remains of their once-magnificent palace are these ruins, which include a 14th-century rose window set into a wall.

Continue on to the first left turning. Here, moored in a slip at St. Mary's Overie ("over the river") dock, is a rather surprising sight, the *Golden Hinde.*

Golden Hinde

The *Golden Hinde* is a full-scale working replica of the 16th-century ship used by Sir Francis Drake. A privateer who set sail from England in 1577, Drake became the first sea captain to circumnavigate the globe. This facsimile ship was sailed around the world before taking up residence here, in one of London's oldest docks. The self-guided tour will give you a vivid picture of life aboard an Elizabethan ship (see Chapter 17).

Return to Clink Street, which now changes its name to Cathedral Street and winds slightly south to **Southwark Cathedral.**

Southwark Cathedral

Southwark Cathedral is one of the oldest buildings in Southwark and also one of the most beautiful. Step inside and take a look at the memorial window to William Shakespeare, whose brother Edmund was buried here, and the 13th-century wooden effigy of a knight, one of the oldest surviving wooden effigies in England (see Chapters 17 and 28).

Continue on Cathedral Street until you reach Borough High Street. Cross here and turn south (right); three streets farther on, turn left into George Inn Yard and find one of the most historically important pubs in London, the **George Inn.**

George Inn

The **George Inn** (☎ 020-7407-2056) is London's only remaining example of an old-style galleried coaching inn. The road to London Bridge, for centuries the only way to cross the Thames, was once dominated by inns like this one. The George was well established by the reign of Henry VIII, and some claim it actually dates back to Chaucer's era, the 14th century. In 1676, it was destroyed by the Great Fire of Southwark but rebuilt within a year; the ungalleried external walls date from then. Up until 1844, when London Bridge Railway Station opened, the George was the main stagecoach inn in Southwark. Among the famous who've drunk here are Winston Churchill, Samuel Johnson, and perhaps even William Shakespeare. Charles Dickens mentioned it in *The Pickwick Papers* and *Little Dorrit*. The inn is open during normal pub hours.

From the George Inn, now head farther south on Borough High Street until reaching Tabard Street, which angles off to the east. On your left as you walk down Tabard Street is a garden containing the **remains of Marshalsea Prison.** Charles Dickens, who grew up in Southwark, knew this place well because it was here his father was imprisoned for debt. Marshalsea wasn't like today's prisons: Dickens's mother and his younger siblings lived in the prison with his father. Charles, who was forced to work in a factory, had lodgings nearby — close enough so he could join his family for breakfast and dinner! By the time Dickens wrote *Little Dorrit*, the novel that reveals much of this miserable period of his life, imprisonment for debt had been abolished and the Marshalsea demolished.

Retrace your steps north on Borough High Street and turn east onto St. Thomas Street. Here, on the north side of the street at no. 9a, is the **Old Operating Theatre & Herb Garret.**

Old Operating Theatre & Herb Garret

The **Old Operating Theatre & Herb Garret** is a vivid reminder of just how much health care has changed (see Chapter 17). Two hospitals and medical schools, St. Thomas's and Guy's, once faced each other across St Thomas Street, but St. Thomas's was forced to relocate in the

1860s with the development of London Bridge Station. In 1956, its operating theater, in use from 1821 to 1862, was rediscovered here. Remarkably intact, it still contains the wooden table where operations and amputations were performed without anesthetics. The **Herb Garret** was where medicines were created from a variety of herbs.

From the **Operating Theatre,** make your way east to London Bridge Station, which contains a new Underground station for the Jubilee Line. Cut through the station and make your way back to the river. Spanning the Thames here is **London Bridge.**

London Bridge

London Bridge was for centuries the only way to get from one side of the Thames to the other. The current bridge, opened in 1973, isn't particularly distinguished, but it marks the site of the oldest river crossing in London. The first London Bridge was built by the Romans in the 1st century A.D. Another span was constructed in 1176 and subsequently replaced several times. During the Middle Ages, the bridge was lined with shops and houses and used to show off the severed heads of enemies of the crown. The London Bridge that went up in 1825 was moved to Lake Havasu, Arizona (of all places), where it's now a tourist attraction. Its replacement is the bridge you see today.

On Hays Lane you are in the midst of one of the several modern developments that are transforming the area around London Bridge. **Hay's Galleria,** a famous wharf that's been restored and converted into a multitude of shops, bars, and market stalls, opens out onto the river. On the lower level is the Southwark Tourist Information Centre (☎ **020-7403-8299;** open Monday through Saturday 10 a.m. to 6 p.m. and Sunday 10:30 a.m. to 5:30 p.m.), where you can pick up details on this fascinating area. Looming ahead of you, to the east, in the Thames, is the **HMS** *Belfast.*

HMS Belfast

The **HMS** *Belfast* is the last surviving example of the big-gun cruisers that once helped Britain to rule the waves (see Chapter 17). Launched in 1938, the ship is now preserved as a floating museum. Holding a crew of 950 men, the *Belfast* went into action in World War II, capturing the German liner SS *Cap Norte* in 1939, sinking the battlecruiser *Scharnhorst* at the Battle of North Cape in 1943, and firing the first shots on D Day, attacking a battery at Ver sur Mer. Later, the *Belfast* saw action during the Korean War before being retired from the Navy in 1963.

Continuing east along the riverside path takes you beneath Tower Bridge and into the riverside development of **Butlers Wharf.** The names of the buildings, streets, and wharves — Saffron Wharf,

Cardamon Building, Cayenne Court, Mace Street, Java Wharf — hark back to the days when Southwark was a teeming warehouse district dealing with all manner of exotic imports. High walkways still link several of the former warehouses, where spices and tea were unloaded and stored after arriving by ship from the far corners of the British Empire. Today, reconstituted into a complex of condos, apartments, offices, and food and wine shops, it's a prime example of what's happening in the new Southwark. You may want to return later for dinner at **Le Pont de la Tour** (see Chapter 14), which has sweeping views of the Thames. Continuing east along Shad Thames brings you to the **Design Museum.**

Design Museum

The **Design Museum** was founded in 1989 to provide an insight into the important role design has played in everyday life from the products of early mass production to the present day (see Chapter 17).

From the Design Museum, take Maguire Street south for 1 block to reach the **Bramah Tea & Coffee Museum.**

Bramah Tea & Coffee Museum

The **Bramah Tea & Coffee Museum** (see Chapter 17) is dedicated to the story of two trades that were of great local importance; it takes you back to the days when tea and coffee were a source of (expensive) wonderment and not something purchased from the supermarket or gulped down at Starbucks. The Butlers Wharf area used to handle 6,000 chests of tea a day.

Retrace your steps back along Maguire Street to **Tower Bridge.**

Tower Bridge

Tower Bridge is one of the most famous spans in the world. In 1876, when horse-drawn carriages lined up for hours to cross **London Bridge** (the only practical route across the river), the city decided to build a new bridge to ease the flow of traffic and allow large masted ships to sail up the river. John Wolfe Barry and Sir Horace Jones designed this raising bridge, which opened in 1894. You can find out more about its history, and admire the spectacular view of London from the walkway high above the river, at **Tower Bridge Experience** (see Chapter 17).

Chapter 26

Strike a Pose: Ten Famous London Statues

*U*nlike pigeons, we don't really pay too much attention to statues of public figures anymore, do we? We prefer creations found in museums, with the names of famous sculptors affixed to them. The whole idea of casting a bronze of a truly important public figure just doesn't fit in with our modern world view. Who'd qualify for such an honor in this day and age?

In England, the only person today who might be considered deserving of such a monument is the late Princess Diana (at least in the general public's opinion). But the city is filled with bronze statues commemorating all sorts of individuals from the past. This chapter offers ten (or so) that may be of interest to you or that you may run into at some point during your London stay and think "Who *is* that?" (for the location of each, see the map "More London Attractions" in Chapter 17). One thing about statues: They can tell you a great deal about the fickleness and fanaticism running through history.

Admiral Lord Nelson

In Trafalgar Square (Tube: Charing Cross), perched atop the 145-foot Nelson's Column, one of London's most famous monuments, is a statue of (you guessed it) **Admiral Lord Nelson.** Horatio, Viscount Nelson, was the victor over the French and Spanish fleet at the 1805 Battle of Trafalgar and is Britain's best-known naval hero. On the column he's 17 feet high (and had to be hoisted up in three sections), but in real life he was all of 5 feet, 4 inches tall. (Also in Trafalgar Square is an equestrian statue of **George IV,** who considered himself a gentleman but was nobody's idea of a hero.)

Charles I

In 1633, French sculptor Hubert LeSueur completed the equestian statue of **Charles I** that stands (or rather sits) at the north end of Whitehall, just south of Trafalgar Square (Tube: Charing Cross). For no discernable reason, royals seem to have elevated egos and think of themselves as larger than life. So Charlie, who came in at just 5 feet tall, had the sculptor tack another foot onto his frame. In real life, alas, the monarch lost whatever symbolic stature the extra foot gave him when his head was chopped off by Cromwell in 1649. However, history has many strange twists and turns: This statue was sold to a scrap dealer who was supposed to destroy it but instead shrewdly buried it in his garden. In 1660, when the monarchy was restored and Charles II ascended the throne, the scrap dealer was able to sell the new king the undamaged statue. It didn't go up in its present spot on Whitehall — with a pedestal by great architect Sir Christopher Wren — until 1765.

Duke of York and Edward VII

Just north of St. James's Park, at the midpoint of Carlton House Terrace (Tube: Charing Cross), is the **Duke of York Monument.** So who was the duke of York (not Prince Andrew) and why did he warrant this massive 7-ton statue? That's a very good question, and one I'm completely unable to answer. He was the second son of George III (who was on the throne when America gained its independence from Britain), and when he died he was massively in debt. Sir Richard Westmacott's 1834 sculpture, resting on a column of pink granite, was funded by withholding a day's pay from every soldier in the Empire. I ask you, was that fair? Some wags have speculated that the duke's statue was placed high up so his creditors couldn't reach him.

The monument looms over Waterloo Place, an enclave of aristocratic elegance and one of London's greatest examples of urban planning. At the entrance of Waterloo Place is a statue of **Edward VII,** chiseled by Sir Bertram Mackennal in 1921 to honor the king who gave his name to the Edwardian era. The son of Queen Victoria, "Eddie" had to wait until he was 60 before he could ascend the throne, and he died 9 years later. But not all is royal in Waterloo Place: There's also a statue dedicated to the victims of the Crimean War.

Henry VIII

Wouldn't you say that Henry VIII is England's best-known king? You've "seen him in plays, movies (such as *Anne of the Thousand Days* and *A Man for All Seasons*), and that great Masterpiece Theatre TV series *The Six Wives of Henry VIII.* Henry VIII was a huge man, with huge appetites, and he wouldn't take no for an answer. (He didn't have to, he was king.) The much-married Merrie Monarch has never been considered anyone's idea of a role model, so maybe that explains why there's only one statue of him in all of London. You can see it atop the **Henry VIII Gateway** on West Smithfield (Tube: Barbican). The gateway itself was built in 1702 by the stonemasons who built St. Paul's Cathedral. It commemorates Henry's giving of St. Bartholomew Hospital to The City — a gift made possible by his dissolution of the monasteries.

James II and George Washington

Two notable statues flank the main entrance of the National Gallery, across from Trafalgar Square (Tube: Charing Cross). On the left is British sculptor Grinling Gibbons's fine statue of **James II,** from 1636, a year after James ascended the throne. Because he immediately levied new taxes and sought to restore Catholicism to England, this monarch never caught on in the public popularity polls. In fact, he was deposed and spent the rest of his life in exile in France. The **George Washington** statue on the right is a Jean Antoine Houdon replica of a statue in the capitol building in Richmond, Virginia. A gift from that state, the statue arrived in London with boxes of earth for the base, so the first American president would always be able to stand on American soil.

Oliver Cromwell

The small garden in front of the Houses of Parliament (Tube: Westminster) contains a statue of **Oliver Cromwell,** Lord Protector of England from 1653 to 1658. This fanatical Puritan was leader of the Parliamentary armies during the Civil War that deposed Charles I. Under Cromwell's "protectorate," at least 30,000 Irish men, women, and children were massacred and vast tracts of Ireland handed over to the English. Small wonder that Irish members of Parliament were outraged when Cromwell's statue, by Hamo Thorneycroft, was unveiled in 1899. In fact, Parliament ultimately refused to pay for it, and Lord Rosebery, the prime minister, shelled out the money himself. Cromwell, a sword in one hand and a Bible in the other, appears to be averting his eyes from the bust of **Charles I** (the king he had beheaded — see "Charles I," earlier in this chapter), which you can see across the street above the doorway of the St. Margaret's Westminster church.

Peter Pan

Children love the famous statue of **Peter Pan,** north of the Serpentine Bridge in Kensington Gardens (Tube: High St. Kensington). Commissioned in 1912 by Peter Pan's creator, J. M. Barrie, the bronze sculpture by George Frampton marks the spot where Peter Pan touched down in the gardens. Of course, this kid could fly — he didn't have to take the tube like the rest of us. Peter Pan was an adored fantasy hero long before he became a psychological "syndrome" for men who refuse to grow up. He was to children of earlier generations what Harry Potter is to the kids of today. Maybe, eventually, there'll be a Harry Potter statue in Paddington Station.

Prince Albert

Prince Albert of Saxe-Coburg-Gotha (a name the royals changed to Windsor at the onset of World War I) was the handsome German consort of Queen Victoria. When he died at age 42 in 1861, the grief-stricken queen donned the black widow's weeds she'd wear for the rest of her long life. There are two statues of Prince Albert. One is at the rejuvenated **Albert Memorial** in Kensington Gardens (see Chapter 16). The other stands in the center of Holborn Circus (Tube: Holborn) — that one has been dubbed "the politest statue in London" because the prince is seen raising his hat.

Queen Boudicca

Who, you may wonder, is the wild-haired superwoman in the horse-drawn chariot at the north end of Westminster Bridge (Tube: Westminster)? She's **Queen Boudicca** (or Boadicea), that's who, with her fearless warrior-daughters. "Bo" was a fierce Celtic queen who fought back the invading Romans and died in A.D. 60. Thomas Hornicraft created the sculpture in the 1850s; it was placed at its current site in 1902.

Winston Churchill and Abraham Lincoln

Parliament Square (Tube: Westminster) boasts more outdoor sculptures than any other place in London. Unless you're a student of British history, most of the bronze gentlemen (**Sir Robert Peel, Benjamin Disraeli,** the **14th earl of Derby,** and **General Jan Smuts**) ranged around the square won't mean anything to you. But you may recognize two of them. **Sir Winston Churchill,** the prime minister during World War II (see Chapter 17) is at his most bulldoggish in Ivor Roberts-Jones's 1975 sculpture, standing in the square's northeast corner. A statue of **Abraham Lincoln** by Augustus Saint-Gaudens stands across the street on the west side of the square. It was a gift from the city of Chicago, which has the 1887 original in Lincoln Park.

Young Dancer

There's much more to public art in London than kings, princes, and politicians. The graceful statue known as *Young Dancer,* by Enzo Plazzotta, acts as a memorial to the dancers of the Royal Ballet who perform at the Royal Opera House. The statue is on Bow Street (Tube: Covent Garden), a block from the opera house.

Chapter 27

Making Amens: Ten Noteworthy London Churches

*W*estminster Abbey and St. Paul's Cathedral (see Chapter 16) are giant repositories of English history and get the lion's share of visitor attention in London. But the city boasts scores of smaller churches also worth visiting. The area known as the City of London is especially rich in neoclassical churches designed by Sir Christopher Wren (1632–1723) after the disastrous Great Fire of 1666. One of England's greatest architects, and certainly its most prolific, Wren designed St. Paul's.

Here are ten London churches you may want to check out on your ramblings around town (for their locations, see the map "More London Attractions" in Chapter 16).

Church of St. Bartholomew the Great

On the east side of Smithfield Square, EC1 (Tube: Barbican), is a rare 16th-century gatehouse, and perched atop it is an even rarer late-16th-century timber-frame house predating the Great Fire. The gatehouse opens onto the grounds of the **Church of St. Bartholomew the Great,** a little-visited gem that just happens to be the oldest parish church in London. It was part of an Augustinian priory founded in 1123. Over the centuries, the building has somewhat miraculously escaped major damage — despite being used at various times as stables and a printing office (where Benjamin Franklin worked in 1725). The 15th-century cloisters are to your right as you enter. Inside the church is a "weeping" 17th-century statue of Edward Cooke (the marble condenses moisture from the air), the tomb of Rahere, the priory's founder, and a lovely oriel (a projecting bay) window.

If you leave the churchyard using the gate in the far right corner, you come out on **Cloth Fair,** a street with gabled houses from 1604. Like St. Bartholomew's, they're among the very few surviving buildings predating the disastrous Great Fire that leveled much of London in 1666.

Church of St. Stephen Walbrook

Walbrook, EC4 (Tube: Cannon St.), a lane in the heart of The City, was the site of a brook that was paved over in medieval times. Today, it houses the **Church of St. Stephen Walbrook,** one of Sir Christopher Wren's finest works. By the 18th century, the fame of this church had spread throughout Europe, and many still consider it the most beautiful church in London. Its splendid dome served as a model for the one at St. Paul's Cathedral. The altar beneath the dome was sculpted from travertine (a porous mineral) in 1956 by British sculptor Henry Moore, who had reservations about tackling the job because he was an agnostic. "Henry, I'm not asking you to take the service," said the rector who offered Moore the commission. "I understand that you're a bit of a chiseler; just do your job."

St. Botolph's

I think it's appropriate to include in this chapter a church dedicated to England's patron saint of travelers: **St. Botolph's** on Aldersgate Street, EC1 (Tube: Barbican), close to the **Museum of London** (see Chapter 17). The church interior has a fine barrel-vaulted roof. Actually, three City churches are dedicated to St. Botolph, and all are located beside now-vanished gates into the city. At one time, instead of being greeted by ATMs and currency-exchange windows, travelers could pause and give thanks to Botolph for their safe journey to London.

St. Dunstan's-in-the-West

The octagonal **St. Dunstan's-in-the-West,** on Fleet Street, EC4 (Tube: Temple), is a fine early example of Gothic Revival architecture. That was the style in fashion when an earlier church that survived the Great Fire of 1666 was replaced between 1829 and 1833. The large clock on the tower is something of a historical curiosity: It dates from 1671 and was installed by the congregation as an offering of thanks because the church hadn't burned down. Every 15 minutes, two giant clubs strike a bell that has been tolling for more than 330 years. People take clocks, watches, and timepieces completely for granted nowadays, but this was the first clock in London to have a double face and to have minutes marked on the dial.

St. George the Martyr Church

Also in Southwark, next to the remains of Marshalsea Prison on Borough High Street, SE1 (Tube: Borough), is **St. George the Martyr Church.** It's probably more famous for its literary associations than for any intrinsic beauty of the structure itself. This is where Dickens's fictional heroine Little Dorrit is baptized and, at one point, is forced to spend the night when she's locked out of the Marshalsea debtors' prison; later she's married in this church. A stained-glass window in the east wall shows her at prayer.

St. Margaret's Westminster

St. Margaret's Westminster, the parish church of the House of Commons since 1614, is on St. Margaret Street, SW1 (Tube: Westminster) and often mistaken for **Westminster Abbey** next door. St. Margaret's is notable for its glorious above-the-altar East Window, whose stained glass was presented by Ferdinand and Isabella of Spain to commemorate the marriage of their daughter, Catharine of Aragon, to Arthur, the son of Henry VII. By the time the glass arrived, Arthur had died and Henry VIII, his younger brother, had wed Catherine, the first of his eight wives (he divorced her for Anne Boleyn). The weddings of poet John Milton (1656) and statesman (and future prime minister) Winston Churchill (1908) were held in this church.

St. Martin-in-the-Fields

St. Martin-in-the-Fields, on Trafalgar Square, WC2 (Tube: Charing Cross), was a stylistic prototype for hundreds of churches constructed in 18th-century New England. It was built in 1726 by James Gibbs, who was obviously influenced by the churches of Sir Christopher Wren. Furniture designer Thomas Chippendale, painters Sir Joshua Reynolds and William Hogarth, and Nell Gwynn, mistress of Charles II, are buried within. For details about the concerts held here, see the description of St. Martin's under "Trafalgar Square" in Chapter 16.

St. Mary-le-Bow

Established in the 11th century, **St. Mary-le-Bow,** on Bow Lane, EC4 (Tube: Mansion House), is one of London's most venerable churches. The structure that originally stood here was a casualty of the Great Fire of 1666; the steepled church you see today is a work by Sir Christopher Wren, who modeled it after Rome's Church of the Basilica of Maxentius. According to tradition, a true Cockney (a native of the East End of London) is someone born within hearing distance of the bells of St. Mary-le-Bow. In the churchyard's garden is a statue of Capt. John Smith, a one-time parishioner who left London to become one of the first settlers of Jamestown, Virginia (he's the one who was saved by Pocahontas).

Southwark Cathedral

Southwark Cathedral, on Montague Close, SE1 (Tube: London Bridge), is one of the oldest buildings in Southwark and also one of the most beautiful (see Chapters 17 and 25). A church has occupied this site for at least a thousand years; before that, a Roman villa was located here.

London's second-oldest church after **Westminster Abbey, Southwark Cathedral,** in the 12th century, was the first Gothic church to be erected in London. Today, you see the 15th-century cathedral (with Victorian restorations) that once served London's rowdy South Bank theater district. Chaucer and Shakespeare both worshiped here, and Shakespeare's brother Edmund was buried here in 1607.

Besides a memorial to the immortal Bard, the church contains a 13th-century wooden effigy of a knight, one of the oldest surviving wooden effigies in England. John Harvard, founder of Harvard University, was baptized in this church.

Temple of Mithras

Not far from **St. Stephen Walbrook,** at the entrance to Temple Court on Queen Victoria Street, EC4 (Tube: Mansion House), are the remains of what's probably London's oldest church site. This isn't a Christian church, however, but a 3rd-century Roman temple, the **Temple of Mithras.** Unearthed during 1954 excavations and raised to its present level, the temple is shaped like a tiny Christian basilica with a central nave and two aisles. It was used by the Mithraic cult, which had its origins in Persia and was brought to London by Roman soldiers in the 2nd century. At one time, when the Roman Empire still ruled the Western world, Mithraism was as popular as Christianity. It's speculated that the pagan temple was destroyed in the 4th century, when Christianity became the official religion of the Empire. Some of the sculptures that were found in the temple are displayed in the **Museum of London** (see Chapter 17).

Chapter 28

A Pint of Ale and a Bit of History: Ten Extra-Special London Pubs

. . . .

In This Chapter

▶ Enjoying some pub history

▶ Finding a pub with character

. . . .

*P*ublic houses, better known as pubs, have been a way of life in London and throughout the United Kingdom for centuries. Chapter 13 offers information about London pubs (and Chapters 15 and 24 also mention some intriguing pubs). But I could write an entire guide just on the pubs of London because there are hundreds. Not all of these pubs are old, of course, and not all have the kind of character that accumulates over centuries of drinking, talking, smoking, and eating. But dozens upon dozens of these pubs date back anywhere from a century to 400 years or more.

This chapter offers descriptions of ten more pubs. Each of these places has some special story, history, or association attached to it (for their locations, see the map "London's Clubs, Pubs, and Bars" in Chapter 24). All are open regular pub hours of Monday through Saturday 11 a.m. to 11:30 p.m.; some are open Sunday noon to 10:30 p.m.

Anchor Inn

The **Anchor Inn** (Park Street, SE1; ☎ **020-7407-1577;** Tube: Southwark) was frequented by 18th-century figures such as Samuel Johnson, who produced the first *Dictionary of the English Language*; playwright Oliver Goldsmith, whose most famous work is *She Stoops to Conquer*; and painter Sir Joshua Reynolds, first president of the Royal Academy. The Anchor Inn boasts a nice riverside terrace. (See Chapter 25.)

Coal Hole

Opened in the early 19th century, the **Coal Hole** (91 The Strand, WC2; ☎ **020-7836-7503;** Tube: Covent Garden) got its name from the coal haulers who unloaded their cargo on the Thames nearby. It's one of Central London's larger pubs, and because it's in the West End, it has many theatrical connections. Famous mid-19th-century Shakespearean actor Edmund Kean used to hire rowdies, get them drunk here, and then send them off to heckle his rivals in other theaters.

George Inn

One of the city's most historically important pubs is the **George Inn** (in George Inn Yard off Borough High Street, SE1; ☎ 020-7407-2056; Tube: Borough). It's the last remaining example in London of an old-style galleried coaching inn (see Chapter 25). The George was doing business during the reign of Henry VIII, and some claim it actually dates back to Chaucer's era.

King's Head and Eight Bells

Chelsea's intimate, clublike **King's Head and Eight Bells** (50 Cheyne Walk, SW3; ☎ 020-7352-1820; Tube: Sloane Sq.) opened over 400 years ago, around 1580. Back then, of course, the area was rural; Henry VIII's country house stood nearby. Later, celebrated artists and writers such as Dante Gabriel Rossetti, Thomas Carlyle (whose house is now a museum; see Chapter 17), Oscar Wilde, and Laurence Olivier and Vivien Leigh made their homes in Chelsea, one of the prettiest (and now one of the most expensive) parts of London. The neighborhood's still filled with literary and other luminaries, so keep your eyes open if you stop in here. You never know who may pop in.

Lamb and Flag

Lamb and Flag (33 Rose St., WC2; ☎ 020-7497-9504; Tube: Leicester Sq.) was once known by the grisly name the "Bucket of Blood" because prize fighters battered one another into a bloody pulp during matches held for betting customers. The pub, a rare survivor of the Great Fire of 1666, has a couple of literary associations to offset its pugilist past. In the 19th century, it was one of Charles Dickens's favorite taverns. A couple of centuries earlier, poet John Dryden was attacked and beaten just outside, probably because of a lampoon he directed at the earl of Rochester. Every year on December 16, the pub commemorates the anniversary of the attack with a Dryden Night.

Red Lion Public House

Red Lion Public House (48 Parliament St., SW1; ☎ 020-7930-5826; Tube: Westminster) is frequented by civil servants and members of Parliament. So many MPs stop in here that the pub rings a special bell before a vote is taken, allowing the lawmakers to get back in time. Charles Dickens stopped in once for a pint of beer — he was 11 years old at the time (life was different back then).

Salisbury

I'm partial to the **Salisbury** (90 St. Martin's Lane, WC2; ☎ 020-7836-5863; Tube: Leicester Sq.) because I used to hang out there. It's right in the heart of the West End theater district, dates from 1852, and has a beautifully preserved art nouveau interior with marble fittings, cut-glass mirrors, and brass statuettes. Like the **Lamb and Flag** noted earlier, the Salisbury was once famous for bare-knuckle prize fights — but that was long before my time.

Williamson's Tavern

Williamson's Tavern (in Groveland Court, off Bow Lane, EC4 ☎ 020-7248-6280; Tube: St. Paul's) was the residence of the Lord Mayor of the City of London before the nearby Mansion House was built. The tavern stands behind a 17th-century gate presented to the Lord Mayor by William and Mary. The building later served as an inn. Inside you can have a drink and one of its famous steak sandwiches.

Ye Olde Cheshire Cheese

Ye Olde Cheshire Cheese (Wine Office Court, 145 Fleet St., EC4; ☎ 020-7353-6170; Tube: Blackfriars) was established in 1667, but there was a tavern on this site as early as 1590 (see Chapter 14). It burned down in the Great Fire of 1666 and was quickly rebuilt — in fact, Ye Old Cheshire Cheese was the first pub to reopen after the fire. Downstairs, you can see charred wooden beams bearing witness to the conflagration that destroyed a large portion of London. This was one of Charles Dickens's favorite hangouts, and he usually sat at a table to the right of the fireplace on the first floor.

Ye Olde Watling

Ye Olde Watling (29 Watling St., EC4; % 020-7248-6252; Tube: Mansion House) is a 17th-century pub that was used by Sir Christopher Wren as an office when St. Paul's Cathedral was being constructed. Timber taken from dismantled sailing ships was used to build the structure.

Appendix

Quick Concierge

American Express

The main AmEx office is at 6 Haymarket, SW1 (☎ 020-7930-4411; Tube: Piccadilly Circus). Full services are available Monday through Friday 9 a.m. to 5:30 p.m. and Saturday 9 a.m. to 4 p.m. At other times — Saturday 4 p.m. to 6 p.m. and Sunday 10 a.m. to 5 p.m. — only the foreign-exchange bureau is open.

Area Code

London now has one telephone area code: **020.** If you're calling a London number from outside the city but within the United Kingdom, use 020 followed by the eight-digit number. If you're calling within London, leave off the 020 and dial only the eight-digit number. The country code for England is **44**; see "Telephone" later in this section for instructions on how to dial.

ATMs

ATMs, sometimes called *cashpoints,* are widely available throughout Central London. See Chapters 3 and 12 for more information on using ATMs.

Babysitters

Babysitting organizations are discussed in Chapter 4.

Business Hours

Banks are usually open Monday through Friday 9:30 a.m. to 3:30 p.m.

Business offices are open Monday through Friday 9 a.m. to 5 p.m.; the lunch break lasts an hour, but most places stay open during that time.

Pubs are allowed to stay open Monday through Saturday 11 a.m. to 11 p.m. and Sunday noon to 10:30 p.m. Some bars stay open past midnight.

London stores generally open at 9 a.m. and close at 5:30 p.m., staying open to 7 p.m. on Wednesday or Thursday.

Climate

See Chapter 2.

Credit Cards

American Express, Diners Club, MasterCard, and Visa are widely accepted in London and throughout the United Kingdom. If your card gets lost or stolen in London, call the following U.K. numbers: **Visa** ☎ 01604-230-230 (☎ 800-645-6556 in the U.S. for Citicorp Visa); **American Express** ☎ 01273-696-933 (☎ 800-221-7282 in the U.S.); **MasterCard** ☎ 01702-362-988 (☎ 800-307-7309 in the U.S.); **Diners Club** ☎ 0800-460-800 (☎ 800-525-7376 in the U.S.).

Currency Exchange

Currency exchange is discussed in Chapter 12.

Customs

Customs regulations are discussed in Chapter 19.

Dentists

For dental emergencies, call **Eastman Dental Hospital,** 56 Gray's Inn Rd., WC1 (☎ 020-7915-1000; Tube: King's Cross).

Doctors

In an emergency, contact **Doctor's Call** at ☎ 07000-372-255. Some hotels also have physicians on call. **Medical Express,** 117A Harley St., W1 (☎ 020-7499-1991; Tube: Oxford Circus) is a private clinic with walk-in medical service (no appointment necessary) Monday through Friday 9 a.m. to 6 p.m. and Saturday 9:30 a.m. to 2:30 p.m. For filling the British equivalent of a U.S. prescription, a surcharge of £20 ($32) is sometimes added on top of the cost of the medications.

Electricity

British current is 240 volts, AC cycle, roughly twice the voltage of North American current, which is 115 – 120 volts, AC cycle. You won't be able to plug the flat pins of your appliance's plugs into the holes of British wall outlets without suitable converters or adapters. Some (but not all) hotels supply them for guests. Experienced travelers bring their own transformers. An electrical supply shop will also have what you need.

 Be forewarned that you'll destroy the inner workings of your appliance (and possibly start a fire) if you plug an American appliance directly into a European electrical outlet without a transformer.

Embassies & High Commissions

In case you lose your passport or have some other emergency, here's a list of addresses and phone numbers:

✔ **United States:** The embassy is at 24 Grosvenor Sq., W1 (☎ 020-7499-9000; Tube: Bond St.). For passport and visa information go to the **U.S. Passport & Citizenship Unit,** 55 – 56 Upper Brook St., W1 (☎ 020-7499-9000, ext. 2563 or 2564; Tube: Marble Arch or Bond St.). Hours are Monday through Friday 8:30 a.m. to noon and 2 to 4 p.m. (there are no afternoon hours on Tuesday).

✔ **Canada:** The high commission is at **MacDonald House,** 38 Grosvenor Sq., W1 (☎ 020-7258-6600; Tube: Bond St.), open Monday through Friday 8 a.m. to 11a.m.

✔ **Ireland:** The embassy is at 17 Grosvenor Place, SW1 (☎ 020-7235-2171; Tube: Hyde Park Corner), open Monday through Friday 9:30 a.m. to 1 p.m. and 2:15 to 5 p.m.

✔ **Australia:** The high commission is at **Australia House,** Strand, WC2 (☎ 020-7379-4334; Tube: Charing Cross or Aldwych), open Monday through Friday 10 a.m. to 4 p.m.

✔ **New Zealand:** The high commission is at **New Zealand House,** 80 Haymarket at Pall Mall, SW1 (☎ 020-7930-8422; Tube: Charing Cross or Piccadilly Circus), open Monday through Friday 9 a.m. to 5 p.m.

Emergencies

For police, fire, or an ambulance, dial ☎ **999.**

Holidays

Americans may be unfamiliar with some British holidays, particularly the spring and summer **Bank Holidays** (the last Monday in May and August), when everyone takes off for a long weekend. Most banks and many shops, museums, historic houses, and other places of interest are closed then and public transport services reduced. The same holds true for other major British holidays: **New Year's Day, Good Friday, Easter Monday, May Day** (the first Monday in May), **Christmas,** and **Boxing Day** (December 26). The London crowds swell during **school holidays:** mid-July to early September, 3 weeks at Christmas and at Easter, and a week in mid-October and in mid-February (when are those kids ever in school?).

Hospitals

The following offer 24-hour emergency care, with the first treatment free under the National Health Service: **Royal Free Hospital,** Pond Street, NW3 (☎ 020-7794-0500; Tube: Belsize Park), and **University College Hospital,** Grafton Way, WC1 (☎ 020-7387-9300; Tube: Warren St. or Euston Sq.). Many other London hospitals also have accident and emergency departments.

Hotlines

For police or medical emergencies, dial ☎ **999** (no coins required). If you're in some sort of legal emergency, call **Release** at ☎ 020-7729-9904. The **Rape Crisis Line** is at ☎ 020-7837-1600, accepting calls Monday through Friday 6 to 10 p.m. and Saturday and Sunday 10 a.m. to 10 p.m. **Samaritans,** 46 Marshall St., W1 (☎ 020-7734-2800; Tube: Oxford Circus or Piccadilly Circus), maintains a 24-hour crisis hotline that helps with all kinds of trouble, even threatened suicides. **Alcoholics Anonymous** at ☎ 020-7352-3001 answers its hotline daily 10 a.m. to 10 p.m. The **AIDS 24-hour hotline** is at ☎ 0800-567-123.

Information

See "Where to Get More Information" later in this Appendix to find out where to get visitor information before you leave home; see Chapter 10 for where to get visitor information after you arrive in London.

Internet Access
Walk-in Internet and e-mail service providers are increasingly common in London. **Office 24,** 38 New Oxford St., WC1 (☎ 020-7616-7300; Tube: Tottenham Court Rd. or Holborn), has high-speed computers available for Internet/e-mail access for 10p (17¢) per minute; it's open 24 hours. Also open 24 hours, **Net House,** 138 Marylebone Rd., NW1 (☎ 020-7224-7008; Tube: Baker St.), charges £1 ($1.65) for 15 minutes (less after 11 p.m.).

Liquor Laws
No alcohol is served to anyone under 18. Children under 16 aren't allowed in pubs, except in certain rooms, and then only when accompanied by a parent or guardian. Don't drink and drive; penalties for drunk driving are stiff, even if you're an overseas visitor. Restaurants are allowed to serve liquor during the same hours as pubs; however, only people who are eating a meal on the premises can be served a drink. In hotels, liquor may be served 11 a.m. to 11 p.m. to both guests and nonguests; after 11 p.m., only guests may be served.

Mail
An airmail letter to North America costs 43p (70¢) for 10 grams, and postcards require a 35p (55¢) stamp; letters generally take 7 to 10 days to arrive from the United States. See "Post Offices" later in this section for locations.

Maps
The best all-around street directory, *London A to Z* is available at most newsagents and bookstores. You can obtain a bus and Underground map at any Underground station. **Stanfords,** 12 – 14 Long Acre, WC2 (☎ 020-7836-1321; Tube: Leicester Sq.), is the world's largest map shop.

Newspapers/Magazines
The *Times, Telegraph, Daily Mail,* and *Evening Standard* are all dailies carrying the latest news. The *International Herald Tribune,* published in Paris, and an international edition of *USA Today,* beamed via satellite, are available daily. Copies of *Time* and *Newsweek* are also sold at most newsstands. Magazines such as *Time Out, City Limits,* and *Where* contain lots of useful information about the latest happenings in London.

Gay Times, a high-quality new-oriented magazine covering the gay/lesbian community, is available at most newsagents.

Pharmacies
Pharmacies are generally called *chemists* in the United Kingdom. **Boots** has outlets all over London. **Bliss the Chemist,** 5 Marble Arch, W1 (☎ 020-7723-6116; Tube: Marble Arch), is open daily 9 a.m. to midnight. **Zafash Pharmacy,** 233 – 235 Old Brompton Rd., SW5 (☎ 020-7373-2798; Tube: Earl's Court), is London's only 24-hour pharmacy.

Police
In an emergency, dial ☎ **999** (no coin required).

Post Offices
The **Main Post Office,** 24 William IV St., WC2 (☎ 020-7930-9580; Tube: Charing Cross), is open Monday through Saturday 8:30 a.m. to 8 p.m. Other post offices and sub-post offices are open Monday through Friday 9 a.m. to 5:30 p.m. and Saturday 9 a.m. to 12:30 p.m. Many sub-post offices and some main post offices close for an hour at lunchtime.

Radio
There are 24-hour radio channels operating throughout the United Kingdom, including London. They offer mostly pop music and chat shows at night. FM stations are **BBC1** (104.8); **BBC2** (89.1); **BBC3** (between 90 and 92); and the classical station, **BBC4** (95). There are also the **BBC Greater London Radio** (94.9) station, with lots of rock, plus **LBC Crown** (97.3), with news and reports of "what's on" in London. Pop/rock U.S. style is heard on **Capital FM** (95.8), and if you like jazz, reggae, or salsa, tune in to **Choice FM** (96.9). **Jazz FM** (102.2) also offers blues and big-band music.

Rest Rooms
The English often call toilets *loos.* They're marked by "public toilets" signs on streets, parks, and tube stations. You'll also find well-maintained lavatories that can be used by anybody in all larger public buildings, such as museums and art galleries, large department stores, and rail stations. Public lavatories are usually free, but you may need a small coin to get in or to use a proper washroom. In some places (like Leicester Square), you'll find coin-operated toilets that are sterilized after each use.

Safety

London is generally a safe city, both on the street and in the Underground. However, be aware that pickpockets may frequent Portobello Market on Saturday. As in any large metropolis, use common sense and normal caution when you're in a crowded public area or walking alone at night.

Smoking

Most U.S. cigarette brands are available in London. Smoking is strictly forbidden in the Underground (on the cars and the platforms) and on buses, and it's increasingly frowned on in many other places. Most restaurants have no-smoking tables, but they're usually separated from the smoking section by only a little bit of space. No-smoking rooms are available in many hotels, and some B&Bs are now entirely smoke-free.

Taxes

The 17.5 percent value-added tax (VAT) is added to all hotel and restaurant bills and will be included in the price of many items you purchase. This can be refunded if you shop at stores that participate in the Retail Export Scheme (signs are posted in the window). See Chapter 19.

Taxis

You can hail a cab from the street; if the "For Hire" light is lit, it means the cab is available. You can phone for a radio cab at ☎ 020-7272-0272. See Chapter 11 for more details.

Telephone

For directory assistance in London and the rest of Britain, dial ☎ 192. The city code for London is 020 within the United Kingdom or 20 outside the United Kingdom. The country code for the United Kingdom is 44. To call London from the United States, dial 011-44-20, and then eight-digit local phone number. If you're dialing a London number from within London, drop the 020 city code.

Three types of public pay phones are available: those that take only coins, those that accept only phonecards (called **Cardphones**), and those that take both phonecards and credit cards. Phonecards are available in four values — £2 ($3.20), £4 ($6), £10 ($16), and £20 ($32) — and are reusable until the total value has expired. You can buy the cards from newsstands and post offices. At coin-operated phones, insert your coins before dialing. The minimum charge is 10p

(15 cents). The credit-call pay phone operates on credit cards — Access (MasterCard), Visa, American Express, and Diners Club — and is most common at airports and large rail stations.

To make an international call from London, dial the international access code **(00)**, then the country code, then the area code, and finally the local number. Or call through one of the following long-distance access codes: **AT&T USA Direct** (☎ 0800-890-011), **Canada Direct** (☎ 0800-890-016), **Australia** (☎ 0800-890-061), and **New Zealand** (☎ 0800-890-064). Common country codes are: **USA and Canada,** 1; **Australia,** 61; **New Zealand,** 64.

Time Zone

England follows Greenwich mean time (5 hours ahead of Eastern Standard Time). Clocks move forward 1 hour on March 28 and back 1 hour on October 24. Most of the year, including summer, Britain is 5 hours ahead of the time observed on the east coast of the United States. Because the U.S. and Britain observe daylight saving time at slightly different times of year, there's a brief period (about a week) in autumn when Britain is only 4 hours ahead of New York and a brief period in spring when it's 6 hours ahead of New York.

Tipping

In restaurants, **service charges** of 15 to 20 percent are often added to the bill. Sometimes this is clearly marked; at other times it isn't. When in doubt, ask. If service isn't included, it's customary to add 15 percent to the bill. **Sommeliers** get about £1 ($1.65) per bottle of wine served. Tipping in pubs isn't expected, but in **cocktail bars** the server usually gets about 75p ($1.20) per round of drinks. It's standard to tip **taxi drivers** 10 to 15 percent of the fare. **Barbers and hairdressers** expect 10 to 15 percent. **Tour guides** expect £2 ($3.30), though it's not mandatory. **Theater ushers** are not tipped.

Transit Information

Call ☎ 020-7222-1234 24 hours.

Weather

Call ☎ 020-7922-8844 for current weather information, but chances are the line will be busy. For the daily London weather report before you go, check the Web sites for the London newspapers listed in the section "Where to Get More Information" later in this Appendix.

Toll-Free Numbers and Web Sites

Major Airlines

Air Canada
☎ 800-361-5373 (Canada and U.S.); www.air-canada.ca

Air New Zealand
☎ 800-262-2468; www.airnz.co.uk

American Airlines
☎ 800-433-7300; www.americanair.com

British Airways
☎ 800-AIRWAYS; www.british-airways.com

Continental Airlines
☎ 800-625-0280; www.flycontinental.com

Delta Air Lines
☎ 800-241-4141; www.delta-air.com

Icelandair
☎ 800-223-5500; www.icelandair.is

Northwest Airlines
☎ 800-447-4747; www.nwa.com

Trans World Airlines
☎ 800-892-4141; www.twa.com

United Airlines
☎ 800-538 2929; www.ual.com

Virgin Atlantic Airways
☎ 800-862-862; 1www.virgin.com

Major London Hotel Chains

Forte & Meridien Hotels & Resorts
☎ 800-225-5843; www.forte-hotels.com

Hilton Worldwide
☎ 800-HILTONS; www.hilton.com

Hyatt Hotels and Resorts
☎ 800-228-3336; www.hyatt.com

Inter-Continental Hotels & Resorts
☎ 800-327-0200; www.interconti.com

Sheraton Hotels & Resorts
☎ 800-325-3535; www.sheraton.com

Thistle Hotels
☎ 800-847-4358; www.thistlehotels.com

Where to Get More Information

Tourist Offices

For general information about London, contact an office of the **British Tourist Authority** at one of the following addresses (see "Surfing the Net" for the BTA's Wed address).

✔ **In the United States**: The main BTA office is at 551 Fifth Ave., Suite 701, New York, NY 10176-0799 (☎ 800-462-2748; Fax: 212-986-1188). There's a branch office at 625 N. Michigan Ave., Suite 1510, Chicago, IL 60611-1977. The Chicago office has no phone; all requests for information go through the toll-free number listed for New York.

✔ **In Canada**: 111 Avenue Rd., Suite 450, Toronto, Ontario M5R 3J8 (☎ 800-847-4885).

✔ **In Australia**: University Centre, 8th floor, 210 Clarence St., Sydney NSW 2000 (☎ 02-267-4555; Fax: 02-267-4442).

✔ **In New Zealand**: Suite 305, Dilworth Building, Queen and Customs streets, Auckland 1 (☎ 09-303-1446; Fax: 09-377-6965).

Surfing the Net

The Web is one of the best places to find information on London. With a click of the mouse you can pull up everything from the latest news emanating from No. 10 Downing Street to current opera and concert schedules. You can even book tickets for a West End show or a concert. You'll find useful and quite specific Web sites scattered throughout this guide. For general information on London, try these sites for starters:

- ✔ **www.visitbritain.com.** The Web page for the **British Tourist Authority** is a good resource for visitors to London and the United Kingdom in general.

- ✔ **www.londontraveller.com.** This is a useful site for browsing, with sections on restaurants, nightlife, and hotels.

- ✔ **www.timeout.com** . The weekly listings magazine *Time Out* will give you the lowdown on cultural events, entertainment, restaurants, and nightlife.

- ✔ **www.guardian.co.uk** . The *Daily Guardian,* London's left-of-center daily newspaper, provides up-to-the minute online news coverage.

- ✔ **www.Sunday-times.co.uk.** The *London Times,* the oldest and most traditional of London daily papers, is a good source for general news and culture.

- ✔ **www.gaylondon.co.uk.** This is a useful list of gay and gay-friendly hotels, services, clubs, and restaurants.

- ✔ **www.heathrow.co.uk.** Information on all of London's airports is available on this site.

- ✔ **http://metro.ratp.fr:10001/bin/cities/english.** Type in your departure station and arrival station on the London Underground and this nifty site will map out a route and how long the trip will take.

- ✔ **www.londontransport.co.uk.** This is the Web site for **London Transport,** which is in charge of all forms of public transportation in the city: tubes, buses, ferry service.

- ✔ **www.royal.gov.uk.** If you want more history, information, and trivia about the Windsors and the British monarchy in general, check out the official Royal Web site.

Hitting the books

Most bookstores with travel sections have at least one or two titles pertaining to London. Many have an entire shelf, because London is one of the world's most-visited cities. Here are a few books that might be useful for your trip. All Frommer's guides are published by IDG Books Worldwide, Inc.

- ✔ *Frommer's London,* updated every year, is an authoratative guide that covers the city and its surroundings.

- ✔ *Frommer's Portable London* is a pocket-size, less-comprehensive version of *Frommer's London.*

- ✔ *Frommer's London from $85 a Day* is a time-honored bible for budget-minded travelers who want to visit London in comfort but don't want to spend a fortune doing so.

- ✔ *Frommer's Irreverent Guide to London* is an entertaining guide for sophisticated travelers who want the basic low-down without a lot of added verbiage.

- ✔ *Frommer's Memorable Walks in London* is an excellent resource for those who want to explore the city in depth and on foot. Each walking tour provides easy-to-follow directions and describes important sights along the way.

- ✔ *Frommer's Gay & Lesbian Europe* contains fun, informative, and up-to-the-minute information on all aspects of gay London, from gay hotels and restaurants to the latest clubs.

- ✔ *London* by Edward Rutherford (published by Fawcett Books), is a sprawling epic novel in which London itself is the main character. It's a fascinating excursion into the city's 2,000-year-old past.

Fare Game: Choosing an Airline

Travel Agency: _____ Phone: _____

Agent's Name: _____ Quoted Fare: _____

Departure Schedule & Flight Information

Airline: _____ Airport: _____

Flight #: _____ Date: _____ Time: _____ a.m./p.m.

Arrives in:_____ Time: _____ a.m./p.m.

Connecting Flight (if any)

Amount of time between flights: _____ hours/mins

Airline: _____ Airport: _____

Flight #: _____ Date: _____ Time: _____ a.m./p.m.

Arrives in:_____ Time: _____ a.m./p.m.

Return Trip Schedule & Flight Information

Airline: _____ Airport: _____

Flight #: _____ Date: _____ Time: _____ a.m./p.m.

Arrives in:_____ Time: _____ a.m./p.m.

Connecting Flight (if any)

Amount of time between flights: _____ hours/mins

Airline: _____ Airport: _____

Flight #: _____ Date: _____ Time: _____ a.m./p.m.

Arrives in:_____ Time: _____ a.m./p.m.

Notes

Making Dollars and Sense of It

Expense	Amount
Airfare	
Car Rental	
Lodging	
Parking	
Breakfast	
Lunch	
Dinner	
Babysitting	
Attractions	
Transportation	
Souvenirs	
Tips	
Grand Total	

Notes

Sweet Dreams: Choosing Your Hotel

Enter the hotels where you'd prefer to stay based on location and price. Then use the worksheet below to plan your itinerary.

Hotel	*Location*	*Price per night*

Places to Go, People to See, Things to Do

Enter the attractions you most would like to see. Then use the worksheet below to plan your itinerary.

Attractions	Amount of time you expect to spend there	Best day and time to go

Going "My" Way

Itinerary #1

q _____

q _____

q _____

q _____

Itinerary #2

q _____

q _____

q _____

q _____

Itinerary #3

q _____

q _____

q _____

q _____

Itinerary #4

q _____

q _____

q _____

q _____

Itinerary #5

q _____

q _____

q _____

q _____

Itinerary #6

q _____
q _____
q _____
q _____

Itinerary #7

q _____
q _____
q _____
q _____

Itinerary #8

q _____
q _____
q _____
q _____

Itinerary #9

q _____
q _____
q _____
q _____

Itinerary #10

q _____
q _____
q _____
q _____

Menus & Venues

Enter the restaurants where you'd most like to dine. Then use the worksheet below to plan your itinerary.

Name	*Address/Phone*	*Cuisine/Price*

Notes

Index

See also Accommodations and Restaurant indexes, below.

General Index

• Numbers •

14th Earl of Derby statue, 338
10 Downing Street, prime minister's residence, 229
21st-century London, trend-setter, 11
24-hour clock, train timetables, 126

• A •

AARP (American Association of Retired Persons), traveling with seniors, 36
About Family Travel, traveling with children, 33
Abraham Lincoln statue, 338
Academy of St. Martin-in-the-Fields, Trafalgar Square, 221
Access America, flight insurance, 111
Accessible Journeys, traveling with disabled persons, 39
Accessible Tours, traveling with disabled persons, 39
Accommodation Bookings Hotline, hotel reservation assistance, 72
Accommodations. *See* Accommodations Index
Admiral Duncan's gay club, 324
Admiral Lord Nelson statue, 335
Admiralty Arch, 221
afters, defined, 160
Airbus Heathrow Shuttle, Underground alternative, 123
airfares, 19, 50–52
airlines
  carry-on luggage, 117
  children's travel guidelines, 35
  discounts for senior citizens, 37
  E-saver e-mail, 51
  full fare, 50
  package tours, 49–50
  toll-free numbers, 351
travel agent commissions, 46
Web sites, 351
airplanes, 122, 126
airports
  bureau de change, 147
  Customs area procedure, 122
  duty-free shops, 255
  Gatwick, 52, 124
  Heathrow, 52, 122–124
  London City, 53, 125
  Luton, 53, 125
  Passport Control, 121–122
  Stansted, 53, 125
Albermarle, ticket agency, 114
Albert Memorial, 211, 338
Alcoholics Anonymous, 349
ale, defined, 318
All England Lawn Tennis Club, 21
All Hotels on the Web, 71
All Zone, Visitor Travelcards, 26
American Airlines Vacations, package tours, 49
American Embassy, Grosvenor Square, 63
American Express
  currency exchange savings, 147–148
  Haymarket, 62
  information, 347
American Express Vacations, package tours, 48
American Foundation for the Blind, traveling with disabled persons, 38
Anne Boleyn Gate, Hampton Court Palace, 243
Anne Hathaway's Cottage, Stratford-upon-Avon, 292
Antiquaris, 269
antiques, shopping venues, 269
Anything Left Handed, Regent Street, 266
Apple Market, 269
appliances, current converter/transformer requirements, 117–118
Apsley House, 15, 238
architectural highlights, 238–239

• *M* •

• *Q* •

• *R* •

Accommodations Index

Restaurant Index

IDG BOOKS WORLDWIDE BOOK REGISTRATION

Register This Book and Win!

We want to hear from you!

Visit **http://my2cents.dummies.com** to register this book and tell us how you liked it!

- ✔ Get entered in our monthly prize giveaway.

- ✔ Give us feedback about this book — tell us what you like best, what you like least, or maybe what you'd like to ask the author and us to change!

- ✔ Let us know any other *For Dummies*® topics that interest you.

Your feedback helps us determine what books to publish, tells us what coverage to add as we revise our books, and lets us know whether we're meeting your needs as a *For Dummies* reader. You're our most valuable resource, and what you have to say is important to us!

Not on the Web yet? It's easy to get started with *Dummies 101*®: *The Internet For Windows*® *98* or *The Internet For Dummies*®³ at local retailers everywhere.

Or let us know what you think by sending us a letter at the following address:

For Dummies Book Registration
Dummies Press
10475 Crosspoint Blvd.
Indianapolis, IN 46256

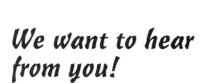

™

...FOR DUMMIES

BESTSELLING BOOK SERIES